CULTURE, COMMUNICATION AND INDIA'S DEVELOPMENT

ABOUT THE EDITORS

Dr. N. Sudhakar Rao is a Professor retired from the Department of Anthropology, at the University of Hyderabad, Hyderabad. He is an alumnus of S.V.U., Tirupati, University, University of Hyderabad, and completed his M.A. (Anthropology) and Ph.D. (Anthropology) from the University of Rochester, USA. He was a J.R. Fellow of AIIS, Chicago, and a Visiting Research Fellow at CDS, Department of Anthropology, University of Bergen, Norway. Served for the Indian Institute of Economics, Hyderabad, ISRO, National Commission for Scheduled Castes and Scheduled Tribes, and TALEEM Research Foundation, Ahmedabad. He also served Assam Central University, Silchar, as Professor of Sociology, and Dean, School of Social Sciences, and as Registrar. Guided students for the award of M.Phil. and Ph.D. degrees and published four books and several papers in reputed academic journals.

Dr. Arbind Sinha, M.Sc. (Anthropology), Ph.D. (Sociology) was on Adjunct Professor and Adviser with MICA, where he worked from 2002 to 2015 holding all senior positions and headed the institution twice. He worked for 22 years with Space Applications Centre–ISRO holding various scientific positions (1974-1996). He was Professor at TALEEM Research Foundation and Director-General of Shanti Business School, Ahmedabad. Dr. Sinha worked for two years as Communication Adviser to the Royal Danish Embassy in New Delhi.

He worked in the field of Social and Development Communication, Health Communication, and Disaster Communication for nearly 30 years and published two authored and two edited books and more than two dozens of papers and chapters in books and journals of national and international repute. His book on *Mass Media and Rural Development* (1985) got worldwide recognition.

Dr. Sinha lectured in Sweden, Canada, and US Universities on fellowship and was in Thailand and Singapore for academic collaborations. He is a life member of more than half a dozen national professional bodies and worked as a member on a few national and international committees.

CULTURE, COMMUNICATION AND INDIA'S DEVELOPMENT

Edited by
N. SUDHAKAR RAO
and
ARBIND SINHA

CONCEPT PUBLISHING COMPANY Pvt. Ltd.
NEW DELHI-110059

ISBN-13: 978-93-5439-023-4

First Published 2022

Published and Printed by

Concept
Since 1974

Concept Publishing Company Pvt. Ltd.
A/15-16, Commercial Block, Mohan Garden
New Delhi-110059 (India)
T : 91 11 25351460, 91 11 25351794
E : publishing@conceptpub.com; W : www.conceptpub.com

Cataloging in Publication Data--Courtesy: D.K. Agencies (P) Ltd. <docinfo@dkagencies.com>

Culture, communication and India's development / edited by N. Sudhakar Rao and Arbind Sinha.

pages cm

"The volume is an outcome of the National Seminar on Culture, Communication and India's Development: Contributions of Anthropology of Communication, Media and Communication"--Acknowledgement.

Includes bibliographical references and index.

ISBN 9789354390234

1. Communication and culture--India--Congresses. 2. Communication in community development--India--Congresses. 3. Mass media--Social aspects--India--Congresses. I. Sudhakar Rao, N. (Nemalladinne), 1953- editor. II. Sinha, Arbind K., editor.

LCC P94.65.I4C85 2022 | DDC 302.230954 23

Dedication

We take it our honour and privilege to dedicate this volume to Dr. Binod C. Agrawal in humble adoration and appreciation of his commitment to anthropology, dedication to research, his love and affection to fellow researchers and academic colleagues; and mentoring young generation of scholars.

Acknowledgements

The volume is an outcome of the National Seminar on Culture, Communication and India's Development: Contributions of Anthropology of Communication, Media and Communication. It is our bounded duty to gratefully acknowledge the logistic and financial support received from various institutions and individuals in organizing the national seminar. The Department of Anthropology and the University of Hyderabad provided the needed logistics and appropriate ambience for holding the seminar. All faculty members, research scholars, students and non-teaching staff are profusely thanked for their unconditional support. Thanks go specifically to Prof. M. Romesh Singh, Head of the Department of Anthropology, for being one of the members of the organizing committee of the seminar. The seminar would not have been made possible had the Indian Council of Social Science Research (ICSSR), Southern Region, Hyderabad not provided the needed major chunk of the financial need, to which we are extremely grateful. Without the academic and moral support from the faculty members and research scholars of the Department of Mass Communication, the University of Hyderabad, and most particularly Prof. Vinod Pavarala, UNESCO Chair Professor for Community Media who has not only provided generous grant but also has given his valuable time being one of the members of organizing community. We are sincerely thankful to the entire team of the Department of Mass Communication. Finally, not least we are immensely thankful to the Association for Development Communication, Ahmedabad, for their financial support granted to the seminar out of their meagre resources. We are also grateful to the Session Chairs and Co-chairs for their time and commitments for conducting the sessions.

We thank all the enthusiastic participants of the seminar, particularly Prof. Ramdas Gambhir, Department of Anthropology, Savitribai Phule University, Pune, who delivered the keynote speech and Prof. B.P. Sanjay, former Vice-Chancellor, Tamil Nadu Central University, Coimbatore, Pro-Vice-Chancellor, the University of Hyderabad, and Senior Faculty Member of the Department of Mass Communication, the University of Hyderabad for delivering the valedictory address for the seminar.

We are grateful to the Concept Publishing Company (P.) Ltd., New Delhi, for coming forward to publish the volume even in the adverse time of Covid-19.

N. Sudhakar Rao and **Arbind Sinha**

About Dr. Binod C. Agrawal

Dr. Agrawal is one of a few anthropologists in India who left his footprint in other disciplines. He is widely travelled, extensively written, and has contributed a lot in bringing anthropological perspective in communication teaching and research.

Dr. Agrawal did his Masters in Social Anthropology in 1963 from the University of Lucknow and was awarded a gold medal for his Masters' thesis on Doctor-Patient Relationship. After his Masters, he worked on a project with Prof. J.W. Elder of the Department of Sociology, University of Wisconsin, Madison, the USA that helped him in getting admission in the Ph.D. programme at the University of Wisconsin in 1964. After completion of M.S. in Cultural Anthropology and Ph.D. in 1970, he decided to return to India in 1971 and joined Indian Agricultural Research Institute, New Delhi as Associate Professor. By the second half of 1973, he joined Space Applications Centre (SAC-ISRO), Ahmedabad to head its Research and Evaluation Cell. It was a major turning point in Dr. Agrawal's career—from Teaching to Research.

At Space Applications Centre, he worked with the world's largest techno-social experiment—Satellite Instructional Television Experiment (SITE) and introduced the new component of a qualitative study in evaluation research—'holistic study'. SITE evaluation study gave worldwide recognition to Dr. Agrawal and he travelled across the world to share this experience. His second landmark study was action research among the Yanadi tribe who were displaced to another corner of the Island for making the island a major satellite launchpad for India. The development work-cum-study continued for five years.

In 1982, Dr. Agrawal was nominated as a member of the P.C. Joshi Committee to guide the Government of India on the Software for Doordarshan. It was an honour to him as well as to the organization.

In April 1993, he joined Mudra Institute of Communications, Ahmedabad (MICA), as its founder Director and worked there for about 15 months and came back to ISRO to retire from Government job and had set up TALEEM Research Foundation, a private non-profit organization of Zee Network in Ahmedabad from where he finally retired in 2015. In between, he also functioned as a founder Vice-Chancellor of Himgiri Zee University, Dehradun from 2005 to 2012.

Dr. Agrawal is a popular teacher and he does not forget to start his classes with examples of culture. It makes the students excited to know more about it. He is also an excellent guide and he piloted a large number of Masters and Doctoral students under his guidance. There are not very many supervisors like him who puts that much effort into preparing the students for writing a quality thesis and for defending the viva exams.

Dr. Agrawal is also remembered as an outstanding organizer. As an Executive Secretary, he managed the Xth International Congress of Anthropological and Ethnological Sciences in 1978 under the Presidentship of Dr. L.P. Vidyarthi. He also steered the 1986 International Conference of the International Association for Media and Communication Research (IAMCR) in Delhi.

Dr. Agrawal is an avid traveller and most of his travels were for attending national and international seminars/conferences, meetings, sometimes relevant and sometimes not so relevant. He established a great network world over.

Publications of Dr. Binod C. Agrawal

Publication of Books

Authored and Co-authored

Year	Title of the Book
2009c	(Co-author) Television and Cultural Crisis. New Delhi: Concept Publishing Company (Co-author Mira K. Desai).
2006	Television in South Asia: Cultural Scenario and Future Directions. Lanham, Maryland: University Press of America.
2004	Ethnography of Communication. Shillong: North-Eastern Hill University Publications (13th Verrier Elwin Endowment Lectures).
2002	(Co-author) Remote Sensing Applications in Brackish Water Fisheries: A Socio-Economic Study. New Delhi: Concept Publishing Company (Co-authors Arbind K. Sinha and Sham Behari Sharma)
1993	(Co-author et al.) Computer Technology for Higher Education (Volumes 1-3). New Delhi: Concept Publishing Company.
1987b	(Co-author) Situational Analysis of Children's Television in India. Commissioned study by United Nations Children's Fund, Ahmedabad: Development and Educational Communication Unit. (Co-authors C. Lal, Kiran S. Karnik and K. Vishwanath).
1986b	(Co-author) Television in Kheda: A Social Evaluation of SITE. New Delhi: Concept Publishing Company.(Co-author M. R. Malek)
1985a	(Co-author) Yanadi Response to Change: An Attempt in Action Anthropology. New Delhi: Concept Publishing Company. (Co-authors N. Sudhakar Rao and P.C. Gurivi Reddi)
1985b	Anthropological Methods for Communication Research: Experiences and Encounters During SITE. New Delhi: Concept Publishing Company. (Assisted by S. Vishwanath)

Year	Title of the Book
1981	SITE Social Evaluation Results, Experiences, and Implications. Ahmedabad: Space Applications Centre.
1980	Cultural Contours of Religion and Economics in Hindu Universe. New Delhi: National Publishing House.
1978	Television Comes to Village: An Evaluative Study of SITE. Bangalore: Indian Space Research Organisation.
1977	(Co-author) SITE Social Evaluation: Impact on Adults (Two Volumes). Bangalore: Indian Space Research Organisation. (Co-authors J.K. Doshi, Victor, Jesudasan, K.K. Verma)

Edited and Co-edited

Year	Title of the Book
2016a	Editor, Media and Religious Communication in Multi- Cultural Asia: An Eclectic Research Agenda. Bangkok: Asian Research Center.
2016b	Editor, Changing Cultures and Religious Practices in Asia. Bangkok: Asian Research Center.
2015	Co-editor, Health, Culture and Development in North-Eastern India. New Delhi: Concept Publishing Company. (Co-Editor Narendra Singh)
2009a	Guest Editor, Communication Anthropology. Eastern Anthropologist Volume 62, No. 4. (Special Number on Communication Anthropology).
2009b	Editor and author, Higher Education Through Television – The Indian Experience. New Delhi: Concept Publishing Company.
2007	(Co-editor) International Satellite Broadcasting in South Asia Maryland: University Press of America. (Co-editors Srinivas R. Melkote and Peter Shields).
2000	(Co-editor) Future of Computerization in Institutions of Higher Learning. New Delhi: Concept Publishing Company. (Co-editor Larry R. Symes).
1989	(Co-edited) Media Utilization for the Development of Women and Children. New Delhi: Concept Publishing Company. (Co-editor B.S. Thakur).
1987a	(Co-edited) Television and the Indian Child. New Delhi: UNICEF. (Co-editor Mira B. Aghi)
1986a	(Co-edited). SITE to INSAT: Challenges of Production and Research for Women and Children. New Delhi: Concept Publishing Co. (Co-editor Arbind K. Sinha)

Year	Title of the Book
1986c	(Co-edited) Communication Research for Development: The ISRO Experience. New Delhi: Concept Publishing Company. (Co-Editor S. R. Joshi and Arbind K. Sinha)
1986d	(Co-edited) Reservation: Policy, Programme and Issues, Jaipur: Rawat Publishers. (Co-editor Vimal P. Shah)
1983	Guest Editor, Social Change. Volume 13 Number 3 Special Issue on Communication and Development (Council for Development, New Delhi).
1982	Editor, Anthropological Approaches to the Study of Complex Societies. Lucknow: Ethnographic & Folk Culture Study.
1974a	(Co-editor) Tribe, Caste and Peasantry. Lucknow: Ethnographic and Folk Culture Society. (Co-editor K.S. Mathur)

Publication of Paper, Chapter in Book and Conference Paper

More than 60 papers in national and international journals and around 50 Chapters in different books published in India and abroad.

Membership in Professional Organizations

Life Member

- Ethnographic and Folk Culture Society.
- Indian Sociological Society.
- Indian Anthropological Association.
- Indian Society of Extension Education.
- Indian Anthropological Society.
- Indian Council for Communication Training and Research.
- National Council for Development Communication.
- All India Association for Educational Technology.
- Asian Media Information and Communication Centre, Singapore.
- Community Aid & Sponsorship Programme (CASP).
- Member, Peoples Council of Education.
- Member, Association of Audio-Video Communication for Development and Education (AV-CODE).
- Member, Indian Association of Social Sciences and Health (IASSH).
- Member, Indian Academy of Social Sciences (IASS).

- Founder Member, Indian National Confederation and Academy of Anthropologists (INCAA).
- Board of Director, AMIC Singapore (2010-).
- President India Organizing Committee (2009), 18th AMIC Annual Conference, New Delhi, July 3-16, 2009.
- Country Representative–AMIC, Singapore (2007-).
- President (1990-1995), National Council of Development Communication.
- Secretary (1984 to 1987), Indian Council for Communication Training and Research.
- Executive Secretary (1986), 15th International Association of Mass Communication Research (IAMCR) Conference, New Delhi.
- Executive Secretary (1978), X International Congress of Anthropological and Ethnological Sciences (ICAES) Conference, New Delhi.
- UGC Panel Member, 'Anthropology Panel' and 'Journalism and Communication Panel' for three years.

Contents

List of Contributors

Mr. Aloysius Sebastian, Research Scholar, Centre for Comparative Literature, University of Hyderabad, Hyderabad. E-Mail:aloysiuspalatty@gmail.com

Mr. Anil Gopi, Research Scholar, Dept. of Anthropology, University of Hyderabad, Hyderabad. E-Mail: kalamboor@gmail.com

Dr. Arbind Sinha, Ph.D. Advisor to CDMC, MICA, Ahmedabad. E-Mail: arbind21@gmail.com

Dr. B. Balaswamy, Ph.D. (Late) Professor, Dept. of Journalism and Mass Communication. Osmania University, Hyderabad. E-mail: baalaswamy@gmail.com

Prof. B.P. Sanjay, Ph.D. Former Professor, Dept. of Communication, Univ. of Hyderabad, Hyderabad. E-Mail: bpssn54@gmail.com

Dr. Delfi Chinnappan R., Ph.D., Doctoral Candidate, Queensland University of Technology (QUT), Australia. E-Mail: delfichinnappan11@gmail.com

Ms. Devina Sarwatay, Research Scholar, Dept. of Communication University of Hyderabad, Hyderabad. E-Mail: devina.sarwatay@gmail.com

Mr. Janga Babu Rao, Research Scholar, Centre for the Study of Social Exclusion and Inclusive Polity, University of Hyderabad, Hyderabad. E-Mail:17siph@uohyd.ernet.in

Dr. Joly Puthussery, Ph.D. Assistant Professor, CFCS, University of Hyderabad, Hyderabad. E-Mail: jputhussery@gmail.com

Ms. Kumari Pallavi, Assistant Professor, Department of Mass Communication, Galgotias University, Greater Noida. E-Mail: pallavi.ranjan@gmail.com

Dr. Krishna Sankar Kusuma, Associate Professor, AJK Mass Communication Research Centre, Jamia Millia Islamia, New Delhi. E-Mail: kkusuma@jmi.ac.in

Dr. M.B, Devadas, Independent Researcher, Bangalore.

Dr. Mira K Desai, Ph.D. Professor, Dept. of Communication, SNDT University, Mumbai. E-Mail: drmiradesai@gmail.com

Dr. N. Sharon Sucharitha, Gold Academic Consultant, Psychology Dept. Yogi Vemana University, Kadapa, A.P. E-Mail: sharon.nemalladinne@yahoo.com

Dr. N. Sivakami, Assistant Professor Department of Social Work, Central University of Tamil Nadu, Thiruvarur, Tamil Nadu. E-Mail: sivakami@cutn.ac.in

Mr. Nitesh Tripathi, Research Scholar, Junior Research Fellow, Department of Journalism and Mass Communication, Banaras Hindu University, Varanasi. E-Mail: tripathinitesh23@gmail.com

Dr. Padma Rani, Ph.D. Director & Professor, Manipal Institute of Communication, Manipal Academy of Higher Education, Manipal, Karnataka. E-Mail: padma.rani@manipal.edu

Dr. Pradeep Mallik, Ph.D. Adjunct Professor. Department of Literature, School of Liberal Studies Pandit Deendayal Petroleum University (PDPU), Gandhinagar, Gujarát. E-Mail: pradeepmallik@gmail.com

Ms. Pragati Paul, Research Scholar, AJK Mass Communication Research Centre, Jamia Millia Islamia, New Delhi. E-Mail: pragatibhalla@ymail.com

Dr. R. Shamala, Ph.D. Assistant Professor, Department of Media and Communication Central University of Tamil Nadu, Thiruvarur, Tamil Nadu. E-Mail: shamala@cutn.ac.in

Dr. Raj K. Kattula, Ph.D. Senior Professional, Centre for Management and Social Research (CMSR), Hyderabad. E-Mail: rajkattula@gmail.com

Dr. Rajesh Das, Ph.D. Asst. Professor, Dept. of Mass Communication, University of Burdwan, Burdwan, Kolkata. E-Mail: rajesh.das.cal@gmail.com

Ratan Naga Deepika, Research Scholar, Dept., of Communication, University of Hyderabad, Hyderabad. E-Mail: ratandeep.621@gmail.com

Dr. Savita Kaushal, Ph.D. Associate Professor, Dept. of Mass Communication, Jamia Millia Islamia, New Delhi. E-Mail: savita@niepa.ac.in

Mr. Satyabrata Das, Asst. Professor, Amity School of Communication, Amity University, Raipur, Chhattisgarh. E-Mail: satyabdas@gmail.com

Dr. Shashikant Bhagat, Ph.D. Faculty, National Institute of Mass Communication and Journalism (NIMCJ), Ahmedabad. E-Mail: shashibhagat4p@gmail.com

Mr. Sreeju V. Nadh, Research Scholar, Dept. of Communication University of Hyderabad, Hyderabad. E-Mail: sreejuviswanadh@gmail.com

Ms. Swati Arjun, Ph.D. Scholar, School of Journalism and Mass Communication, Indira Gandhi National Open University, New Delhi. E-Mail: swatiarjun2008@gmail.com

Mr. Taijrani Rampersaud, Research Scholar, Dept., of Communication, University of Hyderabad, Hyderabad. E-Mail: t.rampersaud@gmail.com

Dr. V.S.J. Wesly Kumar, Ph.D. Assistant Registrar, University of Hyderabad, Hyderabad. E-Mail: weslyhcu@yahoo.com

Dr. Vinod Pandey, Ph.D. Professor, Dept. of Journalism and Mass Communication, Gujarat Vidyapith, Ahmedabad. E-Mail: vinod29@gmail.com

Introduction of the Book by Editors

Development of the underdeveloped societies has been one of the primary agendas for the governmental and non-governmental bodies and it has been the focus of academic discourse as one of the modernization projects wherein intellectual inputs played a significant role after the world wars. India along with several other countries that obtained freedom from colonial rule, proceeded consciously taking the path of modernization and development in the backdrop of her own unique cultural heritage in tandem with the technological advancements and intellectual subtleties. The governments since independence have left no stone unturned towards this end with the formulation of appropriate policies and plans, developing schemes and so on. The utilization of modern communication, both print and electronic media, over more than four decades in this regard has also become a significant aspect. On the academic front, while several disciplines pursued their programmes in the universities keeping the development of the country on top priority, sociology and anthropology have maintained close proximity with the people and the ground realities since the beginning concerning the development issues. These disciplines not only engaged in the production of first-hand empirical knowledge through researches at M.Phil. and Ph.D. levels besides independent researches about Indian society, culture and development covering rural and tribal areas where a large majority of Indian populations live beside the urban population, but also providing academic inputs and evaluating various development schemes implemented. They brought to light the important role of social structural relations and cultural values that resist or hinder change or they may even become instrumental for the promotion of social change. Later joined the discipline of communication that in fact brought together all stakeholders in the development enterprise. From the side of the Government of India, besides several initiatives, two institutions were established at the same time in Delhi: National Institute of Community Development in 1964-65 which was shifted to Hyderabad in 1977 and the Indian Institute of Mass Communication in 1965. The contributions of academicians in these institutions have been of immense value providing inputs to the government bodies and policy-makers for developing and evaluating development policies and schemes. They have also been training different personnel and development agencies in the matters of execution and implementation of development plans and schemes. Further, several departments of communication came into existence either independently or as combined departments along with the extant journalism departments in the universities. Meanwhile, not only the concept of development itself has undergone changes, but also the case of communication with the emergent new technology engendering several media in active circulation. Given these developments over the years, it is imperative to reflect upon the society, culture, communication in the context of development in India for drawing upon the academic contributions made with reference to the intersections of these aspects of Indian society. The uniqueness of the book lies in its focus on the ground realities about transforming India through the lens of new communication technologies.

The chapters in the volume come from various parts of the country and these are written primarily based on first-hand experience and the empirical data collected by the scholars themselves. Few chapters are based on secondary sources also. In terms of disciplinary epistemological strength, these are largely based on anthropological methods and qualitative analysis with certain basic quantification required. They are grouped broadly under six sections described below.

Development in Context: This section essentially draws attention to the theoretical premise on which culture, communication and development come together in the disciplinary confluence of anthropology and sociology in theory and practice. It further sets the stage for the macro-level understanding of the social reality of development in the country by presenting the case of SITE, one of the biggest research work ever carried out in India in the 1970s on the use of Television by satellite technology and its potential for rural and tribal development. It also discusses the contributions of anthropology for development with particular reference to India and also the role of communication for sustainable development.

The section and the volume begin with Arbind Sinha's chapter on 'Culture, Communication, and Development: The Trek of Coexistence'. It traces out the link among the concepts of culture, communication and development to the first International Congress of Anthropological and Ethnological Sciences (ICAES) in London in 1934. The development communication began its journey with the applied ethnography and anthropology that are closely associated with the development of the Third World, and it became communication anthropology. Now development communication has become an area in Communication Studies and an important component in the national development agenda.

B.P. Sanjay's chapter unpacks the background of SITE, its linkages with USAID, NASA, and the Government of India. His analysis mainly focuses on the SITE being the harbinger of change in the communication ecosystem in India and the initiator of the electronic industry on one hand and its connections with academics on the other. While fondly remembering his association with the SITE project, he discusses the contribution of the latter to the SITE as a social scientist and the academic. Sanjay not only gratefully acknowledges the 'holistic' and 'emic' concepts that Dr. Agrawal has introduced in communication studies but also bringing together culture, communication, and development into the academic field along with qualitative methods of research and encouraging research in this area in the university departments.

The chapter 'Culture, Communication and Development' of Balaswamy explores the complex triangular relationship among culture, communication and development. Further, it deliberates on the concept of sustainable development and argues for the necessity of accommodating culture that promotes harmony between nature which is under threat now and human societies for their sustained development.

Communication and Development: This section essentially draws attention to the micro-level observations on the role of communication in the development process. It covers an existing situation about the role of communication in the development of a tribal community in Bihar. The use of communication technology in distance education benefitting immensely a large number of women in the country is another case in the section. It also includes the prevalent communication gap existing among Scheduled Castes in the development planning in the rural sector of A.P. and the lack of communication technology in the schools located in the slums of Hyderabad in Telangana state. This section has four chapters.

Kumari Pallavi discusses in the chapter on 'Communication Practices in the Development of Tharu Community in Bihar' the role of communication in the development of Tharu, a tribal community in Bihar. The discussion is based on the ethnographic data collected by observation and in-depth interviews held with the members of the community and the government officials. The study has employed Sadler's and Baker and McLelland's framework using a bottom-up approach to consider policy implementation and contextualizes it to analyze the impact of the policy.

Wesly Kumar and Babu Rao in the chapter, 'Communication Technology and Education of Scheduled Castes' in the slums of Hyderabad Children' describes the Government of India and state government's efforts to revolutionize the conventional educational practices through education technology and information communication technology for more than four decades. Further, it presents the observation made on these efforts of the government in reaching out to the slum schools. It has been pointed out that these efforts have not been fruitful, some NGOs have donated computers and television sets to the government as well as the private schools. While television sets are hardly used and about 20 per cent of the computers do not work at all.

Raj's chapter on 'Anthropological Reflections on Communication Challenges in Implementation of Special Component Plan (SCP) for Scheduled Castes' in Andhra Pradesh observes partial success of the development. He argues by providing the case of SCP, that public policy both in the formulation as well as implementation actually encounters communication challenges, and without proper communication mechanisms in place throughout these processes, the policy would be maleficent. A qualitative analysis of SCP reveals that the policy of bringing socio-economic development did not yield expected positive results; its partial success is due to not using appropriate communication strategies.

In the last chapter of this section, 'Nurturing Gender Equity through Open and Distance Learning: An Analysis', Savita Kaushal shows that technology-based interventions in open distance learning are making learning more accessible for women. Special provisions for women learners particularly those who are more deprived i.e., marginalized communities, tribal minority groups, disabled are to be made in terms of livelihoods-oriented courses.

Culture and Communication: There are five chapters in this section. It begins with the observation that a new era has been dawn in Indian society that has a large part of it under the oral communication tradition which is now in a clash with writing culture; social media combines both oral and written communication. The remaining chapters discuss the hegemony of dominant culture, religious communication, and ordinary language and communication that reinforce the traditional values of gender that control social behaviour.

Mira K. Desai in the first chapter of this section, 'Clash of Cultures:

Development and Digital Media in Asian Societies' argues by reviewing John Fiske's framework that the digital media mostly developed in Western societies have differential impacts in Eastern societies as regards to written and spoken word, and diverse worlds are consuming digital technologies differently. Thus, the examination of the written versus oral and individual versus collective dichotomies are necessary, and the chapter attempts to examine the digital technologies at the micro as well as the macro level that has a differential impact in Asian cultures.

In the next chapter, 'Hegemonic Indian Culture and Society in *Chandamama* Comics' Aloysius Sebastian, presents an analysis of one of the early Indian comics, *Chandamama*, published from 1947 July onwards, that is, just one month before India gained independence. This initiation had its intention of teaching "Indian tradition and culture" to children and undo what the British education system did. The *Chandamama* represented an idyllic pre-colonial Indian society. However, it is argued in the chapter that *Chandamama* had deliberately attempted to forget and ignore or else peripherize minor communities and cultures under the hegemony of the dominant cultural values.

The following chapter of Anil and Puthusserry, 'Religion in Cyberspace: An Ethnographic Study on *Theyyam* Ritual in Kerala' presents an analysis of three cases where the interplay of digital communication and the ethnic cultic practices occur to create polyphonic discourse in cyberspace. These cases are related to the ritual of *kaliyattam* in Kerala. The study is carried out using ethnographic methods. It reveals that ICTs are providing new perspectives and scenarios in the understanding of religion among the local populations.

Ratan Naga Deepika in the chapter, 'Migrant Community, Communicative Performance and Production of Space' describes the 'Rath Yatra' ritual of immigrant working-class Odiya in Katedan, an Industrial area (IDA) in Hyderabad. The ritual is considered as a "communicative performance" by which it tries to communicate with the larger public and to itself. It is an attempt for a peaceful coexistence of the 'dominant' local community and the 'dominated' immigrant community in sharing the lived urban space.

In the following chapter, 'Use of Mobile Phones and Changing Family Communication Structure within Family of Migrants', Swati Arjun reports on the digital intervention in the form of smart mobile phones, into the lives of the migrant population residing in the Delhi-NCR region and its effect in the communications structure of these migrant families. It has been observed that mobile smart-phones have changed the communication the pattern within the family, contributed to neutralizing gender hierarchy in these families, the man-woman relationship in these families have gone through a change because of this and women have become more expressive and assertive in their approach.

Communication and Health: Three chapters are included in this section. Health, both physical and psychological, being one of the important aspects of life, the role of communication in taking care of health is the most significant aspect with which the section deals. The media used in this regard are several, but some have a positive effect while some other being harmful to the users, and the section deals with three kinds of media.

In the opening chapter in this section 'Community Games: An Instrument for Creating Menstrual Awareness' Pragati Paul and Krishna Sankar Kusuma examine the possibilities of employing community games like Ludo Queen and 'Mahavari: Sabse Zaroori Iski Jaankari' as an approach for creating menstrual awareness in Delhi. They conclude that the concept of engaging youth to prepare floor games is very efficacious. The Field testing of the game has helped these game developers to access the game designed by them in a practical and unbiased manner.

Rajesh Das in the chapter, 'Health Awareness and Television Programme: A Study of the Impact on the Scheduled Caste Community in Rural Bengal' presents an evaluation of the message design, content selection and production technique in television regarding health communication programmes for the rural populations of West Bengal employing health belief model and theory of planned behaviour along with McGuire's Hierarchy of Effects to gauge various stages of the outcome. Based on a study conducted among the scheduled caste families, he argues that TV has an impact and to a certain extent there is an acceptance among the rural Scheduled Caste community. At the same time audience is interested to watch the Entertainment-Education (E-E), model of the programmes.

In the final chapter of this section, 'Social Network Systems, Mental Health and Development: A Study of Medical and Dental Students' Sharon Sucharitha Gold reveals that there is a positive correlation between exposure to cyber-space and depression among MBBS and BDS students in Kadapa town of Andhra Pradesh based on a study. The study has employed Beck's Depression Inventory scale to measure the degree of mental health. However, it points out that more intensive studies need to be undertaken in this regard for causative factors of depression could be multiple and spending time on cyber-space and social network sites are among them.

Community Radio: This section includes three chapters. An alternative to state-run radio is community radio which has come into existence in India after the 2000s only, and it is imperative to study its impact. The chapters in this section discuss the nature of participant communication, participants and the impact of community radios among various populations in different parts of India.

Sreeju Nadh in the chapter, 'Community Radio as a Tool for Gender Sensitization: A Case Study of Gurgaon Ki Awaaz' provides the findings of the study on Gurgaon Ki Awaaz, a community radio station. These include: the radio has provided a space for the community to discuss and debate on various issues ranging from entertainment to development; it has made more approachable and dependable for the community members; it has created awareness on issues of common concern. It has great potential for empowerment for women who largely remain uneducated and financially dependent on men.

Shamala, Devadas and Sivakami in the chapter, 'Community Radio and Disaster Management: A Study on Role of Kalanjiam Community Radio Station during Gaja Cyclone' present the findings of their study about the role played by the community radio station among the fishermen in Nagapattinam District of Tamil Nadu when the cyclone 'Gaja' hit the coast in November 2018. The study concludes that efficacious use of community radio can effectively mitigate disasters, particularly in geographically isolated communities. It argues that the community media, which has tremendous importance, is in a struggling phase. It stands alone, to supporting the voiceless people upholding the value of humanity. There is a need to strengthen the community radio station and broadcasting relevant programmes for the targeted audience.

T. Rampersaud's chapter, 'Who is participating? : An Analysis of Communities in Community Radio in India' is the final one in the section. It provides a generalized description of the types of communities involved in community radio in India. Through quantitative data, it provides insight into the types of participants based on the categorizations of 'children, LGBTQ, men, PWD, women, youth, and other'—classification created through data from secondary sources as well as primary data collected from four community radio stations located in East, West, South and North-East India, It concludes that while there is a need for greater representation of the communities to which community radio stations broadcast in India, the challenges associated with funding is a deterrent.

Media: In this final section there are seven chapters that discuss the utilization of media in contemporary Indian society. It provides the ground realities of media coverage in India in terms of geographical locations, communities and also aspects covered particularly. These chapters, deal with the aspects relating to education, penetration of media in tribal and rural areas, empowerment of women and third gender.

Vinod Pandey and Satyabrata Das discuss in the chapter, 'Media Awareness among the School Going Students: A Study of Math Village in Raipur District of Chhattisgarh' the findings of a study on media awareness and the impact of new media (Social media) among the students in Raipur district of Chhattisgarh. It is found that 70 per cent of the students use new media technology for their studies and other related study materials. The remaining 30 per cent do not have a mobile phone; they depend on the computer classes but the impact is not impressive. About 80 per cent use new technology for entertainment purposes and only 30 per cent use it for getting other facilities like bill payment, online money transactions, online and offline merchandise through this new technology platform.

Pradeep Mallik asserts in the chapter, 'The Role of Social Media in Social Transformation' that in social media the line between media producers and media audience is blurred and the two-way communication between the producers and the audience, and the horizontal communication among the social media users is leading to quick formation of communities and effective communication among the members. He argues that when social media combines with traditional media, the effect of social mobilization would be great, and it would be a step towards social transformation.

Shashikant Bhagat examines in the chapter, 'Role of Social Media in Tribal Development: An Empirical Study of Gujarat Tribes' to what extent social media has reached the Bhil, Scheduled Tribes in Gujarat. It is found that out of 300 respondents only 47 have indicated using social media among which television viewing is the highest (44.3 %) and it is followed by mobile phone (39.7%). Television is used mainly for "news, views and opinion" (93.6 %) followed "entertainment" (89.4%) and "social interaction, social relationships and sharing of information" at the same level (87.2 %). It is also found that the media has not been used for the socio-economic development of the Bhils in any manner.

In 'Giving Voice, Building Community, and Bringing Change One Story at a Time: Can Social Media Live Up to the Hype?' Devina Sarwatay analyses two social media blogs: Humans of Bombay and Momspresso, the author argues in this chapter that there is evidence of communities are being built and bring change in a small way. The Social Media through stories of failures, successes, exclusivity, disappointments and achievements apparently give voice, build communities and bring change. It indicates that despite some differences in terms of tools used in these cases, by and large, social media has a perceptible living up to the expectations.

Delfi Chinnappan in the chapter, 'Hijra Self-representation on and through Facebook: Negotiating *Hijra* identity and Promoting community work in Mumbai' explores the use of social media by trans-genders for community-building and representation in a non-western context, Mumbai-based *hijra gharanas* and their community-based organizations (CBOs). The *hijara* use Facebook to self-represent themselves. She observes that there is an emerging dynamic within *hijra* CBOs through their presentation of the digitally mediated identities on Facebook.

In the chapter, 'Sharenting: An Empirical Study on Online Sharing Habits of Indian Parents and its Effects on their Children' Nitesh Tripathi explores Sharenting, online sharing habits of parents in Indian the context. The study shows that most of the parents who are active on Social Media engage in sharenting but the children are not comfortable with few aspects of Social Media engagement of their parents. Even though the parents don't post or share too much about their children, they rarely take consent of their children before uploading which is unethical.

'Phatic Communication on WhatsApp in the Indian Family Context' is the final chapter in this section. Padma Rani deals with a theoretical issue and its implication of it in the study of the communicative and social function of micro-posts on WhatsApp. Different social networking sites and Instant messaging apps provide an expressive medium to share with others our feelings, needs, current status, or simple statements. Those simple and short statements can carry light information or low information. It can also provoke communication. The chapter attempts to explain such expressive medium through the concept of 'phatic communication' developed in anthropology and semiotics.

Thus the volume provides a wide canvas of culture, communication and development in India. As a maiden attempt, it touches upon the current scenario and emerging themes of communication research. We strongly believe that it will evoke great interest among the students of social sciences particularly anthropology, sociology, communication and journalism besides researchers and development agencies.

N. Sudhakar Rao and **Arbind Sinha**

SECTION 1

Culture, Communication and Development

1

Culture, Communication and Development

The Trek of Coexistence

Arbind Sinha

It is most appropriate to retread back to the essence of anthropology, the history of development communication, and the missions of development to give a proper background of the convergence of these academic disciplines in the context of discourse on the development in India.

Anthropology though traces its origin sometimes from the middle of the 19th century, but got professionally institutionalized on the global plane when the British anthropologists took the initiative to organize the first International Congress of Anthropological and Ethnological Sciences (ICAES) in London in 1934. Travelling through the journey of ICAES, we find how the concepts of 'Culture', 'Communication', and 'Development' were given space for discussion on this international platform over the last 85 years. These are an inseparable blend. Let us travel through time and space to see how subjects that were not part of traditional anthropology were brought to focus.

Through the documentation of ICAES deliberations, we find that the applied side of anthropology has always attracted the attention of the scholars world over. Even during the first ICAES, held in London in 1934, it was not a discussion on only culture, social structure, marriage and kinship. There was a separate discussion on Technology. Of course, the term 'technology' has always been used and was used those days also, in the context of tools and its design to reduce the drudgery of humankind. Can we relate it to today's Information and Communication Technology (ICT) that has changed the face of society? It was taken forward in Brussels Congress in 1948 and the Paris Congress in 1960.

With the advent of new technology developed at every stage of human history, we have enough thought to focus our discussion a bit on how anthropologists diversified their interest and worked in the area of communication and communication technology as communication has also become part of an anthropological discourse, and some of the anthropologists have created their justified positions in communication.

We find that parallel to other streams of anthropology, the applied side of anthropology for solving human problems attracted equal attention in all these deliberations. In the Vienna Congress of 1952, discussion on appiied ethnography was a unique feature. It was followed by Philadelphia Congress in 1956 which discussed community welfare, and Paris Congress specifically deliberated applied anthropology in the context of cultural change in 1960. I am not sure if widening the scope of anthropology had to do anything with the shifting of the venue from European cities to American cities in 1956, but Prof. Vidyarthi commented that "it gave birth to the trend of Americanization of Anthropology" (1978a).

Another sphere of anthropology started when the participants of the 1952 Vienna Congress discussed anthropology on celluloid when an International Committee on Ethnographic Film was constituted with its headquarters at Musee de I'Homme, Paris. During the Paris Congress (1960), a session was introduced on Ethnographic films, mainly depicting the lives of people under study. However, it took another 13 years before a session was organized on Visual Anthropology during the 1973 Chicago Congress. It included the use of film materials in classroom-dissemination of information. The next step was setting up a Commission on Visual Anthropology as part of IUAES in the 1978 Delhi Congress. In his book *Essentials of Cultural Anthropology*, A.R.N. Srivastava (2005) too has listed Visual Anthropology as one of the new subfields of anthropology. He emphasizes the study of human behaviour through visual means –the technology as developed from time to time—films, videotapes, and televisions. We justifiably connect the discussion on people, culture and communication and its applied side that were already on the horizon by the late 1950s.

Communication (we may include visual anthropology as one of the media of communication) is another important feature that appeared in anthropological literature from the beginning. Visual anthropology has a function of 'preservation and communication' through the use of films, videotapes and televisions. These technologies have been proven useful as they are independent of language. These technologies help the preservation of facts—life in action, convey to the audience a 'feel' of the people. Television and visual anthropology were discussed as a new technique of observation and analysis in anthropology. Cyril Belshaw, the

Canadian anthropologist wrote in 1978 about International communication and anthropology. Belshaw (1978) mentioned the wider dissemination of research knowledge and research ideas through verbo-visual and computer-based technology.

On the Indian front, the historical details show that the formative period of Indian Anthropology (till 1919) was dominated by the British influence, followed by the constructive period (1920-1947). After India's independence, the contacts with American Anthropologists increased and the changing trends have been noticeable since then. Hence, the links help in dotting the trajectory of anthropology—traditional anthropology, applied anthropology, and to a limited extent action anthropology. The corresponding role of the social anthropologists have found recognition in applied areas and it has been reflected in anthropologists getting engaged in several non-traditional anthropological roles, but yet using the anthropological approach in the task they handle.

Anthropology turned its focus on the facet of development when the process of urbanization was discussed in Ninth Congress 1973, held in Chicago. Participants also discussed New Approaches to Development at Pre-Congress Conference. It is interesting to know that one of the outcomes of the Chicago Congress was a volume published on *Development from Below: Anthropologists and Development Situation*. Prof. L.P. Vidyarthi (1978b) in his book 'Rise of Anthropology in India' recognized the contribution of anthropologists in SITE project of ISRO, which has been the landmark in the use of communication for national development. He mentioned it and has listed it under the sub-head "Space Anthropology". When he wrote Anthropology for the future will still make the picture clearer, it gave a clear indication that anthropology will not be the same in the future. Many of us remember how excited were we when IUAES decided to have its 10th International Congress in India. The theme of the 10th Congress, under the presidentship of Prof. L.P. Vidyarthi, was "Anthropology and the Challenges of Development".

There is no second opinion that anthropologists can combine their understanding of the cultural context of the target population as well as planner and can help the planners by making appropriate recommendations for the effective use of communication skills for development plans (see L.P. Vidyarthi 1978c). The biggest strength for anthropologists is collecting primary data through extensive 'field research'. Field Work is the differentiator in the management of the development project. It gives a project manager a new perspective of looking at the development issues keeping in mind the social system. This strength was long ago recognized by the British administrators and with most of their development support programmes in developing countries had anthropologists deployed along with their development projects. Many of us here had the opportunity to work with such a development project. I worked for Rotary International that supported the Self-Help Programme of tribal development, in now Jharkhand state.

The strength of anthropology got its due and anthropologists started occupying senior positions in the research units of many other non-traditional government establishments—Planning Commission, Office of Registrar General of India, NCERT, Family Planning, and Media Organisations, Space Applications Centre—ISRO and several other organizations interested in developmental and modernization programmes. The task was to connect the programme and the people. The learning of anthropology started paying a dividend. It may be mentioned here that during that era of post-independent India, Government employments held a bigger pie in a job opportunity, with very few openings in private sectors.

I remember, the top positions in the Research and Evaluation cell of Indian Space Research Organisation, in Monitoring and Evaluation Unit of Planning Commission, Office of Registrar General of India, Indian Institute of Mass Communication, Audience Research Unit, Aakashvani (erstwhile All India Radio) and Doordarshan (Indian Television) were all occupied by anthropologists.

Management education came as the third wave of education in India and it also recognized the strength of anthropologists in teaching the management students the cultural context of business and its management. Indian Institutes of Management, Administrative Staff College of India and MICA are few examples where anthropologists were not only engaged as faculty but also got the top position. Of course, all of them did not only confine to the traditional anthropological practices, rather increased their horizon to other application areas—applied anthropology.

So, there has always been a direct connection between Culture, Communication, and National Development. Communication is culture-bound and the study of communication reflects the reality of contemporary society. It is well documented that communication can be effective only when the coding and decoding of the elements of communication are complete by those who share the same socio-cultural experience—the core of anthropology and sociology. Wilber Schramm (1964: 271) said that the information multiplier is an essential indicator of national, economic and social development and without mass communication; probably the great freedom movements and national stirrings never would have come about at all. S.C. Dube (1976: 107) held the opinion that communication plays a direct and useful role in the areas of community development movement with several communication strategies—traditional channels as well as mass media. I strongly hold the opinion that no development programme can be executed without a strong component of communication.

By the mid-1960s, India realized that a developing country like India cannot afford to wait with a slow mode of communication, and thought of accelerating the pace of development using the contemporary sophisticated technology and planned for satellite communication.

Sarabhai (1969: 5) writes—one of the prime ingredients of development is the dissemination of information and for the rapid and sustained growth of developing countries, the urgent need to disseminate information to the masses is obvious.

There is known evidence of anthropologists working in multi-disciplinary teams and contributing, as part of communication organizations, which aim at national development.

Till the early seventies, the Anthropological Survey of India (ASI) or teaching employment was the only reference point for an anthropologist coming out of the university with a degree in anthropology. Gradually development planning, which otherwise was called 'planning from the ivory tower', realized the need to have realistic participatory planning by analyzing the feel of the grassroots. They did identify the communication gap between the programme and the people whom they wanted to reach out with their plans but did not know their cultural settings in which communication works about their programmes. The emphasis was put on framing development plans in the cultural context of the target population.

REFERENCES

Belshaw, Cyril (1978). "International Communication in Anthropology: Some issues and Alternative." In Demitri B. Simkin, Sol Tax, and John W. Morrison (eds.), *Anthropology for the Future*, Illinois: University of Illinois.

Dube, S.C. (1976). "Mass Media and National Development." In: Wilber Schramm and D. Lerner (eds.) *Communication and Change in Developing Countries*, Honolulu: University of Hawaii Press.

Sarabhai, Vikram A. (1969). *Television for Development*. Paper presented at the 11th World Congress, Society for International Development, New Delhi

Schramm, Wilber (1964). *Mass Media and National Development: The Role of Information in the Developing Countries*. Stanford: Stanford University Press, p. 271.

Srivastava, A.R.N. (2005). *Essentials of Cultural Anthropology*, New Delhi: Prentice-Hall of India Pvt. Ltd.

Vidyarthi L.P. (1978a). *Trends in World Anthropology*, Delhi: Concept Publishing Co.

Vidyarthi L.P. (1978b). *Rise of World Anthropology*, Delhi: Concept Publishing Co.

Vidyarthi L.P. (1978c). *Rise of Anthropology in India. Vol. 2, The Rural, Urban and Other Dimensions*, Delhi: Concept Publishing Co.

2
Satellite Instructional Television Experiment (SITE)
A Holistic Perspective

B.P. Sanjay

PART A: THE ADDRESS[1]

It's indeed an honour to be here. Personally, because of my long and continued association with Binod. I thank Sudhakar for elevating me to this valedictory because I had sent an abstract in response to the first call.

I have deliberately called it SITE, holistic journey. This is to respect the fact that our introduction to the holistic approach was provided by none other than Prof Binod. So I thought that the title is symbolic. It is also symbolic of the synergy that the organizers have between Communication Department and Anthropology in terms of matters concerning Communication and Media. I also borrowed in a way, the anthropological terms of emic and etic. The emic perspective was provided by Binod even before the real world and others and etic was provided by an equally well-known institutional anthropologist, Professor Bob Anderson, whose recent book on nucleus and state and the manufacture of Atomic Bomb in India analyses the Institutional collaboration and the issues pertaining to advanced technologies in a developing country such as India.

The nation is celebrating the birth centenary of Dr. Vikram Sarabhai. It is also coincidental that this seminar is being organised in the birth centenary month of the scientist and creator of the Indian Space Programme. His vision, leadership and institution building profile has been documented and is also being cited as a background to his contribution. Bob Anderson has a separate chapter, where he talked about Vikram Sarabhai as a second and a parallel builder of India's Atomic Energy Programme.

For Sarabhai, SITE was among many other things a launch to the larger aspects of India's space programme that is now evident in terms of India's position in the International Space Club. We as Communication and Media scholars have spent a lot of time concentrating on Sarabhai and SITE. It embedded a developmental approach. One common strand in Sarabhai's thinking was the notion of leap frogging. It is also comparable to the paradigm of Modernisation and leapfrogging that Daniel Lerner talks about in his book *The Passing of the Traditional Society* (1958).

It so happened that Sarabhai and the founder of the Brazilian space programme, were students at an advanced engineering programme at Stanford University. The framework for television for development was persuasively made at this workshop. A substantial body of literature and advocacy regarding television and its potential was put forth in many documents including the Wilbur Schramm authored a report for USAID. Communication satellite as the basis for television expansion was a powerful argument. The Satellite had to be parked by NASA and the considerations leading to this decision needs to be weighed in the context of cold war dynamics as well. Arnold Fruitkin in one of the oral history articulations of NASA recalls certain reluctance to park the satellite based on the USA's experience in the voice of America matter where their offer to set up a powerful transmitter had run into political opposition in the aftermath of the Indo-China war of 1962.

For NASA, the civilian application for the satellite was very important because NASA was not able to push satellites in the USA where the terrestrial cable interests were deeply entrenched. So it was interested in a large country like India, they've chosen India and Brazil. In Brazil, the State Department had assessed that the south coast of Brazil is already inundated with television. So their focus was on India. Going by the VOA episode, the USA as also keen on India stated that it wanted the Satellite. Vikram Sarabhai formally expressed the intent of India leading to the agreement between NASA and DAE for the SITE.

NASA has also formal relationships with the private sector manufacturing communication satellites. SITE was for one year and they refused to extend it even by a day and India had to look for a satellite to continue its television programmes on a nationwide basis via INSAT. It is no coincidence that the Ford Aerospace satellite was the choice and it may be pointed out that part of Ford foundation's long presence in India included its advocacy for television.

Specifically, on SITE, Bangalore University where I was pursuing my Master's had been awarded an external evaluation contract for SITE. This evaluation was commissioned mainly due to the interest and background of Prof. K.E. Eapen who insisted that all our Master's thesis had to focus on several components of SITE for which a research officer (Prof. Leela Rao) was appointed and she set up an office in Gulbarga, one of the three contiguous districts of Karnataka selected for SITE. Part of the evaluation exercise included training by the Space Applications Centre Social scientists and my formal association with Prof. Binod Agrawal began and continues even today. Binod and Eapen were graduate student mates in Wisconsin.

The scientists had already worked on a plan that included a formative (T0), process (T1) and summative (T2). Our work focused on the process dimension and few of us continued in the summative work out of our academic interest.

SITE was conducted during 1975-1976 that coincided with the internal emergency that Mrs. Gandhi had declared. Its impact on the experiment and the overall use or misuse of television in that period is an important factor that we need to understand within the framework of the overall celebration of this experiment.

PART B: THE PAPER

The Satellite Instructional Television Experiment (SITE) was perhaps one of the largest communication projects in the world then called the Third World. It was a culmination of both an academic and institutional persuasion that led to this experiment rooted in the then paradigm of modernisation and development that foreground television as the instructor and teacher in the sky.

For India, the planning of this experiment albeit institutionalised in the vision and work of Dr. Vikram Sarabhai, was also an ideal setting for research to gain and learn from this experiment. It is an academic question now as to whether this experiment took place in the context of the internal emergency and therefore partially shifted the focus to a long term political use of television.

For us, fortunate to be part of a small but outside the established research group, this was both an experience and something that laid the foundation of our comprehensive understanding. The research scientists at Space Applications Centre (SAC) that included Prof Agarwal gave the much-needed direction to the agenda and its implementation. Conceived and stretched over formative, process and summative research, the experiment did lead to the belief and operation of the Indian National Satellite System (INSAT) as the hub of our television system.

By recalling my association with Prof. Agarwal, this paper will reflect partially on my dissertation work. It will analyse the developments since then with regard to not only television but the communication eco-system as it is defined now.

More than the medium that is perceived simplistically as the harbinger of change, the network of other fundamental relations has shaped its development. The now and then dialectics of whether we have forgotten the Nehru-Sarabhai construct of communication and development continues to rankle us. Advocacy and policy groups intervene to try and restore both the medium and the message in favour of the poor and marginalised the digitally divided. Some of the research techniques and lessons that Prof. Agarwal used and applied are perhaps still relevant. Reflecting on SITE is indicative of our respect and regard for Prof. Binod Agarwal. This volume has a more detailed career graph of Binod.

The nation is celebrating the birth centenary of Dr. Vikram Sarabhai whose vision, leadership and institution building profile has been documented and is being recalled with additional perspectives in various forums (Anderson S. Robert, 2010). Satellite Instructional Television Experiment (SITE) is one major contribution that enshrined his belief in science and technology as the framework for India's development within which was subsumed his faith in communication media, particularly television. The fact that Sarabhai had encouraged and permitted the anthropological study of scientific institutions in India is less known but significant as such reflections allow for insights into policy processes, individuals and institution building.

Working through his ideas as part of my dissertation, I realised the continuous thread of the then dominant paradigm of modernisation, national development and leapfrogging embedded in his planning for SITE. What it also reveals is how S&T efforts of a newly independent nation (Anderson S. Robert, 2010, p. 77) are situated within its colonial legacy, geo-political and global competition for supremacy. While the enthusiasm to allow for the use of ATS for SITE was there. It was related to the macro relations of the US and India in the geo-political framework of the Cold War era. Post-Indo-China conflict, part of the help that the US was keen to offer was setting up a high power transmitter in India that could be used for Voice of America (VOA) and India. This raised a political storm in India and the opposition to US help or intervention was evident (Essay, 2013).

The argument for peaceful uses of outer space had to be enshrined as an international mechanism before the actual operationalisation. Specifically, his analysis of the sluggish pace at which TV was to be introduced in India and the need for accelerated consideration of a satellite-based expansion is articulated in his views on television for development (Vikram, 1969). Leapfrogging was his consistent argument. The educational dimension had a US assessment and perspective. Arnold Frutkin (now past 100 and alive) the then director of NASA's international programme in an interview many years after SITE summarised the relationship based on the fact that while NASA was obliquely also interested in satellites for surveillance that was in sharper focus owing to geo-political compulsions. There was a need for demonstration effect of not only satellite but also television more so in large countries that in due course could prove commercially viable. Brazil and India were in the reckoning. Brazil was ruled out as its coastal areas already had television and other areas were not as important. India was not a large country but was debating the introduction of television. However dealing with the US state department was Frutkin's responsibility. He mentions the resistance and how he had to overcome it by persuading Sarabhai to write to him as to how useful the relationship would be. The state department's concern was addressed and articulated as follows:

> Oh, well, that's completely distinguishable from this, because we don't want to build anything on Indian soil, in the first place. Secondly, the Voice of America wants to broadcast American programmes, [which they probably view as] propaganda, good or bad, in India. We don't want to broadcast any American programmes. According to our concept of this thing, all we would do, ... after we have used the satellite for American purposes for a year, [is] nudge it along the equator till it looks at India. Then India can use a ground station which it will build with its own money, broadcast its own programmes, which must be educational programmes, up to the satellite, and the satellite will diffuse [them] down to the receivers. (Frutkin W. Arnold, 2002)

USAID had commissioned a study to Stanford University and the report authored by Wilbur Schramm and Lyle Nelson running into two volumes upheld the utility of television for development and made a pitch for its adoption in other developing countries as well:

> India will make up its own mind on the various satellite plans and proposals before it, and decide whether or where a satellite belongs in its development plans. The purpose of this paper is not to suggest what India should do, but rather to consider the Indian situation as a case, worthy of consideration by other developing countries, by planners and policy makers in all countries who are concerned with the use of satellites, and by aid-granting agencies who may have to decide where to place support.
>
> (Schramm, 1968, p. 3).

To NASA, which loaned us the communications satellite it was a case of realising its technical objectives of testing it on a large area and also the spin-off commercial interests for the commercial satellite manufacturers. It may be recalled that the agreement was fool-proof and for one year only and despite requests and articulation that could the programme continue it did not happen and the television screens in the SITE villages went blank after a year. Subsequently, Ford Aerospace became the supplier for the Indian National Satellite System (INSAT). The spin-off for the Indian electronics industry as Sarabhai had envisioned happened and Indian television has never looked back. In SITE, the reference then was Direct Reception Sets (DRS) and today it is Direct to Home (DTH).

Irrespective of critique and romantic arguments, SITE no doubt is enshrined in the international annals of communication history. Communitarian perspectives in the field are replete with references that touch upon technology, culture, development, dependency etc. Binod Agrawal and many other social scientists occupy a significant place in its formative, process and summative research initiatives. The incorporation of the social science component into SITE planning came much later than the elaborate planning and interaction that went into the agreement. It would be academic now to ask if the SITE programme component and outreach would have been different had communicologists like Binod been associated with it much earlier.

To my mentor and teacher Prof. Eapen and subsequently us, Binod Agrawal was and is a continuous source of inspiration. Our long association began at the Bangalore University particularly during the Master's programme around 1974. The University had seeded the first of its kind in the Indian HE system, a faculty of communication. That historical aspect for a long time lingered across numerous debates regarding nomenclature for what is broadly now accepted as Journalism and (mass) communication studies.

In the Department and for Eapen, SITE was academically significant. He had proposed and was awarded a research project to study SITE and the ongoing first batch of students and us in the second batch of our master's research work had to focus on SITE. An orientation study trip to Ahmedabad and meeting with the social scientists who lead the research exercise was my first introduction to Binod. Our research had to be field-based and we had to stay in the villages. Binod is credited with providing the much needed anthropological input and we had the term, holistic studies from him and his interaction with us.

Binod recalls how for the first time he had heard about SITE from Eapen and was later invited for a social scientists' meeting with Prof. Yash Pal. This meeting was attended by seven University of Wisconsin alumni out of whom only Binod joined the SITE team. Binod and Bella Mody were the first two social scientists to be hired by ISRO. Reflecting on the SITE to commemorate its ruby year, Binod, Bella and Arbind have recalled their association. The political context as in the launch of the experiment post introduction of Emergency and field ramifications in Bihar where the seeds of JP's movement had been sown is also a reference point that Arbind recalls. (Space Applications Centre, 2015).

The experiment social science research component was rooted in the then quantitative approach. However, Binod mentions that anthropological methods in its classical form were factored that led to ISRO documenting it as Television comes to the village. The take-off was a methodological guide and assessment published in 1985 by Binod.

A reference to the utility of his experience and work is contained in the action report that he and his colleagues including Prof. Sudhakar Rao, one of the prime architects of this seminar prepared on the Yanadi tribe whose territory or habitation in Sriharikota had been taken over by ISRO for its programme. While SAC had the benefit of the organisation and its resources, the university could provide support within the scope of the project funding. As stated earlier, the exposure and induction provided by Binod and his team were useful in our work. A formal opportunity to work with Binod and his team in DECU and SAC as a researcher for the SITE continuity project came by but could not be taken up as the organisation I was working for wanted a deferral of acceptance that the then chairman of ISRO politely refused.

> It all started at a dinner party during the first week of August, 1975. Agrawal casually asked Professor Satish Dhawan about the future plans of space research.[1] Professor Dhawan mentioned

> the activities in the Sriharikota High Altitude Range (SHAR) and the problems of the tribal people who were returning to SHAR at the time, in spite of tight security and the disapproval of the SHAR administration. The lands and the forests of the Yanadi (who had been there since time immemorial) had now become the property of the Indian Space Research Organisation. The Yanadi were no longer entitled to live in the forest or eat the fruits and roots. Professor Dhawan asked Agrawal if anthropological knowledge could help in solving the tribe's problem. Agrawal said yes, but that he would first have to visit SHAR. This brief discussion culminated with an abrupt remark by Professor Dhawan: "Please do something about the Yanadi." After dinner, Agrawal asked another scientist from SHAR the name of the tribe living in SHAR. Only next day was Agrawal able to finally pin down the name of the tribe and to collect references on the Yanadi. (Agrawal *et al.*, 1981)

Displacement and identity related aspects including very proactive solutions that included schooling, minimum wages and gender parity were examined and are factored in the report. Peripheral references to the limitations of being a social scientist for the institution and the displacement dynamics of the tribals cannot escape our attention. Anthropologist intervention in persuading the Space agency to start a school for the Yanadi is an institutional dimension.

Both Binod and Arbind defied the many bureaucratic barriers of SAC-DECU and were successful in generating a worldwide network of students and scholars whose interest in SITE was not only engendered but also the data they had and were willing to provide. Apart from SITE itself, the contributions are evident in significant studies and interventions in the Kheda Communications project and also the Jhabua communication project. The many frontiers of the application of space technology with regard to health, education, remote sensing have been analysed at the field level by Binod and his team. At the policy level, the host of educational technology centres including UGC have benefited from his guidance. The appreciation and mentoring Binod was able to provide for my doctoral work pertaining to SITE and its transition to INSAT is of immense value towards understanding technology and the context of its deployment.

SITE factored an organic link with a team of social scientists. However, the nationwide expansion of television following the experiment justifiably divested the technology aspect and the focus was more on related organisational aspects of state-run television and the host of issues that included both news and entertainment content. Binod and his colleagues made substantial contributions to enlarging our perspective on transnationalisation, culture, education, multilingual reception parameters of the audience. Binod was very active and sustained his scholarship through publications and extensive participation in seminars and symposia including leading panels. His guidance to a vast network of scholars is significant and his penchant for institutional building and mentoring of young leaders add to his qualities.

Post SITE, his work in the context of his association with Taleem, the educational arm of Zee has focused on psephology, diaspora, religion, historical analysis of extension and interrogation of theory.

My more than four decades of association with Binod is significant for the fact he was continuously engaged in discussing with us and sharing his ideas and was very quick to publish his thoughts through seminars and publications. I share the affectionate sentiments many of his friends and well-wishers continuously have expressed here and in other events. His career and personality have a holistic dimension.

NOTES

1. Part A is summation of the valedictory address for the national seminar in honour of Prof. Binod Agrawal by Prof. B.P. Sanjay. He shares more than four decades of professional association with him. Part B is the paper edited for this publication.

BIBLIOGRAPHY

Agrawal, B.C., Reddy, P.C.G., and Rao, N.S. (1981). "An Experiment in Action Anthropology: Yanadi Action Research Project in India." *Human Organization*, 40(1), 87–90. JSTOR. www.jstor.org/stable/44125593

Anderson S. Robert (2010). *Nucleus and Nation: Scientists, International Networks, and Power in India, Anderson* (1st ed.). University of Chicago. https://www.press.uchicago.edu/ucp/books/book/chicago/N/bo8156460.html

Essay. (2013). Nehru & VOA. Frontline. *Frontline*. https://frontline.thehindu.com/the-nation/nehru-amp-voa/article4888124.ece

Frutkin W. Arnold. (2002, January 11). *Arnold W. Frutkin Oral History*. NASA Johnson Space Center. https://www.jsc.nasa.gov/history/oral_histories/NASA_HQ/Administrators/FrutkinAW/FrutkinAW_1-11-02.htm

Lerner, Daniel (1958). *The Passing of Traditional Society*, Glencoe: The Free Press.

Schramm, L.N. (1968). *Communication Satellites for Education and Development—The Case of India*. Washington: USAID.

Space Applications Centre. (2015). *Satellite Instructional Television Experiment-Memoirs*. Ahmedabad: SAC.

Vikram, S. (1969, November 16). *Television for Development*. Retrieved August 21, 2019, from PRL: https://www.prl.res.in/~library/sarabhai_v_speeches.pdf

3

Culture, Communication and Development

(Late) Bandi Balaswamy

"Development divorced from its human or cultural context is growth without soul".

—*World Commission on Culture and Development*

Introduction

There is an inseparable relationship between culture, communication and development. They are interdependent and reinforce one another. Communication, it is said, is the lifeblood of society. It is vital to the functioning of the human social order. Communication is constitutive of culture. No culture can breathe without communication (Dissanayake, 2003). As World Commission on Culture and Development (1994) observed, culture is the fountain of our progress and creativity and must be carefully nurtured to grow and develop. Both culture and communication are considered important elements which can propel development. Both in its structures and its content, communication intermeshes with and is dependent on, the economy in many ways. A constant flow of information is vital for economic life. As well as being a great economic force, with incalculable potentialities, it is a decisive factor in development. Information and more specifically, the ability to transmit, store and use information is a key resource on a par with energy or raw materials (MacBride Commission, 1980).

The concept of development can be traced back to the four-point programme announced by Harry S. Truman in 1949. In January of 1949, President Harry S. Truman gave his inaugural address, wherein he elucidated the Point Four Programme. The outcome of this proposal was called development. Relieving Third World suffering consisted of making available the western cornucopia of advances in agriculture, commerce, industry and health (Melkote, 1991). This speech is considered the jumping-off point of international development in the post-war world (Winterhalt, 2018). The Truman doctrine paved the way to the emergence of the dominant paradigm in development. Across the disciplines, the intellectuals and policy makers in the 1950s and 60s believed that by retracing the development path of already developed countries, the Third World countries can develop at a faster rate than the developed countries themselves experienced development. This orientation came to be known as the dominant paradigm. A paradigm is a mental model which seeks to explain a phenomenon. Economists, sociologists, psychologists and communication experts believed that industrialization, urbanization and modernization were the routes to development. Thus, the meaning of 'development' in the 1950s and 60s was the transition of traditional societies as complex modern societies or in other words, the transformation of Third World countries into the form of industrialized, 'developed' countries, such as the USA and UK.

Economic Development

The wealth created by the application of science and technology in the production process became a focal point of development during the dominant paradigm's regime. Development was seen mainly as economic development through industrialization. It was quantified and measured through Gross National Production (GNP) and per capita income. The developmental policies also aimed at increasing GNP and per capita income. Economic growth through industrialization became the obsession of some countries. Due to their prosperity and material well-being the industrialized countries became, subsequently, the models of development for underdeveloped countries. With the emergence of the concept of 'development' as an important concern, it also became the concern of scholars, belonging to various disciplines, including communication. (Narula, 1994).

The role of both communication, as well as, culture, assumed significance in the dominant paradigm. Information was considered as the missing link in the development chain (Melkote, 1991). Some scholars stated that the major problem in developing countries was not a shortage of natural resources but underdevelopment of human resources. For example, Wilbur Schramm felt that the modernization of industry or agricultural sectors in developing nations required the mobilization of human resources (Schramm, 1964). Therefore, the utmost responsibility of modernizing human resources were entrusted to education and mass media. In the dominant paradigm's communication strategies in the 1950s and 60s, there were three approaches: powerful effects approach, diffusion of innovations approach, and mass media and modernization approach. In these three approaches also mass media were thought to have a powerful, uniform and direct influence on individuals, in blowing the winds of modernity to replace the traditional way of life in underdeveloped countries. Thus, the bullet theory model of mass media effects seemed to hold in the Third World countries in the 1950s and 60s, even though this model was discarded in North America in the 1940s (Melkote, 1991).

As this development model aims at modernization of the Third World, all traditional elements including the cultures in developing countries were seen as obstacles to the development. The joint family system and religious beliefs of people in developing countries were criticized by Western scholars. Islam was criticized for tradition-bound rigidity. Hinduism was criticized for Karma Siddhantha. Buddhism was criticized for its ascetic and otherworldly orientation. The protestant ethic was considered to be the right cultural value that can propel change in the developing world. The traditional folk media were also seen as part of traditionalism and therefore as an obstacle for development. On the other hand, mass media were seen as the magic multipliers, which can blow the winds of modernity into Third World countries to replace the traditionalism in these countries with modernity.

Alternative Development

Though many Third World countries followed the model of the dominant paradigm, the rift between the developed and underdeveloped countries, as well as, between the rich and poor within the underdeveloped countries, did not decrease. Rather, it widened. In the 1970s, there was the realization that there is no one single way for development, but each country has to formulate its own development policies taking into consideration the natural resources and the socio, economic, political and cultural conditions prevailing in those respective countries. Given this realization, the role of communication in development and the importance of communication in development were revisited. As the development communication posited by the dominant paradigm could not yield the expected results due to its top-down, authoritarian and hortatory nature, the development support communication, which is bottom-up and participatory in nature was given importance.

The importance of culture in Third World countries was recognized. Since the seventies, there has been renewed interest in studying and pointing out the positive role of local culture in social change. The old paradigm was criticized for the way it conceptualized the role of culture. Theorists in the dominant paradigm held the stereotypical view that culture was necessarily in conflict with modernization (Melkote, 1991). But gradually there was a realization as to how culture and tradition could in fact be employed in social development efforts. In India, Mahatma Gandhi used traditional cultural symbolic systems to propagate new ideas, behaviours, and values among the masses. Thus, traditional elements and particularly, traditional folk media assumed significance in development communication. Today various organizations are using traditional folk media to disseminate developmental messages. To create awareness about preventing the spread of the Corona virus, folk forms like Oggu Katha (a folk form in Telugu states) were used.

Human Development

The notion of development itself had broadened, as people realized that economic criteria alone could not provide a programme for human dignity and well-being. The search for other criteria had led UNDP to elaborate the notion of human development – "a process of enlarging people's choices" –that measures development in a broad array of capabilities, ranging from political, economic and social freedom to individual opportunities for being healthy, educated, productive, creative and enjoying self-respect and human rights. The culture was implied in this notion, but it was not explicitly introduced.

Human development is about giving people more freedom to live lives they value. In effect, this means developing people's abilities and giving them a chance to use them. For example, educating a girl would build her skills, but it is of little use if she is denied access to jobs, or does not have the right skills for the local labour market. Three foundations for human development are to live a long, healthy and creative life, to be knowledgeable, and to have access to resources needed for a decent standard of living. Many other things are important too, especially in helping to create the right conditions for human development. Once the basics of human development are achieved, they open up opportunities for progress in other aspects of life (undp.org). Culture has a key role in promoting human development. For instance, when there are changes in cultural values about the education of girls and empowerment of girls through empowerment, that led to the realization of the goals of human development.

Millennium Development Goals

In September 2000, building upon a decade of major United Nations conferences and summits, world leaders came together at the United Nations Headquarters in New York to adopt the United Nations Millennium Declaration (undp.org). The Declaration committed nations to a new global partnership to reduce extreme poverty and set out a series of eight time-bound targets—with a deadline of 2015—that have become known as the Millennium Development Goals (MDGs). Eight goals range from providing universal primary education to avoiding the child and maternal mortality. The final MDG Report found that the 15-year effort has produced the most successful anti-poverty movement in history:

- Since 1990, the number of people living in extreme poverty has declined by more than half.
- The proportion of undernourished people in the developing regions has fallen by almost half.
- The primary school enrolment rate in the developing regions has reached 91 per cent, and many more girls are now in school compared to 15 years ago.
- Remarkable gains have also been made in the fight against HIV/AIDS, malaria and tuberculosis.
- The under-five mortality rate has declined by more than half, and maternal mortality is down 45 per cent worldwide.
- The target of halving the proportion of people who lack access to improved sources of water was also met (undp.org).

The concerted efforts of national governments, the international community, civil society and the private sector have helped expand hope and opportunity for people around the world. Culture and communication were seen as key players in achieving Millennium Development Goals.

Sustainable Development and Culture

The most widely accepted definition of sustainable development is provided by the UNOs World Commission on Environment and Development (1987), which described it as the development that meets the needs and aspirations of the present generation without compromising the ability of future generations to meet their own needs that sustainable development is a coin that consists of two obligations on its two sides. One side is the alleviation of poverty and the other, the protection of the environment. Sustainable development is very much linked with the involvement and active participation of people. It is a holistic concept that can be on the global, national, local and individual scale. Communication is an intervening variable without which the materialization of different goals of sustainable development is not possible. Therefore, communication has a key role in facilitating the participation of people relating to sustainable development (Bandi Balaswamy, 2006).

Culture is who we are and what shapes our identity. No development can be sustainable without including culture. In September 2015, the United Nations General Assembly adopted the "2030 Agenda for Sustainable Development", with 17 ambitious, universal goals to transform our world. UNESCO ensures that the role of culture is recognized through a majority of the Sustainable Development Goals (SDGs), including those focusing on quality education, sustainable cities, the environment, economic growth, sustainable consumption and production patterns, peaceful and inclusive societies, gender equality and food security. From cultural heritage to cultural and creative industries, culture is both an enabler and a driver of the economic, social and environmental dimensions of sustainable development. UNESCO's work promoting cultural diversity, and UNESCO's Culture Conventions, are key to the implementation of the 2030 Agenda for Sustainable Development (en.unesco.org).

Equitable and Environment Friendly Lifestyle

Sustainable development calls for a lifestyle that is in harmony with nature aims at meeting the need, but not greed; and maintains certain ethical values towards not only fellow human beings but also towards other living beings as well as the future generations (Rao Subba, *et al.*, 1990). As Gyan-Apentang pointed out, the science that produced space travel and nuclear weapons should be able to create an environment-friendly alternative lifestyle (Bandi Balaswamy, 2006). When such a lifestyle emerges which overlooks the national boundaries and other differences, when all people of the world feel that they are the children of mother earth and they should protect her, it resembles the ultimate stage of communism where the state will wither and everyone will work according to the ability and consumes, according to the need, as well as the Indian concept of *Vasudhaiva Kutamba* (universal family). The mass media which influence our lifestyles to a great extent have the potentialities and the responsibility of moulding such equitable and environment-friendly lifestyle. The heroes, heroines and other actors or characters, who are role models to the common people need to become the 'green' role models to the people.

Culture is influenced by the natural resources available in geographical regions. Earlier palmyra leaves, reeds, tiles, etc., were used as the roof to the houses. Such usage of these resources also necessitated the preservation of these trees and grass varieties. Gradually, in view of globalization, there is the homogenization of culture. All people are going for constructing concrete houses with slabs consisting of iron, cement and sand combination. This is causing more pressure on the non-renewable resources like iron and sand and negligence and extinction of trees like palmyra trees. Besides food consumption habits like all people consuming either rice or wheat is affecting the biological diversity of the grains.

As a trend is spreading in the West, in other parts of the world also there is a need to adopt a new lifestyle i.e., productive, equitable and environmentally friendly. In the West, hundreds of thousands of people belong to organizations, such as the National Wild Life Federation, Sierra Club, Audubon Society and Wilderness Society. The environmental movements exist as one of the most important social movements of the 20th century. Environmental movements are not confined to the West. In developing countries also such movements are gaining significance. In India also there are several environmental protection groups and organizations. In the West, in addition to joining national organizations, individual and family lifestyles have changed including behaviours such as recycling aluminum cans, increasing visits to national parks and purchasing environment-friendly products. Manufacturers have responded by featuring green themes in advertising campaigns (Neuzil and Kovarik, 1996). More bio-degradable, compostable and recyclable materials are incorporated in packaging to meet consumer demand. Neighbourhood clean-up programmes enjoy wide participation in all sizes of communities.

Some cultural values and inhibitions restrain the development. Until recent decades, women were confined to their homes. Their free movement and mingling with others were restricted. When the scheme Development of Women and Children in Rural Areas (DWCRA) was launched, many women hesitated to join DWCRA groups. But gradually they changed their attitudes and became members of self-help groups, which widened their horizons. They developed awareness about savings and avoided approaching the moneylenders. Above all, their outlook has changed to a great extent. A more conventional view regards culture as either a help or a hindrance to eco-cultures leading to a call to take "cultural factors into account in development". But the argument advanced in the Report of World Commission on Culture and Development (WCCD, 1994) is that development embraces not only access to goods and services but also the opportunity to choose a full, satisfying, valuable and valued way of living together, the flourishing of human existence in all its forms and as a whole.

Some cultural values created a lot of gaps between ethnic communities. The advent of communication technologies has gradually bridged the gap between the communities and promoted intercultural communication. "In India's remote villages there are many who, after the day's work is done, find time hanging heavily and there must be many officials whose duties carry them into out-of-way places, where they crave the company of friends and solace of human companionship. To all these and many more broadcasting will be a blessing and boon of real value. "These are words spoken by Viceroy of India, Lord Irwin at the inauguration of the Bombay Station of Indian Broadcasting Company on July 23, 1927. His words still hold true to a large extent. People even in the most remote village find peace in the company of a radio (Archana, 2016). It was felt that radio will fill a lot of gaps in Indian society where people are segregated by the social norms and caste system. Now the new media technologies have empowered the marginalized sections also to express themselves, whether their problems, concerns or literary and aesthetic expressions. Social media platforms like Facebook, Twitter, and WhatsApp are empowering people to express themselves.

Communication has Become a Culture Today

With the advent of new media technologies, the emergence of social media and the widespread usage of smartphones there is a phenomenal change in the communication system which has further changed our culture to a great extent. Today we are spending more time with computers and smart phones than with our family members. It has become easier to communicate with individuals and groups. In the wake of the Covid 19 crisis, the importance of Information technology has gained more significance. Online interactions, classes, zoom meetings and webinars have become common. What people are communicating and receiving is a matter of concern. People send and resend both productive and unproductive messages. This is an excellent opportunity to spread the messages which can be used to promote sustainable development.

Conclusion

The meaning and focus of development have changed significantly in the last seven decades. In the 1950s and 60s focus was on economic growth through industrialization. In the 1970s and 80s focus shifted to rural development and poverty alleviation. Instead of mere economic development, human development assumed significance in the 1990s. At the same time, the report of the World Commission on Environment and Development (1987) and Earth Summit[1] (1992) emphasized on sustainable development. Sustainable development is found to be not just for the Third World countries, but for the entire globe and into a distant future, demanding the participation of people at individual, local, regional, national and global levels. From time to time, the importance of both culture and communication in development was recognized. It is realized that development policies and projects which do not take into account the cultural dimension have failed. Culture effectively contributes to policies, strategies and programmes targeting inclusive social and economic development, environmental sustainability, harmony, peace and security. Culture is both a driver and an enabler of sustainable development. Culture plays both an instrumental and constitutive role in development; it is both a means and an end. Identifying communication as a missing link in the development chain in dominant paradigm's modern mass media were seen as the magic multipliers to blow the winds of modernity into Third World to modernize these countries. In the wake of the realization that this communication approach was a failure due to its top-down and hortatory nature, subsequently, horizontal, bottom-up and participatory communication approaches were adopted. In sustainable development, the role of communication is pervasive and vibrant as it is crucial in moulding a lifestyle throughout the globe to protect the interests of both present and future generations.

NOTE

1. The United Nations Conference on Environment and Development, also known as the Rio de Janeiro Earth Summit. It was held in Rio de Janeiro from 3 to 14 June in 1992.

REFERENCES

Archana, K.C. (2016). 80 years of AIR: Remembering the golden days of All India Radio, retrieved from https://www.indiatoday.in/fyi/story/80-years-of-air-remembering-the-golden-days-of-all-india-radio-12987-2016-06-08

Bandi, Balaswamy. (2006). *Communication for Sustainable Development*, New Delhi: Concept Publishing Company.

Dissanayake, W. (2003). "Asian Approaches to Human Communication: Retrospect and Prospect", *Intercultural Communication Studies*, XII-4, 2003.

MacBride Commission. (1980). *Many Voices One World*, Paris, UNESCO.

Melkote, Srinivas, R. (1991). *Communication for the Development in Third World Countries*, New Delhi: Sage.

Narula, Uma. (1994). *Development Communication: Theory and Practice*, New Delhi: Har-Anand Publications.

Neuzil, Mark and Kovarik, William. (1996). *Mass Media and Environmental Conflict: America's Green Crusade,* California: Sage.

Rao, Subba, B.V., et.al. (1990). Andhra Pradesh, Paryavarana Paristhithi, Praja Nevedika (*Status of Andhra Pradesh Environment: A Peoples Report*) Hyderabad: Academy of Gandhian Studies.

Schramm, Wilbur. (1964). *Mass Media and National Development*, California: Stanford University Press.

Winterhalt, Kevin Ray. (2018). Truman's New Deal: Point Four and the Genesis of Modern Global Development, *University of Saskatchewan Undergraduate Research Journal,* Volume-4, Issue-II.

World Commission on Culture and Development. (1994). *Our Creative Diversity*, Paris, UNESCO.

World Commission on Environment and Development. (1987). *Our Common Future*, New York: Oxford University Press.

http://www.agenda21culture.net/sites/default/files/files/documents/en/odm-eng.pdf

https://en.unesco.org/themes/culture-sustainable-development

http://hdr.undp.org/en/humandev

https://www.undp.org/content/undp/en/home/sdgoverview/mdg_goals.html

SECTION 2
Communication and Development

4

Communication Practices in the Development of Tharu Community in Bihar

Kumari Pallavi

Introduction

In India, the concept of 'tribe' has always been an argumentative matter for both practitioners and academicians. They have taken the term 'tribe' differently in distinctive settings. Though much has been written about the tribes, there is a lack of consensus on the definition of the word tribe and their population involved. Using the term "tribe" has been criticized from the mid-20th century onwards by Indian Anthropologists. G.S. Ghurye (1963 [1943], pp. 15-38) argued that there were no sociological grounds on which a fundamental distinction could be made between caste and 'tribe'. One of his main opponents was the self-taught anthropologist Verrier Elwin (1964).

Contrary to Ghurye, Elwin argued that 'tribal' were the custodians of unique cultural traditions that were not just distinct but superior to both the Indian and European mainstream. Elwin feared that a denial of the distinctiveness of the 'tribes' would result in their being categorized as low caste Hindus, despised and rejected for habits that went in many ways against the grain of the mainstream population. Thus perceived, the debate on 'tribe' cannot be disconnected from the efforts made to define mainstream Indian society as centred on a kind of high culture, far removed from what then becomes the folk culture at its margins. In many ways, these juxtaposed positions continue to be of importance in the debate on 'tribe' in India today.

Calling the tribal section of society as a "community" is more logical, as Carol Upadhya defines, "community is a concept to describe a social organization that is considered fundamental to traditional to Indian society such as jati, village or religious section. Such communities are often regarded as natural grouping based on ties of shared blood, language, history, territory and above all, culture (2001, p. 34)." Communities are facing new and more powerful challenges to their survival (Green, 2007). So, they require a reinforcement and endowment for their survival and development.

The concept 'community development' is often used to describe participatory interventions that promote self-help and service delivery when the state is unable to satisfy a community's aspirations. It is "about interacting with people to assist them to find ways to build understanding and co-operation between individuals and groups to enable them to make changes in their own lives and for the greater good" (Bartley, 2003, p. 186).

"Community development supports networks that foster mutual learning and shared commitments so that people can work and live together in relatively coherent and equitable communities" (Gilchrist, 2009, p. 21). For this, they needed different communication practices as every community development initiative requires effective communication among groups of people who are involved in the development process of the community (Aruma, 2018, p. 1). Aruma (1998) profess that the community development process stipulates effective communication practices to achieve a participatory approach in development. Dragon said that "Participation in development programmes and projects cannot occur without communication for one simple reason: participation is communication; the concepts are entangled, intimately knotted as the strings in a fisherperson's net (2009, p. 460)."

Pratt and Boyden rightly indicated that "Every social development project involves communication: Communication between members of a community and a group; communication between development workers and the people among whom they work; communication between funding agencies and field workers and so on. Communication involves the sharing of ideas—information, of emotions, of hopes and fears—and is part of every human activity (1985, p. 156)".

The significance of this is that communication practices are integral tool for the accomplishment of community development to provide sufficient information regarding development policies and plans to the project participants of the participating community. In the social context, effective communication practices can be seen as vital for the success of community development.

Contextual Background—About Tharu and their Need for Development

In common with other tribal communities of India, Tharus of Bihar suffer from pronounced social, cultural, political, and economic imbalances of development. Tharus residing in the urban areas are less in number and are generally endowed with the widely accepted indicators of development while Tharus residing in rural areas tend to be relatively deprived.

The government has attempted many times to improve their developmental condition by providing them various facilities and aid. Then, also these attempts are not sufficient to augment their "standard of living". The major reason behind this situation of Tharus is their social status provided by the Government of India. Even they have all characteristics to possess a category of Scheduled Tribe. Till 2003, the government did not give them the status of Scheduled Tribe in Bihar and they came under the category of Other Backward Class. They had to fight for years to get the ST status. That led them to more dreadful conditions for survival in these years since independence as they cannot avail developmental facilities provided by the Government of India. This tends the Tharus of West Champaran to lead a nomadic life. Only, after 2002, when Jharkhand got separated from Bihar and Tharus got the status of ST then, they were allocated with all the facilities available for the other tribes of India. But, this did not end the problems of the Tharus. Their need for development and endurance was also understood by the Government of Bihar, that's why they came up with a special development wing i.e., Samekit Tharuahat Vikash Abhikaran by the SC/ST Welfare Department of Bihar which is responsible to look after the development process of Tharuahat region of West Champaran district of Bihar as it is the densely populated region of Tharu tribe of Bihar.

Research Methodology

The ethnographic method was adopted to conduct the contextual analysis of the social and cultural context of the indigenous community. This study conceptualized a framework to analyze the effectiveness of policy implementation, with a specific focus on the development of the Tharu community in Bihar, India. This framework suggests what are the measures taken i.e., the policy, what happened i.e., the practice and what were the results i.e., the performance to assess the effectiveness in the implementation of developmental policies and plans. Feedback of the community members based on policy, practice and performance provide suggestions to the policymakers for planning, executing and implementing the policies on the site. For analyzing the effectiveness of policy implementation, policies planned and executed by the Samekit Tharuhat Vikash Abhikaran were considered.

Study Area: West Champaran is a district of Bihar in India. This district has three sub-divisions: Bettiah, Bagaha and Narkatiganj with 18 Blocks. The district has its headquarter at Bettiah. After the separation of Jharkhand from Bihar in 2000, the West Champaran became the highest Scheduled Tribes populated district of Bihar. The state constituted 1.28 per cent ST people of which West Champaran district constitutes about 6.35 per cent of Bihar's ST population. Tharus are the most populated tribe of Bihar. They mainly reside in and around the West Champaran district. So, after the division of Bihar, the West Champaran district became a major concern for Bihar. The significant population of the Tharu community resides in the Bagaha, 1 and 2 blocks of West Champaran. Harnatad village of Bagaha 2 is called the capital of Tharu by the Tharu community. For this reason, Harnatad was chosen as the area of study.

Research Design: The data collection has been conducted in four phases in 2017-18. For collecting the data, the researcher conducted interviews and Focus Group Discussions. The researcher interviewed three categories of essential respondents who gave information related to policy planning, implementation process among the villager groups (lowest administrative level) and the involvement of members of the community in the decision making process for project implementation. The first category of key respondents were: the Head of the village, Village Group leaders, community leaders, and popular community members of the village. The second category of key respondents whom the researcher has also interviewed were government officials of Samekit Tharuhat Vikash Abhikaran with its project officer. And, the third category of key respondents were the Director and other officials of the SC/ST Welfare Department of Bihar.

The researcher has also conducted Focus Group Discussions with men's groups, women's group, people of Self Help Groups, student's groups and members of different organizations related to Tharus. To get a comprehensive picture of the communities' opinions and to ensure that women's responses are not affected by men's perceptions and vice versa, it was important to separate the two groups while conducting the research. The essential informants were not incorporated with the focus group discussions to avoid repetition.

A qualitative analysis was conducted to understand participants' perception of development and how the government is contributing to their development process. Transcripts of the key informant interviews and focus group discussions, notes from field observations, and social maps were used for data analysis (Schutt, 1996). Because the study uses an ethnographic approach and the purpose is to understand, contextualize, and interpret the development process by reaching out to the Tharu community to get to the core of the developmental issue, qualitative methods of data collection and analysis were selected (Castellan, 2010).

Research Objectives

1. To explore the praxis of communication practices in the development process of the Tharu community in Bihar.
2. To examine the Tharu community's involvement and participation in the developmental policies and plans that are implemented by the government.
3. To investigate, what communication strategies were adopted by the government for the dissemination of information.

Framework for Measuring Effectiveness of Policy Implementation

This research paper is based on a modified framework for evaluating the effectiveness of policy implementation in the case of the developmental plans of a tribal community. The modified framework is established based on Pradhan et al. (2017) who suggested a framework which they came up with by considering Sadler's (1996) and Baker and McLelland's (2003) framework to measure the effectiveness of government policy. It pertains policy to practice to performance, as well as associations of performance to policy improvement and the process of development. In addition to Sadler's, Baker and McLelland's framework, and as explained by Matland (1995), the framework incorporates a bottom-up approach to consider policy implementation and contextualizes it to analyze the impact of the policy. Although the major concern is the relationship of policy to practice and practice to performance, this modified framework accentuates an additional step, which is the feedback loop to link performance to policy adjustments and the process of development. The feedback loop is important to devise and implement policy adequately at the local level.

So, in the present research, an attempt has been made to contextualize the same framework for analyzing government policies. Here, I have modified the key questions as per the research requirement but utilize the same elements of Pradhan et al.'s (2017) framework.

Findings and Discussion

Communication Practices of Tharu Community

Communication Pattern/Structure

Communication patterns are networks in which communication flows in an organization, community or society. In this network, individuals are tied and linked to each other by the virtue of the information they transmit. While an individual may simultaneously utilize several communication networks for the transmission of thoughts and feeling with the co-community member of the community the nature of information exchanged in a network is often specific to the interests of network members.

In a Tharu community, the wheel pattern of communication is evident. It is found that community members are directly connected with the group leader as well as the community members as shown in Chart 1. One of the community members, Mr. Shanker Mahto (47, farmer) said that "in our community, everyone is free to talk with any member of the community. No kind of hierarchical caste or creed differences exists here. Even women can approach a community member and community head for discussing their problems freely."

Chart 1

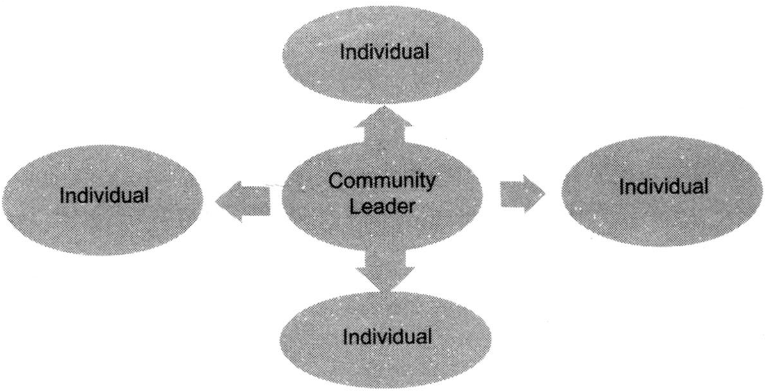

Further, Mrs Maenka Devi (53, housewife) said "if we have any issue in our family or with anyone in our community then we can approach the headman (Gumasta) of our community directly. We don't need permission from anyone to voice our opinion." So, the wheel pattern of communication creates a favourable environment for a flawless flow of information in the Tharu Community. It also helps the community members to share a bond of relationship with each other as cultural practices are largely created, shaped, transmitted and learned through communication.

Communication Channels (Sources of Information)

(*a*) *Formal Source of Information*

The formal source of information like extension personnel, officers of Krishi Vigyan Kendra, NGO officials are rarely utilized by the Tharu Community members. There is a gap of communication between the community members and the government and non-governmental officers. Because of their prior experiences with them, the community members hardly rely on them. They had a bitter experience in the past when in a period of their need the governmental official didn't support them.

Mr. Ravish (28, student) said that "at the time of the flood, we didn't get any support and assistance from the government. We got a limited amount of food supply and other daily necessities. On paper, the government supplied more than the need of this community but the government officials, who are the bridge, only fulfilled their needs and surpassed us.

Mr. Dheeraj (31, businessman) said that even today government has many plans for our development and prosperity but we aren't getting the funds. We don't have proper knowledge and information for availing of those plans. No one is there for providing details regarding governmental plans and programmes. Sometimes, ANM or krishi mitr establishes any special camps for a certain time. There, they informed people about any particular plans. But on regular basis, there is no one to disseminate information.

(*b*) *Informal Sources of Information*

The informal sources of information are mainly used by the Tharu community. The community's social structure is finely knitted by the community members. That's why the social structure helps in a flawless process of communication in society. People are closely connected with one another, which creates a favourable condition for maintaining a proper channel for sharing their knowledge and information. Their close bonding with their family members, relatives, friends, neighbours, community members, has developed into a communication structure in which they can share their feelings and problems. Mrs. Manshi Devi (43, housewife) said that we talk with each other near the hand pump of our village or in the evening we meet at anyone's house. There, we share our feelings, emotions, opinions and many other things like, how to make any different kind of basket, mat, food and many more

(*c*) *Mass Media Sources*

In the Tharu community, the source of information and channel of mass communication is very limited. People don't have access and reach to most of the mass communication mediums. They rarely use the mass communication channels like newspapers, radio and the internet because of the low rate of literacy and proper knowledge for their utilization. The community members perceived these mediums as vulnerable things for them as they don't know how these mediums can benefit them in their development and conservation of culture. Only television is the mass medium that is very popular in the community. Even then, most community members do not have access to it as they can't afford it. That's why for watching television usually they go to other's houses.

Mr. Shekhar (15, student) said that "in my village (Don) which is the most interior area of Bagaha District, mobile network is very weak that's why we don't easily use the internet. And people are not that literate to read the newspaper on their own. So, for entertainment and knowing about what going on around the world, everyone is dependent on television only. But only few people have a television in my village…I have television with a set-top box. So, usually in the evening or whenever community members get time from their work, they come to my place to watch T.V."

Mr. Vishal (19, student) said "I am from Harnatad village which is a more developed place than the nearby areas. It is also called as capital of the Tharuhat region…Here, we can avail all the facilities easily. Almost everyone has a mobile with an internet connection. We are also using WhatsApp and Facebook for connecting with our community members who are staying here or outside our village."

Ms Mamta (16, Student) said "we have television at our home. I usually like to watch daily soap like Yeh rishta kya kahlata hai, Yeh hai

Mohabatten, Naagin and many more. But my grandfather used to watch the news.......We also watch Narendra Modi's mann ki baat show regularly."

Governmental Policies and Plans for the Development of Tharu Community

Samekit Tharuhat Vikas Abhikaran (STVA) registered under Society Registration Act, 1860 was established in 2009. The organization was established by the Bihar Government under the supervision of the SC/ST Welfare Department of Bihar in Bettiah, West Champaran. This organization was formulated for the Tharuhat people to initiate the development process as they are still not have been provided with the basic necessities like road, education, electricity and health.

Objectives of STVA

- To identify small farmers, marginal farmers, agricultural labourers, non-agricultural labourers and artisans, and persons below the poverty line in the rural area.
- To draw up schemes for the economic improvement of the persons identified and in particular to raise the income of the persons below the poverty line as may be defined from time to time by the Government of India so as to take them above the poverty line and to execute such schemes.
- To draw up plans for each of the Blocks in the district and the district as a whole, to contain projects, plans and schemes of development aimed at improving the social and economic infrastructure to subserve the objectives of assisting individuals below the poverty line.
- To review the progress in the execution of these activities as well as the effectiveness of the benefit directed towards the persons below the poverty line.

Policies and Plan for Tharu Community

Samekits Tharuhat Vikas Abhikaran has come up with different policies and plans for the Tharu community as per their requirements. They mainly focused on those problems which are related to their basic necessities like livelihood, education, and health. Some of the major policies and plans made by the SC/ST Welfare Department of Bihar are presented in Table 4.1.

Table 4.1: Plan and Policies for Tharu Community

Livelihood Plans	*Skill Development Plans*	*Infrastructure Plans*
Water Facility for drinking and agriculture	Advance Diploma in Information Technology	Construction of Library and school Buildings
Murgi Gram Yojna (2000 Households)	Diploma in P.C. Hardware and Networking	Connecting Roads, Crossway, Retaining Wall
	D.T.P.	Construction of additional Primary Health Centres and Designated Microscopic Center
	Security Guard Training	

The SC/ST Welfare Department of Bihar came up with these policies and plans based on issues that are included in the memorandum of association of Samekit Tharuhat Vikas Abhikaran which was passed by the Legislative Assembly of Bihar. The official of the SC/ST Welfare Department of Bihar state that "we decide policies and plans under STVA by considering all the aim and objectives mentioned in the memorandum."

He has also mentioned that for proper representation of community members and government officials they have two different types of participatory wings in STVA: one is of Representatives and second is of Bureaucratic and the District Magistrate is the Chairman of this committee. The board of management of STVA includes Tharu community members, Orao community members, MLA, MLC, and Area Pramukhs as a representative. Like, the Project officer of STVA has also mentioned that "for setting up a small-scale industry of handloom in Harnatad was fully suggested by Tharu people. It was their input and suggestion which we executed. Our whole planning and execution process of plans and schemes are participatory in nature."

The STVA has the provision of proper representation of the Tharu and other communities residing in the West Champaran district but they need to implement their provision in the same manner which is prescribed in their memorandum. Most of the time the representatives do not attend their policy-making meetings as sometimes they are not informed before hands and also because of their other works. The bureaucrats are the ones who pass the plans and schemes and execute them. So, mostly the representation of Tharu community is not representational in nature which also hampers the participatory process of decision making in planning and executing the plans.

The Effectiveness of Policy Implementation

The present literature suggests that there is no suitable framework at present that can be used to analyze the effectiveness of policies and plans planning and implementation, especially for the development of the tribal community, this article develops a modified framework. This framework is used to analyze the effectiveness of policy implementation in the development of the Tharu Community, but could also be applied for the policies of Tribal Development of tribes like Asur, Baiga, Bhumij, Chero, Ho, Oraon and others, present in different parts of Bihar.

Though, different developmental policies of the central and state governments are implemented in the West Champaran district of Bihar policies and plans executed by the Samekit Tharuahat Vikash Abhikaran are prioritized based on the intense discussions and interviews held by the officials, community members and key informants. The findings of the study are summarized and presented in Table 4.2.

Table 4.2: The Effectiveness of Policy Implementation Analyzed using the Modified Framework

Framework Element	*Purpose*	*STVA Policies and Plans*
Purpose	What are the issues/problems which need to be solved?	To provide economic stability to the community.
Policy	What are the measures taken?	Skill development, livelihood enhancement and infrastructure building.
Planning	What is the policymaking process at the local level?	The funding and planning for projects are channelized top-down but the Tharu community has some representation in the planning committee.
Practice	Do they include indigenous communication practices of the Tharu community?	The government provided support to address the issue through modern communication tools.
Implementation	How do they implement at the local level?	Infrastructure development, human mobility for employment opportunities.
Evaluation	How do they perform it?	Collecting feedback from the users.

The Tharu community is a tribal community of Bihar as per the central list of the Indian Government. According to the 2001 census the district has a low literacy rate, i.e., 39.63 per cent only. Their percentage of skilled labour in the district is also very low. So, the district faces major problems like education, employment and health along with some other problems related to their cultural and social existence and identity. According to the key informants and interviewees, the most important issues identified by them are unemployment and education. The community members have also problems related to conserving and protecting their culture and identity. But, the government has no policies and plans regarding this. Their major concern is to provide them with economic stability. The community members perceived the causes of unemployment and less literacy are non-availability of schools and colleges, land-use change (constructions of roads), no proper storage for water conservation (fewer dams and canals), and high dependency on government funds.

Almost 90 per cent of the key informants and the participants in the focus group discussions believed that the economic condition of the Tharu community is diminishing. Farming is the traditional occupation of the Tharu community, but in the last few years, they have not been able to follow it due to less favourable conditions. Although the government tried to provide the facilities of modern means of farming—seed production, sowing, fertilization, land preparation, crop protection, etc., these facilities are not sufficient for them to survive. That's why their dependency has been increased on other forms of occupation and also they have to leave their traditional style of agriculture. This tends them to lose their traditional knowledge system too.

The Tharu community has been a traditional society and their way of living is very conventional. So, they don't have modern skills. In this condition, leaving agriculture and switching to a new occupation is tough work for them. Although, the government has initiated many skill developmental plans for them but due to some loopholes in the execution of these plans hampered their effectiveness.

Mr. Vikash Kumar (22, student) said that "I have joined the Advanced Diploma in Information Technology initiated by the STVA. This training programme has given me a good understanding of the usage and handling of a computer. But, after completing the training, I didn't find any related job to it. Even, at the time of training, the trainers are not from our community so, they don't understand our language. That's why there is a communication gap in between us which generates antipathy."

The different measures taken by the government for the upliftment of the Tharu community is also not adequate for them. The government has plans related to skill development, livelihood enhancement and infrastructure building but these are not sufficient for their development. Moreover, the policymaking process of the STVA has a predicament as its funding and planning for projects are channelized top-down but the Tharu community have some representation in the planning committee but the applicability is little different. Although, the selection of problems and planning has been done at the local level the final say of its implementation is in the hands of government officials. They are the ones who have full power to sanction funds for those plans which fulfil their agenda for development, not the Tharu community.

Mr. Shayam Kumar Mahto (42, Member of Akhil Bhartiya Tharu Kalyan Maha Sangh) said that, "We have no participation in these developmental plans of the government. They made developmental plans for us by sitting in district headquarters. Once or twice a year, they came here to ask us about our problems. And every time, we told them about our major problems of survival and they tell us they will address them but those problems which are related to their priority list. Our participation in these developmental plans is only to inform them about which they need to be informed. Like, when we need a canal and bridges then they asked us about what skill development plans we need. Why don't they understand that we are happy with our doing agricultural practices, cattle rearing practices and fishing? But, they persuade us to learn new skills like D.T.P., carpentry, security guard. Even these plans are not adequate as once they provide us with a breed of cow which can't survive in our environmental condition. Government exports those cows because they can provide a good amount of milk but they don't think about their survival condition."

The communication practices of the Tharu community also have been not utilized by the government authorities most of the time. They generally depend on modern communication mediums for disseminating information about the developmental plans for the Tharu community.

Mr. Jeevan Mahto (39, farmer) said "Even, we don't get proper information regarding governmental plans until and unless, we by ourselves inquired about them Mukhiya and Sarpanch of my village is my relative and I used to attend every meeting of our community that's why I have information if any new plans have been introduced. But, other community members, who are busy in their work or occupation then hardly get any information on time. Like, few days' back seeds were distributed by the Krishi Kendra but farmers didn't turn up because don't have information."

Mr. Digvijay (23, Member of Indian Tharu Student Unity) said, "If any skill developmental programme is going to be held in district town then we don't get any information regarding this. In our village, most of the people can't afford to buy a newspaper and they don't even visit district town every time so that they may come across the hoarding or banners utilized by the government for the advertisement. If government utilizes another mode of communication than publishing advertisements in the newspaper, may be our community members get more awareness about it them. As in our village, everyone is connected with one another, and through our gumasta ji, if government have any means to inform him directly then it will be easier for us to get informed."

The evaluation of STVA policies and plans was done by the government officials through collecting feedback from the participants. The Project Officer of STVA said that, "we also collect feedback from the participants of our skill developmental plans at the end of the training. And later on whenever we plan any other such training programmes then, include their suggestions in it. Besides this, we also tried a follow-up session for our security guard training programmes. In this, we called personally every participant to check whether they got any job after taking our training or not."

The perception of participants about the effectiveness of skill development plans is different from the government officials. Mr. Dipak Mahto (23, Participant of skill development training) said that, "after completing the training, there is a provision for providing job to us but only those students got jobs that have skills before joining it. These training programmes are a way for them to get a job and the government also provide jobs to them only who secured good marks in the training exams. The tenure of these jobs is also for just six months or a year. After that, they have to search for a job by themselves. And finding a job of D.T.P. or a security guard in our village is impossible. So, for getting a job we need to leave our village and our family."

Conclusion

The Tharu village has an intricate and well connected community-based communication network whether it's formal, informal or mediated. Their complex communication system comprises extensive local indigenous knowledge and practice system. The study also provides empirical evidence that the Tharu community's perception about the effectiveness of policies and plans contrived by Samekit Tharuahat Vikash Abhikaran.

The government's developmental plans provide the Tharu community to cope up with the economic advancement however, made them aloof from their traditional occupation. They have also taken measures like skill development, livelihood enhancement and infrastructure building but don't try to incorporate their traditional knowledge system in it. This tends them to lose their individuality and cultural assets. At the planning process level also, the inclusion of the Tharu community is very minimal. According to them, they don't have a proper representation at either local or higher level. This creates a communication gap between the beneficiary and the policymaker. The strategies of implementation of these policies and plans have also inadequate communication approach. The government utilizes the modern tools and medium of communication but forgot to consider that they are part of a traditional society and has their own communication tools which are more suitable for them. In addition to this, the government's feedback mechanism also needs to be reconstructed which must have more space for the Tharu community to recommend.

For the development of the Tharu community, participation in the community is necessary. Its applicability is determined by two factors in the wider condition. The first and most critical is the acceptance of government to the engagement of communities in the decision- making process. The government must be approachable for the development of the community. However, this alone is inadequate to determine whether community development will accomplish. The effectiveness of community development of a tribal community like Tharu is also constrained by the complexity of the decision-making process. Thus, for community development like Tharu more awareness campaigns regarding developmental plans, there is a need for participation of the Tharu community at every level of planning, implementation and execution of government's developmental policies and plans. Focusing on the usage of traditional communication tools for information related to the government's policies and plans is essential.

REFERENCES

Aruma, E.O. (1998). *The Contributions of farmers' multi-purpose cooperative societies to community development in Nsukka Zone of Enugu State.* Unpublished Ph.D. Dissertation.

Aruma, E.O. (2018). "Roles of Communication in Community Development", *International Journal of Network and Communication Research,* Vol. 5, No. 1, pp. 1-10.

Baker, D.C. and McLelland (2003). Evaluating the Effectiveness of British Columbia's environmental assessment process for first nation's participation in mining development. *Environmental Impact Assessment Review.* Volume 23(5), pp. 581-603.

Bartley, T. (2003). *Holding Up the Sky: Love, Power and Learning in the Development of a Community*, London: Community Links.

Castellan, C.M. (2010). "Quantitative and qualitative research: A view for clarity." *International Journal of Education* 2(2): 1–14.

Dragon, Alfonso Gumucio (2009). "Playing with Fire: Power, Participation, and Communication for Development." *Development in Practice*, Taylor & Francis Vol. 19, No. 4/5, pp. 453-465.

Elwin, Verrier (1964). *The Tribal World of Verrier Elwin: An autobiography*, Bombay: Oxford University Press.

Ghurye, Govind Sadashiv (1963). *The Scheduled Tribes (The Aborigines So-Called and Their Future)*, Bombay: Popular Prakashan.

Gilchrist, Alison (2009). *The Well Connected Community*, 2nd Edition, USA: University of Chicago Press.

Green, Gary Paul, and Anna Haines (2007). *Asset Building and Community Development*, 2nd Edition. Thousand Oaks: Sage Publication.

Matland, R.E. (1995). "Synthesizing the implementation literature: The ambiguity-conflict model of policy implementation." *Journal of Public Administration Research and Theory*: J-PART 5(2): 145–174. http://www.jstor.org/stable/1181674?seq=13. Retrieved on 17 Feb 2016.

Pradhan, N.S, Y. Su, Y. Fu, L. Zhang, and Y. Yang (2017). "Analyzing the Effectiveness of Policy Implementation at the Local Level: A Case Study of Management of the 2009–2010 Drought in Yunnan Province, China", Int J Disaster Risk Sci, 8:64-77. https://link.springer.com/article/10.1007/s13753-017-0118-9. Retrieved on 6 Sep. 2019.

Pratt, B. and Boyden, J. (1985). *The Field Directors' Handbook: An Oxfam Manual for Development Workers*. Oxford: Oxford University Press.

Sadler, B. (1996). International study of the effectiveness of environmental assessment—Final report. Environmental assessment in a changing world: Evaluating practice to improve performance. Ottawa: Canadian Environmental Assessment Agency

Schutt, R.K. (1996). "Qualitative data analysis." *In Investigating the Social World*, 320–357. Sage. http://www.sagepub.com/upmdata/ 43454_10.pdf. retrieved on 8 Apr. 2015.

Upadhya, Carol. (2001). *The Concept of Community in Indian Social Sciences: An Anthropological Perspective, in Community and Identities Contemporary Discourses on Culture and Politics in India*, Surinder, S. Jodhka, eds., New Delhi-Thousand Oaks-London, Sage Publications in association The Book Review Literary Trust, New Delhi, pp. 33-42.

5

Communication Technology and Education of Scheduled Castes' Children in the Slums of Hyderabad

V.S.J. Wesly Kumar and *J. Babu Rao*

Introduction

India aspires to emerge as one of the superpowers in the world owing to its economic growth in recent times with increasing market potential and human resources available. One of the important stands, on which such an ambitious envisioning has been construed, is based on the impressive progress made over the years in the literacy rate from 12 to 74 per cent. Besides being a major player among the IT capitals in the world with a large contingent of professionals and engineers, India is also surging ahead to become an IT superpower by raising IT skills right from primary education and covering higher education. In this background, education remains the backbone of India's futuristic plan of development.

Though the state is the major supporter of the millions of school-going children, privatization of education began at the primary school level and it is slowly gaining ground fast in higher education as well. It is to be noted in this regard that several state governments have welcomed private universities recently, despite having state-funded universities which will be drastically affected by the new private initiatives. Several of the private schools mushroomed in metropolitan cities in the country have made progress into digital educational technology equipped with tablets, desktops, internet and computer labs in response to the changing global scenario improving the skills of the students to meet the contemporary needs. Contrarily, on the other hand, the government schools are barely equipped to use education technology. While the private and corporate schools stride very fast imparting new learning skills and provide technological skills to young children who find it easy to adapt themselves with the technology-based modern educational learning practices, the government schools struggle with the age-old methods of teaching without any teaching aids. This has created a new digital gap not only among the schools but also among the students. In this regard, the sociological perspective of modern education points out the digital gap and the most affected community is the Scheduled Caste community.

Although the government whether state or central has given top priority to primary school education[1], still most of the Scheduled Caste and Scheduled Tribe community children lag in enrolment as well as achievements compared to others.[2] The governments have not been able to extend support to these children regarding access to education technology. Most government schools in the slums of cities are far behind in this respect compared to the private and corporate schools, despite the government policies and schemes that promote using education technology in schools. But implementation of the same for the upliftment of the slum children especially the Scheduled Caste children remains far from the ideal situation. Therefore, traditional disparity and prejudice against the Scheduled Castes continue even in education in the country. It is a notion that Scheduled Castes are incapable in the field of education and technology and it is a mere waste of time and energy. As such, the Scheduled Caste children are discriminated agaist in all manners in schools. In this background, the present study aims to examine the contemporary situation of communication and education technology available and used for educational purposes in the schools located in the slums of Hyderabad through an empirical study in selected slums. It discusses the general problems of education encountered by the children, and how these stand as obstacles encountered by the children, and how these stand as obstacles and bottlenecks for the development of Scheduled Castes in slums despite having a great desire to educate themselves. It also tries to find out access to education technology outside the school also.

Background: Education Technology–ICT in Schools

Since the concern of the chapter is about the communication technology used for teaching and learning in schools among the Scheduled Castes in the slums of Hyderabad, it is imperative to provide a brief discussion on the Educational Technology that includes ICT in schools. There is a long history of Education Technology (ET) in the country which dates back to 1971 (Lone, 2017). However, it found a place in the National Educational

Policy after two decades in 1992 and since then concerted efforts are being made to make Educational Technology a part of the pedagogy from primary school level through higher education. It is strongly felt that mediated teaching with the aid of technology reinforces and enhances the learning through visual and oral means. Further, the mediated teaching in a distance mode helps to learn "from anywhere and anytime", and thus encourages self-learning. All these in a way outdated the traditional learning, and the teachers are also required to learn the application of technology and reorient their teaching practices and develop skills using new technology. There are various types of technologies of teaching in a classroom situation such as Computer, Class-blog Wikipedia, Wireless classroom microphone, Mobile devices, Interactive Whiteboards Digital video-on-demand, Online media, Online study tools, Digital Games etc. (Goswami, 2014). Thus, the ET is an umbrella term to cover all these technologies.

The Ministry of Education and Social Welfare, Government of India, took the initiative of setting up not only a unit in the ministry but also locating a Centre for Education Technology in NCERT in 1973, while the states also started ET Cells with the support of the Government of India. According to NCERT, the education technology in India till recently has taken two routes: teacher training and support system, and government-sponsored schemes such as Education Technology (ET) Scheme and Computer Literacy and Studies in Schools (CLASS) and partnership with global players.

This technology initiative included the supply of radio-cum-cassette players, colour televisions, microcomputers, present-day computer labs, and even satellite-receiving terminals. The Information Communication and Technology (ICT) came later providing media with multi-centric participation etc. (Anonymous, 2006: v)

The Government of India not only supported the State Educational Technology Cells but also provided the dedicated educational television channels through Doordarshan, besides radio programmes, beginning with the Satellite Instructional Television Experiment (SITE)[3] in 1975. It initiated Gyan-Darshan TV channels in 2000 which are dedicated to education and launched Gyan Vani, a radio channel in 2001 and a project called Vidya Vahini providing IT and IT-enabled education in 60,000 schools. A Centrally Sponsored Scheme of Information and Communication Technology (ICT) in Schools was launched in 2004 to provide opportunities to secondary stage students helping them build their capacity in ICT skills (Anonymous, 2015).

In 2004, Educational Satellite (EDUSAT) came into existence

with the support of the Indian Space Research Organization (ISRO). The other educational projects include ETV of INSAT-B, UGC-Higher Education Television Project (HETV), IGNOU-Doordarshan Telecast, and Gyan-Darshan Educational Channel (Vyas, Sharma, and Kumar, 2002). The Education Departments of the state governments have also been making efforts to develop viable technologies and schemes for imparting new technical skills to teachers, equipping schools with the tools, equipment etc., besides integration of teaching, learning and technological innovations. The Departments and governments have been collaborating with several national and international agencies and reputed national institutions for the development of appropriate means of applying technology for improving the quality of education focusing on the marginal and disadvantaged students covering social and physical space. For example, the Government of Telangana initiated CLIx Intervention in 2016-17. The CLIx, the Connected Learning Initiative, is a technology-enabled initiative at scale for high school students in Telangana, and the Government of Telangana extended its support to the initiative taken up Tata Trusts, Mumbai, with Tata Institute of Social Sciences, Mumbai, and Massachusetts Institute of Technology, Cambridge, as founding partners. It has ventured to provide a hands-on learning experience in mathematics, communication skills in English, digital literacy, and other skills relevant for the 21st century. (Anonymous, 2017)

Another major step taken by the Government of India in this regard is the inclusion of ET in Draft National Education Policy, 2019. The Draft Policy envisages digital literacy at the upper primary and secondary school levels (4.2.1, p. 76 and 4.6.7, p. 95). It desires that technology shall enable reaching the unreached schools located in remote areas (19.5.1, p. 350) Further, it says, 'Appropriate integration of technology into all levels of education—to support teacher preparation and development; improve teaching, learning and evaluation processes; enhance educational access to disadvantaged groups; and streamline educational planning, administration and management'. (Anonymous, 2019: 339)

Apart from the government agencies, several private industries are also coming forward to contribute toward promoting digital literacy among the school children under Corporate Social Responsibility. Notably among them is Ajim Premji Foundation, The HCL Foundation, Infosys etc., wh have been providing equipment, technical support, learning partn and so on in an outreach model (Bajpai, Biberman, and Sharma, 2

As of now, several technologies have been developed as solutions for improving the quality of teaching as well as learning has given the contemporary complex situation in India concerning education—rural and urban, government and private institutions, private high-end international public schools and ordinary private schools etc. Earlier technologies based on Very Small Aperture Terminal (VSAT), Very Personal Network (VPN) and Satellite etc., are no longer necessary while the high-speed internet is available, and similarly, the radio/television sets are giving way to desktops, tablets and mobile phones. Nevertheless, the prevailing situation is such that a variety of resources for learning can be accessed with the availability of various Apps, social platforms from a classroom to online interaction, mobile-based learning management systems. The government has recommended the implementation of ICT in schools and colleges by using free and open technologies including the Free and Open Source Software (FOSS) and Open Educational Resources (OER).

Having discussed the policies, government schemes, programmes, initiatives, public interventions, it is necessary to draw our attention to the ground realities. It is said that the success of ICT so far as the primary schools of India is concerned, remains anecdotal and a lot of money has been wasted. There are at least three barriers to the failure: lack of resources, lack of teachers' participation and lack of local understanding (Byker, 2014: 29). A study has revealed the fact that the ICT has been in the schools with no clear policy of using it, and the teachers have no proper training to integrate the ICT with the regular curriculum (Anonymous, 2015).

A study *Education Technology–Affordable Private Schools* in Hyderabad that covered 250 schools 450 students from 13 schools, has found that 69 per cent of Hyderabad schools have computer labs and 58 per cent have techno-classes. About 34 per cent of computers and 13 per cent of techno-classes are in very poor conditions. Usually, the schools have on average nine computers, a computer lab and administrative technology. The girls seem to have less access to computers and internet access compared to boys. Mobiles are most commonly used by students which are used for games and listening to music also (Campbell, Mehr, Mayer, 2013).

With this background, an attempt is made to examine the Scheduled Caste students in the slums of Hyderabad. A brief account of the slums of Hyderabad which is followed by the methodology adopted for the study is discussed before the findings of the study are presented.

Slums in India and Hyderabad

According to one of the Government of India's reports, the number of slum population which was estimated at 75 million in 2001 is projected to be 102.7 million by 2016 (Anonymous 2015: 2). The same report also includes the following characteristic features of slums in the country: lack of basic services, substandard housing or illegal and inadequate building structures, overcrowding and high density, unhealthy living conditions and hazardous locations, insecure tenure; irregular or informal settlements, which are invasions of non-urban land, poverty and social exclusion (Anonymous, 2015). About 17.36 per cent constitutes the slum population in all cities/towns i.e., 2613, where slums are reported in states and union territories of the country according to the 2011 Census. However, 19 per cent of the child population the above urban population lives in the slums. The Scheduled Castes in the slums range a maximum from 38.9 per cent that is in Punjab to a minimum of 5.3 in Sikkim during the same Census period (Anonymous, 2011).

There are quite few studies of slums in various cities of India since independence: Delhi (Bharat Sewak Samaj, 1958; Prasanta and Majumdar, 1978; Lynch, 1974; Wankhede, 1999); Madras (Balasundaram 1957; Arangannal, 1971; Wiebe, 1975); Bombay (Ramachandran, 1972; Desai and Pillai, 1972); Vijayawada (Rao and Rao, 1984); Vishakhapatnam (Rao and Raju, 1972); Calcutta [Rao, Bhatt and Narayan (ed.)] 1991, Siddique, 1969); Mangalore (Pais, 1999); Panipat in Haryana and Saharanpur of UP (Jodka, 2010) etc. So far, Hyderabad is concerned there are three important studies–the Indian Institute of Economics (1976); Naidu (1978) and Suvvada (2012). All these studies have covered various aspects of the slums and the lives of the slum dwellers. Here it is to be noted that the studies in Hyderabad did not deal with education in the slums, except Kumar (2017) who recently covered for his doctoral dissertation.

Slums in Hyderabad, which is the state capital of Telangana state since 2014, are in existence since 1920 (Iyyengar, 1951) primarily due to the onset of urbanization and industrialization around this time. Mainly migrant rural populations around the city constituted the slum population and later on others from other places of Andhra and Telangana and other states also immigrated to the slums. Since then, there has been a constant increase in population and the number of them also increased over the years. Therefore, in the year 1962, there were 106 slums with a population of 1,20,000 which gradually increased to 1631 by 2001 having a population of 19,51,207; the population has increased to 22,87,014 by 2011 which constitutes 32.70 per cent of the total Greater Hyderabad city population (Anonymous, 2015:26). According to an official report of the GHMC, 22 per cent of the total slums are migrants from different parts of the country.[4]

Table 5.1: Slums in Hyderabad

S. No.	*Year*	*Number of Slums*	*Population*
1.	1962	106	1,20,000
2.	1967	194	1,68,000
3.	1972	282	3,00,000
4.	1976	300	3,20,000
5.	1978	377	3,80,000
6.	1979	455	4,08,000
7.	1981	470	5,40,000

Source: Hyderabad City Development Plan (www.ourmch.com, accessed on 19th April 2012).

Education in Slums and Hyderabad: There are not many studies available about education in slums in India. Some of these include Kundu's (2003) study on slums of Kolkata, Aggarwal and Chugh's (2003) in New Delhi and Shah and Sen's (2008) study of slums and schools in West Bengal. In Hyderabad, the general education in the slum areas is said to be 60-80 per cent and the female literacy is 52-73 per cent. There are 405 government schools, 267 government-aided schools and 175 private schools in the slums of Hyderabad. About 3.72 per cent of the slum children aged 5-14 do not go to school and 3.17 per cent work as child labourers, of whom 64 per cent in boys and 36 per cent in girls. The main employers of child labour are street shops that are by the roadways and highways and construction sites. Among the working children, 35 per cent are engaged in hazardous jobs in the city of Hyderabad even in the 21st century which is called the technological hub.[5] The NGOs like CLAP Foundation, that runs a school on wheels serving over a hundred children with no access to education (www.clapfoundation.org accessed on 10th September 2014) and Alpha which runs a school for slum children at Jubilee Hills (http://aggregate.commuoh.in/slums-schools-in-hyderabad-provide-a-ray-of-hope/ accessed on 9th August 2013) are catering the needs of quality education to the slum dwellers in Hyderabad. Few sporadic studies do indicate the problems of education in slums (Modi, 2006, Prashanthi 2012).

Given the above situation about the education of the slum children in different cities of India, it is thought appropriate to find out the availability and making use of communication and education technology in the schools located in the slums of Hyderabad where a sizable population of Scheduled Castes live in the city.

Methodology of the Study

Given the above objective, the study adopted the methodology of carrying out a survey in Serilingamaplli Municipality of the GHMC that represents one of the municipalities where a large proportion of the slum dwellers are above the poverty line. The selected slums include Gopanpalli, Gopinagar, Kondapur, and Nehrunagar. A sample of 50 students are drawn for the study from seven schools located in these four slums. Out of 50, 48 students are presently attending school and 2 are out of school. Such sample, it is felt, would represent the literate of the slum. The relevant information has been collected with the help of a structured schedule from these students as well as the school teachers, and parents of the students.

Table 5.2: Sample Drawn from the Schools

S. No.	*Name of the School*	*Strength in Schools*			*Sample drawn*				*Total sample drawn*
		Girls	*Boys*	*Total*	*Girls*	*Boys*	*Out of school Girls*	*Out of school Boys*	
1.	MPP-UPS Gopinagar	141	151	292	3	4	-	-	7
2.	MPP-PS Nehrunagar	47	35	82	4	3	-	-	7
3.	ZPHS-Serilingampally	835	455	1290	4	4		2	10
4.	MPP-Gopanapally	146	110	256	3	3	-	-	6
5.	PS- Kondapur	251	200	451	5	3	-	-	8
6.	St.Xavier High School-Gopinagar	175	125	300	4	3	-	-	7
7.	Emmaus The School-Gopinagar	170	150	320	3	2	-	-	5
	Total	**1765**	**1226**	**2991**	**26**	**22**		**2**	**50**

MPP-UPS= Mandal Praja Parishad Upper Primary School; MPP-PS= Mandal Praja Parishad Primary School; P.S. = Primary School; ZPHS –Zilla Parishad High School.

Thus, the data collected from 50 students have been analyzed and discussed in the following pages. Apart from these, about 50 slum residents, 25 school teachers, parents and others are interviewed informally on the objectives of the study. Altogether the total number of respondents are about 125. Table 5.3 shows the distribution of student respondents by age and sex.

Table 5.3: Age and Sex of the Respondents

(Percentage in Parenthesis)

S. No.	Age	Sex		Total
		Boys	Girls	
1.	9-12 years	7 (28.0)	16 (64.0)	23 (46.0)
2.	13-15 years	5 (20.0)	9 (36.0)	14 (28.0)
3.	16-17 years	11 (44.0)	0 (0.0)	11 (22.0)
4.	18 + years	2 (8.0)	0 (0.0)	2 (4.0)
	Total	**25 (100.0)**	**25 (100.0)**	**50 (100.0)**

4. Background of the Slums

Serilingampally: It is a Municipality under the GHMC; it is a Mandal[6] also in Ranga Reddy district. Because of its proximity to Hitech City, Gachibowli, Nanakramguda, Manikonda and Kondapur where several IT organizations are located, there has been a considerable surge in the population. It was constituted in 1987 by merging 23 revenue villages, and it covers an area of around 96.99 sq. kms. The Municipality has more than 24 wards. The aggregate population of Serilingampally Municipality is evaluated to have more than 3,00,000 today. Quick urbanization in Serilingampally is epitomized by the escalating land prices in the recent past. It is also closer to educational institutions like the University of Hyderabad and IIIT. According to the 2011 census, Serilingampally has a population of 3,09,320 which includes 1,60,556 men and 1,48,764 women. The Serilingampally Municipality has an average literacy of 82.17 per cent, of which male literacy is 75.62 per cent and female literacy is 67.75. There is about 10.9 per cent of the population belonging to SCs living in the slums and 9.75 per cent of them are in urban regions of the Municipality. (see Table 5.4)

Gopanapally weaker section colony slum: It is eight kilometers away from Gachibowli 'X' roads, Cyberabad. A huge portion of the houses are situated on the western side of the street, and for those on the eastern side, there is an expansion of old *basthi*. This is originally a village, and

Table 5.4: Social representation in slums and urban areas of Serilingampally Municipality

(Percentage in Parenthesis)

S. No.	Social Category	Area		Total
		Slum	Urban	
1.	SC	8314 (35.71) (10.90)	14966 (64.29) (9.75)	23280 (100.0) (10.14)
2.	ST	1784 (38.35) (2.33)	2868 (61.65) (1.87)	4652 (100.0) (2.02)
3.	Others	66215 (32.82) (86.77)	135530 (67.18) (88.38)	201745 (100.0) (87.84)
4.	Total	76313 (33.23) (100.0)	153364 (66.77) (100.0)	229677 (100.0) (100.0)

Source: http://www.Andhrapradeshstat.com/table/urbnareas/31slums, accessed on 29th December 2013.

with the formation of Serilingampalli Municipality, it became a ward in the municipality. It is dominated by Goud and Yadava castes, and it is located near the southern gate of the University of Hyderabad. Gopanapally has a population of 4,320 distributed in 950 households, and most of the residents are working as temporary and daily-wage workers in the premises of the University of Hyderabad, and some of them are working in the nearby industrial areas of Patancheru. A sizable population belongs to Scheduled Castes and backward class communities. There is a primary school built on government land. And, a Primary Health Centre is at a distance of two to three kilometers located near Gulmohar Park Colony.

Gopinagar slum: This slum is one of the 59 notified slums of the Serilingampally; and it is situated on the way to old Bombay interstate road, by the bank of Gopicheruvu, near aluminium industry (Alind Factory) and close to Bharat Heavy Electrical Limited (BHEL). It was built in the year 1974 and around 1,000 poor households are inhabiting a plot of 60 acres in Survey No. 341/1 of Serilingampally village. The aggregate population of the slum is 9,920 and the number of households is 2,530. There is a primary school with an enrollment of students around 316 which includes 45 SC children. It has been built on government land. A portion of the slum has houses of *pucca* structures, some are semi-*pucca* with tiled rooftops, and few are with mud walls and asbestos rooftops. Drinking water is supplied through tankers besides water pipes and public taps. Though there is a water tank (Gopicheruvu), it has been polluted with sewerage of the nearby residential colonies and it emits a foul smell. Even though, electricity connection is available in many of the households, there is interruption of power supply. On rainy days, the electricity is stopped many times. Few houses that lack electricity depends on kerosene lamps. It comprises castes of backward class, Scheduled Castes, and tribes who are migrants from villages and other slums. And, the majority is a daily-wage workers. Few regular employees are working as low-paid attenders, peons, sweepers, etc. in ALIND, University of Hyderabad, GHMC, shops and stores in Serilingampally.

Kondapur slum: Since the last decade it has grown exceedingly into the latest business hub and also a real estate and commercial zone. It has access to many supermarkets and in the same manner private and government schools as well as medical facilities notably KIMS hospitals and Apollo Cradle which is one of the best hospitals in the city. Some government schools are supported by NGOs but some are not.

Nehrunagar slum: It is located in Papireddy colony and Citizen's colony localities, and is close to Chandanagar railway station. Most of the residents are working as temporary and daily wage workers and some are auto-rickshaw drivers. A majority of them belong to the communities of SC, OBC and ST.

Background of the children: Since the access to educational institutions after primary school is beyond the capacity of the slum dwellers, the children who seek higher education face a hard time. It means that they should invest money and energy to succeed in education at all levels and in all manners including the distance because the schools are not available within the reachable distance of the slum. As money is a constraint for the slum dwellers, the long-distance does matter for them which has an impact on their pursuit of higher education. Many a time, parents do not care for their children's higher education for they have to send them to faraway places and they have to use public transport system. Therefore, they lean toward primary education in the same locality. It is observed that few families send their children to faraway places for higher education even though they consider that the primary schools situated in the slum do not provide legitimate education in comparison to private schools.

About 96.4 per cent of the slum children go to schools within a distance of two kilometers which means that they study either in the same locality or nearby locality and their parents feel that the children can safely commute to the school and thus incur no extra expenditure on education. And in the same manner, 66.4 per cent study at a distance of two kilometers; 20.7 per cent study at a distance of three kilometers; and 11.9 per cent travel more than four kilometers daily. Some children go to school on foot; and some go on a bicycle, and a few children use state road transport buses. Only very few children use auto-rickshaws (Kumar, 2016).

Background of the girls: The slum children, particularly girls, are engaged in domestic works such as babysitting and helping their mothers in sweeping the house, cleaning the vessels and washing clothes etc. It is observed that children attend the household work after school.[7] Therefore, the girl children who attend government schools are more carefree and they are not very serious about their studies. Another reason for such an indifferent attitude towards education could be that the parents are not much concerned about the girl child education as she shall be married off as soon as she attains puberty. According to them, the girl's priority is homemaking than education. But teachers are perhaps not concerned much about the social issues of the girl child in the slum. This results from all the considerations in the attitude of laxity towards education and the physical exhaustion also affect studying at home which impacts their progress in studies.

According to the opinion of the teachers of the schools located in these slums, they are almost unanimous in that the slum children do not show interest in learning; they are weak students in all respects. Undoubtedly, these are subjects of prejudicial statements. But the teachers are unconcerned about the socio-economic background and the social neighbourhood of the children, despite they are sympathetic on these kinds of issues. Their declaration is based upon their performance in various examinations, attendance, and so on. However, the self-assessment of the students is very different from that of their teachers.

Schools in the Slums and the Infrastructure Facilities Available

The data are collected from seven schools as already stated and of them, three are primary schools and the remaining four are high schools as shown in Table 5.5. Of them, two are private schools, the other five schools are run by the state government. It is observed that all the schools are having RCC structures.

School and the Number of Rooms and other Facilities

There are separate rooms for teachers only in two schools where the strength of teachers is maximum i.e., 21 and 15 respectively. Even 12 or 13 teachers and an office have a common hall for sitting. In this regard, it seems there is no difference between a private or a public school. Sitting benches for students are not available in a government school (see Table 5.6).

Table 5.5: Details of Schools Selected for the Study

S. No.	Area of School & Name	School Type	Run by	Structure
1.	Gopinagar	Upper Primary	Government	Pucca
2.	Nehrunagar	Primary	Government	Pucca
3.	Serilingampally	High School	Government	Pucca
4.	Gopanapally	Primary	Government	Pucca
5.	Kondapur	Primary	Government	Pucca
6.	Gopinagar, St. Xavier	High School	Private Agency	Pucca
7.	Gopinagar, Emmaus	High School	Private Agency	Pucca

Table 5.6: Facilities Available in the Schools

S. No.	Schools	No. of Rooms in the School	Separate Room for Teachers	Availability of Sitting benches	Availability of Toilet Facility
1.	MPP-UPS Gopinagar	8	No	Yes	Yes
2.	MPP-PS Nehrunagar	3	No	No	Yes
3.	ZPHS-Serilingampally	21	Yes	Yes	Yes
4.	MPP-PS Gopanapally	6	No	Yes	Yes
5.	PS- Kondapur	12	No	Yes	Yes
6.	St. Xavier High School-Gopinagar	15	Yes	Yes	Yes
7.	Emmaus The School-Gopinagar	13	No	Yes	Yea

Availability of Television Set and the Usage of it

Of the seven schools, two schools are not having television sets while the rest claim to have them. These are provided by the State Bank of India and CYIENT[8] under corporate responsibility. However, only in one school do the students use the television set for watching lessons whereas in other schools these are meant to watch important events such as Republic Day or Independent Day parades etc.

In the schools where television sets are available, there are also DVD players. However, three schools are using the DVD players for teaching lessons while the other two schools are using them to watch some entertainments. Thus, it appears that the technology of television sets is not properly used for imparting education to the slum students. It means that the schools largely depend on the traditional methods of teaching.

Availability of Computers

All the seven schools are having computers which are provided to them by corporate industries as in the case of television sets. The Zilla Parishad High School, Serilingamaplly has the maximum number of computers and has the highest number of students also. On average there are 11 computers in each of these schools. However, 81 per cent of them is in working condition (See Table 5.7) while the rest need repairs.

Table 5.7: Availability of Computers in Schools

S. No.	Name of the School	No. of Computers Available in Schools		Total
		Working	Not Working	
1.	MPP-UPS Gopinagar	5	3	8
2.	MPP-PS Nehrunagar	10		10
3.	ZPHS-Serilingampally	26	1	27
4.	MPP PS-Gopanapally	3	9	12
5.	PS-Kondapur	15		15
6.	St. Xavier High School-Gopinagar	3	2	5
7.	Emmaus The School-Gopinagar	3		3
	Total	**65**	**15**	**80**

Computer Labs

Of the seven schools, four schools have designated separate computer labs, but in the case of others, the computers are housed in the office room itself. It appears no proper care and upkeep of the equipment is being taken by the school authorities.

Computer Instructors

Of the seven schools, in two schools there are teacher instructors, and another three schools the corporate organizations that have provided the computers send volunteers or instructors now and then according to their convenience to take computer classes for the students. In another school, there is no instructor at all.

The teacher instructors are also volunteers; they are not trained by either the government or the corporate organizers. It is their voluntary service; the teachers who are empathetically motivated and desire to share their knowledge with the students become volunteers. They possess basic or minimum knowledge of computers, but most of the other teachers do not have even the minimum knowledge about computers; they are illiterate in this regard.

Curriculum and Computers

Since the syllabi of any of the classes in the school do not include computer lessons, it is argued by the teachers that there is no way there can be regular computer classes. If there is, syllabi of computer lessons, there is an onus on the part of the government to appoint a computer teacher or train a teacher for teaching computer lessons. Therefore, learning about computers is not necessary for the students and it is also not mandatory for the teachers to teach. However, in some schools, there is a 'computer class' which is not part of the regular academic schedule but it is declared as so, as and when the school administration feels about having a computer class.

Patterns of Using the Computers

In the above academic context, the use of computers is based on the interest of the students besides the willingness on the part of the school administration as to when to use them. The computer classes, in practice, appear to be held mostly in the high schools, the students are not prevented to use them in primary schools as Table 5.7 indicates. The version of the school authorities is that the students can use computers any time, while the students say that they can use them during the computer class. Accordingly, Table 5.8 shows that computers are used effectively by high school students.

Purposes for which the Computers are used

According to students, nearly half (45%) of them say the computers are used by the office as well as staff. However, more than one third (35%) of the students say that computers are used for office work only. The remaining (20%) is of the view that only staff use the computers. It can be interpreted from this information that the computers are for general use and common use of all employees of the school.

Table 5.8: Pattern of Using the Computers

S. No.	*School*	*Students' Use at any time of the school*	*Students' Use in Computer Class only*	*Who-ever wants to use*	*Total*
1.	MPP-UPS Gopinagar	1	0	1	1
2.	MPP-PS Nehrunagar	0	0	1	1
3.	ZPHS-Serilingampally	1	1	0	1
4.	MPP PS-Gopanapally	1	1	0	1
5.	PS- Kondapur	1	1	0	1
6.	St. Xavier High School-Gopinagar	1	1	0	1
7.	Emmaus The School-Gopinagar	1	1	0	1
	Total	**6**	**5**	**2**	**7**

About the specific purpose for which the computers are used, more than half (54%) students are of the view that the computers are used for the office work of the school. Another more than one third (34%) have expressed the view of either 'no idea' or 'office use'. Of the remaining, a majority (8%) say that they are used by the teachers and only few (4%) are of the view that they use them to play games or watch some entertainments.

What did Students Learn from the Computers?

Ultimately, did the students learn anything from the computers available in school? The results are not very encouraging. However, given the scenario explained above much cannot be expected also. Table 5.9 reveals that the students are inclined to learn mostly word processing and graphics. On the whole, graphics seems to be more interesting or needed to be learnt for the students in these schools over the word processing or any other. There seems not much difference between boys and girls, though the latter appears to be a little more interested in graphics. It is also important to know that about 12 per cent did not learn anything from the computers available in the school so far.

Apart from the above, it is understood from the discussion with the students that they had learnt the basics like booting up and closing down the computer, searching websites and sending and receiving e-mails. In this regard, the students of private schools are ahead of the students of government schools.

Table 5.9: Learning from the Computers

(Percentages in Parenthesis)

S. No.	*Learnt*	*Gender*		*Total*
		Boys	*Girls*	
1.	Word Processing	3 (60.0) (12.0)	2 (40.0) (8.0)	5 (100.0) (10.0)
2.	Graphics	3 (30.0) (12.0)	7 (70.0) (28.0)	10 (100.0) (16.0)
3.	Any other	6 (40.0) (24.0)	9 (60.0) (36.0)	15 (100.0) (30.0)
4.	Word Processing and Graphics	6 (66.7) (24.0)	3 (33.0) (12.0)	9 (100.0) (18.0)
6.	WP, Graphics and any other	5 (100.0) (20.0)	0 (0.0)	5 (100.0) (10.0)
7.	Not learnt any thing	2 (33.3) (8.0)	4 (66.7) (16.0)	6 (100.0) (12.0)
	Total	**25 (50.0) (100.0)**	**25 (50.0) (100.0)**	**50 (100.0) (100.0)**

It is important to note here that about 70 per cent of the students learnt about computers whatever little it be, they have learnt in the school only. It means that they had no opportunity to learn outside the school given their economic condition and environmental background. For several of the slum children, formal learning begins at the government school, whatever the school offers, and it ends there only in most cases.

Availability of Internet Facility to the Computers

The internet facility is available in all the schools except, the MPPS government school at Gopinagar. This facility is helping the students to learn how to browse different sites on the computer. However, most of the students have no idea of using the e-mail facility.

Technology at Home

Except for one student, all the respondents in the survey asserted to have a television set at home. While there is not a single mobile phone in three homes (6%), one mobile phone in one home (2%), a majority i.e., 41 (82%) of them are having two mobile phones and five homes (10%) have three in each case. The android phone is available in nine homes, and the rest have a regular phone out of 50 households. As regards the connectivity concerning android phones, four have Idea connection, two each with BSNL and Airtel and one with Geo. These phones are mainly used for conversation, and only nine (18%) of the respondents have asserted that these are used for sending messages and watching movies also.

It is interesting to note that four (8%) of the respondents have reported having a computer at home with an internet connection also. But the students do hardly use it for any educational purpose. It is reported to have been used for sending and receiving emails.

Patterns of Visiting Internet Cafe

Out of the 50 respondents, 11 (22%) students have reported having been visiting the Internet Café for various purposes. Among the purposes for which visits are made, chatting and playing games seems to be taking a prominent role as the Table 5.10 reveals. In this regard, boys are much ahead of girls.

Table 5.10: Purpose for Visiting the Internet Cafes

(Percentages in Parenthesis)

S. No.	*Purpose*	*Gender*		*Total*
		Boys	*Girls*	
1.	Internet search	0 (0.0) 0.0)	1 (100.0) (33.3)	1 (100.0) (9.1)
2.	To check and send mails	1 (100.0) (12.5)	0 (0.0) (0.0)	1 (100.0) (9.1)
3.	Play games	2 (66.7) (25.0)	1 (33.3) (33.3)	3 (100.0) (27.3)
4.	Mails and Chat	4 (100.0) (50.0)	0 (0.0) (0.0)	4 (100.0) (36.4)
5.	Chat and Play games	1 (100.0) (12.5)	0 (0.0) (0.0)	1 (100.0) (9.1)
6.	Not Specified	0 (0.0) (0.0)	1 (100.0) (33.3)	1 (100.0) (9.1)
	Total	**8 (72.7) (100.0)**	**3 (27.3) (100.0)**	**11 (100.0) (100.0)**

Expenditure incurred on Internet Cafe: So far as the expenditure incurred on every visit is concerned, the students usually spend between Rs. 20.00 and Rs. 50.00 (see Table 5.11).

Table 5.11: Expenditure Incurred on Internet Café

(Percentage in Parenthesis)

S. No.	*Amount Spent*	*Gender*		*Total*
		Boys	*Girls*	
1.	Less than Rs. 20	1 (100.0) (12.5)	0 (0.0) (0.0)	1 (100.0) (9.1)
2.	Less than Rs. 50	7 (70.0) (87.5)	3 (30.0) (100.0)	10 (100.0) (90.9)
	Total	**8 (72.7) (100.0)**	**3 (27.3) (100.0)**	**11 (100.0) (100.0)**

The Gratification of Learning Computer Operations

By and large, all the students are satisfied with the skills that they have developed about the operation of a computer. Since this is the first generation in most cases in getting educated, and in all cases, this is the first generation of acquiring computer skills, it gives them tremendous satisfaction of handling computers which is the most modern technology found in every walk of life. Table 5.12 demonstrates such satisfaction.

Table 5.12: Satisfaction about the Computer Skills

(Percentage in Parenthesis)

S. No.	*Level of Satisfaction*	*Gender*		*Total*
		Boys	*Girls*	
1.	Greatly Satisfied	17 (51.5) (68.0)	16 (48.5) (64.0)	33 (100.0) (66.0)
2.	Satisfied	6 (42.0) (24.0)	8 (57.1) (32.0)	14 (1.0) (28.0)
3	I do not know	2 (66.7) (8.0)	1 (33.3) (4.0)	3 (100.0) (6.0)
	Total	**25 (50.0) (100.0)**	**25 (50.0) (100.0)**	**50 (100.0) (100.0)**

Discussion

Given the determination and efforts of the Central Government and state governments imparting IT skills to students of primary and secondary schools as discussed above, it is expected that there shall be some impact on the ground. It appears most of the talk about the subject of ET and ICT remains on the paper and government institutions, and hardly does any reach the ground. There could be multiple reasons for such abysmal achievement when we look from the ground. The government has not provided even the television sets to its schools and the teachers have no idea of various educational channels or programmes for the students. As long as the computer science subject is not introduced and trained personnel are posted in the schools, it seems no meaningful effect can be practically found. If this is not possible, at least efforts must be made to integrate ICT with the current syllabi at least at the secondary school level as a vocational programme.

Conclusion

The above discussion makes it very clear that governments do have good intentions and efforts are also made to take forward the Education Technology and ICT to the basic levels of education. Given the trends in global education and development, it is undoubtedly necessary that our children should be imparted the knowledge at an early stage. But it is painfully observed that what is said in the government policies is not found in practice. The study of ICT in the selected slums of Hyderabad clearly shows that there is hardly anything like ET in the schools, and the government's role is not found anywhere. The teachers are not part of the ET programme and there is no instructor. The television sets available in the schools are not used for education; it lacks integration with the curriculum. None of the teachers in these schools is trained to impart ICT to students. They continue to teach in the old conventional way. At the most, students have gained basic knowledge about word processing and browsing websites. The poor Scheduled Caste students of the slums who mostly depend on the government schools are deprived of computer knowledge while their counterparts who are better off are marching ahead in the private schools.

NOTES

1. There are 8,47,118–Primary Schools; 4,25,094–Upper-Primary Schools; 1,35,335–Secondary Schools; and 1,09,318 Senior Secondary Schools. (Anonymous 2016:3).
2. The literacy rates at the level 7 + age group are: 73.0 (All), 66.1 (SC) and 59.0 (ST) as per 2011 Census. The same at 15+age group are: 69.3 (All), 60.4 (SC) and 51.9 (ST). The increase in enrolment between 2001 and 2011 shows 37.49 per cent for SC and 37.92 per cent for ST, but while the dropout

rate for national average remains at 45.13 per cent, for the SC and ST it is 51.72 per cent and 60.51 per cent respectively (Pandita, 2015).

3. This project was launched in India in 1975 by the Indian Space Research Organization (ISRO) in collaboration with NASA with the basic aim of finding out whether the satellite communication can be used for the education and development of rural and remote areas of country.
4. www.cgg.gov.in, accessed on 16th July, 2015.
5. http://en.wikipedia.org, accessed on 2nd May, 2013.
6. Mandal is equal to a Taluk in the administrative setup of the district.
7. It has found that 130 (46.4%) children attend the household work after school; 67 (23.9%) children do their homework after their school. In case of the children studying in private schools, 32.7 per cent children do their homework; about 3.8 per cent children literally while away their time; whereas 10.5 per cent children studying in government schools do their homework (Kumar, 2017).
8. Global engineering and technology solutions company.

REFERENCES

Aggarwal, Y. and Chugh, S. (2003). *Learning achievement of slum children in Delhi*, New Delhi: National Institute of Educational Planning and Administration.

Anonymous (2006). *Position Paper–'National Focus Group on Educational Technology*, New Delhi: National Council for Education Research and Training (NCERT).

Anonymous (2011). *Primary Census Abstract for Slum*. New Delhi: Census of India. http://www.censusindia.gov.in/2011-Documents/Slum-26-09-13.pdf

Anonymous (2015). *Slums in India–A Statistical Compendium*. Ministry of Housing and Urban Poverty Alleviation. New Delhi: National Buildings Organization, Government of India.

Anonymous (2015). *Use of Information and Communication Technology in Secondary Schools*, Research Report, Study Commissioned by NITI Ayog, Govt. of India. New Delhi: Education Quality Foundation of India.

Anonymous (2016). *Educational Statistics at a Glance*, New Delhi: Ministry of Human Resource Development. Department of School Education and Literacy, Government of India. https://mhrd.gov.in/sites/upload_files/mhrd/files/statistics/ESG2016_0.pdf.

Anonymous (2017). *CLIx–Connected Learning Initiative*, New Delhi: TATA Trust. https://clix.tiss.edu/wp-content/uploads/2018/05/CLIx-Telangana-State-Report.pdf.

Anonymous (2019). *Draft National Educational Policy 2019*, New Delhi: MHRD, Government of India.

Arangannal (1975). *Socio-economic survey of Madras slums (1971 Survey)*, Madras: Tamilnadu Slum Clearance Board.

Bajpai, N., Biberman, J. and Sharma, A. (2019). "Information and Communications Technology in the Education Sector in India". Towards a New Indian Model of Information and Communications Technology-Led Growth and Development, 3. Center for Sustainable Development, Earth Institute, Columbia University. https://doi.org/10.7916/d8-9anm-mc81.

Balasundaram, D. (1957). *History of Slums in Madras City and Scheme for Improvement*. Madras: Corporation of Madras.

Bharat Sevak Samaj (1958). *Slums of Old Delhi: A report of socio-economic survey of slums*, Delhi: Atmaram and Sons.

Byker, E. J. (2014). "ICT in India's Elementary Schools: The Vision and Realities", The *International Education Journal: Comparative Perspectives*. 13(2): 27-40.

Byker, E.J. (2015). "The One Laptop School: Equipping Rural Elementary Schools in South India through Public Private Partnerships", *Global Education Review*, *2*(4): 126-143.

Campbell, K. Mehr, H. and Mayer, B. (2013). *Education Technology in India: Designing Ed-Tech for Affordable Private Schools*, https://edtechindia.files.wordpress.com/2013/01/education-technology-in-india-designing-ed-tech-for-affordable-private-schools.pdf.

Desai, A.R. and Pillai, S.D. (1972). *A Profile of an Indian slum*. Bombay: Popular Prakashan.

Goswami, C. (2014). *Role of Technology in Indian Education* https://edtechindia.files.wordpress.com/2013/01/education-technology-in-india-designing-ed-tech-for-affordable-private-schools.pdf

Iyyengar, S.K. (1951). *Rural Economic Enquiries in the Hyderabad Sate, 1949-51*, Hyderabad: Government Press.

Jodhka, S. (2010). "Dalit in Business: Self-Employed Scheduled Castes in Northwest India", Working Paper Series, New Delhi: Indian Institute of Dalit Studies.

Kumar, Wesly (2017). *Education and Social Exclusion of Dalits in slums of Hyderabad*, Unpublished Ph.D. thesis. University of Hyderabad. Hyderabad.

Kundu, N. (2003). "The Case of Kolkata, India, understanding slums: case studies for the global report on human settlements", www.ucl.ac.uk/dpu-projects/global_report/pdfs/kolkotapdf.

Lone, Z.A. (2017). "Technology in Education in Rural India", *International Journal of Engineering Science and Computing*.7(7): 13953-13955.

Lynch, O.M. (1974). "Political Mobilisation and Ethnicity among Adi-Dravidas in Bombay Slum", *Economic and Political Weekly*. *9* (39): 1657-1659.

Modi, S. (2006). "Poverty premium in Rasoolpura, Hyderabad", CCS working paper No. 163, Summer internship programme, New Delhi: Centre for Civil Society.

Naidu, R. (1978). "A study of slums in Hyderabad-Secunderabad", *The Indian Journal of Social Work*, *39*(3): 297-312.

Pais, Richard (1999). "Scheduled Castes, Employment and Social Mobility." In: S.M. Michael (ed.) *Dalits in Modern India: Vision and Values*, New Delhi: Vistaar Publications, pp. 334-339.

Pandita, R. (2015). "Dropout Percentage of Scheduled Caste & Scheduled Tribe Children in India: A Decadal Analysis up to Secondary level", *Journal of Indian Education.* Volume 41: 97-117.

Prasanta, S. and Ila Majumdar (1978). *Rural Migrants in an Urban Setting : A Study of Two Shanty Colonies in the Capital City of India*, New Delhi: Hindustan Publishing Corporation.

Prashanthi, B. (2012). *Practices of Untouchability in Schools of Hyderabad*, Unpublished M.Phil. dissertation, University of Hyderabad. Hyderabad.

Ramachandran, P. (1972) *Pavement Dwellers in Bombay City*, Bombay: TISS.

Rao, M.S.A., Bhat, C. and Kadekar, L.N. (1991). *A reader in urban sociology*. New Delhi: Orient Longman.

Rao, Ranga and Raju, B.R.K (1992). *Slums of Vishakapatnam: A Perspective*, Vishakapatnam: Andhra University Press.

Rao, Ranga. K. and Rao, M.S.A. (1984). *Cities and Slums: A study of a squatter settlement in the city of Vijayawada*, New Delhi: Concept Publishing Co. Pvt. Ltd.

Shah, M. and Sen, S. (2008). "Education Mapping in A Slum Area: An Analysis of the Dynamics of Demand and Supply". CCS Working Paper No. 201, Summer Research Internship Programme, New Delhi: Centre for Civil Society.

Siddiqui, M.K.A. (1969). "Life in the Slums of Calcutta", *Economic and Political Weekly*, Vol. 4, No. 50, Dec., pp. 1917-1919.

Suvvada, Srinivas (2012). *Coping with Degrading Work: A Study of Mehtars in Hyderabad City*, Unpublished Ph.D. dissertation, University of Hyderabad. Hyderabad.

The Indian Institute of Economics (1976). *Sample Survey of Socio-Economic Conditions of Slums in 1975- 76*, Hyderabad, Hyderabad: TIIE.

Vyas, R.V., Sharma, R.C. and Kumar, A. (2002). Educational television in India. *Turkish online Journal of Distance Education*, *3*(4). 1-9. http://tojde.anadolu.edu.tr/yonetim/icerik/makaleler/72-published.pdf.

Wankhede, G.G. (1999). *Social Mobility and Scheduled Castes*, Jaipur: Rawat Publications

Weibe, P. D. (1975). *Social Life in Indian Slums*, Delhi: Vikas Publishers.

6

Anthropological Reflections on Communication Challenges in Implementation of Special Component Plan (SCP) for Scheduled Castes

Raj K. Kattula

Introduction

This chapter is a part of larger research undertaken for my Ph.D. programme to explore policy and practice of the Special Component Plan (SCP) from an anthropological perspective. The fresh attempt essentially is to understand the role of communication in policy processes. First, it highlights key areas of policy processes and then it explains how these processes work as communication between authorities and later the beneficiaries. Further, it shows challenges in communicating policy, especially at the grassroots. For this purpose, a case of SCP is presented in this chapter.

What Does Communicating A Policy Mean?

The policy process is generally considered in India as a result shaped by how a web of institutions created by the Constitution (Mathur and Bjorkman, 2009, p. 26). However, in this chapter, policy processes are not strictly examined on these lines rather as a process of a unique communication system, through which social problems are narrated, understood, translated into a policy document and executed to reach out back to beneficiaries to solve the existing problem.

Therefore, whenever it is to do with communicating a policy there are two important components to be considered without a miss i.e., the process of policy formulation and the process of policy implementation. These processes are nothing but manifestations of several decisions, views, requests and suggestions of stakeholders in connection with how to go about with a particular policy. It is important to consider the inputs of all the stakeholders in the process of policy-making. However, the stakeholders are usually stratified by their association with their position, identity and ability in society i.e., a public representative, a government official, a peer-group/pressure-group, a member of NGO, a beneficiary/a target-group etc. Bringing such diverse stakeholders together into a common platform to make an inclusive decision and to get goals-set for policy to resolve the existing problem is the first and foremost step in the process of policy-making.

The entire exercise requires not just the right communication but most importantly the suitable mode of communication. Right information added with a suitable mode of communication would empower stakeholders about the scope and the importance of their participation in the process of policymaking. However, there is no single suitable mode of communication that can be adopted to disseminate the information to and among all the stakeholders involved because they are stratified and diverse. For example, for a government official, information on an official letter/ notice is an appropriate mode of communication, which he/she will pay due attention to. But, for an illiterate and uninformed targetgroup or person at the grassroots, informing through an official letter/notice may not be appropriate. Perhaps, conducting an awareness camp may be more suitable for them. Likewise, choosing an appropriate communication method for an appropriate stakeholder group is a very important step in the process of achieving a common platform and formulating policy thereof.

Bringing diverse stakeholders onto a common platform is required not only for formulating a policy but also for executing it. This means that the implementation of the policy requires proper administrative set up to perform necessary processes to deliver the intended benefits to the target group/individuals so that the purpose of the policy is achieved. On the other hand, beneficiaries should also be given proper information/ guidelines on how, where and when to access the benefits.

Hence, as mentioned above, both policy formulation and policy implementation play a crucial role in communicating a policy between authorities and the target-group. So, the challenge involved in communicating a policy is nothing but effective execution of its processes. Therefore, these processes are considered as forms of communication rather than mere components of policy in this chapter.

Before going further, it is appropriate here to have a glance at SCP.

What is SCP?

Special Component Plan (SCP) is a comprehensive development policy for Scheduled Castes (SCs) also known as Scheduled Castes Sub-Plan (SCSP). The government of India has adopted it as a national policy in the Financial Year 1979-80 due to pressure built upon the government by Scheduled Castes against their oppression. It is supposed to be mandatory upon all the State and Central Governments as well as Governments of Union Territories to make sure that all their Departments and Ministries implement the policy without fail. It is an umbrella policy which means that number of programmes and schemes can be designed and implemented for the benefit of SCs. Funds should be allocated from State, Central and UT budgets on par with the SC population percentage in their respected territories. Further, the allocated funds should be spent in a way that is directly and exclusively beneficial for SCs. Funds should be mentioned under minor head 786 in the budget, which bars the funds allocated under this head to be diverted to other programmes.

However, SCP was a result of many factors (Kattula, 2016). During the 1960s due to the introduction of the Green Revolution in India farmers and landowners across the country started receiving fruits of it, as it resulted increased in agricultural production. On the other hand, despite increased production, the market prices of daily commodities have gone up, unemployment increased, and the economic growth has almost come to a stall. Consequently, ongoing welfare programmes were seized to be implemented. The victims of the situation were the socially and economically weak section of Scheduled Castes. Since the majority Scheduled Castes were agricultural labourers, and could not stand the prices of the market, have started demanding the landowners for more pay for their labour. The landowners did not agree to the demand put forth by the labourers, which sparked the conflict between landowners and labourers. Many incidents of the conflict took place across India, at Kanchikacherla (Kafir, 2010; Satyanarayana and Suisie, 2013), Kilvenmani (EPW, 1973), and Marathwada (Morkhandikar, 1978) to mention a few. At this point, the lack of government's intervention. In favour of SCs has resulted in losing faith in the Indira Gandhi led government. After which, she had to take slogans like "*Garibi Hatao*' to gain sympathy back from SCs. However, due to political instability, which came later in the form of an emergency, the economic situation of SCs had further affected. However, this time, the SCs who were the largest vote bank for the Congress Party started to move away from the party. The parting of Babuji Jagjivan Ram from Congress had been one of the strongest indications that the Congress had lost a majority of its party people since Babuji leads a strong mass of people. So, for the first time, Indira Gandhi led Congress party has lost the majority in many states.

After political instability and before going for the 1980 general elections Gandhi had to gain the sympathy of SCs once again to win the elections. So, a Central Committee was formulated in 1975 with all the CMs of the states and UTs, and called for a meeting and initiated a Special Component Plan for the overall development of SCs in the similar format already existing as Tribal Plan for STs.

However, one needs to pay attention to how this decision of adopting a Special Component Plan was communicated for implementation. In the capacity of Prime Minister of the country, she wrote in a letter to all the Chief Ministers about the importance and need of implementing the SCP without a fail. Later, Dr. Manmohan Singh the then Member of the Planning Commission has communicated guidelines to all the CMs in India through a letter to implement SCP. The gist of the guidelines was that SCP should be supported by allocating funds at the center, state and UTs in their respective budget at par with their respective SC population proportion, and the funds allocated should be spent in a way that they are directly and exclusively beneficial for the development of SCs.

What Went Wrong?

In the above context, the Government boasted about the efforts that it had put in the form of SCP for the benefit of SCs. However, contrasting observations and findings resulted in the studies undertaken, to study status of the SCP and SCs, not only by scholars and NGOs / Pressure Groups, but also by Committees appointed by Government itself.

For example, it was found that the criteria through which beneficiaries were identified to be benefitted under programmes intended for SCs were faulty. Many non-SCs were included in the list as beneficiaries, which is denying or hijacking the benefits of qualified SC beneficiaries. This resulted due to the influence of the local elites who play a crucial role in identifying the beneficiaries for several government programmes at the grassroots based on their personal relations (NABARD, 2004). Further, a comprehensive study on the status of SCP, which was sponsored by the then Planning Commission of India (2006) has highlighted the fact that the allocation of funds towards SCP is not according to the proportion of the SC population in the majority of the states, and even the states which were allocating the funds under SCSP were allocating a major portion i.e., 60-65 per cent of funds to the sectors like irrigation, agriculture, industry, power, roads and bridges whereas the major proportion of the SC population fall in the land-less daily wage labour category. In the above mentioned sectors, the percentage of SC population is between 10 per cent and 15 per cent. It means that fund of the SCP has benefited non-SCs (SEEDS, 2007). As a consequence, a large SC population remains far away from the mainstream development of the country. Besides economic poverty, they have been found to occupy lower positions in all the human development indicators i.e., nutrition, mortality, access to agricultural land, capital assets, employment rate, non-agricultural wages and are spotted at a higher rate of discrimination and atrocity (Expert Group, 2008). A report prepared by the Task Force which was constituted by the Government itself has pointed out that all the Ministries and Departments at the Centre and in several states have fallen of short meeting the requirements in implementing SCP (Task Force, 2010). An appointed State Cabinet Sub-Committee to look into the status of SCP and SCs in the erstwhile Andhra Pradesh in its report states that the state governments are not maintaining proper records of fund flow of SCP to different development projects (Cabinet Sub-Committee, 2012). In a study on the economic status of SCs, it is found that desired goals could not be achieved due to insufficient budgetary allocation and a lack of an effective monitoring system (Rajamma and Siddaraju, 2013). The National Campaign for Dalit Human Rights has revealed the fact that most of the States/UTs are not holding on to the given basic methodology for the operation of SCP. Some State governments have evolved their own methodologies for the implementation of these strategies which gave a way to deviation or diversion of the funds allocated under the SCP (NCDHR, 2014).

As mentioned above, two version statements exist about the effectiveness of SCP on the lives of SCs i.e., the positive all good version of the government on one hand, and the critical version which emerged out of findings of studies conducted by NGOs/Pressure Groups, the government appointed committees and scholars. These contrasting claims can generally provoke one to search the truth. Therefore, the following section gives an ethnographic description of the sociological situation in Pasarlapudilanka, East Godavari District of Andhra Pradesh within which SCP was implemented.

Pasarlapudilanka

The Indian village was studied and described by veteran anthropologists like S.C. Dube (1955) in his "Indian Village", Mc Kim Marriot (1960) in his "Village India", and M.N. Srinivas (1955) in his "India's Villages", and by contemporary anthropologists like N. Sudhakar Rao (1998) in his "Organized Power and Un-organized Resistance". They observed that villages in India maintain a social hierarchy, which is majorly based on caste. Accordingly, their social and economic relations are shaped. So, any event or activity that involves these groups will inevitably have the effect of these relations on it. The present chapter essentially tried to explore the effect of these relations on communicating policy to the beneficiaries in rural areas.

Pasarlapudilanka is not different from the observations on villages mentioned above. It is a multi-caste (including SC, BC, and OC) village with few tribal households. Each caste is again divided into sub-castes. There are in total 12 sub-castes in the village. These include SC– Mala and Madiga; BC–Agnikulakshatriya or Markad (Fisherman), Chakali, Kummari, Mangali, Settibalija and Vishwabrahmin; OC–Kapu, Komati, Brahmin, Kshatriya. Besides, a very small number of tribal population, who identified themselves as Yerukala also inhabit as a tiny cluster in the village.

Table 6.1: Castewise Population of Pasarlapudilanka Village

Sl. No.	*Category*	*Population*	*%*	*No. of H.H*
1.	Kapu	1120	29	306
2.	Mala	798	21	235
3.	Settibalija	782	20	230
4.	Komati	375	9.9	175
5.	Brahmin	157	4.1	35
6.	Yerukala	145	3.8	32
7.	Chakali	125	3.3	27
8.	Kummari	74	1.9	15
9.	Markad	58	1.5	12
10.	Kshatriya	45	1.1	10
11.	Mangali	29	0.7	6
12.	Madiga	23	0.6	5
13.	Vishwabrahmin	21	0.5	5
	Total	**3752**	**100**	**1093**

Source: Records of the Pasarlapudilanka Village Panchayat.

The location of households of different castes in the village is not an accident but a conscious choice made by the villagers themselves. The arrangement tells us something, it is a sign of socio-economic hierarchy. In Pasarlapudilanka, the area at the entrance of the village is considered a prime-area by the villagers due to its importance. All the government offices (including village Panchayat office, village revenue office, village co-operative society), village goddess temple, village market are all located in this area. Further, this area is directly connected to the highway so one can move out to nearby towns easily as auto-rickshaw and bus facility is available only at this point in the village. Therefore, this area is generally occupied by the most powerful ones in the village. Kapu are numerically the largest caste in the village. The numerical strength (see Table 6.1) of Kapu made them one of the strongest political groups in the village. This is the reason why multiple numbers of Panchayat Presidents emerged from the Kapu caste. Komati, on the other hand, are not as big as Kapu numerically, but they hold the majority of lands in and around the village (see Chart 6.1), which made them economically powerful. This economic power empowered them to play as strong opponents to Kapus in village politics. The houses of Kapu and Komati castes are located in this area. So, this location of the village signifies not only social but most prominently political and economic power.

The rest of the village can be divided into two broad parts, of which the first part is inhabited by all the other castes except Scheduled Castes and Scheduled Tribes household, and the second part which is considered as the most backward area in the village where semi-*pucca* houses and mud-roads are seen. This area is inhabited by SC and ST households. However, the eastern part of the village is called Agraharam where Brahmins, houses are located; this area has social and religious significance, unlike the area where Kapu and Komati houses are located. Similar observations were made about villages in previous studies as well (Hiebert, 1971).

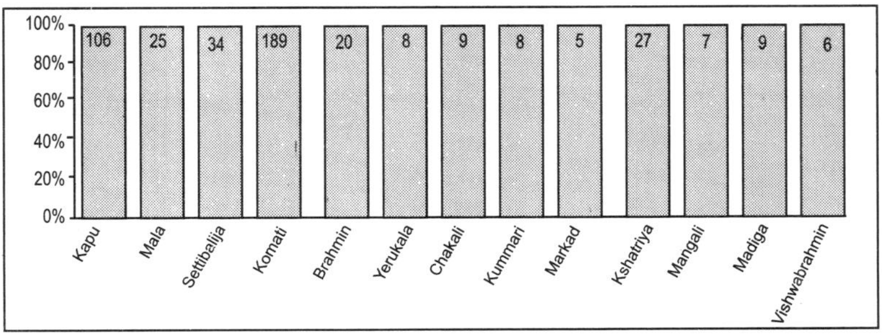

Chart 6.1: Caste-wise Landholdings in Pasarlapudilanka.
Source: Revenue Records of Pasarlapudilanka Village.

A typical day in Pasarlapudilanka starts with early morning scenes of labourers gathering at the village entrance to show themselves to their respective Komati and Kapu masters/landowners (see Chart 6.1) to confirm whether or not there is work for them for the day. It is a daily routine for these labourers to come and show their faces to their masters/ landowners without which the labourers are afraid that they will not be counted while landowners assign work in their agricultural land to the labourers on a daily basis. Showing their faces to their masters appears as a ritual. However, it is a sign by which they want to communicate to landowners that they are available to complete the tasks if assigned. So, it is a necessary daily routine for labourers regardless of the availability of work to show up and present themselves. Most labourers who are usually present there belong to Scheduled Castes.

Since the major livelihood source in Pasaralpudilanka is agriculture (see Table 6.2) (Coconut farming and paddy cultivation), and Kapu and Komati castes hold a large extent of lands in and around the village, people in the village across all the castes, excluding Brahmins, depended on these landowners for work. However, as mentioned, the majority of them belong to Scheduled Castes.

Table 6.2: Castewise Occupation Details of the Pasarlapudilanka Village

Name of the Caste	*T. HH**	*Farmers*	*Agricultural Labour*	*Daily Wage Labour*	*Shopkeeper*	*Trader/ Business*	*Jobholders*	*Others**
Kapu	30	12	00	00	03	09	06	00
Mala	24	00	15	07	00	00	02	00
Settibalija	23	05	01	00	10	04	03	00
Komati	17	07	00	00	05	05	00	00
Brahmin	03	01	00	00	00	00	02	00
Yerukala	03	00	02	01	00	00	00	00
Chakali	02	00	01	01	00	00	00	00
Kummari	02	01	00	00	00	00	00	01
Markad	02	00	00	00	00	00	00	02
Kshatriya	02	02	00	00	00	00	00	00
Mangali	02	00	01	00	00	00	00	01
Madiga	02	00	01	01	00	00	00	00
Vishwa-brahmin	02	01	00	00	00	00	01	00
Total	114	29	21	10	18	18	14	04

Note:* T.HH–Total Households, Others–including Drivers of vehicles (i.e. tractor, lorry, and auto-rickshaw) and Caste associated occupations (i.e. barber, potter, fisherman and purohit.)

Kapu, due to their numerical and partially economic strength and Komati due to their economic strength have become alternative dominant castes in the village. Further, to retain and uphold their dominance against each other as well as over other castes in the village, they have entered into village politics. When it is to do with politics it is the method of election, which brings them into power, and the election is to do with the number of voters. Kapu do not have to worry about numbers as it is the largest caste in the village in terms of population. On the other hand, Komati falls short in numbers. This is the reason why they started grooming the SC community, which is the second largest population in the village. Kapus started offering employment for SCs in their Coconut fields as part of mobilization. This is the reason why the majority of the SC workers in the village work in Komati Coconut fields. In return the SCs show loyalty to their Komati landowners.

The situation in the village is such that since Komati and Kapu are active in village politics and administration, information related to government schemes and programmes is first accessed by them and the rest of the village has to rely upon them for the same. It is already known that SCs are loyal to their Komati landowners, and Kapus are political rivals of Komati. Hence, Kapus have become unfriendly with SCs in the village. Therefore, whenever an SC man approaches a Kapu for some information, they either delay giving the information to a possible extent or are denied information. So, accessing information from a Kapu is a difficult process for an SC man. Such kind of incidents happened when Kapu man became Panchayat President of the village.

On the other hand, the process of accessing the information from Komati is not simple either. An SC respondent who is working in the Komati coconut field explains that: "Komati cannot be demanded information by SCs as they are their employers. If an SC goes to a Komati to ask whether there is any scheme or programme that is beneficial for him/her, a Komati would say, 'if there is any such information available I would have informed you already' in a witty manner." But, in fact, the information is not passed on to them freely. This means that he will only pass it on to someone from the SC community in the village who is loyal to him for circulating it among only those who are loyal to this SC man. This works in two different ways for a Komati: One, those SC men who closely move with Komati will become leaders in the eyes of other SCs as they carry some useful and authentic information, which otherwise is difficult to access. Therefore, creating some aspiration for SCs to move closer to Komati, and Komati will choose the best out of them for the purpose. Two, the SC men who move closely with Komati is recognized by the SC community as information carriers will be useful for Komati at times of elections to mobilize the community. To say it in other words, by doing this, Komati intentionally made these loyal SC men resourceful persons for the whole SC community in the village. So, whenever there is a need to mobilize the community then the loyal SC persons come in handy for the Komati. He is creating a network for a purpose.

Concerning the implementation of SCP in the village, identification of beneficiaries was done using this network mentioned above. For example, few years back land distribution programme was implemented in Pasarlapudilanka and few people from the SC community were given land as they don't have any. This programme was intended to improve the economic condition of the beneficiaries as it is projected that the land will generate revenue for the beneficiary once it is brought under cultivation. Two such beneficiaries were identified and interviewed to understand the impact of the land distribution programme. Their cases are presented as follows:

Case 1

Suri Yanna Boppi (Pseudo Name) a 66 years old man with three sons, two daughters and wife says, "the government has never bothered to look into the realities of SCs at the grassroots". He is illiterate and has very limited knowledge about the functioning of government departments. For him, the government is a Gram Panchayat and the Office of the District Collector and nothing else. Even the position of the Chief Minister according to him is just a political position and he only does politics. He has very little idea about how government and administration are linked together. All he does throughout his life is work as a daily wager in the fields for himself and his family.

Few years back, he also became a beneficiary under the land distribution programme in the village. But, he expresses his hopelessness about the government and the way it functions. When asked about why and how he has got the land, he said "I worked for the Gram Panchayat and it gave me". It means that he did not know about the land distribution programme that was implemented years back for the benefit of poor SC families in the village.

However, he says, "The land he got is not viable for cultivation". He is entirely dependent on daily wage labour and he hardly saved anything. Over the years, he was able to save twenty-five thousand rupees with great difficulty. Few years back when he got the land, he started cultivating it with an investment of fifteen thousand rupees. In the same year, his agricultural land, including many others (most of the lands belonging to SCs), was affected by unseasonal floods and backwaters from the Bay of Bengal. In this way, his entire efforts and investment of fifteen thousand rupees had gone to waste with the flood. He did not get any relief from the government or any other source afterwards. With that incident, more than half of his lifelong savings have gone into the waters.

He continued to be a daily wage labourer. After two years, he again invested his remaining savings of ten thousand rupees in banana farming. This time due to heavy rains the banana farm was ruined and he got only half of what he has invested. Afterwards, he does not dare to invest any more in farming or agriculture in the government provided land.

What is observed is that lands which were provided by the government under the land distribution programme for the poor SC families are not useful for cultivation or any farming activity. The lower altitudinal levels and the proximity to the Godavari and the Bay of Bengal make the land almost impossible for any kind of agricultural activity.

Suri Yanna Boppi said that he was very happy when he got the land. But, he realized that the lands were useless when he started cultivating. He said, "It may be a political drama to woo the SC voters towards a particular political party". He recollected and explained what has happened at the time of land distribution. He used to work for a Komati landowner as a daily wage labourer. The owner preferred to give him work since he was a very loyal servant who worked at low wages. At times when the work is scarce, poor villagers mostly SC wage labourers used to approach the Komati landowners seeking work in his field. Suri Yanna at such times managed to get work for the Komati and brought work for others as well. As such, over the years, he became a mediator between the wage labourers and the landowners.

Few years ago, a relative of the Komati landowner contested for the post of village Sarpanch as a TDP candidate for which they need the support of SC voters, who are the second largest community in the village. However, traditionally, SCs have not been supporters of TDP. Hence, there was very little chance of getting votes from the SC community for this candidate. At this juncture, Suri Yanna, already popular among SCs in the village came in handy for the Komati landowner. He was used by the landowners to motivate the SC voters. The Komati landowner managed to include Suri Yanna's name in the land distribution programme, which also took place some time back in the same year. As a result, Suri Yanna campaigned for the Komati candidate and announced on behalf of the landowner that if the TDP candidate wins, the SCs will be given priority to work in the fields of Komati and the daily wages will be hiked to Rs. 150.

This announcement attracted the majority of the SC voters for the TDP candidate. Thus, the Komati candidate won the elections. However, the wages were never hiked during the entire tenure of the Komati Sarpanch. Besides that, Suri Yanna is now realizing that he was used for political ends. What was given to him was useless land, despite the good land that was available in the village. Now, all his lifelong savings were lost on the unviable land for cultivation and he became dependent on his children, who are again wage labourers?

The notable point in the case of Suri Yanna Boppi is that the efforts of the government have reached the bottom level for sure. But, the local politics and personal networks have ruined the effectiveness of the programmes. The problem cannot be linked to only local politics and personal networks but also most importantly with governments' inefficient implementation process. The absence of a systematic process for identification of land that is good for agriculture along with the systematic identification of the beneficiaries shows the negligence of the government on part of the development of the SC community.

Case 2

Satty Cetta (Pseudo Name) is a 51 years old man with wife, son and daughter who depend on daily wage labour. He is not illiterate but had studied up to the sixth standard. His forefathers and father never had a piece of land before until his father got a piece of land under the land distribution programme. Since his father could not educate him, he was needed to help his father. He was forced to discontinue education at the sixth standard. Since then, he had been contributing to his family's economy. His father got the land when Satty Cetta was 28 years and he inherited the land after his father. Since then he has been taking care of the land and earning his bread.

However, now his land is not safe for cultivation anymore. The ONGC pipelines are laid through his agricultural land. This may turn out to be very dangerous for life at any time. He recollected the past experiences of gas leakage in 1995 in the same village, and in 2005 in Thandavapalli village, which is close to the Pasarlapudilanka, and Nagaram incident in 2014 in which 14 people died and 15 people were injured. He says this happened because of the caste politics in the village. According to him, the actual pipeline laying plan was different from what it is now. Initially, the pipeline plan route was to go through the other parts of the village so that the pipelines could be straight. Later, the plan changed; originally the pipeline had to go through or nearby the Komati and Kapu caste habitations in the village. Since they are politically influential and were able to lobby with the government officials, they were able to change the plan. According to the new plan, the pipelines are running through the lands that mostly belonged to SCs and STs. In his words, "Due to the pipelines and their maintenance I had to give up agriculture in that land. The compensation paid also is meagre. I have no other land to cultivate anymore. The government only gave and the government only took it away. Finally, I was left with daily wage just like my father".

The notable point here is that the case of Satty Cetta reveals the government contradicts its own activities. It is paradoxical that on one hand it aims at improving the living of the most backward and unprivileged sections of the society, especially SCs, through various welfare measures but on the other hand, in the name of national development activities, the benefits of SCs are taken away. It is the local political game that affected the land of Cetta along with the other SCs, but, the government should have taken measures to protect SCs as it takes care of the privileged sections in the village.

The above two cases demonstrate how dominant communities in Pasarlapudilanka i.e., Komati and Kapu have influenced the government programmes and schemes, which have ultimately resulted in a way that SCs subsided and were given the least priority in participation of decision making. This proves the point that despite of the existence of a mechanism to include beneficiaries in the decision making process in the implementation, the government only has an ear to listen to dominant voices. As a result, Satty and Suri Yanna though they have got land, nothing productive came about but had to end up as wage labourers.

At this point, it is worth noting that the landlessness among SCs has increased since 1991. In 1991, 70 per cent of total *Dalit* households were landless or near landless (owning less than one acre). This increased to 75 per cent in 2000. The prevalence of such high levels of poverty and economic disparity among the most vulnerable and marginalized population indicates, at best, the limited success of a planned and redistributive economy (SECC, 2015).

On the other hand, the Mandal Development Officer (MDO) of Mamidikuduru Mandal within which jurisdiction Pasarlapudilanka falls under said that few schemes (though there is no clarity whether or not these schemes come under SCP, as the mentioned schemes were not exclusively implemented for SCs) were implemented for the welfare of SCs, and the officer holds the list of beneficiaries from Pasarlapudilanka under the schemes already implemented in the village. However, when verified the names of the persons in the village the list actually includes many non-SC beneficiaries as well. Among SC beneficiaries most of them were found to be working in Komati coconut fields and are loyal to Komati.

The list consists of 352 names under different schemes, which include loans for petty shops, distribution of sewing machines, loans to start a farm, and loans for agriculture related activities/purchase of materials and tools etc. It is found that out of 352, only 150 were SCs in the list. If the above mentioned schemes were implemented under SCP then it is surely malpractice because any scheme or programme implemented under SCP should be implemented in a way that it is directly and exclusively benefited for SCs. The point over here is that the MDO office was not clear as to whether or not the mentioned schemes come under SCP. However, he acknowledges that SCP funds are utilized to implement these programmes. In fact, such is the situation at the Mandal and Village level as there is no clarity on how SCP funds have been channelized. It is only at the Ministry and Department level there is some clarity on the spending of SCP funds. This blurring situation on the spending down the line is actually making SCP funds vulnerable to diversion or improper utilization.

Previous studies on SCP suggested that the above mentioned situation is not confined to one place but it is more or less the same across the country as there is lack of awareness among SCs about SCP. Therefore, a survey was conducted to assess the awareness level among SCs in Pasarlapudilanka about SCP. Out of 150 listed beneficiaries 100, were approached and interviewed. A set of 15 questions was used to gain information from each respondent. The results are given in Table 6.3.

Through Table 6.3, it is clear that the basic information about SCP is not distributed among SCs in Pasarlapudilanka. Neither government officials nor non-government agencies, neither media nor awareness programmes have brought the news of SCP to the masses at the villages. Therefore, they do not even have basic information about it.

Lack of awareness about SCP among SCs in Pasarlapudilanka is making SCs vulnerable in two ways. One, the very purpose of the policy is not served i.e., SCP came into existence as a response to improve the poor living conditions of SCs at villages, as they have been socially and economically disadvantaged for a long time. It is just a lack of an appropriate administrative system to bring awareness among the masses that are

Table 6.3: Basic Awareness Among SCs about SCP in Pasarlapudilanka

Q. No.	*Question*	*Responses*	
		Yes	No
Q. 1	Do you know what SCP or SCSP is?	8	92
Q. 2	If yes, how?		
	Through News Papers	0	100
	Through TV News/ Ads	0	100
	Through Internet	0	100
	Through Social Media	3	97
	Through a Government Official	0	100
	Through an NGO	0	100
	Through Landowner	0	100
	Through an Awareness Programme	0	100
	Through Handouts/ Pamphlets/ Wall posters	0	100
	Through Friends and Family Members	5	95
Q. 3	Do you know where to enquire information about government programmes?	78	22
Q. 4	Do you think you can get official information at Panchayat or govt. officials?	90	10
Q. 5	Have you ever tried to access information from any government offices?	15	85
Q. 6	Have you ever tried to access information from the land-owner?	62	38
Q. 7	Do you think the landowner gives reliable official information?	60	40
Q. 8	Do you think the landowner gives information on demand?	35	65
Q. 9	Has your the landowner ever given you information about SCP?	0	100
Q.10	Were there any awareness programmes in the village about government programmes?	10	90
Q. 11	If yes, is it related to SCP?	0	100
Q.12	Do you read the newspapers?	23	77
Q. 13	Do you watch the news on Television?	40	60
Q. 14	Do you discuss government and governance with your fellowmen/ women?	32	68
Q. 15	Who has referred you as a beneficiary for the scheme you benefited from?		
	Village Sarpanch	15	85
	Landowner	42	58
	Government Officials	18	82
	Any other	25	75

largely poor, illiterate and living in rural places, to communicate the policy efficiently that the living conditions of SCs are improved through the benefits it provides. But it did not happen. Two, the lack of an information system has created a gap between policy implementing authorities and beneficiaries, which has been utilized by the local dominant communities for their political benefits. This gap of an information system has become— a source for the local dominant to recreate master and servant relations which was then called the *Jajmani* system, under which castes used to receive grains against services rendered (Wiser, 1936). But, in Pasarlapudilanka it is not grains but work and information received by Scheduled Caste persons against services rendered to the dominant caste.

Conclusions

Public policies are made to resolve existing problems, at least that is what beneficiaries expect. But, when policies are not able to adopt an appropriate administrative system then it will be not only difficult to communicate policies as intended to the target group but may lead to dangerous consequences. In the case of SCP, an appropriate administrative mechanism was not in place to communicate necessary processes to SCs in villages. It resulted not only in defeating the very purpose of implementation of SCP but contributing to the resurgence of the age-old practice of the *Jajmani* system. The case of SCP shows that communicating policies is not just having guidelines but most importantly having an efficient method that works in a given sociological situation because the very existence of the policy is to change that situation.

REFERENCES

Cabinet Sub-Committee (2012). Report of the Cabinet Sub-Committee on Special Component Plan for Scheduled Castes and Tribal Sub-Plan, submitted to Government of Andhra Pradesh, Hyderabad.

Dube, S.C. (1955). *Indian Village*. London: Routledge and Kegan Paul.

Economic and Political Weekly. (1973). Gentlemen Killers of Kilvenmani. *EPW*, Vol. 8, No. 21, May 26, pp. 926-928.

Expert Group. (2008). Report to Planning Commission on Development Challenges in Extremist Affected Areas. New Delhi: Government of India.

Hiebert, Paul, G. (1971). *Konduru: Structure and Integration in a South Indian Village*. Minneapolis: Minnesota University Press.

Kafir. (2010). Dalit Massacres in Andhra. Blog post, Casteism in India and the Fallacies of Hindu Religion, April 1. Online Source (accessed on 21/06/2020) http://justicefordalits.blogspot.in/2010/04/dalit-massacres-in-andhra.html

Kattula, R.K. (2016). "The Hollowness of a Hallowed Policy: Emptiness of a Special Component Plan for Scheduled Castes." *The International Journal of Humanities & Social Studies*. Volume 4, Issue 9, September, pp. 197–203. Online Source: http://theijhss.com/2016-2/september-16.

Marriot, Mc Kim. (1960). *Village India*. Chicago: University of Chicago Press.

Mathur, K. and Bjorkman, J.W. (2009). *Policy-Making in India: Who Speaks? Who Listens?* New Delhi: HAR-ANAND Publications Pvt. Ltd.

Morkhandikar R.S. (1978). "Marathwada Riots: The Background." *Economic and Political Weekly*, Vol. XIII, No. 34, August 26, pp. 1461–1462.

NABARD. (2004). *Impact Assessment of Special Component Plan (SCP) and Tribal Sub-Plan in West Bengal–An Ex-Post Evaluation Study*. NABARD, Kolkata.

NCDHR. 2014. *Report on Status of Special Component Plan for SCs and Tribal Sub Plan for STs*. NCDHR.

Planning Commission. (2006). *Report on Scheduled Castes Sub Plan: Guidelines for Implementation*. New Delhi: Government of India.

Rajamma, N. and V.G. Siddaraju. (2013). "An Economic Analysis of the Special Component Plan for Scheduled Castes: A Case Study of Mysore District." *International Journal of Social and Economic Research,* Volume-3, Issue-1, pp. 65–70.

Rao, Sudhakar N. (1998). *Organised Power and Unorganised Resistance*. New Delhi: Aravali Books International.

SECC. (2015). *Socio-Economic Caste Census. Ministry of Rural Development*, New Delhi: Government of India. Online Source (accessed on 21/06/2020): http://www.secc.gov.in/welcome

SEEDS. (2007). Research Study on Livelihood Options, Assets Creation out of Special Component Plan (SCP) & Tribal Sub Plan (TSP) Schemes and its Impact among SCs and STs in India'. Planning Commission of India, New Delhi.

Satyanarayana, K. and Susie Tharu (2013). *From those Stubs Steel Nibs are Sprouting: New Dalit Writing from South Asia, Dossier 2: Kannada and Telugu*, New Delhi: Harper Collins India.

Srinivas, M.N. (1955). *India's Villages,* Calcutta: West Bengal Government Press.

Task Force. 2010. Review of Guidelines of Scheduled Castes Sub-Plan and Tribal Sub-Plan. New Delhi: Planning Commission, Government of India.

Wiser, H. William (1936). *The Hindu Jajmani System*. Lucknow: Lucknow Publishing House.

7

Nurturing Gender Equity through Open and Distance Learning

An Analysis

Savita Kaushal

Women's Education: An Overview

The benefits of educating women are manifold ranging from improved productivity, income and economic development on the national level to better quality of life, healthier and well-nourished population and greater autonomy among women. It is also well documented that there is a positive link between mothers' education and their childrens' readiness for learning and between female education and productive self-employment. Therefore, the education of women is a contributor towards a substantial economic and social return to a country.

Despite the various initiatives and interventions, the gender gap in the field of education since independence has existed in India. This dismal situation has been stated in the various policy documents published by the Government of India from time to time. The Programme of Action (POA), 1992 in the context of National Policy on Education mentioned that "there are significant rural-urban disparities among women". The National Policy on Education (Government of India, 1986) admitted that the school would not reach all the children, particularly millions of girls and working children whose participation in the school system was thwarted by socio-economic conditions of life.

Though the female literacy rate increased from 8.86 per cent in 1951 to 65.5 per cent in 2011, it is still considerably lower than the male literacy. As per the 1991 Census, the female literacy rate was 39.42 per cent compared to 63.86 per cent for the males. In 2011, the scenario changed. As per the 2011 census, the female literacy rate rose to 65.5 per cent and male literacy rate to 82.2 per cent. This shows that gap in the male-female literacy rate narrowed from 24.4 per cent in 1991 to 16.7 per cent in 2011 (Fig. 7.1).

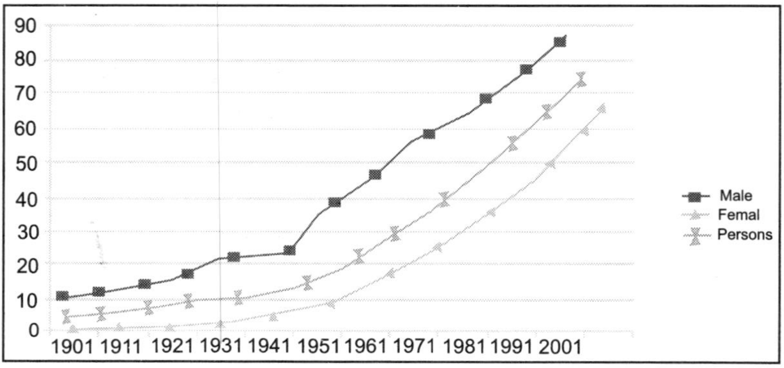

Fig. 7.1: Growth of Literacy in India (in terms of percentage from the Year 1901-2011)

Source: Government of India (2001a) & Government of India (2011): Provisional Population Totals Paper 1 of 2011 India Series 1, Office of the Registrar General & Census Commissioner, India

There are 940 women per 1000 males as per the 2011 Census in India. It is more than 49 per cent of the total population. For the growth of the country, it is essential that women are educated and participate in economic activities in an equal proportion. The state-wise data also reflects that there are gender disparities in literacy. (Table 7.1)

Table 7.1: Literacy Rates—State-wise

Sl. No.	*State*	*Literacy Rate (2011 Census)*	*Male Literacy Rate (2011 Census)*	*Female Literacy Rate (2011 Census)*
1.	Andaman & Nicobar Islands	86.3%	90.1%	81.8%
2.	Andhra Pradesh	67.7%	75.6%	59.7%
3.	Arunachal Pradesh	67.0%	73.7%	59.6%
4.	Assam	73.2%	78.8%	67.3%
5.	Bihar	63.8%	73.5%	53.3%
6.	Chandigarh	86.4%	90.5%	81.4%
7.	Chhattisgarh	71.0%	81.5%	60.6%
8.	Dadra & Nagar Haveli	77.7%	86.5%	65.9%

(Contd.)

Sl. No.	*State*	*Literacy Rate (2011 Census)*	*Male Literacy Rate (2011 Census)*	*Female Literacy Rate (2011 Census)*
9.	Daman & Diu	87.1%	91.5%	79.6%
10.	Delhi	86.3%	91.0%	80.9%
11.	Goa	87.4%	92.8%	81.8%
12.	Gujarat	79.3%	87.2%	70.7%
13.	Haryana	76.6%	85.4%	66.8%
14.	Himachal Pradesh	83.8%	90.8%	76.6%
15.	Jammu & Kashmir	68.7%	78.3%	58.0%
16.	Jharkhand	67.6%	78.5%	56.2%
17.	Karnataka	75.6%	82.8%	68.1%
18.	Kerala	93.9%	96.0%	92.0%
19.	Lakshadweep	92.3%	96.1%	88.2%
20.	Madhya Pradesh	70.6%	80.5%	60.0%
21.	Maharashtra	82.9%	89.8%	75.5%
22.	Manipur	79.8%	86.5%	73.2%
23.	Meghalaya	75.5%	77.2%	73.8%
24.	Mizoram	91.6%	93.7%	89.4%
25.	Nagaland	80.1%	83.3%	76.7%
26.	Orissa	73.5%	82.4%	64.4%
27.	Puducherry	86.5%	92.1%	81.2%
28.	Punjab	76.7%	81.5%	71.3%
29.	Rajasthan	67.1%	80.5%	52.7%
30.	Sikkim	82.2%	87.3%	76.4%
31.	Tamil Nadu	80.3%	86.8%	73.9%
32.	Tripura	87.8%	92.2%	83.1%
33.	Uttar Pradesh	69.7%	79.2%	59.3%
34.	Uttarakhand	79.6%	88.3%	70.7%
35.	West Bengal	77.1%	82.7%	71.2%
	INDIA	**74.04%**	**82.14%**	**65.46%**

Enrolment of boys is more than girls at all levels of school education and drop-outs rates for girls are also higher which is indicative of a gender gap that needs to be bridged (though in recent years, it has narrowed considerably).Though the situation continues to improve, girls still have lower enrolments, lower attendance rates as well as higher drop-out rates compared to the boys.

In the higher education sector, it is seen that India has made considerable progress since Independence, with there being a significant rise in women's enrolment in higher education.

Table 7.2: Gross Enrolment Ratio (GER) in Higher Education: 2010-11 - 2012-13

Category	*2010-11*	*2012-13 (P)*
Male	20.8	22.3
Female	17.9	19.8
Total	19.4	21.1

Source: Annual Report 2014-15, Ministry of Human Resource Development, Government of India, p. 81.

Table 7.3: Women Students Per Hundred Men Students (2014-15)

Year	*Total Women Enrolment (000s)*	*Women Enrolment Per Hundred Men*
1950-1951	40	14
2014-2015	12,476	88

Source: UGC Annual Report, 2014-15, p. 61.

The total students' enrolment in Universities and Colleges for the year 2014-15, through conventional face to face mode, stood at 26,585,437 (26.58 million). Of this, the total number of women was 12,475,669 (12.47 million), which amounts to 46.93% (UGC, 2015 p. 53-54).

Open and Distance Learning

The advances in technology have revolutionized the way in which open and distance learning institutions are functioning. Open and distance learning with advanced technological developments like TV lessons, radio lessons, interactive web-based lessons, online learning, mobile-based communication channels etc., is certainly more helpful to women for achieving their educational goals. In addition to the usage of technological interventions, the Open and Distance Learning (ODL) system involves cost-effective and flexible norms of entry qualifications. Evaluation studies reveal need for programme accessibility in the preferred technology medium of women learners. There is also a need for programmes that empower women even if enrolment is low. In view of this, there is a need to introspect and revisit the system to reflect whether ODL has achieved all that it was set up for, in terms of physical accessibility, courses, technology and other provisions that facilitate women's learning. The Open University the system has contributed to the growth of the higher education sector. As per the All India Survey in Higher Education (2017-18), "Total enrolment in higher educational institutions is estimated to be 36.6 million students, with 19.2 million boys and 17.4 million girls. Girls constitute 47.6% of the total enrolment. Gross Enrolment Ratio (GER) in Higher education in India is 25.8%, which is calculated for the 18-23 years of age group. GER for the male population is 26.3% and for females, it is 25.4%. For Scheduled Castes, it is 21.8% and for Scheduled Tribes, it is 15.9% as compared to the national GER of 25.8%. Distance enrolment constitutes about 11.0% of the total enrolment in higher education, of which 41.9% are female students" (Government of India, 2018).

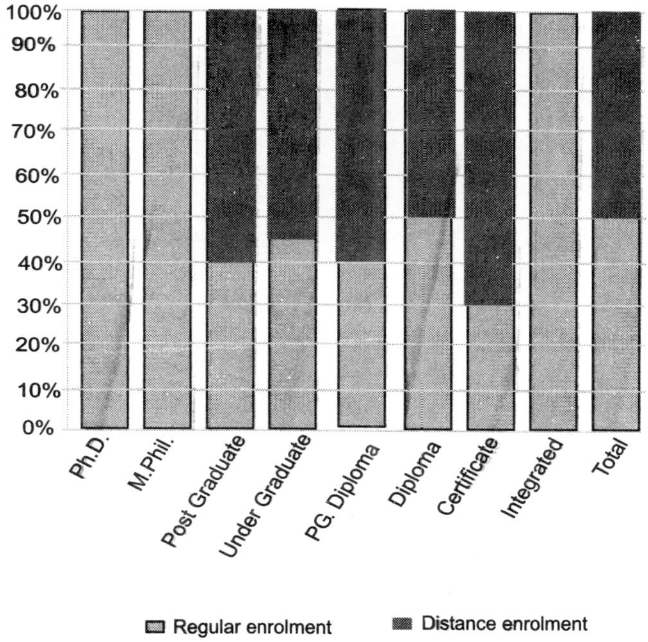

Fig. 7.2: Enrolment in Formal and Distance Education (AISHE, 2017-18).
Source: All India Survey in Higher Education Report (2017-18), p. 17.

According to Srivastava (2015), "the total enrolment in 2013-14 in the 14 Open Universities of the country stood at 2.10 million. The review of the student's enrolment figures shows that Open Universities are able to attract a large number of women learners. As per university reports, the student profile of YC Maharashtra Open University, Nasik for the year

2013-14 shows that 35.5 per cent of learners were female, while women's enrolment of B.R. Ambedkar Open University, Hyderabad stood at 43.3 per cent for women for the same period. The Tamil Nadu Open University, Chennai reported 49.1 per cent women's enrolment for 2013-14, while at KKH State Open University, Guwahati, the women's enrolment in the year 2013-14 stood at 43.9 per cent". The gender-wise enrolment in Higher Education through distance mode depicts that the enrolment of women is more than men in Certificate programmes (All India Survey in Higher Education Report, 2017-18) however in other courses it is lower than that of men. (Fig. 7.3)

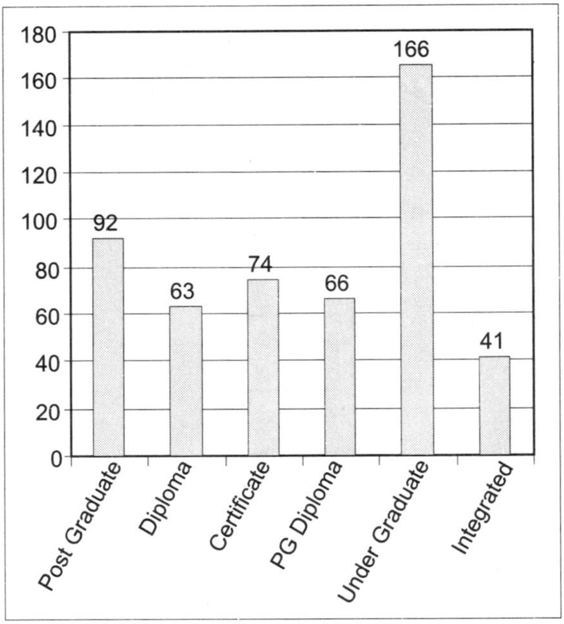

Fig. 7.3: Gender-wise Enrolment in Higher Education through Distance Mode.
Source: All India Survey in Higher Education Report (2017-18), p. 17.

Kulandaiswamy (1993) observed that Distance Education is neither a supplement nor a mere alternative to the conventional system, but a new stage in the evolution of education which recognizes the fact that in many situations, it is easier to transport knowledge to people than transport p to knowledge. This also facilitates women's education as they are able to study anytime on their own. The research evidence also indicates that "Women learners could particularly benefit from open learning systems as it provides a viable alternative, reducing social opportunity costs and weakening cultural constraints" (Thomas 1996; Rathore, Singh and Dubey 1996).

Keeping the above aspect in view, two national-level institutions e.g., IGNOU and NIOS have been examined from the perspective of their role in the education of women in this chapter.

I. Indira Gandhi National Open University (IGNOU)

IGNOU is a mega university in the global arena with more than 2.88 million cumulative enrolment figures. It has witnessed an impressive rise in student enrolment from 4,528 in 1987 to a significant number of 7,96,127 students during 2015-16 admission cycles. An analysis of data of enrolment from 2004 -05 to 2015-16 reveals that the enrolment of women has steadily increased from 35.8 per cent to 45.5 per cent thereby providing a significant social spread towards inclusive education (IGNOU Annual Report, 2016, p. 7). (Table 7.4)

Table 7.4: Enrolment Profile of Male-Female Learners of IGNOU

Sex	*2004*	*2005*	*2014*	*2015*	*2016*
Male	64.2	63.6	55.2	54.2	54.5
Female	35.8	36.4	44.8	45.8	45.5

Source: Based on Chaudhary and Shankar (2015a) and Annual Report, IGNOU (2016).

It is significant to note from the above data analysis that IGNOU has been able to achieve close parity with the formal education system in terms of enrolment of women. Both face to face as well as ODL systems show a similar gender ratio of around 46 per cent with respect to the enrolment of females in higher education.

It has 4000 learner support centres and 67 regional centres with a strong student support service network. As mandated in the IGNOU Act and statutes, the University has developed several programmes in many allied areas of diverse disciplines of study with the use of the expertise of the teachers in the country for educational empowerment of the population.

Usage of Technology

IGNOU has contributed to equity and access to higher education and in using education technology and ICT in the delivery of quality higher education through ODL. The remarkable ICT enabled initiatives of the University include designing, developing and launching Massive Open Online Courses (MOOCs), accessing learning resources through Shodhganga (UGC-INFLIBNET project), and National Digital Library (MHRD project), contributing to Skill Assessment Matrix for Vocational Advancement of Youth (SAMVAY), re-starting of Gyan Vani FM radio stations, reactivating eGyankosh, Wi-Fi campus connectivity, Cloud-based IT infrastructure and Digital Locker. Moreover, the University has taken initiatives to augment the use of ICT in academic and administrative transactions and introduced e-tendering for the purchase of items for the University through the Central Public Procurement Portal of India. For capacity building of its teaching, academic and non-teaching staff, the University organizes refresher and orientation programmes with an emphasis on design and delivery of online education and designing of online education. The University also plays an important role in the training of in-service teachers from schools. It has been engaged in the training of teachers employed by the Kendriya Vidyalaya Sangathan (KVS) and Governments of North-East states for which it uses its widespread Student Support Network and technology for training in-service teachers on a large scale without displacing them from their place of work.

Admission

Flexibilities of the open learning system with regard to entrance policy make it possible for the girls/women engaged in household responsibilities to join the IGNOU programme at a time suitable to them. They have the freedom as well to discontinue their studies for a while to attend to socio-economic responsibilities. The IGNOU provides them with an opportunity to rejoin the course at a point where they had left it due to compulsions of life as such, instead of leaving educational pursuits forever.

Special Study Centres

IGNOU as a role model among ODL institutions in the country has established special study centres for women learners in all parts of the country in higher educational institutions enrolling only women students. Such a measure is highly helpful to women learners to pursue their educational programmes hassle-free with female peer groups without any gender discrimination at the study centres.

Fee Concessions

IGNOU offers free education to transgender, jail inmates and sex workers as a rehabilitation strategic approach for educational empowerment of such people in the society. The war widows of army personnel are given 50 per cent fee concession in all programmes of IGNOU, and moreover, 50 per cent fee concession is given to rural learners in the agricultural programmes of IGNOU, and such concession is extended to the below poverty line students of urban areas also.

Programmes Offered

The Government of India has launched Digital India, Skill in India and Make in India schemes aiming to cover the population to develop knowledge and skills for the needs of the future. The programmes at IGNOU are designed keeping in view of the fact that there is a strong need for women education through awareness and sensitizing programmes and the potential need for participation of women in technical and vocational education for their educational empowerment, livelihood improvement and socio-economic development.

IGNOU has developed many programmes of study to suit the needs of women that can contribute to bringing about significantly transformational changes in women empowerment. The curriculum content serves as a role model for students and plays an important role in breaking gender stereotypes. Gender-specific knowledge is integrated into the curricula in all subjects. Also, the course teams involve the participation of women and men. Care is taken while presenting the graphics and pictures in the course material so that it is gender-sensitive. Many female learners of conventional higher educational institutions in India, in particular degree and masters level programmes, simultaneously pursue the IGNOU certificate and diploma programmes for gaining knowledge and increasing their potential for future employment. The enrolment data of IGNOU shows that short-duration certificate programmes in the areas of health care, food and nutrition, guidance, childcare, primary teacher training are able to attract higher female enrolment (Chaudhary and Shankar, 2015b). As per the Vice-Chancellor (IGNOU), "the University has enrolled a larger number of women students in academic programmes of Gender and Development Studies, Humanities, Health Sciences, Continuing Education, Vocational Education, Social Work and Translation Studies. It is reflected in the fact that the strength of female students is more than 50 per cent of fresh enrolments in these Schools "(IGNOU, Annual Report, 2015-16, p. 3). Some of the popular programmes among the women learners are described below:

Food and Nutrition

Certificate Programme in Food and Nutrition (CFN) offered by IGNOU is an example of a course that sensitizes the majority of women learners on effective nutrition required for the well-being of humans, and since the introduction of the programme, many women learners have benefited by enrolling in it. The CFN programme of IGNOU is a major boost in society, as today several thousands of *anganwadi* workers, especially females pursue the programme for their professional knowledge and practice at the workplace.

Empowerment of Self Help Groups

IGNOU undertook a project on empowering the Self-Help Groups (SHGs) of women in India, which has been recognized as the effective strategic measure for women empowerment in rural and urban areas. Many women in the self-help groups work for the cause of social issues like women rights, agriculture, forestry, health and nutrition besides their active role of earning income through microfinance and microcredit. The women empowerment project of IGNOU created an avenue for training the master trainers towards training others for a sustainable future approach. The training was conducted through satellite-based broadcasting of lessons in the network of 150 programme centres across the country. Master trainers at various parts of the country are trained through teleconferencing facilities available in IGNOU, Gyan Darshan TV channel and GyanVani FM radio station available at various places of India. Further, training programmes sensitized the SHGs on their legal literacy in various aspects for getting their rights in the government.

Courses in Gender Development Studies

The University Grants Commission [UGC (2015] in its Eleventh Plan guidelines highlighted the specific need to emphasize Women and Gender Studies in all universities, and accordingly most of the universities and autonomous colleges have established separate Centres/Departments for Women and Gender Studies to increase research studies. Masters level degree in Women and Gender Studies is being offered by IGNOU to cover the distance learners and also to increase research attitude amongst the scholars for developing strategies on women development. The School of Gender and Development Studies (SOGDS) of IGNOU coordinates with the regional centres and learner support centres for increasing access to women empowerment programmes to cater for the needs of distance learners.

Other Programmes

The IGNOU programmes on health, child care, organic farming, water harvesting, teacher education, environment, sustainability, law, nursing, community radio, computer literacy etc., have attracted many women learners in the country, particularly from north-eastern parts of India since IGNOU has entrusted the network of learners support activities through its Educational Development of North East Region Unit (EDNERU) and the Regional Centres in such states.

Placement of Women

The University is proactive in promoting activities pertaining to women empowerment/development through its various initiatives by the way of organizing programmes, seminars and conferences. It also organizes an exclusive job fair for female students reaffirming the University's commitment towards the cause of women for their empowerment.

II. National Institute of Open Schooling

A popular model for girl's/women's education in India is that of the National Institute of Open Schooling (NIOS). In addition to this, there are also State Open Schools. Eleven states have already got State Open Schools. These are located in Andhra Pradesh, Delhi, Haryana, Jammu & Kashmir, Karnataka, Kerala, Madhya Pradesh, Punjab, Rajasthan, Tamil Nadu, and West Bengal. There are 8 states namely Uttar Pradesh, Orissa, Maharashtra, Gujarat, Assam, Chhattisgarh, Uttaranchal and Bihar which are in the process of setting up State Open Schools.

In order to sustain interest and commitment in continued schooling of girls/women, open schooling provides a viable and workable solution to the challenges of equity in educational provisions for girls and women. Some salient features of open schooling programmes that are addressed to the special needs of the girls/women are as follows:

Policy Regarding Entry to NIOS Courses

Open schooling ensures access to education of the learners as it addresses the shortcomings of the traditional system in terms of its rigidity. The NIOS (2016), expects a minimum level of competence for entry into its courses. Any student who has passed primary school can enrole himself/herself in the Foundation Course or the Secondary Level course. To enrole in the Senior Secondary course, however, a candidate must have a secondary pass certificate, to maintain equivalence with other examining bodies.

Admission to the Programme

In NIOS, there are no rigid entry qualifications and no upper age limit for admission. It has a diverse student profile at the secondary stage having young and old learners ranging from 14 years to 89 years, distributed throughout the country. There is online admission and round the year admission. Flexibilities of the open learning system with regard to entrance policy make it possible for the girls/women engaged in household responsibilities to join the NIOS programme at a time suitable to them. They have the freedom as well to discontinue their studies for a while to attend to socio-economic responsibilities. The NIOS provides them with an opportunity to rejoin the course at a point where they had left it due to compulsions of life as such, instead of leaving educational pursuits forever.

Fee Exemption

This is yet another motivating factor that promotes girl's/women's education. Many parents cannot afford expenses on the private cost of education of their children. Due to this, they have to choose as to whom they should send for education; for which they prefer the son, as he is seen as the future earning member of the family. To encourage greater participation of women/girls, the NIOS allows partial fee exemption to them for different levels of courses. To promote the involvement of women, the NIOS accepts the name of the mother as a parent in the relevant column of the Learner's Admission Form.

The Programme Focus

Objectives of the programme, especially under the NIOS vocational and life enrichment stream are to empower women with required knowledge, life skills, pre-vocational skills, vocational skills and attitudes for their sustainability. Broadly some of the significant aspects of NIOS programmes that accelerate girl's/women's education are:

- extending the knowledge of recent advances in science and technology and skill-oriented education to the large population of women/girls including those residing in remote and isolated villages;
- Changing their mindset about their perceived role towards family, society and country, at large thereby improving their quality of life.

Nature of Courses and Course Structure

The NIOS offers a wide spectrum of courses of general and continuing education for different categories of learners through distance education mode. It has worked out a course equivalent to Class III and V. These courses provide an avenue to the women/girls who had to drop-out due to various factors, such as, migration of parents/guardians to another village, death of a family member etc. The other academic courses offered by the NIOS, such as the foundation course (equivalent to class VIII), which serves as a bridge course to those joining the secondary level programme (equivalent to ten years of schooling); and the secondary level programme

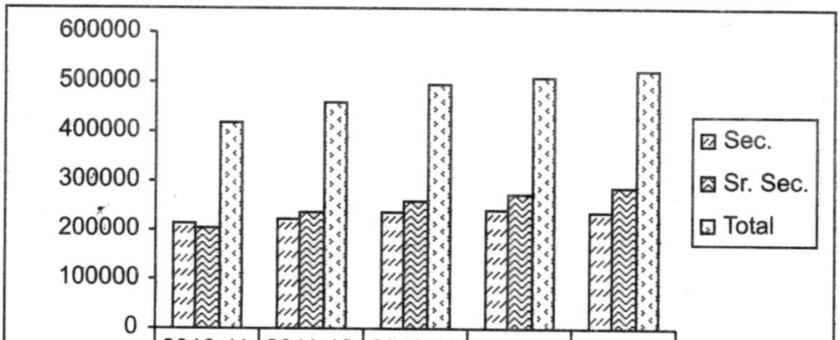

	2010-11	2011-12	2012-13	2013-14	2014-15
Sec.	213337	222336	234317	239163	237211
Sr. Sec.	206365	235719	259217	271625	286574
Total	419702	458055	493534	510788	523785

Fig. 7.4: Enrolment Trend in Academic Courses

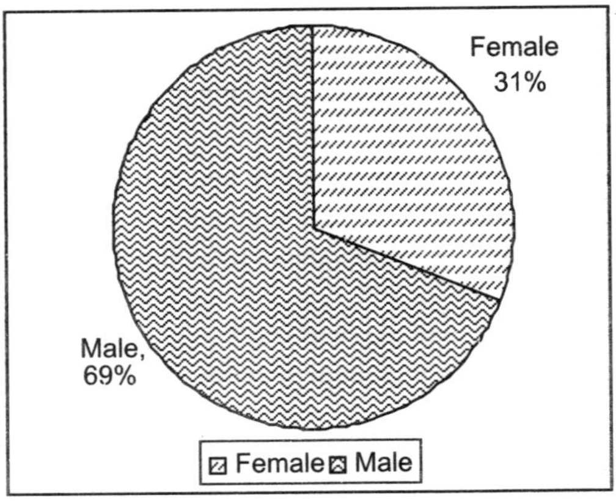

Fig. 7.5: Male and female perecentages.

which leads to senior secondary programme (equivalent to twelve years of schooling) provides a graded continuity to the female learners. The learners can take up subjects according to their preference/area of interest.

It also provides vocational education courses and life-enrichment courses. In this context it is worthwhile to mention that it offers life-enrichment course for adolescent girls and adult women, named, the Paripurna Mahila (completely empowered women). This course covers a vast range of areas of women's empowerment, namely, legal literacy, health, nutrition, general awareness and the like. The major objectives of the courses are to equip, especially, rural women with better skills and enhance their knowledge so as to prepare them to face new challenges due to technological development. There are several subject areas in which the NIOS is working for the betterment of women. Some such subject areas are – Jan Swasthaya (public health), early childhood care and education, cutting and tailoring, beauty culture, computer applications and poultry farming. Because of the diversity of the courses offered and the flexibility of the NIOS programme, there has been a gradual increase in the number of NIOS learners and also of the female learners (Fig. 7.2). In fact, female learners outnumber males in the vocational education courses can be seen from Fig. 7.2 and 7.3. Approximately 61 per cent of the Vocational admission is that of girls and women in the age group of 14-20 years.

The curriculum content serves as a role model for students and plays an important role in breaking gender stereotypes. Gender-specific knowledge is integrated into the curricula in all subjects. Also, the course teams involve the participation of women and men. Care is taken while presenting the graphics and pictures in the course material so that it is gender-sensitive.

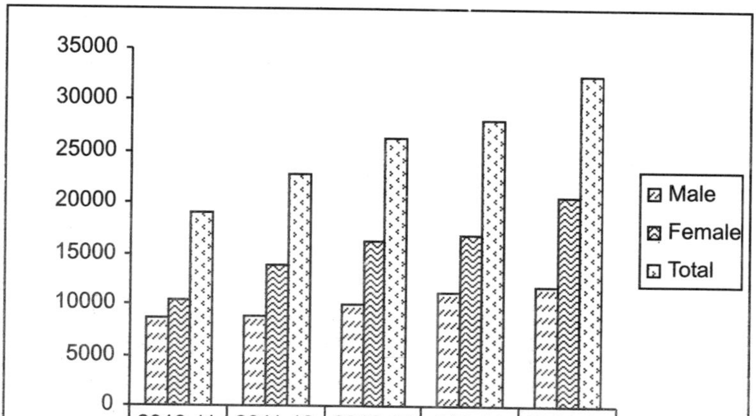

	2010-11	2011-12	2012-13	013-14	2014-15
Male	8562	8902	9972	11158	11840
Female	10511	13877	16382	16877	20632
Total	19073	22779	26354	28035	32472

Fig. 7.6: Enrolment Trend in Vocational Courses

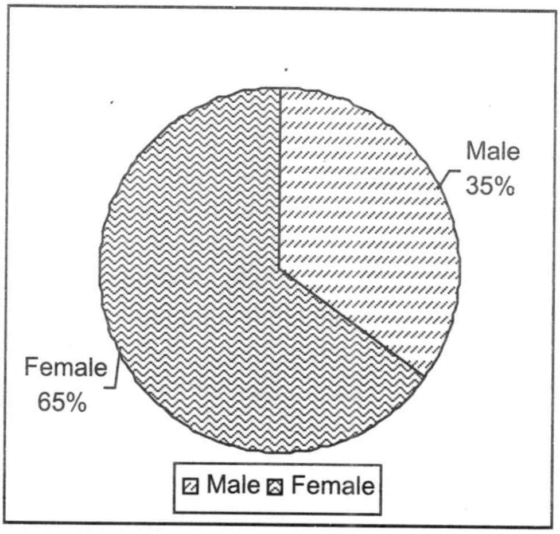

Fig. 7.7: Gender-wise Enrolment in Vocational Courses (2014-15).

In addition to this, the students can choose the subjects according to their own needs and interests. There is ample choice before the girls/women to select any combination of courses from among the given alternatives. The students can take up vocational subjects along with academic subjects. For example, a senior secondary student may choose play-centre management courses along with any three academic subjects and one language. The comparison of the enrolment in academic programmes *vis-a-vis* vocational programmes shows that percentage of women enrolling in vocational education programmes is more than the men. Perhaps it is the diversity of the courses that are gender-sensitive in nature that is enabling the enrolment of women.

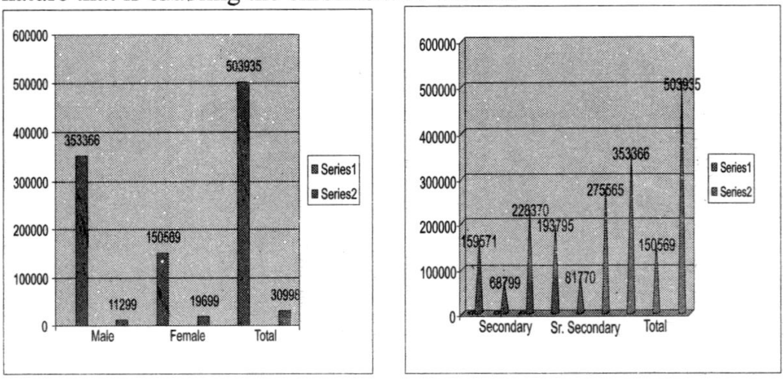

Fig. 7.8: Gender-wise Enrolment in Academic and Vocational Course (2015-16), NIOS.

Source: NIOS Profile, 2017.

Hunar Scheme

The NIOS in collaboration with Bihar Education Project has implemented the Hunar Scheme which has turned out to be a huge success in Bihar with over 13,000 learners joining the programme. The scheme was jointly launched by the Union Ministry of Human Resource Development and the Bihar Government to make women from minority communities' self-dependent. Under the scheme, started on an experimental basis in July 2008, women from minority communities are being trained in computers and other skills like weaving, knitting, and child and maternity care. A total of 13,768 Muslim girls have been imparted skill training in courses like Gram Sakhi, Cutting, Tailoring and Dress Making, Basic Rural Technology, Jute Production, Bakery and Confectionery, Beauty Culture and Early Childhood Care and Education. Out of 13,768 girls, 11,347 girls passed the examination and got a certificate in respective trades. It is interesting to note that not even one learner, dropped out of this programme. The success of the Hunar Project in Bihar encouraged NIOS to launch the project in Delhi also.

Student Support Services

Carefully designed self-instructional printed material, audio-video programmes (that also includes web -radio), teleconferencing and personal contact programmes at the study centres give enormous potential to learning through an open learning system as it provides the women/girl opportunity to learn at their own pace and place.

Realizing the fact that the distance education methodology is still new to the learners, the NIOS gives importance to face-to-face instruction also. The Student Support Services are provided through the study centers. The study centers are located in formal schools, colleges; teacher's training institutions and non-governmental organizations with the capacity to provide academic support to the learners.

Study Centres for Women

One of the reasons why fewer number rural parents is sending girls to schools is the co-educational status of the schools. Surprisingly this feeling exists as much in the urban areas as in rural areas. NIOS has sought a way out by having study centres (N=4,102) for 'girls only' in good schools and vocational institutes in semi-urban, rural and remote parts of the country in areas where their strength is significant. These schools usually have lady teachers who can understand the problems of girl students better. It is because of these features that its coverage has been expanding. Classes are held on Saturdays and Sundays or evenings of working days. Some study centres have special timings for women. Sometimes, classes are held in the afternoon when women are free from their domestic responsibilities. This has widened the scope for gender equity in access to educational opportunities for girls/women.

Usage of Technology for Teaching

The self-learning material is supported by the audio-visual material and also audio programmes that are made available to the learners. All Secondary Courses and Diploma in Elementary Education (D.El.Ed) programme are also delivered by the National Institute of Open Schooling (NIOS) through SWAYAM Portal. NIOS has also taken various steps to promote E-Learning at the school level, such as Virtual Open Schooling (VOS), Eklavaya–Massive Open Online Courses, Mukta Vidya Vani.

SWAYAM courses are available on the SWAYAM.gov.in website in four quadrants: video lecture, specially-prepared reading material that can be downloaded/printed, self-assessment tests through tests and quizzes and an online discussion forum for clearing the doubts.

Learner Evaluation

In pursuance of its policy of learner-friendly approach, the National Institute of Open Schooling allows students to take examinations when they are ready. Examinations are held twice a year and students are free to take the examinations according to their convenience. This allows the girls/women to study at their own pace and convenience. In addition to this, the NIOS has introduced a scheme of transfer of credits through which learners who have cleared one or two subjects from the Central Board of Secondary Education (CBSE) but are not qualified in the full course can seek admission in the NIOS and take the remaining subjects in the Secondary/Senior Secondary programmes. The learners cannot only take admissions online but also register for examinations online.

The NIOS has a an On-Demand Examination (ODES) which is a technology-enabled examination in which the computer generates a unique question paper of equal difficulty level for every examinee. This has opened up wider opportunities for appearing in the examination by parts as per the date and time suitable to the learner.

A Few Emerging Issues

It is relevant to review the positioning of certain programmes in terms of gender-wise enrolment. As per data given earlier in this paper. A gender ratio of around 46 per cent and 31 per cent (in NIOS academic programmes) can be seen with respect to the enrolment of females in IGNOU and NIOS respectively. Which however shows that still there is a disparity among beneficiaries of the open learning system in terms of gender-wise enrolment as male enrolment is more. But the position is reversed in the case of the NIOS vocational programmes. Enrolment of female learners in many popular vocational courses of NIOS is more than that of the males. No doubt the enrolment in traditional courses such as

Certificate Courses in Early Childhood Care and Education, Certificate in Play Centre Management is far above their male counterparts. The figures are also encouraging as they show that the women have taken admission in some of the non-traditional courses such as web designing, a certificate in computer applications. The entry qualification of the NIOS vocational programmes is variable in nature and it varies from class VIII to Secondary to Senior Secondary Level pass outs. (Table 7.5)

Table 7.5: Enrolment in Popular Vocational Courses of NIOS (2015-16)

No.	*Trade*	*Male*	*Female*	*Total*
1.	Certificate in Basic Computing	603	1207	1810
2.	Certificate in Beauty Culture	28	5052	5080
3.	Certificate in Community Health	2994	975	3969
4.	Certificate in Computer and Office Applications	30	107	137
5.	Certificate in Computer Applications	877	746	1623
6.	Certificate in Cutting and Tailoring	46	5350	5396
7.	Certificate in Data Entry Operations	91	162	253
8.	Certificate in Desk Top Publishing	115	237	352
9.	Certificate in Dress Making	23	362	385
10.	Certificate in Early Childhood Care and Education	51	2111	2162
11.	Certificate in Indian Embroidery	6	48	54
12.	Certificate in Library Science (CLS)	244	255	499
13.	Certificate in Rural Health For Women (Gramsakhi)	8	33	41
15.	Certificate in Play Centre Management	0	64	64
16.	Certificate in Secretarial Practice	4	48	52
17.	Certificate in Stenography (English)	45	48	93
18.	Certificate in Typewriting (English)	28	34	62
19.	Certificate in Web Designing	91	84	175
20.	Certificate in Typewriting (Hindi)	202	82	284
21.	Certificate in Yoga	263	252	515
22.	Cutting, Tailoring and Dress Making	51	1509	1560
23.	Diploma in Secretarial Practice (PA/PS)	118	223	341

Source: NIOS, Annual Report (2015-16).

In 2015, IGNOU offered 228 programmes, which were at different levels and each programme had its own eligibility criteria for admissions. The educational qualifications required for admission into these programmes varied from being merely literate to have a degree in a subject.

The total percentage-wise share of learners in the IGNOU programmes is shown in Tables 7.6 and 7.7:

Table 7.6: Level-wise % Share in Total Enrolment (1986-87–2014-15)

Level	*Enrolment*	*% Share*
Adv. Diploma	18123	0.19
Bachelor	4531896	47.67
Certificate	636561	6.70
Diploma	567211	5.97
Master	3119548	32.81
PG Certificate	6793	0.07
PG Diploma	273095	2.87
Other	352544	3.71
Online	1226	0.01

Source: Chaudhary & Shankar (2015a), p.10.

Table 7.7: Male-Female Programme Level-wise Distribution (%)

Programme level	*Male Enrolment*	*Female Enrolment*
Ad Certificate/Diploma	0.25	0.12
Bachelors Degree	50.32	42.70
Certificate	14.30	13.59
Diploma	6.88	9.59
Masters Degree	24.43	30.44
PG Certificate	0.16	0.10
PG Diploma	3.58	3.01
Others	0.09	0.07

Source: Chaudhary and Shankar (2015a), p.16.

It is seen that the Bachelors and Masters Degree programme are most popular and attract 80 per cent of the student enrolment. Another interesting outcome is that the number of women enrolled in Masters Degree programmes is, in fact, higher than the number of males enrolled. This auger well for women and their usage of the ODL system for furthering their education.

The long list of alumni of these institutions such as MC Mary Kom, winner of bronze medal of London Olympics, L. Athira Krishna, international violinist/ Guinness world record holder, Dipika Rebecca Pallikal, professional squash player who is 13th rank holder, Sudipta Chakraborty, notable film actress strengthens the belief that the open and distance learning delivery system enables girls and women to pursue their educational efforts without disturbing the normal rhythm of life and the needs of the family. Open learning can benefit the family without taking the wife/mother away from the house or career opportunities to pursue her studies. The strength of the open learning system is that it allows women a bit of breathing space within an overpowering situation of bringing a balance between her desire for career advancement and meeting the family expectations. It suits the requirements of those who want to carve out their own educational path.

The present policy of these institutions that aims at providing concessions to girl/women candidates addresses to some extent the constraint of poverty in relation to the education of the girl child. Where girls' work is concerned, the diversity of open learning programmes must address to generate sustainable livelihoods pertaining to their local context. So in that context, it seems that these institutions need to widen their horizon by offering more livelihoods-oriented courses and also focused on catering to girls from all walks of life. Programmes should be developed for marginalized sections even if enrolment is low. Special provisions for women learners and within women, special measures for those who are more deprived i.e., marginalized communities, tribal minority groups, disabled be made. Further, there is sufficient research to show that gender differences exist in learning behaviour. The treatment of content has to be conducive to women's learning. Gender theme should be included in all SLMs, along with regular gender editing and content analyses to prevent stereotyping.

Using Technology

There can be no doubt about the value of ICT in the learning process. Several factors need to be taken into consideration when deciding upon the use of the available technologies for conducting admissions, examinations, course delivery and other purposes. However, if technology must effectively contribute to the ease of access knowledge, then the appropriateness of technology must be considered. The socio-economic, political, cultural and geographical background of learners can influence their ability to learn using different forms of technology.

There is a misconception that the appropriate use of media and technology has provided information access to all students in remote, rural and urban areas. There are various other factors such as affordability, availability, access to the technological application, the financial status of the learners that can work as barriers. In a recent programme evaluation, it was seen that most learners had easy access to radio and mobile phones (Priyadarshini, 2016).

Women in rural and disadvantaged areas may not be able to access the online, e-learning support at home, this again puts across another challenge i.e., safeguarding the rights of women to pursue education in a safe and dignified environment. A disturbing challenge related to women learners is the issue of their safety and security both within and outside the learning environment. Moreover, the other challenge is the fact that how much these women are technology-friendly.

Another problem that can arise when programmes are telecast through time slots that are unsuitable for women. In rural areas, the reality is that the time slot reserved by women for milking cows, filling water, feeding cattle, or organizing the household cannot be given up for viewing educational programmes. Providing admissions and examination related opportunities by online mode sound to be very attractive and seem to make the system very much open. But these facilities become a barrier when the learners are not capable of working online and are devoid of such facilities.

Conclusion

The case studies of both the institutions demonstrate that the rigid mould of the formal system of education can be broken. The flexibility in timings and schedules for studies and provision of academic support indicate that these factors can prevent girl child from becoming workers by default, and the entry of older girls into the workforce can be delayed. But still, there is a need to reach out to the unreached sections of the women through livelihood targeted local specific courses. To further strengthen the skill empowerment of these women through meaningful programmes, it is recommended that the Distance Education Bureau (DEB) can support research studies on the impact of ODL programmes on the empowerment of women and other socially weaker sections in the country. This would help in strategizing and planning the vocational and skill empowerment programmes by distance learning institutions to increase women enrolment as well as to support the real cause of sustainable development in society.

Secondly, the selection of appropriate media and technology for a learning package is a complex decision influenced by a variety of considerations, such as the specific learner's background and experiences, the characteristics of the target group as well as practical constraints including the availability of infrastructure and financial resources. Managing technology is no simple task as it needs a certain kind of capacity development in the learners too so that they can take its benefits. There are approaches that can work in such environments, especially where they utilize the technologies with which people are already familiar (e.g. low-end mobile phones) in ways that are simple to use and very user-friendly. These sorts of practices and projects are just the tip of the iceberg, of course.

REFERENCES

Chaudhary, N. and Shankar, G. (2015a). *Three Decades of Distance Education, A Statistical Report on Enrolment Trends in IGNOU Programmes from 1986-87 to 2014-15*, New Delhi, Planning and Development Division (P&DD), IGNOU.

Chaudhary, N. and Shankar, G. (2015b). *Nurturing Social Equity Through Distance Education, A Social Category-wise Statistical Report of IGNOU Programmes from 1999 to 2015*, New Delhi, Planning and Development Division (P&DD), IGNOU.

Government of India (1986). *National Policy on Education (NPE) – 1986*. New Delhi: Department of Education, Ministry of Human Resource Development.

Government of India (2001a). "Literacy in the Context of the Constitution of India". A Consultation Paper of the National Commission to Review the Working of the Constitution. New Delhi: GOI.

Government of India (2001b). Census of 2001, Series 1 India: Provisional Population Totals, Paper 1 of 2001. New Delhi: Registrar General and Census Commissioner.

Government of India (2011). Provisional Population Totals Paper 1 of 2011 India Series 1, New Delhi: Office of the Registrar General & Census Commissioner.

Government of India (2018). *All India Survey on Higher Education 2017-18, Ministry of Human Resource Development, New Delhi:* Department of Higher Education. http://epsiindia.org/wp-content/uploads/*2019/AISHE-2017-18.pdf.*

Indira Gandhi National Open U niversity (1985). *Indira Gandhi National Open University Act and the Statutes of the University,* New Delhi: IGNOU.

Indira Gandhi National Open University (2015). *Vice Chancellor's Report on 28th Convocation*, New Delhi: IGNOU.

Indira Gandhi Open University (2015). Annual Report, New Delhi: IGNOU.

Indira Gandhi Open University (2016). Annual Report, New Delhi: IGNOU.

Kulandaiswamy (1993). "Open University." In Chitnis, S. & Altbach, P. (Eds). *Higher Education in India*, New Delhi: Sage, p. 36.

National Institute of Schooling (2016). Annual Report 2015-16, NIOS, NOIDA, UP, (https://www.nios.ac.in/media/documents/annual_reports/FINAL_ANNUAL_REPORT-2015-16_Website.pdf).

Priyadarshini, A. (2016), *Report: Brainstorming Workshop on Gender Concerns in Open and Distance Learning, New* Delhi: STRIDE, IGNOU (unpublished).

Rathore H.C.S., Singh S.K. and Dubey, G. (1996). "Problems of Women Students in Distance Education in India", *Indian Journal of Open Learning,* Vol. 5, No. 1, pp. 17-27.

Srivastava, M. (2015). *Report: Status of the State Open Universities in India*, New Delhi, CEMCA.

Thomas, J.A. (1996). "Empowerment of Women: An Analysis of Gender Training Frameworks for Open Learning Systems", *Indian Journal of Open Learning*, Volume 5, No 2, pp.1-9.

University Grants Commission (UGC) (2015). *Annual Report (2014-15)*, New Delhi: University Grants Commission.

SECTION 3
Culture and Communication

8

Clash of Cultures

Development and Digital Media in Asian Societies

Mira K. Desai

Development and Technology

Development for any society gets defined from infrastructure to equity in distribution and human justice. While most often infrastructure provides possibilities for growth, it is not the precondition since the distribution of resources, quality of life of people and their rights and freedoms do not come with the physical infrastructure. Technology has a unique relationship with development. While on one hand technology democratizes development processes, on the other; it creates its own hierarchy and divides within the given society.

Desai (2017) based on the analysis of about 66 ICT4D projects in India using secondary sources, remarks that telecentre information access to its population is the most frequently used model of ICT4D in India. The ICT policy and structure supports the market economy of globalization and there does not seem to be much space for people' needs and people's participation. The paradigm of development that the majority of the ICT4D projects address, though offering successful models for Public-Private Partnership, does not seem to be making people partners in bringing about change, whereby negating their roles of active agents in taking charge of their lives.

While centre to periphery arguments for development discourses of the fifties and sixties have long been rejected and nineties and twentieth-century processes of globalization have led to the liberal, private and convergent world across economics, much is to be achieved. It was voiced by Millennial Development Goals and now Sustainable Development Goals; today sustainability is the mainstay of development of 'Third World' economies. But most often it is forgotten that in most Asian societies where resources are scarce for most of the populations, sustainability is the inbuilt character for the large majority. It is a compulsion and not a choice!

With technologies come visuals and languages both of which are highly contextual cultural artefacts. For most Asian societies the diversity and complexity are part of the day to day life. In order to reach out to large masses, using technology and standardization of messages, the space of diverse and complex message construction shrinks dramatically. Besides most Asian societies are 'oral' cultural compared to the expectations of 'literate' societies of the West.

East versus West

Gautam (1994) in his article 'Perspectives' make a remarkable point where he argues that the major source of threat to the autonomy of the people of the Third World can be seen in the Western tendency to continue its domination with its control over technologies of communication, armaments, transportation and production. This needs to be understood not merely in cultural and political terms but also in terms of the requirement on the part of the West to control and perpetuate the existing patterns of consumption of the global resources by which its high standards of living are maintained. The West (also known as the north these days) manages to do this by keeping control of the global trade and financial markets through various mechanisms. Western domination; achieved by means of employing unequal and unbalanced exchange of material goods, ideas, and skilled persons is very much a part of the culture, politics and economy of Indian society. Socio-political and economic decisions at the government level continue to be taken under conditions of lack of autonomy.

With digital media and digitization of culture, there is a huge search for 'identity' and efforts in the direction of documentation, leading to increased content in local languages. Written and visual content in multiple world languages wrestle to make their presence felt. As shreds of evidences have indicated more global one goes, the more strongly one clings to their local identity. And on the face of it, while the semantics may vary, the values embedded in the content may become more hegemonic. Values of consumerism, competition and individualism make their presence felt over the Asian values of collectivism, cooperation and conservation.

Agrawal (2000: 297) remarks that in India, little distinction has been considered essential between culture and communications while discussing development. Punathambekar and Mohan (2019) also highlight the India-centricity of South Asian studies as a challenge.

Speaking Versus Writing

Speaking is a higher form of communication compared to writing. That is the reason that earlier communication literature gave a lot of emphasis on 'speaker' and not on the 'text'. Aristotle (384-322 BCE), a Greek philosopher, gives the model of communication focusing on speaker and speech. He provided five primary elements: Speaker, Speech, Occasion, Audience and Effect. In the Indian context, Bharatmuni in his work *Natyashashtra* refers to the process of *rasa swaad* where speaker and listener become one with each other.

While oriental language is about performing, they are not about naming. Indian philosophy assumes that 'I' can be 'you' but I cannot represent you. You only can represent yourself. Western thoughts emphasise 'writing' but Asian/Eastern thoughts survived on 'speaking'. Asian philosophy lays importance on '*vyak*' (grammar) as well as '*vyavhar*' (behaviour) which becomes irrelevant in writing since writing is two dimensional as opposed to speaking which is three/multi-dimensional and multimodal.

John Fiske (1987) in his landmark cultural studies work titled 'Television Culture' notes his earlier work of 1978 listing differences in oral versus literate modes.

Oral Modes	*Literate Modes*
Dramatic	Narrative
Episodic	Sequential
Mosaic	Linear
Dynamic	Static
Active	Artifact
Concrete	Abstract
Ephemeral	Permanent
Social	Individual
Metaphorical	Metonymic
Rhetorical	Logical
Dialectical	Univocal 'constituent'

Source: Fiske and Hartley (1978).

Way back in 1986, P.C. Joshi wrote in *Economic and Political Weekly*, "The disjunction between culture and political economy, values and interests, has emerged as a fundamental disorienting and destabilising force in India in the recent period. Modern communication technology, which has arisen as a qualitatively new element, is tending to accentuate this disjunction instead of reducing it". Agrawal (1996) a decade later noted, "analysis of contemporary 'political economy' of communication technology, and related software provides some concrete clues as to how the "whites" living in the Euro-American countries are able to have communication domination over the "non-whites" of Afro-Asian countries.

Punathambekar and Mohan in their 2019 work on global digital culture in the context of south Asia categorize the sections as infrastructure, platforms, and publics. They point out, that "the story of digital media in South Asia is, on the one hand, about the phenomenal expansion of communication infrastructures since the mid-1990s has in the span of a decade, industry discourse in the digital and mobile media sectors, shifted from educating new consumers about devices and data services to a generation "born for the Internet."

Santhosh (2016) argues that the internet, particularly social media, which was expected to revitalize the public sphere to bring about a new civic culture, has instead allowed for the selective return of the "written word" in support of fascist ideology. Cyberspace, along with the mass media, has enabled the coming together of many virtual "participants" to hurl masculinist abuse and silence their opponents.

People as Stakeholders of Development

Desai (2019a) concludes that life in 'Third World' is still 'physical'. Life in most Asian societies has created a disconnect between micro and macro. An individual may create a digital world for him/herself but the 'world' outside his/her life is disconnected from the digital world. While the real world has started acknowledging the 'digital world' in media spaces, a disconnect of the 'real/physical' world with the 'digital' world still persist and probably growing.

Desai (2019b) researched women students in university hostel setting over the period of a decade and suggested that women and digital technologies seem to be having a differential relationship with time and research suggested that from being an 'empowering tool' in year 2009 it is becoming 'dependent device' in 2018 and absence of which is making women sad and helpless. The study also lends evidence to the active audience premise as women recognize their dependence and value real life more than virtual life.

The government of India initiated a Digital India (https://digitalindia.gov.in/) as "a flagship programme with a vision to transform India into digitally empowered society and knowledge economy". The ecosystem of the programme lists 32 agencies that provide support and backbone to digitize India. The assessment of goals and vision indicates that it is ICT4D and E-governance programme with a strong focus on infrastructure and delivery. Being a programme of the Department of Electronics and Information Technology, it is the technology and not people that drive the programme. Moses (2018) evaluates its performance of three years and remarks, "The focus and priorities of 'Digital India' need to be aligned with the larger rural population, while a clear roadmap with execution discipline from the center and state government will give a much-needed reboot for the programme".

Schroeder (2017) taking an example of four countries–India, China, Sweden and the U.S. comments "In all four countries, despite their differences, digital media, in contrast to traditional broadcast and interpersonal media, have led to a more differentiated media landscape.... In terms of popular culture, all four countries have experienced a proliferation of media offerings and greater togetherness between people. Hence, new divides are emerging between more active and variegated as against more passive and restricted media uses".

Punathambekar and Mohan (2019) note, "when assessed in relation to this longer media and cultural history, it is evident that platform localization cannot be merely about local language implementation, subtitling, or technological tweaks that respond to concerns like data speeds and cost".

World Bank (2016: 77) states that more than 90 per cent of firms in high-income countries, and 46 per cent in low-income countries, used electronic mail (e-mail) to communicate with clients between 2010 and 2014. The differences are greater when the internet is used for more demanding business activities. For instance, 42 per cent of firms in upper-middle-income countries had a website, and 30 per cent purchased goods or services online. Only 14 per cent of firms in low-income countries purchased goods or services online and only 11 per cent delivered them online.

Analysis of WhatsApp Status lines

As known to people using WhatsApp, the company gives defined status lines which remain their status of the user does not change it specifically. The given options are 'available', 'busy', 'at school', 'at the movies', 'at work', 'battery about to die', 'Can't talk WhatsApp only', 'in a meeting', 'at the gym', 'sleeping', 'urgent calls only'.

In order to examine how urban Indians use 'written' and 'spoken' words, few status lines of people were examined. A management professor from Mumbai notes in his status line "Voice call preferred" and "Prefers a voice dialogue". Another professor again from Mumbai notes, "SMS is the fastest way to reach me". Not necessarily status line has references the researcher is looking for but the ones above are distinctly opposite to each other.

The researcher had been part of a number of interpersonal and group conflicts on digital technologies in general and WhatsApp in particular suggesting an individual preference for 'spoken' versus 'written' worlds and word. The people who have grown in spoken traditions prefer to be in Fiske's words be rhetorical and social compared to those interested in the written world are logical and individualized. Personal observational analysis indicates that people who were from spoken cultures were not interested in being sequential and linear. They were active, dramatic, episodic and dynamic. Their readiness to engage in the written word was minimal and they did not appreciate abstract, static narrative. There is also a reluctance to engage with the written world. Once a person wrote in her e-mail to the researcher, "why don't you pick up a phone and talk to me in place of sending e-mails!" At another incident, a person in response to the written comment on WhatsApp called up and argued "you do not seem to be understanding what and how things should be written". Such clashes though are micro in nature are occasionally becoming evident in cases of lynching, intolerance and violence in the day-to-day life of India. In the recent past, chocking of communication in conflict areas while viewed as a temporary solution, again indicate a clash of two worlds.

Clashes or Convergence?

World Bank (2016) reports titled "digital dividends" point to findings of academic research related to technology and complements. It notes that Rules, Skills and institutions are critical for digital adaptation. While technologies can be global in nature, while implemented it follows local rules which may not be in alignment with the global expectations. Technologies demand skills and not all the tasks can be leveraged. Within the institutional domain, if people are not inclined, technology may not bring about the difference. The report further adds that (2016: 32-33) the lives of the majority of the world's people remain largely untouched by the digital revolution. Only around 15 per cent can afford access to broadband internet. Mobile phones, reaching almost four-fifths of the world's people, provide the main form of internet access in developing countries. But even then, nearly 2 billion people do not own a mobile phone, and nearly 60 per cent of the world's population has no access to the internet. The world's offline population is mainly in India and China, but more than 120 million people are still offline in North America.

When it comes to digitization, issues of algorithms, privacy and transparency, people as numbers and well-being and representation becomes critical. Digital technology cannot be contextual. It is standardized, becomes a tool only if used on the principle of 'economies of scale' otherwise it becomes a liability for the governments.

Algorithms: The 2018 case of the Facebook Cambridge Analytica data scandal gives rise to questions of data theft, data protection, identity targeting, manipulation of public opinion and so on. In Asian societies where people most often trust and believe what they are seeing, reading, listening, and watching (especially written word) such narrowed targeting can be not only dangerous but also can lead to clashes of opinions.

Privacy and Transparency: While personal-public spheres are Western connotations, most Asian cultures do not have so much division of life. Most often people who meet each other on public transport or social occasions immediately start talking about intimate details of their personal life to strangers even in the first meeting. Agarwal (2006) examines it elaborately.

People as Numbers: Digital technologies make human beings as mere numbers. While all Asian societies are diverse societies, digital media is more of a uniformity. The marriage of digital media and Asian societies is the marriage of international pressures on Asian governments to introduce technologies whereas helping capitalist economies to benefit themselves.

Well-being and Representation: It has been documented that there are more mobiles than toilets in India. What populations need for well-being may not be digital media and how people are being represented in digital media.

Conclusion

There is no doubt that Asian societies have a multiplicity and long history of oral traditions. The recent revival of visual content in the forms of videos, Over The Top (OTT) platforms and video calling in digital space clearly suggest how the 'written' world is being replaced by the 'spoken' worlds in digital spaces. The review and limited empirical data clearly suggest that while digital technologies are as of now converging written and oral cultures, occasional clashes of on written and spoken cultures demand more investigation in years to come.

REFERENCES

Agrawal, Binod (1996). Euro-American Communication Domination Over Afro-Asian Countries, Keynote presented at Western Association of Asian Studies at Weber State University, Ogden, Utah, USA, October 25, 1996.

Agrawal, Binod (2000). "Culture, Communication and Development: An Indian Perspective", In: Gore, M.S. (ed.) *Third Survey of Research in Sociology and Anthropology*, Vol. 1, New Delhi: Manak, pp. 296-325.

Agarwal, Binod (2006). "Culture, Communication and the Meaning of Intellectual Property Rights in South Asia: A Critical Analysis," In: Thomas, P.N. and Jan Servaes (ed.) *Intellectual Property Rights and Communications in Asia: Conflicting Traditions*, New Delhi: Sage. pp.164-173.

Desai, Mira (2017). "ICT4D projects in India: Continuation of Dominant Pradigm...?!," *Quest in Education*, 41(1): 12-36.

Desai, Mira (2019a). Disconnect of Micro with Macro: Digital world for the "third" world, Paper presented at AMIC Annual Conference at Chulalongcorn University, Bangkok-Thailand, May 2019.

Desai, Mira (2019b). "Understanding Women and Digital Media Relationship: Changes and Challenges", *Interaction*, Vol. XXXVII: 24-32.

Fiske, John and Hartley, John (1978). *Reading Television,* London: Methuen.

Fiske, John (1987). *Television Culture*, London: Routledge.

Gautam, Satya (1994). "Cultural and Political Autonomy in Indian Society", *Economic and Political Weekly*, 29 (20): Perspectives.

Joshi, P.C. (1986). "Role of Culture in Social Transformation and National Integration", *Economic and Political Weekly*, 21(28) Special Articles.

Moses J.J. (2018). 3 Years of Digital India, Here is what has worked and what has not, 23 May 2018, URL: https://www.peoplematters.in/article/industrial-relations/

Punathambekar, A and Sriram, Mohan (ed.) (2019). *Global Digital Cultures: Perspectives from Asia*, Michigan: University of Michigan Press.

Santhosh, S. (2016). "Making the 'Modi Effect' Questions on the Technologies of Fascism", *Economic and Political Weekly*, 51(3) Commentary.

Schroeder, R. (2017). "Towards a Theory of Digital Media, Information Communication & Society", 21(3): 323-339.

World Bank (2016). Digital Dividends, International Bank for Reconstruction and Development, Washington DC. URL: https://www.worldbank.org/en/publication/wdr2016.

9

Hegemonic Indian Culture and Society in *Chandamama* Comics

Aloysius Sebastian

Chandamama was a comic published in India from 1947 July, that is, one month before India gained Independence from British imperialism. It was immensely popular and had a significant influence upon Indian children in immediately Independent India. It was begun with the agenda of teaching Indian children "Indian tradition and culture" and history and myth when the prevalent comic culture in the country was highly Westernised due to the import of material from the West. This chapter analyses how the Indian community represented in *Chandamama* is a hegemonic Indian community with a hegemonic culture that justifies precolonial and even *Vedic* Indian power structures that are Hinduistic and even casteist.

The following passage is from the editorial of the July 1955 issue of *Chandamama*:

> There is great joy in reading or listening to a nice story. In olden days, some kings engaged story-tellers to derive this joy. Teachers told their pupils tales of wit and wisdom instead of dry lessons. These pupils got educated by listening to them. Those days are gone, but the stories have remained. *Chandamama* brings you these wise, old stories and gives you the same joy that kings of old derived from their story-tellers. (Editor 1955)

The reference to the "olden days" when "some kings engaged story-tellers to derive the great joy" of "reading or listening to nice stories" indicates nostalgia for an earlier society of kings. Most of the stories in *Chandamama* are set in a pre-colonial, feudal Indian society ruled by monarchs, and in many of these stories, the protagonist is a king. These monarchs are usually presented as chivalrous and wise, and as acting in the interest of the people, while depictions of unruly and corrupt monarchs in the stories in *Chandamama* are comparatively very few. Such representations indicate nostalgia towards the pre-colonial, feudal and monarchical Indian societies, which was probably a result of newly democratised Indians' psychological turmoil while getting gradually adapted to the new democratic system. For newly Independent India, the newly formed democratic government was as foreign as the British government that preceded it. Maybe this is the reason why there are many stories in this comic that present feudal societies ruled by monarchs who are very efficient in ruling the kingdom and always act towards the welfare of the people. In some such stories, the protagonist makes use of his talents to gain the favour of the monarch and is thereby awarded several gifts and often permanent employment in the court. Such monarchical societies in these stories are presented as reminiscences of India's glorious past, thus instilling among its young readers' inclination and longing for such a monarchical, feudal past.

The editorial refers to "some teachers" who "told their pupils tales of wit and wisdom instead of dry lessons." The predominant system of education in India before colonisation was the *Gurukul* system of education. This editorial of *Chandamama* refers to such a system of education as having constituted wit and wisdom, unlike the "dry lessons" that constituted the contemporary education system. Thereby, the older *Gurukul* system of education is presented as better than the contemporary one. In the *Gurukul* system, a scholarly *guru* or teacher imparted knowledge to his students who stayed at his residence for several years to learn from the *guru*'s knowledge gained through texts as well as from experience. This was mainly liturgical education, and it was Hindu liturgical education through *Vedas*, *Puranas* and *Upanishads*. "The philosophy of education in Ancient India was based primarily on the philosophical offerings of the scriptures, namely the *Veda*, *Upanishad*, *Brahmana* and the *Bhagavad Gita*" (Gupta, 2006 : 15), constituting "verses and scriptures compiled in an archaic form of Sanskrit as early as 2000 B.C." (*Ibid*., 37). Thus, in precolonial India, education was predominantly Hindu liturgical. Precolonial Indian society considered liturgical knowledge as the highest form of knowledge. All other forms of knowledge were considered secondary or tertiary. This liturgical knowledge was handled by *Brahmins*, and thus, Brahmanical knowledge was considered the highest form of knowledge. "The body of literature called *Puranas* was a central repository for the circulation, affirmation, and renewal of various Brahmanical schemas about the origins of the world, its topographical ordering, sacred geography, and genealogies of gods, sages, and kings" (Goswami, 2013 : 155). The *Kshatriyas'* knowledge of warfare or the Vaishyas' craftsmanship and skills of innovation or trade were not considered equivalent to Brahmanical knowledge.

Moreover, education in pre-colonial India was discriminatory based on caste since the *Sudras* were denied education. "Education was available to most during the early Vedic stage but became more discriminatory as the caste system began to evolve" (Gupta, 2006 : 38). "The business of higher education became more concerned with the requirements of priesthood as the rituals of sacrifice began to gain increasing prominence in Vedic society" (*Ibid.*, 40). "Education was available to most except members of the *Sudra* caste, who, although they could train in menial jobs, were denied religious and spiritual learning.

The cover page of the July 1955 issue of *Chandamama* depicts one of the *avatars* of Vishnu, the *Matsya avatar*. On page number ten is a description of the front cover. It is about how Vishnu in the form of the *Matsya avatar* rescued Vaivaswata and the other seven *rishis* along with the seeds of all important plants from a great flood that devoured the entire world.

The description begins like this: "Many of you, no doubt, have heard of Noah and his Ark and the Flood. There is a similar, but slightly different, story in our mythology." Here, the reference to the Biblical tale of *Noah and the Great Flood* before saying there is a similar Indian mythological tale is indicative of the comic's ambition of making Indian children read "Indian stories". Even though the tale of *Noah and the Great Flood* is from the *Bible*, and most Indians are Hindus, the writer seems to be quite sure his readers are more familiar with the Biblical tale rather than the Hindu mythology. Therefore, the writer refers to the Biblical tale to introduce the readers to the "Indian/Hindu" tale. This happens because the producers of comics like *Chandamama* and *Amar Chitra Katha* started these comics as "Indian comics" since they were unhappy that in newly Independent India left with the colonial legacy, the influence of Western literature was powerful; most of the available and favoured comics were Western, usually the super-hero comics of DC or Marvell. This trend was magnified by the kind of school curriculum introduced by the new educational policies derived mainly from the education system the British had introduced in India. The English language was a compulsory subject of the new school curriculum, and the English syllabi mostly constituted not Indian but Western literary pieces, which led to the younger generations' of newly Independent India growing up under the strong influence of Western literature and culture. This was the scenario in which comics like *Chandamama* and *Amar Chitra Katha* began to be published.

By the 19th century, the provincial government in India began to issue rules and regulations intended at controlling or banning Hindu religious practices and customs they looked upon as uncivilised and pre-modern. They began to exert deliberate force to shape Indian society by banning child marriage and widow burning (*sati*) as well as other religious practices that contravened British morality. When the "modern" British colonisers thus began to question several traditional and religious beliefs, practices and customs, nationalism began to emerge as a feeling to protect traditions, beliefs, practices and customs. The British had been using the services of the local literati, who came from the Hindu upper castes, mostly *Brahmins* and, as a result, a new elite of upper-caste British-trained white-collar workers took shape, which was more prominent in Bengal. They admired Britain for its remarkable scientific, technical, legal, and social achievements. However, even though they were inclined to reform their traditions along modern lines, they did not want to abandon or disown them. They often wanted to reform these traditions to save them. For instance, even though

> Ram Mohun Roy supported Western reformist ideas, including the abolition of *sati*, at the same time he was very critical of the proselytising work of Western missionaries. He steadfastly vindicated Hinduism against Christian expansionism, though in the reformist way. Roy admitted that missionaries were right when they stigmatised polytheism, the caste system and the condition of Hindu women. However, he argued that these retrograde practices were latter accretions in Hinduism, and that in its original form, Hinduism did not lay itself open to such opprobrium (Jaffrelot, 1996 : 7).

Gradually, Roy founded the 'Brahmo Samaj' in 1828, which believed in the notion of a Vedic "golden age". After returning from England, Keshab Chandra Sen, who was a member of the Samaj, promoted the idea that India was technically less advanced than England but spiritually superior (Jaffrelot, 1996 : 7). "Dayananda Saraswati argued that Indian antiquity was imbued with cultural and social greatness" (*Ibid.*, 9) contrast to the old reformists like Ram Mohan Roy, Dayananda did not look upon British colonialism as a providential development but rather as posing a threat to Hindu civilisation" (*Ibid.*, 9). "His effort was to dissuade the British from changing Hindu customs by law, as well as to dissuade Hindus from admiring the West" (*Ibid.*, 9-10). Thus, nationalism initially originated in India as cultural nationalism against the British, and people who had remained fragmented and separated began to come together.

After India's Independence, the newly formed Indian Government wanted to unify the Indian people who were very fragmented since they were ethnically, culturally and linguistically different, and different communities of people in the country had different problems and goals. Therefore, the state tried to instil nationalism among the people to bring them together and unify them through patriotism. The icon of Bharat Mata offered a potent origin myth for national history and territory.

> The figure of Bharat Mata (Mother India) embodied par excellence the organicist self-understanding of popular nationalism. Bharat Mata worked as an enduring matrix of nationalist identification and desire. It enabled and rendered plausible constructions of the nation as an organic formation rooted in an ancient past. (Goswami, 2013 : 199).

Glorification of the past is a technique frequently used to instil nationalist sentiment among the people of a state. Voluntarily and involuntarily, this technique was used by the Indian state, its thinkers and artists to instil nationalism and patriotism among the people of India. Thus, there was much discussion and representation in popular culture of "a glorious and honourable precolonial past". According to Romila Thapar, "what we regard as tradition may well turn out to be our contemporary requirements fashioned by the way we wish to interpret the past" (1998 : 267). In this process, the goodness of the precolonial past is exaggerated, while the negativities are often forgotten or neglected. "In creating a tradition, we sometimes select from the past those normative values which may have a contemporary appeal, but which may even be contrary to historical actuality" (*Ibid.*, 271).

The Indian community represented in *Chandamama* is a pre-colonial, feudal yet idyllic Indian community, and sometimes the narratives in this comic are set in as early as "the glorious Vedic period". Religion is at the centre of this feudal community. In *Chandamama*, many stories are based on or derived from Hindu mythologies and *Puranas*. In some stories and narratives, the protagonist is an ardent Hindu devotee who is eventually blessed by the God or deity whom he worships. In such an idealistic, feudal, religious and monarchical community, the protagonist is usually a figure closely associated with the running of the monarchy or the institution of religion, like the king or the *Brahmin* respectively. In such narratives in *Chandamama*, while the *Brahmin* who is the religious head is presented as holy, pious and wise, the king who is the head of the monarchy is presented as chivalrous, wise and as always acting towards the welfare of the people. Such narratives are often set in significant Hindu religious centres.

Such a trend of cultural nationalism with a religious inclination in Indian popular culture like comics was part of the rise of Hindu nationalism in India. The proliferation of such content in visual media like comics, television and cinema led to the development of cultural nationalism into Hindu nationalism. Eventually, the Janata Party, the predecessor of the BJP (Bharatiya Janata Party), won the general election in 1977, even though mass discontent towards the State of Emergency declared by Indira Gandhi had also created support for the opposing BJP.

Synonymous with popular cultural nationalist discourses, according to Catarina Kinnvall, the *Hindutva* movement has aimed:

> to construct a chain of events where a glorified past is connected to the present and where it justifies future actions. It is a nationalist homogenising narrative that is deeply rooted in religious discourse. Hindu nationalism is not a modern phenomenon in India. Instead, its provenance is held to go back to Vedic times, and it is therefore enmeshed with the history and culture of the Hindu "race" (2006 : 139).

During the rule of the BJP government from 1998 to 2004, the educational policy was highly in tune with the Hindu nationalist leaning. The Minister for Human Resource Development, Murli Manohar Joshi, "appointed personalities who had been close to the Sangh Parivar as heads of the directive body of the Indian Council of Historical Research (ICHR), the Indian Council of Social Science Research (ICSSR), and the search committee for faculty appointments in the National Council for Educational Research and Training (NCERT) which was entrusted with the task of designing a new school curriculum. One of Joshi's priorities was to create new textbooks, including those dealing with Indian history, rewritten in a vein more in line with Hindu nationalist ideology" (Jaffrelot, 1996 : 22).

Hinduism takes the central place in *Chandamama* through several stories based on or adapted from Hindu epics and mythologies. Contributing to the Hindu nationalist discourse, *Chandamama* depicts Hinduism as an Indian tradition and culture. Apart from stories based on

Hindu *Puranas* and mythologies, several creative stories in *Chandamama* portray, as already described, an idyllic, monarchical and feudal society. In these stories, the protagonists are usually upper caste Hindus like the stereotypical *Kshatriya* warrior king who was the head of the monarchy, or the "pious and holy *Brahmin*" who was the head of the institution of the Hindu religion. Thus, these stories are always narrated from the perspective of upper-caste Hindus. A reason for such representations may have been the newly democratised middle class and upper-caste Indians' nostalgia for the precolonial, monarchical and religious past. However, this is hegemony at work since these narratives always pertain to the taste of upper caste and middle-class Indians, which was quite inevitable since both the producers as well as consumers of comics like *Chandamama* and *Amar Chitra Katha* were upper-caste, urban middle classes.

The main reason behind the colonial British government's introduction of the English language and Western education in India was its requirement to employ Indians as clerks and officers since it proved more efficient than importing people from Britain. The British mostly chose upper-caste Hindus for such positions because it was easier to educate them institutionally since they already had some exposure to institutional education that the low caste people had been denied. Moreover, since the British knew about the caste system in India and how it operated, they knew the upper caste Hindus were more suitable for smooth functioning as mediators between the British and the Indians, especially the more powerful sections of the Indian society who were mostly upper-caste Hindus. Such Indians became one of the first middle classes in India. They were some of the first to read newspapers and to get more exposure to emerging discourses. Thus, in the latter 20th century, most producers and consumers of newspapers, journals and comics were upper-caste Hindus, and therefore, these forms of media usually spoke from an upper-caste Hindu perspective.

In *Chandamama*'s upper-caste Hindu Indian society, non-Hindu religions like Christianity and Islam and their followers are presented as to foreign. They are often "othered", and Muslims are even represented as hostile invaders through "historical narratives" of battles between "chivalrous Hindu warriors" and "hostile Muslim invaders", which is synonymous with the Hindu nationalist discourse that considers Islam and Christianity as foreign religions and also talks about the destruction of several Hindu temples by "Muslim invaders", as in the book *Hindu Temples and What Happened to Them* by Goel, Shourie, Swarup, Narain, and Dubashi (1990). Many Hindu nationalists consider Hindus as the descendants of "Vedic fathers" who have been living in this geographical area since antiquity. Christianity and Christians, if ever represented in *Chandamama*, are represented in stories or narratives situated in the West, and non-hostile representation of Muslims happens only in stories situated in West Asia or "the Middle East."

> According to Ritu Khanduri,
>
> To authorise the cultural claims of their comics, Indian publishing houses frequently inform readers of a historian or cultural expert among their staff, who ensures the accuracy of the research for their narratives. Anant Pai, the founder-editor of *Amar Chitra Katha*, emphasised that *Amar Chitra Katha* comics were a product of primary research and the script was not arbitrary (2010 : 174).

However, theorists like Hayden White have described how even historiography is often a fiction-making operation since history is narrated from the usually hegemonic perspective of the historian.

> Hayden White states,
>
> historical sequences can be emplotted in many different ways to provide different interpretations of those events and to endow them with different meanings. How a given historical situation is to be configured depends on the historian's subtlety in matching up a specific plot structure with the set of historical events he wishes to endow with a meaning of a particular kind. This is essentially a literary, fiction-making operation (1986 : 85).
>
> Further,
>
> the overall coherence of any given series of historical facts is the coherence of story, but this coherence is achieved only by a tailoring of the facts to the requirements of the story form. The historical narrative does not reproduce the events it describes but tells the reader in what direction to think about the events and charges the reader's thoughts about the events with different emotional valences (*Ibid.*, 91).

The representation of Christians in *Chandamama* history is mythicised. However, Buddhism is represented as though it is an offshoot of Hinduism, which may be because Buddhism did originate from Hinduism, even though that happened not as an offshoot of Hinduism, but by questioning certain beliefs and practices within Hinduism.

Chandamama internalises Hindu nationalist ideas. For *Chandamama*, synonymous with the Hindu nationalist discourse, India is a Hindu nation where other religions are foreign. Such an Indian community was being represented in *Chandamama* in the 60s, 70s and 80s when Hindu nationalism was on the rise, which indicates this immensely popular comic's symbiotic relationship with Hindu nationalism.

Godliness (Chandamama 1956 p. 42-48) is a story about two elderly friends, Govind and Gopal, going on a pilgrimage to the famous Hindu Kashi Vishwanath Temple. On the way, they come across a poor peasant family on the verge of death due to starvation. Govind helps them using all the money he had with him. Govind offers to help them cultivate on their small plot of land. However, the peasant says even that small plot has been mortgaged. Therefore, if he cultivated anything on that land, the yield would go to the creditor.

Moreover, he sold his cart and buffaloes. However, Govind helps the family by paying the debt to free the land from the moneylender. Moreover, he purchases for them a cart and a pair of buffaloes. Thus, after making sure the family can begin farming again and live a comfortable life, Govind decides to leave them and continue his pilgrimage, guessing his friend Gopal would already have reached Banaras. However, he realises now he does not have with him enough money for the pilgrimage since he has spent most of it for the peasant family. So, he decides to return home instead.

Meanwhile, Gopal continues his pilgrimage and reaches Banaras. As Gopal reaches the pilgrim centre, the central place of worship is very thickly packed with devotees touching the *linga* to purify themselves. Gopal's old age health does not allow him to make his way through the crowd to the *linga*.

However, Gopal is surprised to see Govind at the front, rising after touching the *linga* with his forehead. Gopal intends to meet Govind as everyone came out. However, even though he observes everyone very carefully, he is surprised when he is unable to find Govind. He just seems to have disappeared. Gopal stays at Banaras for three days. Every day he goes to the temple, and every day he sees Govind touching the *linga* with his forehead. However, he never sees Govind anywhere else.

So, Gopal leaves Banaras and visits Gaya, Prayag and other sacred places before returning home. On the way back, he visits the peasants whom Govind had helped. He learns from them that Govind had stayed with them for three months, but he had never reached Banaras.

Now Gopal realises Govind has passed away, and it is his soul that now visits the temple every day and even touches the *linga* with his forehead as he is now very close to God because of his goodness, especially his generosity towards the poor peasant family. Thus, even though Gopal was unable to accomplish his pilgrimage in his lifetime, he has achieved much more through his helping mentality and goodness, that now he is constantly close to God. Perhaps this indicates Govind has achieved *moksha* or salvation.

This story has as its theme Hindu spirituality and how the protagonist reaches the culmination of this spirituality through his charitable deeds. The protagonist is a very religious and devout Hindu who is also hugely charitable and helpful. By presenting such a character as the protagonist, this story tends to stimulate among its young readers' inclination towards Hindu religiosity.

In several stories in *Chandamama*, the protagonist is a *Brahmin* who gets blessed by the god/s not only because of piety but also because he belongs to that particular caste. Through such representation of *Brahmins*, *Chandamama* internalises the caste hierarchy and the *Varna* system. Other than "the pious and holy *Brahmin*", "the chivalrous *Kshatriya* warrior king" is also a frequent protagonist in many stories in *Chandamama*. *Brahmin* and *Kshatriya* kings in *Chandamama* are described as having the characteristics attributed to them by the *Varna* system. Thus, while *Brahmins* are presented as holy, pious and wise, kings are presented as brave and noble warriors who always act very wisely towards the welfare of the subjects. Such representations could have been part of the cultural nationalist sentiment accompanied by an inclination towards the precolonial past in newly democratised India with a new and unfamiliar centralised democratic government. However, such representations in *Chandamama* and the intensity of such representations aggravated during the 70s when Hindu nationalism was on the rise.

In such stories, *Brahmin* characters are usually very good. They are pious, benevolent and charitable. They are very wise but devoid of deceit. The *Brahmin* in *Chandamama* is selfless and is not interested in accumulating riches. He is respectful and devoted to the gods and is good-natured and helpful towards his fellow men. The Indian community in *Chandamama* respects *Brahmins* because of two reasons; their caste and also their characteristic goodness. Thus, by presenting *Brahmins* as characteristically good and as respectable, "the idyllic" Indian community in *Chandamama* is casteist in nature.

In some of these stories, *Brahmin* protagonists are capable of even superhuman feats because of having been blessed by some god or deity.

Such divine interventions and feats are usually seen only in *Brahmins* and not in characters belonging to any other caste, which internalises the *Varna* system that attributed *Brahmins* as the caste of people most closely associated with the gods and *Sudras* as the caste of people the farthest from the gods. Sometimes such supernatural capabilities are inherited by *Brahmins* from one generation to the next, which further strengthens the casteist nature of *Chandamama* since according to the *Varna* system, each caste of people has certain hereditary qualities that enable them to engage in their respective caste-prescribed occupation efficiently.

Thus, *Brahmins* who are at the centre of the Indian community in *Chandamama* are presented as very likeable and humane, thereby insinuating the reader's affection and respect towards them. Such glorified representations of *Brahmin* characters can have the effect of inspiring young readers to become like the *Brahmin*, which is an invitation towards sanskritization prevalent in *Chandamama*, whereby readers belonging to other castes are inspired to go up higher in society by attempting to become like the *Brahmin* through the process of imitation. However, this imitation is like the process of colonial mimicry described by Homi Bhabha (1984) in *Of Mimicry and Man: The Ambivalence of Colonial Discourse* where he talks about colonial mimicry and its ambivalence. Similarly, in the case of sanskritization as well, mimicry is accompanied by ambivalence, whereby people belonging to other castes can aspire and imitate the *Brahmin* to try to become "almost *Brahmin* but not completely" since that is allotted only for the hereditary caste of *Brahmins*.

In *Chandamama*, while *Brahmins* are presented as inheriting qualities like wisdom, intelligence and divinity, and sometimes supernatural abilities like the power of prediction, *Kshatriya* kings and warriors are presented as inheriting qualities like strength, valour and courage. The stories in *Chandamama* instil among its young readers' nostalgia and inclination towards a pre-colonial, feudal, monarchical Indian society through tales of righteous monarchs who strive for the welfare of the subjects and rule the kingdom with peace and prosperity. In some stories, the protagonist, through his talent/s, captures the favour of the king who rewards him generously. Such stories, being narrated from the perspective of the protagonist, makes the reader rejoice along with him as he is rewarded by the righteous monarch whom the protagonist looks upon with great respect and adoration.

In *Chandamama*, the glorification of upper-caste Hindus like *Brahmins* and *Kshatriyas* and the representation of these castes of people according to the attributes made to them by the *Varna* system is casteism. While upper caste Hindus are glorified, people belonging to lower castes are usually not represented in the stories in *Chandamama*, and if represented, they serve as foils to upper-caste Hindus. Through such representations, *Chandamama* internalises the characteristics and qualities attributed by the *Varna* system not only to upper-caste Hindus but also to those belonging to the lower castes as well. Thus, the discourse of *Chandamama* is casteist and discriminatory towards people belonging to lower castes. Such representations may not have disturbed most of the readers of *Chandamama* since they were mostly the urban, upper-caste, middle classes.

Krishna Came to the Poet's Rescue (Chandamama 1975 pp. 39-41) is a narrative of a mythological incident associated with the Sanskrit poet Jayadeva. Apart from the glorification of the poet who is the *Brahmin* protagonist of the story, the event in the narrative induces among faithful Hindus admiration and worship towards Krishna, a major Hindu god. The narrative starts as follows: "In the shade of a tree, behind the great temple of Jagannath at Puri, sat a young *Brahmin*, engrossed in engraving his verses on a bunch of palm leaves" (1975 : 39). Here, the temple of Jagannath at Puri has been referred to as "great." After that, when the poet is initially introduced, he is not introduced by his name, but as a *Brahmin* sitting in the shade of a tree behind the "great" Jagannath temple, engraving his verses on a bunch of palm leaves. Such addressing of the poet by his caste name as *Brahmin* rather than by his name itself attributes the activity he is engaged in, namely that of engrossing verses, as something commonly pursued by *Brahmins* and not just Jayadeva himself. Thus, this narrative seems to claim proudly that *Brahmins* of the past were often engaged in engrossing and studying verses and scriptures, and thus, it seems to take pride in *Brahmins*' "capability" to create and engage with verses and scriptures like the *Vedas*, which implies glorification of not only *Brahmins* but also of Hindu verses and scriptures. Thus, it supports a *Veda* centric society in which only *Brahmins* and *Kshatriyas* had the right to engage with the scriptures while those who belonged to the lower castes were prohibited from reading the scriptures or even studying Sanskrit. The verses the poet was engaged in engrossing are the *Gita Govinda*, a major Hindu poem about the relationship between Krishna and the *gopis* (cowgirls) of Vrindavana, particularly Radha. However, the name of the poem is revealed only by the end of the narrative. Till then, the narrative talks about the commitment as well as the devotedness of the poet Jayadeva, and it describes the event of divine intervention in the writing of the poem. Such a technique instils curiosity in the reader until the end when it is finally revealed the poem is the *Gita Govinda*.

The narrative continues as follows, "It was a quiet mid-day, with no sound heard except the roar of the sea which was not far and the cooing of a couple of cuckoos from the tree. However, of course, there was another faint sound too – joining the cuckoos' song from time to time, which was the sweet voice of our poet Jayadeva. He was reciting his verses as he went on writing them" (1975 : 39). Here the poet is described as engrossing and reciting his verses sitting in a very idyllic environment. He was sitting in the shade of a tree behind the temple of Jagannath at Puri. There was no other sound other than the roar of the sea and the cooing of a couple of cuckoos from the tree under which the poet was seated. Thus, the temple of Jagannath, as well as the *Brahmin* poet, is situated in an idyllic environment and such a representation can inevitably induce among its readers, especially young readers, some inclination towards such an idyllic setting as presented in the story, with massive, renowned temples, and highly devoted and talented *Brahmins* to support and strengthen such establishments.

Moreover, he is referred to as "our poet Jayadeva", thus instilling a feeling of familiarity with the poet. Apart from this, referring to him as "our poet" implies an all-encompassing Hindu nationalist perspective that sees all the readers of the comic as Hindus even though the comic was read by children belonging to other communities as well.

"With deep concentration, Jayadeva was writing about Krishna and Radha, about the great love that the two felt for each other. He was narrating an episode in which Krishna had to be shown trying to appease Radha who had grown a bit angry with him" (1975 : 39).

However, the poet murmured, "O Krishna, my Lord! I know your great love for Radha. Even then, how can I show you humbled before her, apologising to her" (1975 : 39-40). The poet repeatedly tried to write down the lines he has in his mind, but his reverence for Krishna would not allow him to do so since he was reluctant to write about God bowing before a human being, *especially a woman*. Here, Jayadeva's reverence for Krishna is illustrative to young readers of how they also should, like the "great" poet, love and respect God with humility.

When it was time for lunch, the poet's wife Padmavati came out of their hut nearby and said, "The sun is already overhead. Food is ready. Will you not go for your bath" (1975 : 40).

The poet said, "Oh, is that so? I was not aware of time. Very well, Padmavati, carry home my manuscript and the pen. I will be back soon, after a dip in the lake" (1975 : 40). Jayadeva is thus presented as so immensely interested in composing the poem about Krishna that he forgot time and even hunger.

The piousness of the *Brahmin* poet is emphasised by saying that for him bathing included reciting long hymns and performing certain rites. Thus, by presenting him as always very keen on performing rites, his exclusive right to clergyship is internalised.

After a bath, he went home to take food. As he reached home, Jayadeva was surprised to see his wife preparing to take food, which was because, throughout their married life, it had been Padmavati's habit to eat only after her husband had finished eating. So, he was surprised why she was now behaving in this strange fashion. He asked her, "How is it, Padmavati, that you were in such a hurry to take food today" (1975 : 40).

Padmavati seemed to be surprised at this and said, "Isn't your conduct rather unusual today? A little while ago you rushed in and asked for your manuscript, saying that you wanted to write down a couple of lines before you forgot them. I gave you the manuscript, and after writing down those lines, you finished your meal and went out, saying that you had some urgent business to attend in the temple. You are back in no time, and you say that you are hungry!" (1975 : 40) Jayadeva was stunned. However, something occurred to him in a flashlight, and he wanted to see the manuscript. Padmavati washed her hands and brought it out. As Jayadeva looked at the manuscript, he trembled with emotion. Tears rolled down his cheeks, which was because he saw added to the manuscript the same lines he had been hesitant to write down since he did not want to offend Krishna in any possible manner. The lines described Krishna humbly bowing to Radha to please her. It was Krishna who had come in Jayadeva's guise to help him complete the poem.

Jayadeva said to Padmavati, "Great is your luck, Padmavati, although you do not know yet whom you saw a little ago. He who came assuming my form was none other than Krishna himself. Who else could have known what was going on in my mind?" (1975 : 41) Thus, in this narrative, it is presented as very befitting for Krishna to take the form of the *Brahmin*. Krishna took the form of the poet since he wanted to help him to perfect and complete the poem he was writing about Krishna himself. Here, God took the form of the *Brahmin* without any hesitation, which seems to suggest it was not only the poet's devotedness or the theme and quality of the poem but also the caste of the poet that caused God to help him by taking his form. Through such an instance of a major Hindu god helping a *Brahmin* poet, this story elicits among its readers' respect for the *Brahmin* poet, apart from inducing love and worship towards Krishna. By talking about God taking the form of the *Brahmin*, the *Brahmin* is raised to godliness, which is what the Brahmanical caste system always tried to do. Such an effect is highly achieved in this narrative since it is about a real poet, the writer of the *Gita Govinda*.

After realising Krisha has visited their house, Jayadeva and Padmavati sat down at the same spot where the god had sat and eaten the remains from the dish from which Krishna had eaten. Thus, the opportunity to eat from the remains of what the Hindu god ate is presented as a divine blessing. The narrative ends like this, "Jayadeva's lyric poem, in the writing of which Krishna had played such a role, is famous as the Gita Govinda" (1975 : 41). Thus, the name of the poem is revealed only by the end of the narrative, thereby providing an answer to the curiosity of the reader after building up a glorified image of the poem through the portrayal of the poet Jayadeva as a highly talented and devoted poet, and through the description of an event of divine interference in the writing of the "great" poem.

"Jayadeva lived in the twelfth century. For hundreds of years past his immortal lyric poem, the *Gita Govinda*, is regularly recited in the temple of Puri. It is said that the Lord does not go to sleep without listening to this sweet composition" (1975 : 41).

In Fig. 9.1, the *Brahmin* poet Jayadeva is placed in front of the famous temple of Jagannath at Puri. Since the poet is sitting at the front under the shade of a tree, he appears very large in the image, which is a voluntary or involuntary technique of emphasising the greatness of the *Brahmin* poet who is presented as sitting before a very famous Hindu temple. Through such a representation of the *Brahmin* poet sitting in front of the temple, engaged in engraving scriptures, the *Brahmin* is presented in a divine light. Thus, this image makes use of two significant Hindu symbols that instil among its readers' inclination towards such a culture. Like this image, there are other images too in this comic that depict *Brahmin* characters reading or writing scriptures. Because for the pre-colonial Indian society depicted in *Chandamama*, liturgical knowledge was the highest form of knowledge, such portrayals of *Brahmins* dealing with scriptures is indicative of the comic's belief and interest in presenting them as the caste of people most suited for and experienced in dealing with "true knowledge." Thereby, they are presented as the true scholars, while according to such a discourse, people belonging to other castes are not as suitable and talented as the *Brahmin* to deal with the scriptures or "true knowledge."

Even though the glorification of upper-caste Hindus in several stories in *Chandamama* implicitly supports sanskritization as a means for upward mobility, through some stories in this comic, there is the implication it is never actually possible for a lower caste individual to ever become as perfectly sanskritized as an upper-caste individual, which is implied through some stories that present lower caste protagonists as foils to upper-caste protagonists in other stories.

LEGENDS OF INDIA

KRISHNA CAME TO THE POET'S RESCUE

In the shade of a tree, behind the great temple of Jagannath at Puri, sat a young Brahmin, engrossed in engraving his verses on a bunch of palm leaves. It was a quiet mid-day, with no sound heard excepting the roar of the sea which was not far and the cooing of a couple of cuckoos from the tree.

But, of course, there was another faint sound too—joining the cuckoos' song from time to time. That was the sweet voice of our poet Jayadeva. He was reciting his verses as he went on writing them.

With deep concentration he was writing about Krishna and Radha, about the great love that the two felt for each other. He was narrating an episode in which Krishna had to be shown trying to appease Radha who had grown a bit angry with him.

But the poet had faced a dilemma. He murmured, "O Krishna, my Lord! I know your great love for Radha. Even

Fig. 9.1

Source: "Legends of India: Krishna Came to the Poet's Rescue." *Chandamama*, June 1975, p. 39.

The story *The False Mendicant* (Chandamama 1974 pp. 59-61) is about a fake mendicant who is exposed by a clever man. The protagonist is a financially poor man named Dolu who acts as a mendicant and makes money by deceiving the highly superstitious people of a village called Andhapur. However, the fake mendicant is exposed by a clever man named Bolu, who had been considered as the village idiot. The villagers beat up Dolu and chase him away.

As described through many examples, in several stories in *Chandamama*, the protagonists are often *Brahmins* who are highly devout and pious. Some of them are wise mendicants and advisers to the king. In some of these stories, these *Brahmins* are even capable of superhuman feats through divine intervention that can be called superstitious. Moreover, these *Brahmins* are usually very good men: Apart from being devoted and dutiful towards the gods who grant them blessings, they are also very benevolent and helpful towards fellow human beings. However, if ever any stories talk about fake mendicants, then these frauds are never *Brahmins*, and the caste of the protagonist is not mentioned.

Thus, in the society represented in this comic, *Brahmins* are usually pious devotees who are mendicants, advisers and ministers to the king; *Kshatriyas* are chivalrous warriors who are kings, generals or soldiers, and the middle caste usually constitutes prosperous merchants who are often in good terms with the king and the aristocracy. Therefore, in such a society, when a man is not indicated as belonging to any caste, he probably belongs to a lower caste.

Thus, in *Chandamama*, people belonging to lower castes are sometimes presented as foils to upper caste people. Through the glorification of *Brahmin* mendicants and the representation of fake mendicants coming from lower caste backgrounds, *Chandamama* implicitly gives the idea that only *Brahmins* can become and serve as true mendicants. According to the narrative of *Chandamama*, this is because, by belonging to that caste, *Brahmins* are rightfully endowed with the right as well as the requisite talents to practice their occupations as *gurus*, ministers, advisors, mendicants and soothsayers, which indicates *Chandamama*'s implicit support for the caste system, and it instils such casteist beliefs and feelings among its young and thereby gullible readers.

In this comic, such casteism is implied and instilled more strongly by emphasising the goodness of upper caste people like *Brahmins* and *Kshatriyas*; by presenting both as acting for the welfare of the subjects, and by representing *Brahmins* as benevolent and *Kshatriyas* as noble. On the other hand, as with the case of Dolu, *The False Mendicant*, lower caste people are presented as self-centred, deceitful and greedy. This supports the caste hierarchy and implies that if upper caste people possess all the better qualities and *vice versa*, they should be rightfully appointed as the rulers and caretakers of such a society.

REFERENCES

Bhabha, Homi (1984). "Of Mimicry and Man: The Ambivalence of Colonial Discourse." *October*, vol. 28, pp. 125-133. *Jstor*, www.jstor.org/stable/778467.

Chandamama, "Godliness." June 1956, pp. 42-48.

Chandamama, "Legends of India: Krishna Came to the Poet's Rescue." June 1975, pp. 39-41.

Chandamama, "The False Mendicant." June 1974, pp. 59-61.

Dubashi, Jay (1990). "November 9 Will Change History." In: *Hindu Temples: What Happened to Them?*, Edited by Arun Shourie *et al.*, vol. 2, New Delhi: *Voice of India*, pp. 28-29.

Editor, Chandamama, 1955.

Goel, S.R., Shourie, A., Swarup, R., Narain, H., and Dubashi, J. (1990). *Hindu* Temples: What happened to them. vol. 1 and 2, New *Delhi: Voice of India.*

Goswami, Manu (2004). *Producing India: From Colonial Economy to National Space.* University of Chicago Press.

Gupta, Amita (2006). *Early Childhood Education, Postcolonial Theory, and Teaching Practices in India: Balancing Vygotsky and the Veda*. Palgrave Macmillan.

Jaffrelot, Christophe (1996). *The Hindu Nationalist Movement in India*. Columbia University Press.

Khanduri, Ritu G. (2010). "Comicology: Comic Books as Culture in India." *Journal of Graphic Novels and Comics,* vol. 1, no. 2, pp. 171–191, DOI:10.1080/21504857.2010.528641.

Kinnvall, Catarina (2006). *Globalisation and Religious Nationalism in India: The Search for Ontological Security*. Routledge, 2006.

Thapar, Romila (1998). "Tradition." In: *Between Tradition and Modernity: India's Search for Identity*, edited by Fred Dallmayr and G.N. Devy, SAGE Publications, pp. 265–277.

White, Hayden (1986). *Tropics of Discourse: Essays in Cultural Criticism*. Baltimore, Johns Hopkins University Press.

10

Religion in Cyberspace

An Ethnographic Study on *Theyyam* Ritual in Kerala

Anil Gopi and *Joly Puthussery*

Introduction: ICT and Ethnography

Social science researchers have started to look at digital technologies and internet-mediated communications (IMC) soon after their budding. The digital and cyber became a matter of serious scholarly enquiry for the social and cultural aspects associated with it and the novelty in it. In the field of anthropology, the early 1990s saw the beginning of researches on it. Escobar's (1994) contribution can be considered as one among the pioneering works through which anthropological enquiries stepped on-to cyberspace. The mutual interaction between humans and technology; computer and internet-based ones particularly is a matter of wide debate on various matters ranging from time, space, identity, reality and so on and the subject field of psychology has made a special deal with these. Sociality, knowledge, and language especially in the social and cultural life of humans is an essential part in the studies related to the new information and communication technologies (Kelty, 2010).

Morton (2001) argues that computer-mediated communication (CMC) with the technologies associated with it, like electronic mail, the internet, CD-ROMs has a profound influence on social interactions. It has an influence on the academic field also on teaching as well as in research. The author observes the challenges CMC poses on the various basic aspects of community, society, identity, authenticity and subjectivity. At this juncture, cyber-ethnography that exploits the scope of the same new technologies has advantages in dealing with the research. Here the text in the electronic medium acts as the field and the social group being studied scatters across the world (Morton, 2001: 5). Regarding the methodologies in this Morton finds two different groups of research based on the participation of the researcher, one from a distance and the second one is involved form. The first one does not require the direct interaction of the researcher (like for example content analysis, survey etc.) and in the second, the researcher directly interact with the informants by interviewing through chats or so (Morton, 2001: 6-7).

Cyber anthropology may be defined as the 'study of human in virtual communities and networked environment' (Stockl, 2003). That is whenever we engage with people in cyberspace in which the internet is the base with an objective of anthropological enquiry it can be considered as cyber anthropology. In the ethnographic venture what is happening is the engagement in a cyber 'field'. Notable early anthropologists encountered with the area are Turkle (1984), Benedikt (1991), Rheingold (1994) and especially Escobar (1994). In the ethnography part, one of the major dilemmas was on the 'participant observation' while being in cyberspace. The use of e-mails, online questionnaires and live chats that differs from 'participation' in terms of embodiment (Stockl, 2003) and such methods are considered have many advantages.

The involvement of the researcher with the informants often produced conflicting arguments regarding the physical presence in the field. The traditional ethnographic methods demand direct involvement to get the factual information and to understand the reality. In cyber ethnography too, the information can be factual and real based on the way the researcher interacts with the subjects and the specific medium one uses. Compared to the early days of internet-based communication technologies, contemporary times offers technologies that are so advanced that the researcher can avoid misleading and wrong information. The social networking sites and various social media (like Facebook, WhatsApp, Instagram, Telegram etc.) provide a 'field' in which an ethnographer finds information.

Focusing specifically on the social networking platform of Facebook which is the largest of this type with over a billion individuals present we can understand how an internet-mediated communication channel plays what roles in society. Randi Zuckerberg, an executive for Facebook Inc., explains how the platform was used to raise substantial monetary funds for the social causes, in political issues, campaigning, or even disaster management around the world (Zuckerberg, 2010). Researchers have tried to understand various social and cultural effects of such social media platforms (Buchner and Zaniewska, 2012; Wilson *et al.*, 2012, Billow,

2012). There are also researches conducted to understand the scope of cyber ethnography that gives a detailed idea about the whole deal.

Isomaki and Silvennoinen (2003) wrote an interesting essay on ethnographies to understand the research in the online setting. This work is significant for the reason that the comparative analysis unfolds sixteen different types approaches that include netnography, webnography, network ethnography, cyber-ethnography and digital ethnography. This typology is based on certain specific features embedded in it. The netnography is a six-phase process that involves both online and offline (Kozinets, 2010), similar is the case with connective ethnography [Dirksen, Huizing & Smit, 2010; Fields and Kafai (2008, 2009, 2010); Hine, 2007]. More interesting in the present essay is related to the digital ethnography that mainly deals with social media and social networking sites, for example, those works by Wesch (2009) and Murthy (2008). Closely related to digital ethnography is cyber ethnography which is again related to work with social networking and online communities. Based on the work of Rybas and Gajjala (2007), Isomäki and Silvennoinen (2003) say that cyber-ethnography is about the studies on the "production of identities in social networking sites and online communities through multifaceted social settings in the intersection of online and offline worlds in which ICT, for instance, the Internet is used." This method is considered to be the best in studying online communities with the advantages it has in using various techniques for data collection like the use of semi-structured interviews (Ward, 1999). Possibilities of being Multi-sited is another advantage in this type of ethnography because of the wider range of connectivity, the researcher can contact informants spread across the world (Marcus, 1995; Wittel, 2000). The main drawback related to the cyber or internet-mediated research is that of the connectivity between the researcher and the informant as it is determined by the digital electronic channel as well as the apparent attitude of the participants. It is from this stage we take the impetus to research the religious activities of people in South India. The participants of the ritual are huge both online and offline, and what becomes the reason for the special interest in studying the online participant is purely related to the salient features it shows. The diaspora from the North Malabar region is huge and the only way they can be in connection with the native religious practices is through online media and the people who stay in the area also get involved in the online mediated spaces with special interests in various aspects of the ritual and the belief system associated with it.

The ritual of *Kaliyattam* in North Malabar

The present study of the 'culture' centers around a highly performative ritual of *kaliyattam*. The ritual of *kaliyattam* is a very much localized form of religious worshipping which has a history dating back to several centuries. The archaic form of rituals that shares similarities with the present-day ritual is believed to have existed in the *Sangham* era in South India. The early colonial writers mention this ritual as a form of devil dance or animistic form of rituals. European traveller Barbosa in his account on Malabar discussed this ritual and it was one of the main oldest historical documents. Edgar Thurston (1909, p. 192) in his book on *Castes and Tribes of Southern India* while discussing the Malayan castes gives a detailed description of the ritual particularly focusing on *theyyam*, supplemented with photographs of the *theyyam* cults.

When academic research became prominent, especially in the post-Independence time, the ritual of *kaliyattam* became a focus of scholarly studies. Various subject specializations like history, sociology, anthropology, folklore etc., took up this religious activity because of the distinctive socio-cultural, political and economic significances in addition to the core religious importance.

The ritual of *kaliyattam* can have different definitions, like the dance of *Kaali* or play-dance (*Kaali*–the deity, *kali*–play, *aattam*–meaning dance) of which the latter is more common. Whatever may be the word meaning of it, a *kaliyattam* is a religious ceremony that is conducted in a festival manner. In the event, a series of rites are performed and the core ritual consists of the dance of the deity. The deity is called *theyyam*, which actually means god (derived from the root word *daivam* meaning god in the Malayalam language). In the event specialized performers put on a characteristic costume, accompanied by music, conduct a series of rites, recite songs and *mantra* and go into a trance. When this transition happens, the human performer becomes divine and people worship him as god or goddess according to the deity under propitiation at that rite. The god turned man performs fast dance and after finishing it starts blessing the devotees. The worshippers approach the *theyyam*, talk to him, and explain their worries and problems. The *theyyam* then consoles the devotee, often holding their hands and gives a reply to their queries and finally blesses them by touching their head.

Definitions are given by scholars who studied *theyyam,* form various dimensions which can be taken into consideration for a brief understanding of what it is. One folklorist Payyanad (2001:11) defines that "*Teyyam is the total of the belief system, the mythology and religious factors regarding the local Gods and Goddesses. There are more than 300 Gods/ Goddesses with their own mythologies that each one narrates how a particular deity is originated, journey from place to place and how the deity got the right to have ritual performances in different shrines... mythology as well as a belief system are latent in the minds of the people which are expressed through the ritual performances of the local God/Goddess.*" According to Tarabout (2005:187) *theyyam* is a ritual. According to the author "*Teyyam ('deity') is a village, family or caste cult celebrating localized deities. It is also called teyyattam ('dance of the deity') or kaliyattam ('play-dance'), as well as other names. As part of the ceremonies, the God or Goddess is incorporated temporarily in a male specialist who is said to be possessed and who speaks as the deity itself.*"

Wayne (1979:100) following his theatre-based research orientation discusses *theyyam* with regard to the folk performance element of it. According to Ashley, *theyyam* which is also known by names like *teyyattam, tereyattam*, is a "*colloquial expression which means gods and generally refers to numerous spirits, ancient heroes, ancestors and various Puranic deities.*" He also observes that by *theyyam kettu*, the people mean 'to prepare the god' which is what actually happens at the event. Apart from these in most of the studies on *theyyam* and *kaliyattam* scholars have given individual observations on it often focusing on aspects that are of special attention to them (Freeman, 1991; Koga, 2003; Dinesan, 2010; Wayne, 1979).

The ritual of *kaliyattam* and *theyyam* can be considered as a symbolic representation of almost every aspect of the social life of the people of North Malabar. For every individual *theyyam* there are myths and stories associated with it and it narrates life and incidents of people. In the *theyyam* pantheon, there are different types of deities as earlier mentioned like spirits, mythical characters related to mainstream Hindu deities, animals, dead ancestors and so on. Of all these different types of deified humans after their tragic and untimely death are most significant concerning to the social system of the region. Such myths narrate incidents like the death of warrior heroes in a feud, the assassination of women and lower caste men for reasons of acquiring knowledge and challenging patriarchy, caste conflict etc. A common theme is that all these dead individuals rising to the level of gods and goddesses, take avenge on their enemies and protect common people.

The portrayal of the prevailing caste system and related injustices and inhuman acts perpetrated, patriarchy and evil acts of politically, economically and religiously powerful section in society can be noted in performing these rituals. In a way, during the performance of the *theyyam*, especially in the first part of the event which is known as *thottam* or *vellattam,* the complete story is narrated and demonstrated before the audience. This is a re-construction of the past social life through which the older generation passed. Damodaran (2008) had studied this aspect and he observes that *theyyam* is a tool for reconstructing the history of the people of North Malabar. He is emphasizing the differentiation in roles and statuses of the castes and communities who take part in the ritual and portrays the hierarchy existing in socio-religious terms in this ritual event. Similarly, Menon (1993) also studied the aspects of the caste system in this ritual. Katheleen Gough (1958) in her studies on ancestor spirits and rituals also discussed *theyyam*, especially those related to the Nayar caste.

Irrespective of the intense religiosity and the socio-political aspects embedded in this ritual *theyyam* are celebrated as a festival in a village elaborately. Just like the different types of *theyyam* in the pantheon, there are different types of shrines too where the deities are being worshipped. Based on the caste that owns a shrine and the main deity under worship, shrines are known by names like *ara, kottam, podikkalam, thara, kalari, kazhakam, muchilodu, madappura*, to name a few. While these are the specific names, generally a *theyyam* shrine is known as a *kaavu*. A *kaavu* is a small forest with thick vegetation and is considered a sacred grove. The presence of trees like banyan, peepal, *paala, kanjiram*, etc., which have special religious significance to the people is often central to these sacred places. The sacred groves as the main worship place of the *theyyam*, which is mostly animistic in original form can be associated with nature worship. In the present days, most of the traditional sacred groves of *kaavu* are disappearing and people are converting such shrines, which was actually a part of nature into well built concrete constructions of modern Hindu temple complex.

Based on the ownership of the shrines they can be classified into three main types. Family shrine, which is situated in the courtyard of traditional lineage households of *tharavadu* is the first type. In such shrine, the respective families worship their ancestors and specific family gods and goddesses. The propitiation rituals and festivals are a matter of concern to respective family only. The second type, which is considered a community shrine belong to a particular caste people in a village. The *Muchilodu* of Vaniya caste, *Kannangadu* of Maniyani, *Kalari* of Thiyya, *Kottam* of Pulaya etc., are examples for such shrines. In a third type, a shrine may be owned and operated by the public, that is by the villagers irrespective of caste.

The festivals in these shrines are considered as festivals of the whole village if not the neighbouring community. If the event is large with extensive celebration and festivities entire village becomes a part of it by contributing whatever one could cater. The *kaliyattam* event specifically involves conducting a series of rites and the propitiation of the *theyyam* and performing the dance of the *theyyam* being the main one. In a *kaliyattam* different castes have to play specific roles according to custom. Irrespective of the caste of the owners of the shrine, the performers always come from Vannan, Malayan, Pulayan, Anjoottan, Munnoottan, Velan, Koppalan etc. All these castes were considered untouchables in the past and in the present day they belong to the Scheduled Caste category. Other caste people play roles related to their traditional caste-based occupation, for example, Thiyya gives country liquor of toddy, Vaniyan gives oil, Artisan communities (Viswakarma or *Nankuvarna*) serve metal works, carpentry and so on. The communities who were higher in the social strata like Nayar and members of the ruling families act as the patron of the event. In the olden days, in the chiefly agriculturally based economy, the land belonged to the higher caste people and lower caste people were serving them. This hierarchy and power relations are maintained in the religious sphere too. Whatever may be the social realities behind the whole religious practice in the present day *kaliyattam* is celebrated as a religious festival of all the people. The people of North Malabar consider *theyyam* as a special cultural element indigenous and native to themselves.

Cultural Production through *Theyyam*

The context that drew attention was the changes that occured in the way people approach *theyyam* in recent times. This happened mainly with the advancements in digital technologies, like that of photography, and the Internet. Social networking sites (SNS) played a prime role in this. Dinesan (2014) in his studies has noted how the people started to incorporate their religion into cyberspace too. He was focusing on one of the first such platforms which gained popularity, the Orkut and later Facebook. The people were highly receptive to these communication platforms to share information regarding their belief system. The digital photography and spread of cameras incorporated mobile phones and later smartphones acted as the major source for information in cyberspace. The popularity of digital cameras can be considered as a second stage or even a completely new phenomenon that intensified the process of digitization of this religious event. The number of young men who purchased digital cameras of varying levels (amateur entry-level to professional) exploded in a short period. This group consists of professional photographers and enthusiasts who are attracted to the spectacular visuality of the performing ritual. The photographs they take are uploaded to the internet and shared via social networking sites. These photographers were able to organize and form special interest groups and occasionally conducted gatherings. Exhibitions of *theyyam* photographs by these people during the festival times at shrines became a new event.

People started to use cyberspace, websites, social media sites, blogs, video-sharing platforms in recent years. The number of dedicated social media public groups, and chat groups are countless in the present times. Most of these groups were named after *theyyam* and its associated concepts. Apart from the groups created by the public, the shrines also started pages to deal with their information. The administers of shrines were able to start pages on Facebook and WhatsApp and also economically sound shrine management started websites too. In such a context, it was no surprise when some shrines created dedicated mobile phone applications to deal with their information during the time of grand scale *kaliyattam* festivals. Interestingly when the new media appeared it democratized and opened up the possibilities for many people to get connected, comment and participate in the discourse on *theyyam*. This explosion in communication and interactivity along with the growth of visual literacy and greed for visuality started affecting and converting the complex phenomena of *theyyam*. Within the parlance of visual communication with the focus of *theyyam* phenomena as reflected in the new media context, the present chapter tries to analyze how cultural communication triggered with anthropological spirit gave rise to imagined communities to participant social activists to politico-religious revivalists. The discourse has grown and expanded the scope for the study of the anthropology of communication in the digital era.

It is at this juncture an anthropological venture is attempted to understand the entire religious phenomena and ICT. In short, the chapter tries to see how new media and cyberspace can be used in analyzing discourses on cultural communications with a focus on *theyyam* cosmos.

Methodology

In both data collection and analysis, novel methodologies and techniques are adapted apart from the conventional ones. Documenting information from the online platform requires non-conventional techniques. While following the discussions, the text is copied and saved for further reading and analysis. Participating in online discussions is done by posing questions that are aimed at all the group members. Whenever needed specific questions are asked to a particular informant to know the details or specific comment. The question-answer method in social media groups forms a group discussion of conventional type. One advantage of this method is that if the number of discussants is large, the researcher can collect comments and opinions in a well-focused manner. Depending on the necessity, each of the informants can be contacted directly in person or through the internet to probe into the matter of concern. With this mode of data collection, it can be also considered as a kind of multi-cited ethnography.

Data collection of the conventional methods in ethnography is also adopted in the present study. Extensive fieldwork is carried out to learn the whole religious complex associated with *theyyam* and the *kaliyattam* ritual. Interviews, group discussions, participant as well as non-participant observations are used to get first-hand information about the subject under study. Being a highly performative religious festival visual documentation is a core method of data collection. Documentation is made through photography and videography, more importance is given to the first. It was photography that became a matter of particular attention because of its special place in the internet-based communication among online communities.

In the first two case studies, the researcher was present at the scene in person. It also included photographing the activities and making sense of the discussions that followed it. In the third case, the original photographs and video are contributed by a key informant. What is special about these two different approaches is the role of the researcher as participant and observer. It is found that the methods and techniques so far discussed were very fruitful in the studies of those aspects of culture which have a greater 'visual element'. A second speciality and advantages are the quantity of data a researcher can collect in a short period which is also economical and efficient. Any chance of false information and unreliability can be avoided by communicating the informant directly out of the group.

Case one: "The *Gulikan theyyam* and the passenger bus"

The incident that became the starting point of a discussion in social media occurred during the ritual of the deity *Gulikan theyyam*. This *theyyam* is believed as a demonic spirit (*bhoota*) of Shiva and is a widely worshipped cult. Performed as a very funny character this *theyyam* often makes several acts to entertain the audience, like playing with fire, climbing trees, chasing children, and doing whatever act based on the circumstance in which the ritual is taking place.

The shrine where the particular ritual performance took place was close to a road and the *theyyam* was on its display of playful mood running around and entertaining people who gathered there. During this, a noticeable incident happened. A bus came by this road and suddenly the *theyyam* stood in front of the bus, stopping it. For a while the *theyyam* started teasing the passengers in the bus and then lay in front of the bus on the road, blocking the bus from passing. The *theyyam* making acts which are very common in the demonstration of the character of the cult. The researcher photographed this incident which clearly shows like the *theyyam* blocking a bus. This photograph was later uploaded in a social media group that is dedicated to *theyyam* related matters, all the members being enthusiasts of the ritual. Several people noticed this photograph for the odd acts of the *theyyam*. Usually such acts of the *theyyam Gulikan* are taken as very silly and natural by those who are familiar with this *theyyam* and its mocking and entertaining behaviour.

Fig. 10.1: *Gulikan theyyam* confronting a passenger bus.

This photograph later was shared with several other social media groups, which are hundreds in numbers. After a couple of months, another incident took place. The particular bus which was blocked by the *theyyam* met with an accident and fell in a paddy field. Again, a photograph of this the accident was also uploaded into the social media space and once one individual noticed this. He suddenly compared the incident of the bus accident with that of the *theyyam* blocking the bus. This person, supposedly a firm believer of the *theyyam* interpreted the accident was a punishment or curse of the god as the bus (or the driver in turn) played against the god. That is, though in reality, it was the *Gulikan theyyam* that blocked the bus during a funny act of entertainment, but this particular devotee interpreted that it was the bus that made the problem. This particular observation and comment spread across and became an example of the malevolent nature of the god, which in turn increased the fear and devotion over the *theyyam*.

In this case, the ethnographic data collected by the researcher was primarily based on the cyber channels. Also, this case can be taken as an example for a mode of engagement of the researcher with cyberspace in an experimental basis by citing an activity to the respondents to understand the social dynamics of the study group. Here on this particular occasion, the religious belief and its propagation through people are traced via the online platform.

Case two: The second incident is about the influence of a photograph posted in social media that revived a traditional *theyyam* shrine of *kaavu* which was in a complete ruined state and under utter neglect. Once, a member of a social media group (Theyyakkazhchakal, a WhatsApp group) while passing through a village noticed a small shine on a river bank, covered and surrounded by wild bushes. The shrine was about fifty-meter away from the tarmac road and the area is less populated and largely covered by agriculture fields. This person took a photograph of the shrine, which conveys a clear picture of the ruined state of the shrine and the beautiful and scenic place where it is situated.

After a short enquiry on the shrine with the villagers, he identified that it is a shrine named Aryakkara Kottam, after the main goddess. The photographer shared the image in the social media group with a short description. He came to know that this was the shrine of a Pulaya family named Maadan. About five to six decades ago this was an active shrine with yearly *kaliyattam* ritual and a series of incidents happened with the owning family that pushed the shrine to ruin. The Maadan was a large family that lived in the area associated with agriculture activities. When agriculture and farming declined, the people lost jobs and started to move into nearby places. Later, no one remained in this village to take care of the shrine and to conduct the expensive *kaliyattam* rituals. This is what led to the current state of the shrine.

Fig. 10.2: Aryakkara Kottam on the day when discussion on revival took place

The particular internet community with which the image and information were shared consisted of people of various backgrounds, like *theyyam* performers, researchers, enthusiasts, photographers etc. The striking image and the description caught attention very fast and the members decided to revive the shrine. More enquiries were made by several members by directly contacting the Maadan family members and the villagers and started to revive and rebuild the shrine.

A monetary fund-raising campaign started and they were able to raise a considerable sum of money, around seven hundred thousand rupees in a short period. This particular social media group has a considerable number of members who hail from Kannur and work in Middle East countries who are economically sound and they engaged with any matters related to *theyyam* with great enthusiasm and interest. This diasporic community was a major factor in this revival initiative. Later, the internet community was able to arrange a meeting with the Maadan family members and villagers at the premises of the shrine. They also organized a programme to overcome the traditional astrological problem for restarting the worship and the rituals.

In the identification of the astrological problem, it was found that there is the presence of about a dozen of different deities in the shrine and a proper propitiation is required to be organized after rebuilding the shrine. The reconstruction of the shrine was a laborious task that required acquiring sufficient land from the surrounding landowners who were demanding a huge sum of money. All the initiatives were spearheaded by the social media group of *theyyam* enthusiasts, most of them except a handful not belonging to the village where the shrine is situated. There are certain factors that are socially relevant here. The shrine owning family belongs to the Pulaya community and it is one of the most downtrodden ones among all *theyyam* performers and worshippers and they were considered untouchables in the past. Even in the present days, caste discrimination is still present within the *theyyam* religious sphere. It is in this context, an internet-based cyber community that has members of various social and economic statuses come together to help and revive the religious practices of the community with all its originality. When once the shrine was mentioned as a '*kshetram*' during the discussion it drew strong criticism from the majority as naming the shrine as *kshetram* has the notion of installing the Vedic type religious system of mainstream Hinduism. Critics commented that such a name change would destroy the real identity of the shrine, which is a *kottam*, a specific Pulaya community *theyyam* worshipping shrine. At present, the works are afoot at a good pace to achieve the goal.

Case Three: The *theyyam* in non-religious space

The use of the *theyyam* cults in non-religious and non-ritual spaces is always a matter of heated debate in North Malabar. Originally associated with the rituals of religious worshipping, the *theyyam* started to appear on other occasions too in the last four or five decades. It started with the display of a *theyyam* by an eminent *theyyam* ritual specialist in its full costume in the Republic Day parade in New Delhi in the late 1970s. The cult was intended in representing the culture of Kerala as an icon. Later, a greater number of such incidents started to be seen within North Malabar and also in other parts. The *theyyam*, with its spectacular outlook and distinctive features, became synonymous with North Malabar and particularly to the Kannur district.

The growth of the tourism industry suddenly embraced *theyyam* as a symbol of Kannur and became an essential part of the publicity campaigns and advertisements. Apart from this, *theyyam* as a symbol started to be used in various cultural programmes, rallies of political parties, and also it became an interesting subject for creative works like drama, literature and so on. Among all the different non-religious contexts tourism industry has been the major one and the present discussion focuses on such an incident. One tourism festival was conducted in Kannur with the support of a government organization in 2017. In the festival where several foreign tourists were also invited, one man in complete *theyyam* costume (*kolam*) was

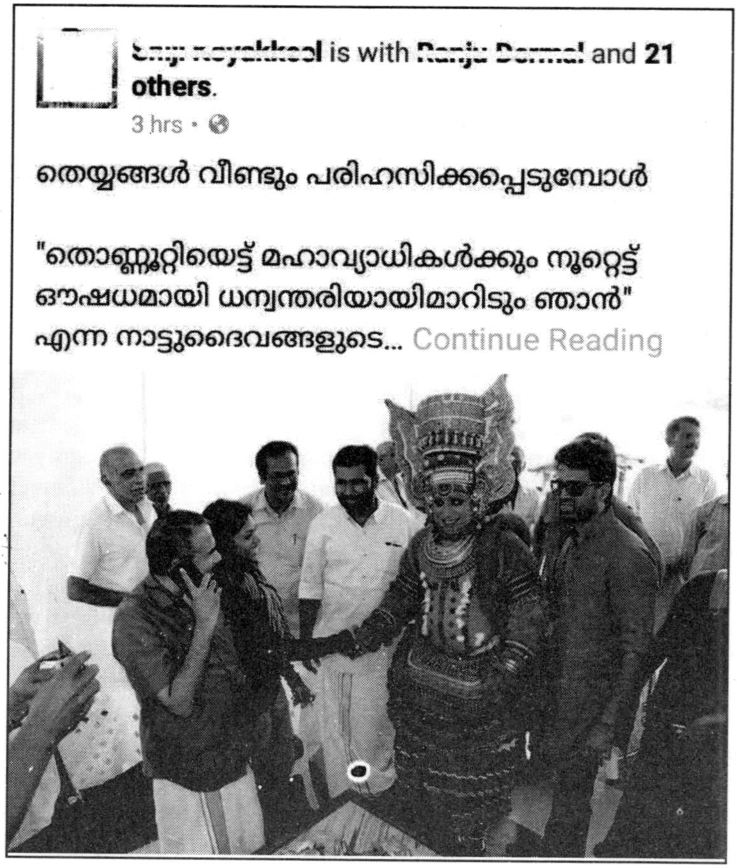

Fig. 10.2: A screengrab of the social media post on the tourism event.

arranged to welcome the guests. No rituals were happening and it was just the form of the *theyyam* being used here. This incident was an occasion for the people who are aware of *theyyam* to think loudly on the significance, use and misuse of the ritual cult and the artistic elements in it.

One participant who is a strong believer of the *theyyam* god took photographs and videos of this incident, the 'god' welcoming guests to a public function and shared in the social media with a critical comment and this led to a serious discussion. The discussions dealt with various aspects of *theyyam*, *kaliyattam*, belief, involvement of political parties and non-religious organizations of governmental as well as non-governmental bodies. The person who shared this was expressing his concern over such an incident including the necessity of rethinking the whole concept of the social relevance of *theyyam* and for the preservation of its originality. He said, 'for some people *theyyam* is an art and for some others, it is a ritual and posed questions on this and clearly expressed his refutation in considering *theyyam* exclusively as art by neglecting its religious values.

According to the informant, it is the responsibility of everyone to preserve *theyyam* in its purity which is handed over to them by their forefathers. For the people of North Malabar, *theyyam* is a ritual that balanced social inequalities from the time of its emergence because in the olden times there was a strong social hierarchy and injustice prevalent in the society as regards to caste. Earlier, *kaliyattam* was an occasion when higher caste people came before the lower caste people who become gods in the ritual. Over the time, the ritual achieved the current status and state. Though one could not say that caste discrimination is completely absent in the present day there is a huge change in it compared to the olden days.

The informant observes that there is no system of worshipping that stands so close to the heart of the devotees which is comparable to *theyyam*. The forefathers had made the worship and shrines well integrated in a way that resonate with the ecology and environment. But what contemporary society doing to it is non-justifiable. The people are making *theyyam* as clown and display them before some random audience by calling it the symbol of culture. He angrily asks what tourism development is planning to introduce by doing such mockery? What we must have done is to invite the enthusiasts or tourists in traditional Keralite way and took them to the shrine where the ritual events are taking place in real life and inform them about it instead of displaying some performers at random *theyyam* costume on stage.

Organizers of the event argue that the *theyyam* performers are living a life in poverty and a performance on the stage will fetch them a good sum of money. But the informant says that it is only to satisfy the ego of the organizers they conduct such events. He appeals to the ritual specialists who perform *theyyam* in places other than religious space that they should think about the place where they have in the minds of devotees. *Theyyam* are in the hands of the performers and the ancestors have given the *theyyam* in the right hand and never forget about that. On the contrary, one group argues that earlier also men performed *theyyam* in non-ritual occasions and questions what is wrong in the present incident?. Whenever one did such an act it is a fault only and an exception is there if they did not make the performance into a commodity. If people are looking at *theyyam* as a way of making money in the tourism industry, one should take care of *theyyam* from not going beyond the religious places and if it does so *theyyam* will also have a fate like *Kathakali* (though it is not a ritual) that completely got modified into an entirely new form for the entertainment of tourists. The heated debate goes like this.

Conclusion

The study reveals that the factors contributing and playing important role to dynamics of the ritual in cyberspace and its consequences are so vast that it would be possible to make any meaningful generalizations. Nevertheless, there are several specific features that required more attention to show particular characteristics solely related to 'cyber'. The dynamics of *theyyam* and the connoisseur of it becomes a specific reason behind the whole engagement of people across Northern Malabar. The whole *theyyam* ritual is so dynamic with theatrical and entertainment elements which also offers a spectacular by colourful show before an audience. The digitization of these shows is made by enthusiasts who are connected to cyberspace through their pages as well as through their membership in groups. The increased access to the internet makes their participation extensive. Cyberspace then nullifies the dimensions of space and time by connecting people across the world at any point in time.

The democratization of space is also significant. The participants receive an equal opportunity to engage with the discussions and sharing of information here. In this regard, one of the most important features to be mentioned relates to the social system associated with the ritual. Being a highly caste specialized event that stratifies people into hierarchically differentiated strata with varying degrees of status in the actual ritual practice and space in the online space no such differences prevail. Cyberspace can mask the caste identity which otherwise plays a significant role in real time and space.

Special focus given to three cases reveals those aspects which are associated with it. Regarding the first case, it provides an understanding of how rumours are metaphors in religious beliefs and how they multiply even in cyberspace. People can interpret and misinterpret facts based on occasions and this in a way contributes to the belief in their god and goddesses. It is almost like the creation of new myths, legends and folktales. The second case reveals how nostalgia and affection towards one's own culture help forming a group that takes special initiatives to make a real contribution to 'do something' for the religious-cultural system. The third case is related to the idea that how people handle a religious practice and belief to preserve the authenticity. Or in another way, it portrays how the people being skeptical about the new technologies which potentially destroy the sanctity of a sacred religious system. This concern is connected to the urge of the highly profit-driven mind of one section of the people to make a business out of sacred culture of one's own.

REFERENCES

Benedikt, M. (1991). *Cyberspace: First Steps*. Cambridge, Mass: MI.

Billow, *R.* (2012). "Facebook as 'Social Fact'." Group, *36*(3), 213-222.

Buchner, A., and Zaniewska, K. (2012). "Facebook as a Catalyst for Beneficial Participation in Culture." *Polish Sociological Review*, 177, 107-116.

Damodaran, M.P. (2008). "Teyyam is the Best Tool for Reconstructing the History of North Malabar." *Anthropologist* 10, No. 4, 283-287.

Dinesan Vadakkiniyil (2010). "Images of Transgression: Teyyam in Malabar, Social Analysis." *The International Journal of Social and Cultural Practice*, Vol. 54, No. 2, 130-150.

Dinesan Vadakkiniyil (2014). *Anushtanam Kalam Samooham, Kottayam:* Sahithya Pravarthaka Co-operative Society Ltd.

Dirksen, V., Huizing, A., and Smit, B. (2010). "Piling on layers of understanding: the use of connective ethnography for the study of (online) work practices." *New Media and Society*, *12*(7), 1045-63.

Escobar, Arturo *et al.* (1994). *"Welcome to Cyberia: Notes on the Anthropology of Cyberculture* [and Comments and Reply]." *Current Anthropology*, 35, 211-231.

Fields, D. and Kafai, Y. (2008). "Knowing and Throwing Mudballs, Hearts, Pies, and Flowers: A Connective Ethnography of Gaming Practices." In: V. Jonker *et al.* (Eds.), *8th international conference on International conference for the learning sciences*. Utrecht, Netherlands: University of Utrecht.

Fields, D. and Kafai, Y. (2009). "A connective ethnography of peer knowledge sharing and diffusion in a tween virtual world." *Computer-Supported Learning*, *4*(1), 47-68.

Fields, D. and Kafai, Y. (2010). "Knowing and throwing mudballs, hearts, pies, and flowers: A connective ethnography of gaming practices", *Games and Culture*, (Special Issue), *5*(1), pp. 88-115.

Freeman, J.R. (1991). Purity and violence: Sacred power in the Teyyam worship of Malabar. PhD Dissertation, University of Pennsylvania.

Gough, Katheleen (1958). "Cults of the Dead among the Nayar". *Journal of American Folklore*, *71*(281), pp. 446-78.

Hine, C. (2007). "Connective Ethnography for the Exploration of e-Science", *Journal of Computer-Mediated Communication*, *12*(2), Article 14.

Isomäki, H. and Silvennoinen, J. (2003). "Online Ethnographies." In: Isaias, P. and Miguel Babtista Nunes (Eds.) *Information Systems Research and Exploring*

Social Artifacts: Approaches and Methodologies, Edition: 1st, Hershey: IGI Global. pp. 124-141.

Kelty, C. (2010). "Introduction: Culture in, Culture Out", *Anthropological Quarterly*, *83*(1), 7-16.

Koga, M. (2003) "The Politics of Ritual and Art in Kerala: Controversies Concerning the Staging of Teyyam." *Journal of the Japanese Association for South Asian Studies*, No.15, 54-79.

Kozinets, R.V. (2010). *Netnography–Doing Ethnographic Research Online.* London: Sage.

Marcus, G.E. (1995). "Ethnography in/of the World System: The Emergence of Multi-Sited Ethnography", *Annual Review of Anthropology*, 24, 95-117.

Menon, M.D. (1993). "The moral community of the theyyattam: Popular culture in late colonial Malabar", *Studies in History*, *9*(2), 209-217.

Morton, H. (2001). "Computer-Mediated Communication in Australian Anthropology and Sociology: Social Analysis, *The International Journal of Social and Cultural Practice*, *45*(1), 3-11.

Murthy, D. (2008). "Digital Ethnography: An Examination of the Use of New Technologies for Social Research", *Sociology*, *42*(5), 837-855.

Payyanad, R. (2001). "Teyyam and our times", *Indian Folklife 1*(1), 11-12.

Rheingold, H. 1994. *The Virtual Community: Finding Connection in a Computerized World*. London: Minerva.

Rybas, N. and Gajjala, R. (2007). "Developing Cyberethnographic Research Methods for Understanding Digitally Mediated Identities", *Forum: Qualitative Social Research*, *8*(3), Article 35, 1-33.

Stöckl, A. (2003). "The Internet, Cyberspace, and Anthropology", *Cambridge Anthropology, 23*(3), 67-78.

Tarabout, G. 2005. "Malabar gods, nation-building and world culture: On perceptions of the local and the global", In: Assayag, J. & Fuller, C.J. (eds.) *Globalizing India: Perspectives from Below*. London: Anthem Press. pp. 186-209.

Thurston, E. and Rangachari, K. (1990). *Castes and Tribes of So*uthern India. Madras Government Press, p. 192.

Turkle, S. (1984). *The Second Self.* New York: Simon and Schuster.

Ward, K.J. (1999). "The Cyber-Ethnographic (Re) Construction of Two Feminist Online Communities", *Sociological Research Online*, *4*(1). pp. 51-64.

Wayne, Ashley (1979). "The Theyyam Kettu of Northern Kerala", *The Drama Review*: TDR. *23*(2), 99-112.

Wesch, M. (2009). "YouTube and You–Experiences of Self-Awareness in the Context Collapse of the Recording Webcam." *Explorations in Media Technology*, 19-34.

Wilson, R., Gosling, S., & Graham, L. (2012). "A Review of Facebook Research in the Social Sciences", *Perspectives on Psychological Science, 7*(3), 203-2[illegible]

Wittel, A. (2000). "Ethnography on the Move: From Field to Internet", *Forum: Qualitative Social Research*, *1*(1), Article 21.

Zuckerberg, R. (2010). "Accidental Activists: Using Facebook to Drive Change", *Journal of International Affairs, 64*(1), 177-180.

11
Migrant Community, Communicative Performance and Production of Space

Ratan Naga Deepika

By foregrounding Henri Lefebvre's (1991) *The Production of Space* this chapter seeks to argue that there are possibilities of resistance and negotiation between the 'dominant' conceived and 'dominated' lived spaces. Though not as revolutionary as the idea of 'differential space' imagined by Lefebvre, the contestation between the conceived and lived spaces is manifested in the form of cultural performativity of a subaltern migrant community. Here, the term 'performativity' is used to denote the construction and sustenance of identity by a migrant community through various cultural acts which are performative in nature. By analyzing and discussing the annual chariot festival, this chapter proposes that a community festival can be considered as a "communicative performance" (Kuutma, 1998) of the community by which it tries to communicate with the larger public and to itself and in the process 'produces' space.

This work should be seen in a wider context of the internal migration and rapid urbanization happening in India, largely triggered by the neo-liberal economic policies of the government. India has 25 of the 100 fastest-growing cities in the world and a significant source of this growth is rural-urban migration. This has led to a crisis in the cities and 'space', and latter is at the center of this crisis particularly in the context of migrants.

This study is part of my ongoing doctoral research project on industrial working class Odiya (people from Odisha, south-eastern state of India) migrant community in Katedan, an Industrial area (IDA) on the outskirts of Hyderabad, the capital city of Telangana, India. This community celebrates *Rath Yatra*, the annual chariot festival which is a local chapter of the original chariot festival of Puri, pilgrim city of Odisha.

Introducing the Field

Located in the Rajendra Nagar Mandal of Rangareddy district, Katedan Industrial Area was developed by APIIC in 1983. Spanning across 110 hectares the industrial area mainly houses small and medium enterprises producing various products like biscuits, oil, carton boxes, rubber, polymers etc., but chiefly plastic products. Talking about the demographics, it has a mixed population constituting both intra- and inter-state migrants. However, migrants from Odisha, Bihar and Uttar Pradesh are dominant in terms of numbers and certain pockets are geographically marked as belonging to particular state migrants.

Introducing the Odiya Migrant Community

As claimed by the community elders, Odiya migrants were one of the early migrant workers coming to the Katedan Industrial Area. Most of these migrants are from three districts: Bhadrak, Balasore and Ganjam. So it can be assumed that migration in this context is via kin relations. People who migrated in the late 1990s and early 2000s are more settled and own small factories but their number is very less. There are few other migrant workers who after finding financial opportunities bring the women from their families to either work in factories or run small grocery stores. There are also single male migrant workers who reside in the rooms provided by the factory owner within the compound walls of the factory. The more settled migrants have formed an organization called Jai Jagannath Odiya Society with an agenda to conduct *Rath Yatra*. However, over the years it has become a representative body that negotiates, arranges compensations for wounded or dead Odiya workers, builds tie-ups with local politicians and actively engages in community building.

Understanding Space

One of the few influential thinkers who conceptualized space as something beyond the 3D understanding of its physical aspect is Henri Lefebvre. Till then the concept of space was confined to the field of geography. His work on space has influenced the urban theory and resulted in the ideation of concepts such as spatial justice, right to the city, third space etc.

For my analysis, I would like to use his theory of space, particularly the lived space which I would be explaining in a short while. My understanding of Henri Lefebvre's space is informed by Kanishka

Goonewardena's et.al's book 'Space, Difference and Everyday Life'. According to this book, Lefebvre opined that space is a product and thus it cannot exist in itself but be produced (Goonewardena, Kipfer, Milgrom, & Schmid, 2008, p. 28). And since he says it is a social product, space is to be understood as an intricate web of relationships that is continuously produced and reproduced (Goonewardena, Kipfer, Milgrom, & Schmid, 2008, p. 41).

As to the question of how is this space produced he put forward a two-fold approach. One is based on the phenomenological notion and the other has a semiotic base. Using these approaches, he said three interconnected processes go into the making of space.

Phenomenological Approach

My interest lies in the phenomenological approach and the three processes which are explained by this approach are perceived, conceived and lived. Perceived space is the space that can be grasped by the senses. This is the physical aspect of the space.

The second one is the conceived space, the space created first in mind and then communicated through some visual element.

And the third one is the lived space which is created by human experience and expressed symbolically. It is this space where I am placing my analysis of a community festival. So I discuss the festival both as a lived space and a way of producing lived space.

Resistance and Negotiation

Henri Lefebvre being a Marxist philosopher argued that the conceived space which is the space produced by architects and city planners is the dominant space and the lived space which is created by experience is the dominated space. Lefebvre was very much aware of the power relations implicit in the polarising characterisation of conceived and lived spaces and hence proposed a utopian idea of differential space, where the lived space overpowers the conceived space through a revolution. However, I would like to argue that processes of resistance and negotiation are continuous and these contestations get manifested in subtle forms like the cultural performativity of a working-class migrant community.

Cultural Performativity

Here I am using the term performativity to denote the construction and sustenance of identity by a migrant/ethnic community through various cultural acts which are performative in nature. The most important of these acts is the annual *Rath Yatra* festival which falls in June or July.

Rath Yatra though has various connotations, I am using it concerning to the annual chariot festival which is celebrated in Puri where the deities Lord Jagannath, Balabhadra and Subhadra are taken out in procession. This procession reaches the Gundicha maa temple where for the next nine days, deities are placed and worshipped. On the 10th day, these deities are brought back to their main abode.

This same *Yatra* is enacted in Katedan by the Odiya community which has a Jai Jagannath Odiya society exclusively formed to serve this purpose. However, over a period of time, society has taken up other roles too.

Based on the interviews, the *Rath Yatra* of Katedan was started in 2003 a year after the construction of Jagannath temple on the old Mumbai highway. Like in Puri, it is a ten-day festival including 2 processions, evening *bhajans* and *keertans*, daily *anndaans*—morning and evening and *havans*. The procession like in Puri starts from the Jagannath temple in Katedan and ends at Gundicha maa temple in Laxmiguda housing board colony where the Odiya population is very high. Though the Jagannath temple was constructed in 2002, the Gundicha maa temple was constructed in 2015 owing to the unavailability of land and funds. Later due to local political leaders' interventions, the temple was finally constructed. Now they have plans to construct a bigger temple for Jagannath since the present one is smaller than the Gundicha temple which shouldn't be the case as per the Puri temple topography.

Rath Yatra through Pictures

Pic. 1: is the *Rath* and the procession. As you can see, it is a single *Rath* unlike in Puri where there are three, one for each deity. But due to space and funds limitations, only one *Rath* is used. The *Rath* construction is done on the same day and by evening the procession starts. The *Rath* is built every year anew like in Puri. The procession takes nearly six hours to reach Gundicha maa temple which is 3 kms from the Jagannath temple. There is police *bandobast* and traffic diversion during the procession

2: is the core committee members of the society wear t-shirts designed exclusively for the procession which make them stand out in the community

3: is *anndaan*: the first day they claim nearly 2000 people eat and on other 9 days nearly 700 people eat during *anndaans*. The money for the festival is raised from local donations, political leaders and individual contributions of society members.

4: is the *bhajans*: this is the first day of the festival. From the early morning, the *bhajans* start and as people keep thronging to the temple the music group increases in size. Children are made to sit and listen to the *bhajans*.

5: is the traditional music group brought from Odisha specifically for the festival. The playing of *mardaa*, the drum and the *manjeera* stand out. However, there is a local brass band and a DJ placed on the trolley playing film songs.

6: is the idols are carried on the heads of the devotees on the way to the chariot. There are dancing and singing and high pitched slogans of Jai Jagannath during this process.

7: is the corporator, Srinivas Reddy being felicitated by the society members. The corporator is invited for every event of the community and personal events of the society members. Not just the corporator, the local MLA also attend the festival. During the procession, the chariot was stopped in the middle of a street to allow the MLA to perform *puja*.

The one in the *pagdi* is the president and he serves as the ceremonial raja of the procession. Not only does he direct the procession but also performs the '*chera phera*' ritual that is sweeping the road and around the chariot before the start of the procession.

8: is the brass band, the glittering lights and the twinkling umbrellas all add to the grandeur of the procession. This is the *vapasi* procession and this band was playing devotional songs from Hindi films.

9: is the desire for political affiliation is very much visible in their banners placed at the entrance of the *pandal*s. The society banner is placed somewhere behind the temple.

Festival as Communicative Performance

Milton singer was the first person who highlighted the performative aspect of a culture and listed certain characteristics which are observable in a cultural performance (Madison, 2005). Applying his cultural performance idea, I would like to analyze the *Rath Yatra* festival as a communicative performance of the community enacted through a series of cultural acts. Here I am trying to center the communicative aspect of a festival and suggest that a festival can be analyzed as a mode of communication used by the community to communicate with the larger public and with itself. Kristin Kuutma tries to build the festival, performance and communication nexus in her analysis of the Estonian song festivals (Kuutma, 1998). She says "a festival provides opportunities to observe the communicative system of a culture conveyed through semiotically complex performance events" (Kuutma, 1998).

As said earlier, the Odiya community through its *Rath Yatra* performance tries to communicate with the public and with itself. To highlight these two communication processes, I would like to borrow the terms demonstration and experience from Beverly Stoelje's essay "Festival" where he uses them to highlight the specific objective of a festival (Stoeltje, 1992).

Demonstration and Experience

So what are they demonstrating and what are they experiencing by performing *Rath Yatra*?

1. Cultural uniqueness

The annual celebration of the *Rath Yatra* gives an opportunity to the Odiya community to underline the Odiya customs and traditions centred on Lord Jagannath which they think is specific to their culture. This kind of assertion is possible in two cases: (1) when the community has over a period of time settled down and is now looking for an opportunity to express its identity, and (2) in a mixed population like Katedan where there are other migrant groups from various other states. Then it becomes important for the Odiya community to talk about their legacies and customs which make them different from other migrant groups.

Every element of the festival speaks loudly of the specificity of Odiya culture. Like the '*shankas*', the white bangles which the married women wear, the traditional music troupe with the '*marda*' which is also very specific to Odiya culture. Moreover, the food served during *anndaans* is also from Odiya cuisine.

2. Community size and strength

When the people of a community walk on streets with a common purpose then its size and strength are highlighted. A migrant community trying to negotiate with the local agencies has to demonstrate its strength so that it can influence power. As Jacobsen puts it "Since size is important for minority groups seeking public recognition, the gathering of the whole group on a public street becomes a sign of strength and might be a sign that the group is seeking influence" (Jacobsen, 2008, p. 218).

3. Marking of community presence

Flowing from the point above, the large scale participation of people from its community in an event like *Rath Yatra* symbolizes the marking of community presence. Women, children and old participate thus showcasing their community life. The common t-shirts of the society members also symbolize the organized nature of the society which enables it to represent the community. The presence of an organized body to represent shows the desire of the community to mark itself on the social, cultural and political landscape of the region.

4. Negotiation of the sacred pathway, time and space (Kong, 2001)

As described earlier, the procession starts from the Jagannath temple and reaches the Gundicha maa temple. So all through the route, the participants (rope pullers, dancers, musicians, organizers) are barefooted. So for a brief moment, the pathway becomes sacred to this community. The procession attains the nature of performance when its participants try to demarcate the space by enacting sacredness and thus the route becomes a 'performative space' (Booth, 2008).

What are they experiencing?

1. Constructing, confirming and celebrating collective identities

Celebration of a festival which is the centre of a community's identity, in a place far from their original state gives an opportunity and a reason to the community and its people to construct a collective identity. This process helps them to cope with the "disrupt and disorientation" (Jacobsen, 2008) caused by migration. Once constructed then it has to be confirmed and celebrated through these cultural performances which would reassure their collectiveness and belonging. A new Odiya migrant struggling to adjust to the new locale finds relieving and reassuring to find the extent of his community presence.

2. Emotional attachment

Knut Jacobsen writes that religion in the diasporas secures "the emotional attachment to the culture of origin" (Jacobsen, 2008). Similarly, participating in *Rath Yatra* keeps them connected to their home. As one of the respondents puts it "since everyone cannot attend the festival of Puri, a similar version in Katedan would help poor Odiya people to be part of their lord's celebration".

3. Social interaction and cohesion

Any festival has the basic objective of bringing people together and builds social relations. *Rath Yatra* festival also provides an opportunity to the people of the community to find and interact with 'their' people. As one of the respondents says "*Rath Yatra* brings Odiya community together and gives a cause to work together".

4. Self-confidence, pride and loyalty

Conscious display of community strength and unity in the presence of other migrant groups instills self-confidence and loyalty in the people. The fact that they are able to serve such huge numbers during *anndaans* builds a sense of pride which leads to other cultural performances. For example, since the construction of Gundicha maa temple in Brindavan colony where they have found their own space to perform culture, the society organizes *anndaans* on full moon day of every month citing community unity and loyalty as the primary intention.

5. A Shift from 'everyday'

Listing the characteristics of a professional performance Barbara Krischenblatt-Gimblett and Brooks McNamara write, "The procession employs distinctive elements to distinguish it from everyday movement through space. These elements include special scenography, costume, music and sometimes elaborate movement patterns. The procession, however, is designed to compete with the existing environment around it, becoming for a time the dominant element" (1985, p. 2). Most of the migrants in the community are factory labour. A festival of this nature not only brings them close to their community but also relieves them from the tensions of their everyday lives.

Conclusion

Not undermining the experiences of migrants, this chapter has tried to locate a festival as a mechanism of negotiation and resistance built by the migrant community in their destination city. The cultural performativity described above helps the migrant community to cope with the ever-changing political, socio-cultural and economic landscapes of the city. However, the migrant community cannot be considered as a homogeneous lot and the performativity cannot be assumed to run across all the segments of their community singularly. Factors like caste, class and gender are expected to play pivotal roles which could lead us to multiple performativities and consequently to the ways of producing space.

REFERENCES

Booth, G.D. (2008). "Space, sound, auspiciousness, and performance in North." In K.A. Jacobsen, *South Asian Religions on Display*, pp. 63-76. New York: Routledge.

Goonewardena, K., Kipfer, S., Milgrom, R., & Schmid, C. (2008). *Space, Difference, Everyday life.* New York: Routledge.

Jacobsen, K.A. (2008). "Conclusions and Future Prospects." In: K.A. Jacobsen, *South Asian Religions on Display*, pp. 217-219. New York: Routledge.

Jacobsen, K.A. (2008). "Procession, Public Space and Sacred Space in the South Asian Diasporas in Norway." In: K.A. Jacobsen, *South Asian Religions on Display*, pp. 191-204. New York: Routledge.

Kirshenblatt-Gimblett, B., & McNamara, B. (1985). "Processional Performance: An Introduction." *The Drama Review: TDR,* 2-5.

Kong, L. (2001). "Mapping 'new' geographies of religion: politics and poetics in modernity." *Progress in Human Geography*, 211-233.

Kuutma, K. (1998). "Festival as Communicative Performance and Celebration of Ethnicity." *Folklore: Electronic Journal of Folklore.*

Lefebvre, H. (1991). *The Production of Space.* (D. Nicholson-Smith, Trans.) Cambridge: Blackwell.

Madison, D.S. (2005). *Critical Ethnography: Method, Ethics and Ethnography.* California: Sage Publications Inc.

Stoeltje, B.J. (1992). "Festival." In R. Bauman, *Folklore, Cultural performances, and Popular Entertainments,* pp. 261-271. New York: Oxford University Press.

12

Use of Mobile Phones and Changing Family Communication Structure within Family of Migrants

Swati Arjun

Introduction

The use of mobile phones is neutralizing the gender hierarchy amongst the middle-class family of migrants living in Ghaziabad, an urban set-up, 30 kms away from the national capital of Delhi. A typical Indian middle-class family is usually not only the harbinger of change but also the class, which takes pride in carrying forward the legacy and traditions of radical feudal society at large. So, while on one hand, it wants to upgrade its lifestyle and adhere to basic norms of modernity, on the other hand, it carries a sense of déjà-vu regarding the basic tenets of family structure, that serves as a pillar of strength to them.

But, with the liberal use of technology and communication gadgets like mobile (smart) phones, the communication pattern and relationship structure between man and woman in such families is going through a sea change. Mobile phones are still out of reach for millions of Indian women because of gendered (gender-based) power dynamics and the dearth of gender sensitivity.

As much of rural India remains highly patriarchal, women lack the disposable income to purchase their own mobile phones. But, with the increasing number of middle-class migrant working families living in bigger cities, comparatively less and moderately educated dependent women are also coming in contact with newer means of communication like mobile (smart) phones to make their life easier. This contact with mobile phones is not only bringing a change in their communication pattern but also, in their interpersonal relationship within the family. Thus, augmenting a change in the communication structure and the nature of relationship between men and women members of the family.

According to the National Family Health Survey (NFHS) in the year 2015-16, less than 46 per cent of Indian women own and use a mobile phone. This has had the effect of limiting independence for many women, as well as access to various opportunities. A closer look we will find that the problem is worse when the data is examined carefully. In urbanized centres, 62 per cent of women use their own handsets, but in rural regions/areas, the figure is under 37 per cent. This stark discrepancy doesn't exist in countries like the US, where rural and urban cell-phone penetration is at par and close to 95 per cent for both urban and rural women populations.

The 25 per cent of a point difference in mobile usage between women from the urban and rural sections of the country was present in most of India's 36 states and union territories. This NFHS data was extracted by the English Daily *Hindustan Times*. Phones are still out of reach for millions of Indian women as a result of gendered power dynamics (Dynamics is the force or properties which brings change, growth or development within a system or process). Much of rural India still remains highly patriarchal and feudal. Women still lack the disposable income and freedom to purchase their own mobile phones.

In addition, as the men of these families namely fathers, brothers and husbands often share the luxury of also being the decision-makers of the household, exclusion from the decision-making process– often bars the women from communicating through mobile phones.

According to a report published in *Wall Street Journal*— even in states like Haryana which are barely few kms away from Delhi, there is a common view that "If girls will have free access to mobile phones then they will start talking to boys and the next thing that they will do, will be to either have a love marriage or elope with a boy". But, with the migration of more and more middle-class families to cities, the ever dependent and relatively less-educated women have not only started venturing out of their houses but are also coming in contact with newer means of communication to make their life easier than before. And this change has a lot to do with the free use of mobile phones in their day to day lives. This could be either through the immediate expansion of social space or through the technological intervention of mobile phones.

Hypothesis (how?)

The researcher assumes that "Use of mobile phones is neutralizing the gender hierarchy within the family communication set-up amongst the middle-class income group of migrants residing in the region of Delhi/ NCR." And, she expects that the findings of this study will help in establishing the assumption that, "the communication pattern as well as relationship structure between men and women of such families is undergoing thorough a change." The contact with mobile phones is not only bringing a change in their social communication but, also in their interpersonal relationship pattern within the family.

Significance/Rationale

The reason for the researcher to do a study on this subject was while keeping in mind the fact that, India being largely a closed society in various capacities is still not open to the idea of a girl/women communicating freely with the outer world that constitutes her immediate surroundings. According to the global mobile industry monitor GSM Association, "In the year 2015, 114 million fewer women than men owned a mobile phone in India. This was despite the population being split almost evenly between the two gender, mobile phone penetration by woman was 28 per cent, which was much lower than the 43 per cent of figure by men. A total of 81 per cent of Indian women have never accessed the internet on their phones, therefore, the researcher wanted to base her study on the assumed understanding that, has this newly acquired empowerment of these women from under or less privileged background has brought any change or shift in the 'man-woman' discourse taking place within the four walls of their homes (GSM 2015, p. 1)?"

Relevance of the study: Lies in the fact that with the changing demography and changed mode of communication, how the mildly privileged but otherwise traditional and radical family systems and values are undergoing a change, after being connected with modern communication tools like mobile phones and the internet. Thus, augmenting a change in the man-woman relationship as well as their communication structure.

Objective

The aim and objective of this study is to primarily find out the comparative usage of mobile phones between the men and women residents of a family within the urban and rural set-ups simultaneously. Identify the change in the man-woman relationship in those families who are first-generation migrants to the industrial town of Ghaziabad. Also, to examine and find out—if post introduction of mobile phones to the women members of these families, has there been a change in the communication structure between both the sexes, and has it evolved from a unilateral to a bilateral process? Finally, has this in any way contributed to the neutralization of gender hierarchy within the family?

Review of Literature

Study on the present subject has not been done in a specific sense but, much literature has appeared on the use of mobile phones, which is based on families who normally use mobile phones in their day to day communication. Some of the studies are based on regular family set-ups to find out how mobile phones are helping them in coordinating as a family organization.[1] Ling and Yttri called this practice 'micro-coordination'. The concept bears a resemblance to the idea of using mobile phones for 'nuanced instrumental coordination' (Ling and Yttri, 2002:139-169).

The previous studies mentioned above basically dealt with the instrumental dimension of family and the use of mobile phones. However, later on, it also tried to incorporate the perspective of expression or expressive emotion. i.e. the emotional content of calls and text messages. One of the strongest reasons in the sample families of these studies for purchasing a mobile phone was the sense of security that it provides (Røpke, 2003). Even Mante-Meijer and Loos (2001) suggested, that security threats and daily eventualities have been the major driving force in their life which has persuaded people in general to own one of them. This could be in the form of unplanned and uncontrolled incidents like accidents, delays, emergencies or any kind of externally enforced situation.

The studies which had been done around micro-coordination, remote parenting and security contribute immensely to the different dimensions of communication that take place within the family with the help of mobile phones. Here mobile phone acts as a facilitator or an aggregator, which has far reached phenomenological and micro-level social implications.

In the study, 'Are mobile phones changing social networks? A longitudinal study of core networks in Kerala', Palackal *et al.*, (2011 p. 9) found 'that average number of relationships involving mobile phones (over four) is more than those involving face-to-face interaction (about two), and much higher than those involving e-mail communication (less than one)'.

In her study 'Mobile technology in Indian villages: ICTs culture and social logistics' Tenhunen opines, "Mobile technology, like other ICTs, facilitates the dispersion of transnational capital. Mobile phones often facilitate a multiplicity of relationships in areas that used to be relatively isolated before." (2008).

Therefore, the more there is an increase in the growing numbers of individual media technologies like mobile and smartphones, along with television channels that serve programmes keeping in mind the individual need of the target audience like women, adults and adolescents based in-home (Røpke, 1999). It is creating a temporary and material life within the households as normally is available outside the house. As described by Gergen and Gergen: "Even within the family, geographic propinquity now means little. In large measure, each family member lives a psychologically separated life" (2003 p. 17).

On a more general level, it is also believed that if someone calls a family member frequently within a stipulated time frame then they are establishing a relationship of 'mutual accountability' and trust by collecting information about the physical, social and psychological whereabouts of the partner in conversation. Berger and Luckmann, (1966) noted that the face-to-face situation forms the basis for social interaction and social relations; it is the 'prototypical case of social interaction' from which all other forms of communication can be derived. However, with the proliferation of personal and portable communication technologies, the question arises as to what degree this phenomenon challenges the position of the face-to-face situation as the prototype of social interaction. According to Fortunati "The use of ICT undermines the role of mutual-physical communication as the primary mode of interaction. Even blurring the demarcation line between mediated and non-mediated communication" (2005 p. 218). Fortunati also highlights the dynamics of modern society, where the social network of a human being is continuously extending which in turn is leading to separate paths for them.

From a communicator and constructivist perspective, Licoppe has described relationships as something which has a genesis on the continuous interactions happening through mediated tools. Licoppe has identified that "[each] of these mediated interactions not only reactivates but also reaffirms and reconfigures the relationship between two people" (2004:138). In Punyanunt-Carter, (2008) study, father-daughter relationships were focused on in an effort to examine family communication patterns and interpersonal communication satisfaction. The focus of this study was to see how the communication between fathers and daughters have affected their relationship and their level of satisfaction with regard to their relationship. This particular research focused on four types of families: consensual, pluralistic, protective and laissez-faire.

The findings of this study dictated that the two types of families which held the greatest satisfaction with regard to communication were those in the middle range, the pluralistic and consensual types. In the styles of communication where there were less satisfaction daughters tended to rebel or look to other people for comfort, rather than their fathers which in turn could cause their fathers to think that, their thoughts are not valued in the lives of their daughters. Further resulting in divergence of the relationship between the girl child and their paternal heads.

The study conducted by Schrodt Witt, and Messersmith (2008: 248-269) focused on a meta-analytical review of family communication patterns and their associations with information processing, behavioural, and psychosocial outcomes. This study looks at various communication patterns to see how these methods shape family communication both inside and out of the family. This research was conducted via compiling 100 mass media and family communication articles written between 1968-2007. Of these 86 were chosen for the study. Results indicated that there was an association between family communication patterns and how family members responded to them. Besides other things, it created a healthier environment in the family and individuals were better equipped to handle any difficult situation. If a family allows the members to express themselves openly without fear of criticism this will, in turn, promote the health and well-being of family members. These types of open families also equip children to be better equipped to handle relationships with people who are not part of the family.

Devitt and Roker, (2009) focus on the role of mobile phones in family communication. They conducted interviews with 60 families including parents and kids of 11-17 years. The purpose of the interviews was to learn of the role mobile phone plays in a person's family life. Research conducted by Haddon (2006) focused on how miscommunication (between generations) can transfer into mobile phone usage. The emphasis here is on other members of a household. In another study, the focus was on the privacy invasion of the telephone with regard to children and how it carries over to young adult college students. This may be helpful in deciding how the boundaries between parents and children (or spouses) may be affected with respect to the fact that, how much the family is open to the idea of openness or is liberal of the idea where a member could freely reveal his/ her thoughts and feelings.

Geser (2006) raises an important question as he describes a set of four regressive impacts on social and societal structures, because of the heavy use of mobile phones. In this particular study, it was more likely than those who had multiple members in a household were more likely to possess and use mobile phones than single people. Mobile phones were found to strengthen existing social ties rather than to start new ones.

There is extensive literature in relation to parent-child, and a parent with–young member relationships, particularly in relation to monitoring and supervision, surveillance, independence and autonomy (Kerr, Stattin and Trost, 1999); (Stattin and Kerr, 2000). Theoretically, this study draws a view on those kind of notions within a family which involves surveillance, family constructions of relationships, and the impact of new technologies on family life, as well as the life of the child. There is growing literature on the role of technologies in the lives of young people and families. Much of it focuses on how individuals and families use the Internet (for example Holloway and Valentine, 2001); (Kerawalla and Crook, 2002); and a Canadian study into mobile phone use and independence among teenage girls (Campbell, 2006) involved interviews with 11 girls aged 14–16. Despite its small sample size, the author provided some interesting insights, including identifying three types of discourse in relation to mobile phone use amongst girls — first a media discourse that emphasizes image and independence, second a parental discourse that focuses on danger and safety, and third a youth discourse that emphasizes self-determination, privacy and sociability.

Summary of Literature Review

The review of the literature available online for this study has largely been based on the other European and Asian countries. It was also noted that the area of research of these studies focused more on the interpersonal relationships of parents and children using mobile phones than spouses in middle class educated and urban families. However, what could be easily construed by these studies is the fact that there has been an evident increase in the ownership and usage of mobile phones individually by all family members, be it husband and wife or growing children of both the sexes.

In certain cases, elderly occupants of the family are also using mobile phones. The reason for using mobile phones for all of them has been different. Youngsters use it for recreation and expression, but couples are seen to use it for communication and to be in touch or even to instil a sense of safety regarding their kids or elderly family members in the family. Sharing is also a necessity in cases where both spouses are working. In reference to women of the family whether young girls or adult women, expressions like independence, self-independence, privacy, rebellion and sociability has been extensively used, which the author felt is an important area for further study and research in the Indian context. The current chapter is a step taken ahead in the same direction.

Theoretical Framework

After a detailed study of the above cited research studies, the theoretical framework that the researcher found apt for this research has been Cultivation theory and Uses and Gratification theory. This was chosen keeping in mind the fact, that one of the two chosen sample groups had come in contact with the usage of mobile phones for the very first time in their lives. Therefore, they are cultivating a habit of using mobile phones in their new set-up which is their migrated space in the urban settlement. Since the exposure is new to them therefore they have their own set of indulgence and fulfilment attached to it. For example, being in touch with their native people, language, music in their local dialect, local food recipes via YouTube channel, local news etc. But at the same point in time, it has also become a need for them to survive in their new set-up where they are faced with a new challenge of survival on a daily basis. Therefore, the researcher felt that her study very minutely encompasses the features of cultivation theory also, along with the features of Uses and Gratification theory.

Research Questions

In a world that is fast changing "*CHANGE*", has become synonymous with technological intervention in our day to day lives. With voluntary and to some extent compulsive uses of newer means of technological products and devices into our lives. Slowly and gradually a change has made space between the confined boundaries of a modern home. As it was said in a countrywide study done in 19th century Europe the invention of the washing machine had ushered in the most impactful liberation into the lives of women, living in then Europe. Therefore, in the current study, the focus area lies in the internal and psychological liberation of women residing in an urban set-up, with the help of a communication tool like mobile phone, which has made inroads into their lives just a decade ago. There is also an effort to try to explore the family set-up, educational background, financial independence and political awareness of women from these families. The study also aims to locate a comparison between women who belong to financially stable family background, but their social background is different. This means that they come from a different set of social-milieu (rural), that comprises of a patriarchal and feudal set-up and a closed society with confined physical boundaries living in a village.

So, the essence of this research study was to examine the mental emancipation and visible self-dependency of these family women brought in through a more democratic communication structure facilitated with the help of a device that is called mobile phones.

Methodology

The methodology adopted for the current research to collect data had been to administer a questionnaire of 25 questions covering 25 families from a village called Galand, under Hapur Tehsil and 34 families from Indirapuram an urban town both falling under the district of Ghaziabad in Uttar-Pradesh. The rural family had a minimum seven members in a family, which could easily exceed eight or nine. So, the average number of residents covered under the survey in the rural area was roughly around one hundred and seventy-five (175). Whereas the urban household had a minimum of four members in a family, which very rarely went ahead to five. Therefore, the average number of residents covered in the urban landscape of Ghaziabad district were about one hundred and thirty-six (136). An additional 11 more questions were asked to urban families to ascertain the change in their communication structure, with the help of mobile phones. These questions were not administered to the village samples, as they had made it clear in advance, that their women did not use or own a mobile phone. The whole survey was done with the motive of undertaking a comparative study between urban and rural families.

The study was aimed at exploring the magnitude and measurement of expressions and decisions both verbal, non-verbal and emotional occurring in such set-ups. Therefore, it was decided to proceed ahead with a quantitative approach. This was applied by designing a questionnaire to collect the necessary data. The quantitative approach to this study was considered with the objective, to find out the *change* in the relationship status of men and women in those families who were using mobile phones and are living in urban set-ups compared to those living in rural establishments and not using mobile phones. The aim was to find and channelize diverse opinions and experience into predetermined response category to a limited set of questions.

This was done because the research was based on the assumption that, the free and liberal use of mobile phones in such households, has been the catalyst in changing the whole process of communication within the already set and established family system. This has eventually culminated into the more evolved and emancipated status of women in the family *vis-à-vis* their relationship with their men. Thus, the focus was on finding the *extent of impact* brought through the liberal use of mobile phones within these families.

The study universe has been the district of Ghaziabad in UP, which is also known as gateway of UP, because of its propensity to the national capital Delhi and New Okhla Industrial Development Area or Noida. It is a large and planned industrial city and as per the official census of 2011, it has a population of 46,81,645. Of which 24, 88,834 is men and 21,92,811 is women population. As per the same official census of 2011, 67.55 per cent of the Ghaziabad population lives in urban regions of the district which makes for a total of 31,62,547. Of these 16,80,612 is men and 14,81,935 is women. As per the 2011 census, 32.45 per cent population of Ghaziabad districts lives in rural areas of the villages; which counts to 15,19,098. Both, the urban and rural sample falls in the same district of Ghaziabad.

The village Galand which was the rural sample of this study falls into the Nagar-Palika Parishad of Hapur Tehsil of Ghaziabad Municipal Corporation/District. The total population of Galand village is 12,500 of which 52 per cent (6500) is of men and 48 per cent (6000) is of women. The population of Indirapuram is around 4,50,000. Of which 53 per cent (2,38,500) is of men and 47 per cent is of women (2,11,500). Both the sample sizes were 0.3 per cent representation of the total population of Ghaziabad as a whole. The rural sample was 0.0037 per cent of the total population of Galand village and the urban population was 0.0029 per cent of the Indirapuram area.

The data for the survey was collected in a period of 21 days. The researcher essentially tried to use the triangulation method, which means using more than one method to collect data so that a good understanding is gained of the subject from different perspectives, and strengthen the researcher's standpoint from various aspects. Once the data was collected, then the quantitative data was converted into qualitative content by analyzing and interpreting the gathered data. To conduct these tests aimed at extracting information from the sample population, 'Likert Scale' was used by the scholar and the data collected was later converted to ordinal data.

As per the planning, the researcher worked on her questionnaire, logistics, contacts and identification of villages where she wished to take her survey forward focusing on such families where mobile phones were not being used by women folks. A village called Galand was chosen as a sample village for his study. It is situated some 30 kms away from Indirapuram and falls under Hapur Tehsil of Ghaziabad district on NH24.

Galand village is majorly agrarian in nature and has a feudal set-up. The women of these villages were all homemakers and were cutoff from exposure to the outer world. Here, they do not own a mobile phone of their own. In most cases, the family used a basic handset or even a smartphone which is owned by the men of the family. The maximum connection that the women had with the mobile phones was just limited to either receiving a call from their families or making a call to them. Most of the times this exchange of pleasantries was done in the presence of the owners of the mobile phones, who happened to be the men of the family. These men were very stringent, averse to their women talking to strangers. The researcher could somehow manage to talk to 25 such families where mobile phones were not used. She was introduced to the Gram-Pradhan of that village by a local TV stringer. The Pradhan happened to be a teacher himself, thus convincing him became easier, but only after producing the researcher's I-card.

The process that she undertook for the collection of data or while administering the questionnaire in Galand village was to orally administer the questions in front of the women folks to answer the queries noted in the questionnaire. This was done for an individual as well as 2-3 women participant basis, with some help from local children.

The second set of respondents (urban) were taken from the Indirapuram area which falls under Ghaziabad district. In the past 10 years, Indirapuram has acquired the status of a residential area which is being populated by migrants of diverse and vivid professional as well as rural background. However, still the majority of the population belongs to people from the Hindi speaking belt, who had migrated from the Hindi speaking states of (Bihar, UP, Madhya Pradesh, Uttarakhand, Rajasthan) belonging to middle-class services and businesses background. The researcher took the responses of 34 middle class nuclear families, where the women were a mix of house-wives and working women with exposure to their outer world and freely using mobile phones.

Justification of Sample Area: Ghaziabad is well connected to roads and railways and is the administrative headquarters of Ghaziabad district. Besides, it is also a primary commercial, the industrial and educational centre of Western Uttar Pradesh and a major rail junction for North India through Anand Vihar railway station. Recent construction works have led to the city being described by City Mayors Foundation survey as the second fastest-growing city in the world. Therefore, all these characteristics of this city have attracted migrants from all sectors, segments and strata of society from different states and cities. Prime among them are migrants from lower and middle-class income group households, who come here in search of work as daily labourers, workers in factories and support staff in shops and malls, private jobs, tech-media sector, government jobs etc. In most cases, these migrants come here with their families and live in modest set-ups. In many cases, women from such families also start working as there is no social confinement for them too.

Sampling: The provisional data derived from the 2011 census shows that Ghaziabad urban agglomeration had a population of 46,81,452, of which men were 24,79,710 and 22,01,742 were women. The literacy rate was 93.81 per cent. According to the data shared online by CDP-Delhi, the NCR region of Delhi comprises eight districts of Haryana, one of Rajasthan and five districts of UP. These sub-regions of NCR-Delhi have accommodated 37.33 per cent, 23.42 per cent, 8.07 per cent and 31.19 per cent of NCR's population respectively. Delhi has witnessed the fastest growing numbers of the population in the past two decades—clocking over to 47 per cent, which is double the national rate. A large part of this rapid growth is because of the high level of migration taking place in these cities. Both the sampling (Urban and Rural) for this study was purposive in nature, selection was made on the basis of those families who had migrated to Delhi/NCR in the last decade or so and those rural families where women were not using mobile phones. Once the data was collected, it was chronicled into a data analysis plan, as a premise for data analysis.

Data Analysis and Interpretation

The researcher went ahead with this research with three objectives in mind. The first was to identify the general behaviour or inclination of middle-class urban migrants towards the usage of mobile phones. Therefore, in this qualitative study, she implemented the process of triangulation to understand the phenomenon of change in the communication pattern and family structure in migrant families.

During the time of fieldwork it was discovered that out of all the 25 rural families and their 175 members approached 85 per cent of their women were not exposed to the usage of mobile phones, in their day to day lives as compared to the urban migrant families where hardly 10 per cent women did, had a very basic functional relationship with their mobile phones, otherwise the rest of 90 per cent of the respondents had a pro-active relationship with their mobile phones. This was evident in the visible difference between the man-woman relationship in both the set-ups.

Rural women were primarily homemakers and financially dependent, with a lesser level of education and larger family size. Women were incapable of taking decisions on their own and were dependent in nature. They were politically disconnected, keen to have a male child. Men were not expected to take active part in cooking or other household chores. In contrast to this, urban women were more outspoken of their rights. Enjoying their newly acquired freedom most of them were graduate and postgraduate. The family size was less than five. 85 per cent of them were financially independent, some even working from home, politically aware, self-dependent and forthright. Despite being a homemaker they had ample exposure to the outer world; there was a remarkable difference in the manifested man-woman relationship in urban set-ups. More emancipated and open than feudal and patriarchal, there was a visible changed behaviour pattern within the family. Usage of mobile phone in their day to day dealings within and outside the family seems to have significantly improved the communication pattern among urban couples and had a positive effect in their inter-personal relationship.

After going through the whole research process and studying minutely the findings, the interpretation of the data collected highlights few important points. First, education among the rural and urban samples too played an important role. Besides, the system of joint family, feudal and patriarchal set-up, dependency on male folks of the family and village had become a habit for them. Lack of ownership also played a major role–compared to the urban women who were left on their own to run the family in the absence of their men, who would leave for work. This in turn made them more responsible, independent and demanding, which led to a say in the family, financial, political and matters related to daily chores. Though there was an evident and remarkable difference in communication structure and relationship pattern in the urban and rural set-ups, it would be difficult to say if this happened just by the free usage of mobile phones in one of the two sample groups. What it did signify was that the use of the mobile phone has definitely played a very important role in the frequency of communication between both the sexes. The time spent on communication by urban women was much higher than rural ones, both for functional and personal reasons, which in the long run helped in the process of breaking gender hierarchy and gender neutralization.

Conclusion

The above presented study of, 'Use of Mobile phones and Changing family communication structure amongst middle-class family of migrants', undertaken in the city of Ghaziabad, which is geographically 30 kms away from Delhi, shows how by the usage of mobile phones the traditional and conservative ways of communication structure is going through a change in those urban families who a decade ago were a part of traditional and feudal set-ups.

The study consisted of those migrant families who had migrated to city life in the past 9 to 15 years. However, mobile phones could not be described as the only guiding force behind the change in their communication structure. But, its significance cannot be undermined too, as all the migrant families who were a part of this study, despite using mobile phones frequently were exposed to the same just a few (5-6) years ago. Whereas, their migration occurred more than a decade ago. The migration in itself was a major catalyst for change in their lives resulting in nuclear families, better education level, employment, income, financial independence and self-reliance. All these factors led to a need for better coordination at the family level, which was facilitated by the usage of mobile phones.

While, there had been earlier studies where factors like security, remote parenting and connectivity were addressed. (Røpke, 2003), with some studies even emphasizing the instrumental dimension of families and mobile phone use, and some others broadening the perspective by including the expressive dimension, which is the emotional content or message of texting or making a call. It is here through this study, that some value could be added to this already touched upon aspect.

The present study aims at decoding the unsaid or the unexpressed; identifying the changes taking place within urban migrant nuclear families of Ghaziabad. The research has definitely improved the understanding of this subject gives a clear picture of the potential as well as the limitation of mobile phones in relation to certain behavioural and communication patterns in the migrant population of Ghaziabad.

The findings of this study cannot be generalized to any larger group but it can definitely pave way for similar studies pertaining to a larger population. As the study suggests, the use of mobile phones even if not acting as a catalyst–do have a role in changing the communication structure within these families. However, this role is supportive or facilitative, which is open for discussion and further investigation.

NOTE

1. For example, Ling and Yttri (2002:139-169).

REFERENCES

Berger, L.P. & Luckmann, T. (1966). *The Social Construction of Reality: A Treatise in the Sociology of Knowledge,* Garden City, NY: Anchor Books: 31-49.

Campbell, Rachel (2006). "Teenage Girls and Cellular Phones: Discourses of Independence, Safety and Rebellion". *Journal of Youth Studies, 9*(2):195-212.

Devitt, K. and Roker, D. (2009). *"The Role of Mobile Phones in Family Communication. Children and Society"*, National Children's Bureau, 23(3):189-202.

Fortunati, L. (2005). *Mobile Communications–Renegotiation of the Social Sphere*, London: Springer Verlag Publishers.

Gergen, M. and Gergen, J.K. (2003). *Social Construction: A Reader,* London: Sage Publications.

Geser, H. (2006). "Is the cell phone undermining the social order? Understanding mobile technology from a sociological perspective". *Knowledge, Technology and Policy*, 19:8-18.

Global System for Mobile Communications (GSM) (2015). "Bridging the gender Gap: Mobile access and wage in developing countries"—Weblink (pl. see email).

Haddon, L. (2006). "Communication Problems". *Knowledge, Technology and Policy*, 19:19-27.

Holloway L.S. and Valentine, G. (2001). "It's only as stupid as you are: Children's and adults' negotiation of ICT competence at home and at school". *Social and Cultural Geography Journal*, *2*(1):25-42.

Kerawalla, L. and Crook Charles (2002), *Children's Computer Use at Home and at School: Context and Continuity*. British Educational Research Journal, Volume 28 (issue 6), pp. 757-771.

Kerr. M., Stattin. H. and Trost. K (1999). "To know you is to trust you: Parents' trust is rooted in child disclosure of information". *Journal of Adolescence 22*(6), p. 737-52. DoI: 10.1006/jado.1999.0266.

Licoppe, C. (2004). "Connected' Presence: The Emergence of a New Repertoire for Managing Social Relationships in a Changing Communication Technoscape." *Environment and Planning D: Society and Shape, 22*(1):135-156.

Ling, R. and Yttri, B. (2002). "Hyper-Coordination via mobile phones in Norway". *https://www.researchgate.net/publication/234788498*. Pages 139-169.

Mante-Meijer, E.A. and Loos, E.F. (2008). "Risk takers and choice makers: Their (non) use of new media. Age and risk perception during a choice process." In: J. Pierson, E.A. Mante-Meijer, E.F. Loos and B. Sapio (eds.), *Innovation for/by users*. Brussels: Office for Official Publications of the European Communities. pp. 53-64.

Palackal, A., Mbatia, N. Paul, Dzorgbo. D, Duque, R.B., Yualvez, M.A. and Shrum, W.M. (2011). "Are mobile phones changing social networks? A longitudinal study of core networks in Kerala." *New Media and Society*. (sagepub.co.uk/journalspermissions.nav), *13*(3) p. 1-20.

Punyanunt-Carter, M.N. (2008). "Father-daughter relationships: examining family communication patterns and interpersonal communication satisfaction". *Communication Research Reports, 25*(1): 23-33.

Ropke, I. (1999). "Theories of practice — New inspiration for ecological economic studies on consumption." *Ecological Economics–Science Direct. 68*(10): 2490-2497.

Ropke, I. (2003). "Consumption dynamics and technological change—exemplified by the mobile phone and related technologies." *Ecological Economics – Science Direct. 45*(2):171-188.

Schrodt, P., Witt. L.P., and Messersmith, S.A. (2008). "A Meta-Analytical Review of Family Communication Patterns and their Associations with Information Processing, Behavioral, and Psychosocial Outcomes." *Communication Monograph: National Communication Association, 75*(3):248-269.

Stattin, H. and Kerr, M. (2000). "Parental Monitoring: A Reinterpretation." *Child Development: Society for Research in Child Development, 71*(4):1072-1085.

Tenhunen, S. (2008). "Mobile technology in the village: ICTs, culture, and social logistics in India." *Journal of the Royal Anthropological Institute, 14*(3):515-534. DOI: 10.1111/j.1467-9655.2008.00515.x

SECTION 4
Communication and Health

13

Community Games

An Instrument for Creating Menstrual Awareness

Pragati Paul and *Krishna Sankar Kusuma*

Games and Edutainment

Games are expressions of play that allow people to go beyond instant imagination and direct activity. Games are like ice-breaking activities which are conducted in a way that can be an effective tool for community participation and creating a dialogue between players. They can enhance participatory processes discreetly placed in the learning process. It helps people to reflect, relax, energize, bring a sense of interest, create humour, "grab people in the gut", feel emotions, and induce meditation. They provide multiplicity, discovery and surprise through various play methods and thus keep players involved. It triggers both sides of the brain–the cognitive, logical side and the emotional, creative side and stimulates perception, affection or expression, creating interest through the demonstration of a thought-provoking situation. According to Schrier (2016, 2019), games can be considered moral knowledge because they build new knowledge that does not yet exist and generate new approaches to issues and problems. The striving point in any game is the sense of accomplishment when the players get some kind of reward and appreciation and different strategies adopted to win any game. An important component of any game is feedback which makes the player motivated to play till the end.

ZMQ Development is a non-profit organisation practising 'Games for Development' through interactive means of communication. The methods are not only interactive but also conscientize the participants to think innovatively and approach the diverse societal needs with better solutions. It used sustainable methods or models to bring positive change among the players/participants. The role-play based games are being used as a successful way to create behaviour change among the users. Through this approach, participants will be able to relate with real life issues and contexts that ultimately push them to handle by themselves. The founder of the organization Subhi Quraishi says, "Understanding knowledge, attitudes and practices level enables us to design a more efficient process of awareness creation and capacity building through customized performance tools appropriate for community needs." (personal communication)

Singhal and Rogers state, "When two words education and entertainment are put together, the meaning becomes encouraging individual growth and development in a learning environment that commands and holds the emotional attention of the learners." (2001:343) Edutainment cultivates understanding by introducing the element of fun for enhancing and retaining knowledge imaginatively and engagingly. Entertainment in education is the method of intentionally creating and executing a media message to entertain and poster the participants or audience knowledge about a problem and to transform the actions of individuals and communities. Edutainment is an effective method for education by bringing some element of entertainment as well in the game and breaking the monotony as well.

Menstruation and Adolescence

The World Health Organization defines, "Adolescence as a period of life with specific health and developmental needs and rights. It is also a time to develop knowledge and skills, learn to manage emotions and relationships, and acquire attributes and abilities that will be important for enjoying the adolescent years and assuming adult roles." (quoted in Takahashi, 2019:3) Menstruation is often dealt with in secrecy in many cultures and communities (Rajagopalan & Mathur, 2017). It is often dealt with a myth that food cooked by menstruating women turns bad and cannot be served to the deity as it is considered impure (Kumar & Srivastava, 2011).

A study has revealed how menstruation is a taboo among women in the South Asia region. It is shocking to learn that "one in three adolescents had no information about menstruation before their first period" (UNICEF, 2018:2). The study further finds that the majority of teenagers thought that menstruation was a disease. It is often considered disgraceful, unclean and the secrecy surrounding menstruation has permeated every aspect of society, nurturing superstitions and taboos that are passed on between generations. Most teenagers believed menstruation was a disease. The concept of 'purity and pollution' is implemented here. It is often considered disgraceful, unclean, and the secrecy surrounding menstruation has permeated every aspect of society, nurturing intergenerational superstitions and taboos.

Game Design: Method and Practice

The study adopted the practices of design research which has been considered to provide training to the students (co-creators) involved in the development of games, which in turn are expected to adopt this approach when working with the relevant stakeholders and team members in their respective communities through experiential learning.

The research explores menstruation as an issue that can be potentially associated with board games on both theoretical and practical levels. The game aims for behavioural change in communication (BCC) by trying to change the prejudices and practices of women in the context of menstruation. The game procedure was discussed in the background of a number of players, limited time, putting the game into play and method of playing.

The important component to be deliberated while designing the game is the structure of interaction between a player, the game system, and any other players. The game is described in terms of the rule or how to use the play sheet so that it can be placed into action by the game players. The game aims to bring behavioural change among women in the following aspects: awareness about menstruation in the context of lack of material and facilities and how it is a normal biological process that is a sign of a healthy body. The change in practices related to the material used during periods by women and leading a healthy lifestyle. Keeping the above background in mind following are the objectives of the study: To develop games for creating a dialogue on menstruation among women, to study and document the process of development of the games and to ascertain the role of community games among the co-creators and players who are actively involved in the development and engagement of games for change.

The study engaged practice-based methodology, where the process and participation are key elements of the research. The study was conducted at two levels. One is a workshop for the postgraduate students and field testing with the need-based community. The games were developed by the students of development communication, Jamia Millia Islamia as a part of their workshop titled 'Games for Change'. The workshop enabled the students to co-create interactive games on different social issues using various human-centric design methods. The co-creators were actively involved in the inspiration, ideation, designing, implementation and field testing phase. The prototypes were created based on mind mapping sessions in context to design, visuals and content. Among the games developed by the students/co-creators, two games were selected for the study (field testing). First is *Mahavari: Sabse Zaroori Iski Jaankari* (Menstruation-Information is necessary) is a participatory floor game that explores three aspects of menstruation and relies on a participatory approach involving two generations of females; the young girls who just entered puberty age and their mothers. The second is Ludo Queen which is a popular game played by all age groups. It has four pink boxes with questions on them that talk about the Dos and Don'ts about menstruation.

Mahavari Sabse Zaruri Iski Jaankari (Menstruation-Information is necessary)

Mahavari Sabse Zaruri Iski Jaankari
(Menstruation-Information is necessary)

The game is designed to impart to users what is happening inside the female body and how to maintain cleanliness and well-being during menstruation days. It is co-created by Aradhana, Shikhar, Tarique, Upma and Ishita (Batch of Development Communication, 2018). The game endeavours to turn an uneasy situation into an entertaining, learning and constructive experience. The method of playing creates an engaging environment where players can acquire healthy practices to be undertaken during those days. The game will be played in three phases—Chit system, *Stappoo* (hopscotch) and *Pitthu* (lagori). Rinnie is a 12 years old girl, who has just entered the puberty phase and her menstruation cycle has just begun. She is a bit uninformed about the practices related to menstruation. Razia is 27 years old woman who is familiar with the practices. Radha is 35 years old woman. She disseminates her existing knowledge about menstruation to girls and also learns healthy practices from young girls.

The method of playing includes various stages. The player has to pick one chit from the bowl of 10 chits of different colours. Each player will pick up one colour which states the question number they will disclose in the second phase of the game and take the game forward. In the *Stappoo* (hopscotch) phase, there are ten questions (through an interaction between the three characters) in 10 different colours in a systematic order. The player with number 1 starts the *stappoo* game. The last and the final stage of the game is *pitthu* (lagori) which will be played by other players who are sitting around the game. They will be the ones providing answers to the questions by placing the *pitthu* blocks in an order they think is right. In the end, the co-creators will give an awareness ball to the players standing on the *Stappoo* which they will hit and break the *pitthu* (lagori). Inside that ball, there will be a chit providing the best possible answer.

Ludo Queen

Ludo Queen helps the players to observe and analyze their own growth process. The game was co-created by Sadaan and Asna (Batch of Development Communication, 2018). There will be different pads at different places which denote a safe house. It has four pink boxes with questions on them which highlight the Dos and Don'ts about menstruation. The four colours boxes include symbols related to women like freedom, courage, breaking the stereotypes and hard work. The game can be played between 2-4 players. The player will throw the dice and will

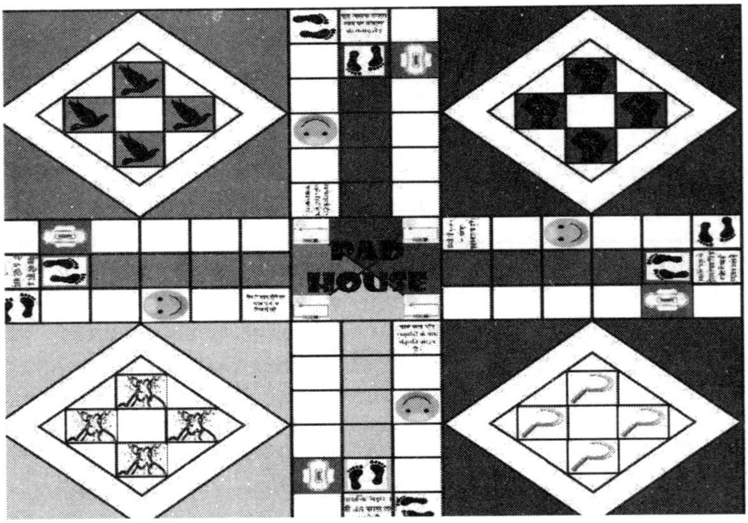

Ludo Queen

move accordingly on the floor game. The player who comes to the safe house has to answer a question related to the issue; a correct answer will get another chance. Each player has to reach a pad house and answer a simple question.

Field Testing of the Games

Rigorous fieldwork is conducted after designing the games. For the field testing of the community games, the group consists of ten co-creators who are actively involved in designing games to initiate conversations on menstruation. Field testing was done at two sites: DMST-Delhi Mahila Samaj Trust, Sangam Vihar, New Delhi, and Vidya Foundation, Saket, New Delhi. Approximately 80 participants played the games divided into various groups. The age group of the participants was ranging from 15 to 40 years. The focused group discussion was conducted with 80 participants who were actively involved in game sessions. Five groups were formed (16 participants each) to understand their views on games for change in context to menstruation. The participants were informed about the objectives of the study and it was entirely voluntary participation. Participants consented to the study and the audio recording of the focus group discussion. The researcher ensured the participants, anonymity with no names used in the data reporting. The games engagement process began with a short introduction about the purpose of the game. The game session was conducted for three hours. The two-floor game 'Ludo Queen' and 'Mahavari Sabse Zaruri Iski Jaankari (Menstruation-Information is necessary)' were displayed, and one of the players was asked to read out the method of playing the respective games in the group. As part of the game, each group had to identify a group facilitator. The facilitator was asked to read the instructions carefully and explain the game to the players. After the games, a focused group discussion was conducted to understand the views of the players in context to the game design, behaviour change and content.

The Co-creators Creating a dialogue with the Game Users

Source: Personal archive.

Observations and Experiences from the Field Testing of the Games

The players found the game was very innovative, visually appealing and engaging. The visuals were found to be realistic and made the game appear very attractive. The multi-coloured characters in the games (Rinnie, Radha and Raziya) were appreciated by all the players. The method and design of the game were found to be very new and innovative. The players were able to identify themselves with the characters and the situation in the game. One of the players said "When I was playing the *stappoo* (hopscotch) game, I was visualizing my elder sister Razia communicating information to me. Razia (Character in the game) looks like my elder sister." The majority of the players stated that the language (Hindi) used in the game was simple and was easily understood by the players. The game co-creators' presence made the players comfortable in understanding the method of playing the game for the first time. They also encouraged the group to speak up and overcome their hesitation in conducting various ice-breaking activities during the session.

The feedback was analyzed in the context of the four broad categories:

1. **Design and layout:** All the players liked the simple design of the game. They found all the visuals very attractive. The players were very keen to play Ludo Queen. One of the players said this is the most interesting game because she loves playing Ludo on her phone and playing live is exciting and participatory.
2. **Method for playing the game:** Around 70 per cent of the adolescents said they were able to understand the instructions and play accordingly. The method of playing triggered them to create a dialogue on menstruation as the method was very flexible and easy to comprehend. But 30 per cent felt that they were not able to follow the instructions as they found the instruction sheet boring as there was a lot of content placed on it.
3. **Visuals of characters and situations:** The majority of the players liked the characters a lot, especially the characters in *Mahavari Sabse Zaruri Iski Jaankari* (Menstruation-Information is necessary). The players could easily identify all the situations and characters shown in the game. They all found all the characters very close to their lives.
4. **Content:** Most of the adolescents were able to express their opinions and experiences on the issue of menstruation during the game. A few were a little hesitant. The majority of the players felt

that all the questions discussed in the game were very much related to their lives and had great relevance for them. The information given in the game was very relevant and informative. The game highlights the various aspects of menstruation in context to hygiene, safety during those days, food habits, taboos, and ways to cure menstrual pain. The game can be played in various schools, NGOs, and health organizations. The majority of the players wanted to acquire the game and keep it with themselves to explore it further and play with their community people.

Focus Group Discussion

As a part of the study focused group discussion was conducted with the stakeholders involved; the participants and the co-creators.

On game design one of the co-creators shared their intimate relationship with the development of the concept. She said, *"the game is very close to my heart from the time I started visualising it"*. She was very keen to use the concept of *stappu* (hopscotch) and *pitthu* (Lagori) in the game and amalgamate menstruation as an issue in the game. Three characters in the game enabled them to create a dialogue with the target audience.

One of the co-creators expressed perceptions during the field study. While taking this game to the community they were apprehensive that menstruation being a sensitive issue, will we be even allowed to play the game and will the players participate as it is taking place in their own locality. But to their surprise, everyone really enjoyed playing the game and they also felt that through this game their misconceptions have been cleared out about menstruation. One of the players shared, "when I first got my period, I thought I was suffering from blood cancer. I had no information about menstruation". These taboos and misconceptions are spread all over Indian society for generations.

All the co-creators after the field testing felt that the games have a power that no other medium has–they provide information, entertainment, create a dialogue among people especially when sensitive issues to deal with. It was revealed through one of the players that she was scared talking about such issues in front of men and felt initially *"periods are related to women only and men are not involved in it"*. After playing the games she is now open to discussion. It was clearly evident that various societal stigmas obstruct her from talking about such issues.

Another Co-creator revealed that "*I was also very shy talking about periods during my teens, but my mother informed me about the biological process and said it's absolutely fine to talk about periods*". Now she is confident to talk about menstruation with anyone and would actually like to educate more people about the issue and break the stereotype which we all have about it.

While discussing menstruation, participants spoke about the various changes women experience in their bodies in the form of bad blood. Most of the players revealed that "we are not allowed to be a part of the family rituals during those days, as we are considered impure." It reveals that it is prevalent across various sections of Indian society.

Conclusions

The whole process of coming up with this in a workshop and the concept for a game is a journey in itself involving various drafts. It was interesting to see people appreciating the games and coming, again and again, to play them, as well as retaining the knowledge they gained while playing.

Gray and Malins (2004, p. 2) believe that there is a connection between experiential learning and constructive learning. The classification was done on the basis of constructivism in three learning experiences. "First experience states, learning is constructed as a response to each individual's experiences and prior knowledge. Secondly, learning occurs through active participation and exploration. The last experience includes learning occurs within a social context in context to an interaction between learners" (2004, p. 2). It is clearly indicated that active participation is the key to learning. Learning cannot take place in isolation in fact one needs to consider the social and cultural context which shapes the conversations around learning.

The concept of engaging young people to prepare floor games was very efficacious. The testing of the game helped these game co-creators to access the game designed by them in an applied and balanced manner. The game becomes a very good medium to educate and explain concepts that may become ordinary and boring if given in a lecture pattern. The introduction of visual characters in the game creates a sense of proximity amongst the users as well as other visuals making the game aesthetically rich and interesting while also stating facts and messages through it.

By and large, the co-creators found that games are powerful tools, and through games, they can educate women on sensitive issues like mensuration and bring it to the mainstream. They have succeeded in conscientizing the participants that menstruation is not a disease but normal hormonal changes that a woman goes through in her lifetime. The message is powerful and had its impact not only on them but also their peer groups.

REFERENCES

Gray, C. and Malins, J. (2004). *Visualizing Research: A Guide to the Research Process in Art and Design*. Hants GU11 3HR, England: Ashgate Publishing Limited.

Kumar, A. and Srivastava, K. (2011). "Cultural and Social Practices Regarding Menstruation among Adolescent Girls", *Social Work in Public Health*, 26:6: 594-604, DOI: 10.1080/19371918.2010.525144.

Rajagopal, S. and Mathur, K. (2017). "Breaking the silence around menstruation: experiences of adolescent girls in an urban setting in India", *Gender and Development*, 25:2: 303-317, DOI: 10.1080/13552074.2017.1335451

Singhal, A. and Rogers, E.M. (2001). "The Entertainment-Education Strategy in Campaigns." In: R.E. Rice and C. Atkins (eds.) *Public Communication Campaigns*. 3rd Edition. Thousand Oaks, CA: Sage Publications.

Schrier, K. (2016). *Knowledge games: How playing games can solve problems, create insight, and make change*. Baltimore, MD: Johns Hopkins University Press.

Schrier, K. (2019). "Designing Games for Moral Learning and Knowledge Building". *Games and Culture, 14*(4): 306–343. https://doi.org/10.1177/1555412017711514.

Takahashi, K.D. (2019). *Serving Teens with Mental Illness in the Library: A Practical Guide*, (e-book), Santa Barbara, California: Libraries Unlimited.

UNICEF (2018). "Menstrual Hygiene Management in Schools in South Asia". *Country snapshot – India*. Water aid. https://washmatters.wateraid.org/sites/g/files/jkxoof256/files/ WA_MHM_SNAPSHOT_INDIA.pdf.

14

Health Awareness and Television Programme

A Study of the Impact on the Scheduled Caste Community in Rural Bengal

Rajesh Das

1. Introduction

It has been observed in health communication and health promotion that significant researches have been carried out relating to health messages in popular media layouts over the last decade (Atkin and Wallack, 1990). These include an interdisciplinary and multifaceted dimension of media mix between news media, broadcast entertainment media, and the Internet. Again, 'Health communication' has witnessed an attempt of hybridization of different components. It derives from communications studies including journalism, sociological studies, psychological analysis marketing and public relations, and also overlaps with health education, health literacy, health promotion and health advocacy (Woodruff, 1996).

Health communication can take place across different levels– individual, group, organisational, community or through mass-media. Communication of health messages is still transactional in nature as regular communication. However, for promoting health, specific attention is paid to disseminating health messages or information related only to health – the process of communication and messages are further streamlined. 64 per cent of the country's social capital lives in villages. Again 16.63 per cent population is under the Scheduled Caste (SC) category and in West Bengal, it is 23.51 per cent as per the 2011 Census of India.

With the development of society, we find that the rates of different kinds of diseases are increasing, and again the nature and the rates are different in an urban community from those in a rural community. In urban areas, we find more incidences of cardiac disorder, blood pressure, asthma, diabetes, cancer, peptic ulcer, etc. whereas in rural areas the incidences of malaria, polio, jaundice, tuberculosis, diarrhoea etc., are prominent. A more remarkable difference between rural and urban communities is in the rate of child mortality and death of pregnant women. The causes behind these diseases are also different. In urban areas, most of the diseases result from modern living, business, tensions, pollution, etc., whereas rural areas lack medical facilities, awareness (about symptoms, early prevention etc.), and superstitions may be considered as the main causes of disease. If we can increase their awareness regarding good health, then definitely they can work more effectively and may contribute to rural development. Here mass media can create a significant role through its message designing about health awareness programmes. Significantly, TV reaches the vast area of rural society (considering the geographical domain i.e. footprint area as well as among audience), particularly Doordarshan and its family. Doordarshan and the other private channels are broadcasting the health awareness programme on regular basis. In this context, it's an important question whether these programmes of health are accepted or not by the rural audience. If accepted, then it will be another relevant discussion that how much they are benefited by these programmes in their daily life. On the other hand, if the programme fails to reach the rural people, then what are the reasons behind it? This research work tries to reveal the usefulness of the health-related programme among rural people more specifically among women. Again, it will also explore the rate of acceptance of health programmes among them. A large section of rural women is illiterate. They are housewives, agricultural labourers or workers of small scale industries. When it comes to the question of health problems, they may be driven by their social and religious orthodoxy (like Polio) which may lead them to quack therapy instead of proper medical treatment. Sometimes it becomes fatal. Children are our greatest prize and the growth and development of the fetus and newborn child depend solely on the mother. Therefore, the awareness of health about herself and her family is the basic requirement of an integrated rural development programme (Dalal and Misra, 2006). The basic objective of the chapter is to examine the potentiality and utilization of television in developing the health standard of rural people of Scheduled Caste community, to study the attentiveness, method of listening, viewing behaviour and time spent of rural villagers for television programmes and also try to find out whether there is any relationship or not between the degree of exposure to the television programme and the health awareness of rural Scheduled Caste community.

Communication is an important factor in the development process, more so in a planned development. SC community is one of the deprived populations in our country. A portion of the SC community in rural India is a vulnerable group of people considering their social dignity. Communication has different meanings as well as different definitions. At the same time, the term 'communication' has its own sociological, cultural, psychological, and bio-cultural orientations. After Denis McQuail (2005), the central idea is of a process of increased commonality or sharing between participants based on sending and receiving 'messages'. In this process, two important dimensions are: (i) the degree of response or feedback, and (ii) the degree to which a communication relationship is also a social relationship. India has witnessed revolutionary changes in the media ecology since the last decade or so. Thus, it will be the right time to introduce a multidisciplinary research work so that a comprehensive model could be worked out regarding message design, content selection and production techniques in television regarding health communication programmes for rural villagers. Two major issues were analysed in this study, first one is: (i) to reveal a perspective of a changing notion of communication paradigm of health and hygiene from its existing scientific extension system to the transfer of technological information on need-based orientation for a specific community and second one is, (ii) issues, ideas and scopes of applications of cultural proximity and dialogic action in health communication in television programme for rural viewers. From this discussion, the research problems may be stated as the following:

(i) how to problematise health communication?,
(ii) conceptualizing a rural media community as distinct or similar to the real-time cultural community for media effects, and
(iii) devising scales to measure media effectiveness in the face of segmentation of audience.

After explaining the issues, ideas and structure of health communication and health advocacy considering a rural subaltern community the basic objectives for the present study may be stated as the following:

(i) to enquire into the prevailing patterns of media consumption (more specifically television and their corresponding impact on awareness about health-related issues among rural communities,
(ii) to ascertain the relationship, if any, between the degree of exposure to a segment of media, i.e., television programme and the health awareness among the segment of the media community, i.e., rural Scheduled Caste community, and finally
(iii) to identify emerging patterns of newer media platforms

for informational needs about health and their respective effectiveness *vis-a-vis* the real-time health needs of different communities

Since the study is grounded on an interdisciplinary notion, then theoretical frameworks have been mapping on different aspects of communication, sociological and anthropological understanding. By framing the study as above (focusing on outcomes and impact), it may look at how the prevailing mass media consumption patterns affect health outcomes—which can include awareness about health, favourable predispositions to healthy living, higher rates of health-seeking behaviour, and higher practice of healthy behaviours. This study has considered the Health Belief Model and Theory of Planned Behaviour as Possible Theoretical Frameworks, along with McGuire's Hierarchy of Effects to gauge various stages of the outcome.

2. Overview of Literature

The entire review has been conceptually organized and presented under different heads as given below:

A. Socio-Economic and Personal Characteristics of Rural Women

Radhakrishnan (1988) from his study on the impact of the agricultural telecast on farmers reported that since agricultural programmes were telecasted in a very interesting way, it had attracted more young farmers as compared to the old and middle-aged ones.

Nayak and Jhadav (1996) said that the maximum proportion of the respondents knew the correct name, days and time of the telecast of the agricultural programme. Most of the respondents thought that television served entertainment purposes (58.5%) followed by an agricultural programme (46.89%). The size of the family, socio-economic status, work orientation and extension contact had a significant association with the televiewing behaviour of respondents.

Johnson (1999) made a detailed analysis about the impact of the widespread introduction of television on the rural life of India. He examined the social environment of village life in India and looks at the impact of television on the aspirations, values, ideas, relationships, and traditions of the villagers themselves.

B. Health Communication: An Overview

A study was conducted by Jaggarajamma *et al.* (2008) in 51 villages of Ellapuram block, Tiruvallur district, Tamil Nadu in the year to identify the channels of communication available in rural areas by interviewing key informants. The final result revealed out of 9893 households (for their project) the main occupation was agriculture (86%). Electricity was available in all the villages. More than 80 per cent of the villagers had community TV/cable connections, >50 per cent of the villages had cinema star fan associations, Mahila Mandals, youth clubs, self-help groups, Anganwadi centres and ration shops. The main source of communication as per the interview was television (100%), wall posters (55%); publicity through panchayat office meetings (53%) and *dandora* or beat of drums (43%). They concluded that the main communication channels, commonly used to disseminate information were TV and wall posters.

Another research work was done by Karnik (2008) on rural women health care, more specifically on reproductive health. Media planning or building up the communication strategies for health care were not the objectives of this research work, but to discuss the community influence on health communication or importance of socio-demographic factors on health care—the research work will help a lot.

C. Effectiveness of Television to Create Awareness of Primary Health in Rural Society

Pallikadavath and Sanneh's (2005) study aimed to identify socio-cultural and reproductive health correlates of knowledge about AIDS among rural women using multivariate analysis of 1998-1999 National Family Health Survey (NFHS) data from two Indian states, Maharashtra and Tamil Nadu. Analysis using multiple logistic regressions was undertaken, modelling women's knowledge of AIDS, of whether the disease can be avoided, and of effective means of protection.

Sharada (1992) commented TV has now emerged as the most potent medium for raising awareness especially among illiterate and semi-illiterate populations. She explained whether it can bring about desirable social changes including modernization, civic and economic awareness, political rights etc., and how far rural populations have become politically conscious through television media based on factor analysis such as age, sex, education, occupation, economic status, social participation etc.

D. The Usefulness of Television Programmes on Health Issues

Wallack states the following: "...media advocacy reflects a progressive approach to health promotion in that it explicitly recognizes the importance of the environment and defines health problems as matters of public policy and not just of individual behaviour. It tries to empower individuals by providing the knowledge and skills necessary for participation in efforts to change the social and political factors that influence health status. The health of the community, not necessarily that of the individual, is the main concern." (1990: 428-437)

Centre for Disease Control and Prevention, in its Annual Report (2008), pointed out media advocacy involves understanding and working with the news media to turn public attention to an issue and pressure policymakers to act. Furthermore, media advocates craft a story to focus on specific solutions involving change through policy development. Focus on the news media as a far-reaching channel of communication. Whereas social marketing tries to influence individual behaviour change, media advocacy aims to improve health by influencing the social and political environment in which decisions are made.

3. Methodology

A comprehensive media consumption survey can allow capturing the degree of mass media consumption and various hierarchies of health outcomes, including associations between them and also study various theoretical frameworks and operationalise to gain a deeper understanding of how to implement them in the local context. A Mixed method design classification on public health and education has been followed for the study. It means qualitative methods to develop quantitative measures and qualitative methods to explain quantitative findings, like:

I. Focused group discussion–three in each village – one for male, one for female, rest one represented by both male and female.
II. In-depth interview–from a social scientist, academician, media practitioner and media editor, extension workers, people's representatives (like PRIs members), ICDS/ASHA workers and NGOs personnel representatives.
III. Content design on health programmes in TV channels would be classified in four broad areas, likely chat show or panel discussion, live/phone-in programme, features or special report and daily hard news.

Survey

i. Population definition—In the administrative set-up, each district comprises Blocks and each Block again some villages. As a domain of the coverage of the study Jamalpur Block (under the District of Purba Bardhaman, West Bengal) was selected considering the rural population, rural Scheduled Caste population and number of television sets in households.

ii. Now stratified three-stage sampling technique was followed to collect data from the field. The selected Block was taken as a stratum. From each stratum (selected Block) all the villages were considered as a first-stage unit. Two villages were chosen randomly (second-stage unit) from the Block, and it was assumed that the size of all villages is equal. If not, then it was chosen by proportional sample size. Finally, from each selected village 50 households (third-stage units) were chosen randomly. A household should be treated as the ultimate sampling unit of the study. Any adult people of the household normally were taken up as the respondent. In this present study, 102 respondents were considered from two selected villages.

4. From Health to Health Communication: An Integrated Concept

According to the Medical dictionary, health is a status of an individual, more specifically a phenotypic status and a functional status also. Health is a condition of one's physical, mental, social and, spiritual function. According to WHO, (1948) "Health is a state of complete physical, mental and social well-being and not merely the absence of disease or infirmity." Again in the year 2000, WHO, clarified that Public and private health service provision is the most visible product of the health care system. In the present days, considering some phenomena like the growing urban life, professional pressure, quantum of global pollution, social and corporate tension, psychological pressure, conflict in society or in family etc., redefine the concept (WHO, 2007).

Definition of Health Communication – After Recognized Organizations

a. According to WHO (2014), in the year 1957 health communication was defined as a combination of three parameters– the words "information", "education", and "communication" (IEC). The

Information, education and communication (IEC) combine strategies, approaches and methods that enable individuals, families, groups, organizations and communities to play active roles in achieving, protecting and sustaining their health.

b. The major objective of health communication is to induce individuals and communities. Since health communication aspires to improve health outcomes by sharing health-related information, the objective becomes commendable. The Centres for Disease Control and Prevention (CDC) (1967) describe health communication as "the study and use of communication strategies to inform and influence individual and community decisions that enhance health".

c. Health communication is a multi-faced and multidisciplinary approach to reach diverse audiences and share health-related information to influence, engage and support individuals to communities, health professionals to special groups, policymakers to the public in general to espouse or maintain a behaviour, practice, or policy that will eventually proceed towards the attainment of better health outcomes (WHO, 1979).

d. The study and practice of communicating health-related information such as health education, health awareness, public health related campaigns and communication between doctors and patients can be termed as Health Communication. Thus, influencing personal health choices by improving health literacy becomes the main purpose of disseminating health-related information. (NACO, 2000)

e. The Sociological notion of Health Communication: Health has turned out to be an omnipresent motif in our culture. Health and illness receive substantial attention from the media such as television, radio, newspaper, magazines and video all devote significant space and time to health-related issues. Information and knowledge about health are therefore no longer just the area of health experts. Everyone has at least some experience and knowledge. The progress of the sociology of health has to be thus understood in terms of its relations to the dominant paradigm of western medicine—biomedicine. A lot of the central concerns of the sociology of health have thus emerged as reactions to, and critiques of, this biomedicine.

f. Wellness concept of Health Communication: The era of post-globalization was witnessed as its complexity of life, tension, a high degree of pollution, socio-psychological pressure and nucleus family structure. Now health communication is a key strategy not only to inform the public about health concerns but also to maintain important health issues on the public agenda. Here health communication defines a specific 'public sphere'. This kind of communication needs the applications of mass and multimedia and other technological improvements like 'new media' and 'social media' to disseminate useful health information to the public. Health communication believes in collective wellness through an individual's "feel-good" on his biological and psychological level. Health communication is directed towards improving the health status of individuals and populations.

So health communication is an integrated conception that includes the conception of health, hygiene, health education, health literacy, health campaign and health advocacy. Collectively it offers a holistic sphere of 'health system'—an interconnectedness among patients, his/her family members, communities, government officials, academicians/researcher in science and health communication, health provider's agency/organizer, pharmaceutical companies, media personnel and insurance companies.

Television and Social Behaviour

A study could be carried out on the broad aspect of examining the impact of media on the general public. Similar studies done by George Gerbner in the US has proven that TV medium is by far violent and induces violent behaviour. This medium affects the general population of the United States negative way and that effect can be seen in the way people tend to behave after getting exposed to television (Subbarayan, 1991). Gerbner in his report to the Surgeon General of the United States has found out that TV generally reaches a large population in many ways and the impact is marvellous. He terms what calls as 'Light Viewer' and 'Heavy Viewer' of television and that generally apply to the large audience it reaches. A light viewer is one who is exposed to television for a lesser period than what he calls a heavy viewer who watches TV more often than so. It is needed to be mentioned that the average American family watches television for 7.5 hours a day and that they spend more waking hours in front of the television than any other activity put together. TV has become this popular that the effect it has on the audience is tremendous. TV can be compared to a vast land in which a person can trek into indefinitely exploring new vistas but never be able to get away from it. Once a person becomes addicted to T.V watching, lifelong he remains so. This is the major problem with television. (Subbarayan, 1991)

5. Demographic Configuration of the Field Study

A survey was conducted in the Jamalpur Block of district Purba Bardhaman (West Bengal) considering the total population of Scheduled Caste. Two villages, Balarampur and Salimabad were selected for this survey and finally, 48 households were visited to conduct the survey and collected the required data.

Table 14.1: Demographic Particulars of Field Survey: Gender

S. No.	*Gender*	*No. of Respondents*	*Pecentage*
1.	Male	48	47.1
2.	Female	54	52.9
Total		102	100.0

Table 14.2: Demographic Particulars of Field Survey: Educational Qualification

S. No.	*Education*	*Number of Respondents*	*Percentage*
1.	0	30	29.4
2.	1	5	4.9
3.	2	3	2.9
4.	3	20	19.6
5.	4	12	11.8
6.	5	8	7.8
7.	6	14	13.8
8.	8	10	9.8
	Total	102	100.0

[General Educational Level: literate without formal schooling–0, literate but below primary–1, primary–2, middle 3, secondary–4, higher secondary–5, certificate course–6, not literate–8]

Table 14.3: Demographic Particulars of Field Survey: Employment Status

S. No.	*Employment Status*	*Number of Respondents*	*Percentage*
1.	Employed	30	29.4
2.	Unemployed	72	70.6
	Total	102	100.0

The above shown three consecutive tables reveal that around 40 per cent Scheduled Caste population of total Scheduled Caste are either illiterate or has no formal school level education (Table 14.2). Possibly, it brings about two-staged negative interferences, first one on socio-demographic scenario followed by to collect and share the scientific information related to health and hygiene. It's a general presumption that extent of access to get a skill-based job is rightly proportionate with a formal educational degree. It is being proved again, when (Table 14.3) shows that 72 per cent of the total adult population is still unemployed or engaged as marginalized and/or landless farmers. On the other side, if we consider the ecology of the health communication system, then it verbalizes a scientific communication network within a defined socio-psychological dimension. The Information Education Communication (IEC) method or health literacy help to enhance an integrated health advocacy system within the community. This structure needs a minimum degree of formal information—knowledge system. Even to decode some terminologies, (about the disease, its symptoms or process of diagnosis) that are used in a television programme, formal knowledge may help as a reagent.

6. Analysis and Interpretation of Media Credibility on Heath Communication

Here we try to analyse the collective scopes and advantages of the Health Information System through Television in any developing society like the Indian rural community. The designing message of health communication through television may develop the following concerns:

- Providing personalized self-management tools and resources.
- Building social support networks.
- Delivering precise, easy to get to and actionable health information that is targeted or customized.
- Facilitating the meaningful use of health and the exchange of health information among health care and public health professionals.
- Providing new opportunities to connect with culturally diverse and hard-to-reach populations

These traits are significantly related to the media behaviour of an individual. There are three major conventional forms of media i.e., newspaper, radio and TV. The present study also observed that a high degree of mobile communication is working (less quantity of android device) in these selected villages. At the same time, it also studied that villagers are involved more in 'entertainment' forms of communication compared to 'learning'—'practice' through their mobile set.

A. Mass Media Participation of Rural Villagers

Table 14.4: Radio Usage

S. No.	*Usage*	*No. of Respondents*	*Percentage*
1.	Regularly	2	2.0
2.	Occasionally	14	13.7
3.	Rarely	86	84.3
	Total	102	100.0

Table 14.5: Television Usage

S. No.	*Usage*	*No. of Respondents*	*Percentage*
1.	Regularly	86	84.3
2.	Occasionally	16	15.7
3.	Rarely	-	-
	Total	102	100.0

Table 14.6: Newspaper Usage

S. No	*Usage*	*No. of Respondents*	*Percentage*
1.	Regularly	2	2.0
2.	Occasionally	16	15.7
3.	Rarely	84	82.3
	Total	102	100.0

Tables 14.4 to 14.9 reveal that television gains its highest accessibility (84% of total), compared to other conventional mass media (radio and newspaper) in a rural domain. Perhaps, audio and visual effects make an extent of the effect of fairness, openness and immediacy format of TV programme towards audience's mind. But, at the same time, it is also true that the degree of attraction of a TV programme does not reciprocate the usefulness or utilization of content at right time at the right place by an individual (viewer).

During the past decade, there has been a growing recognition of the usefulness of behavioural theory in the development of behaviour change intervention (see, e.g., National Institutes of Health, 1997). Theories of behavioural prediction and behaviour change are useful because they provide a framework to help identify the determinants of any given behaviour, an essential first step in the development of successful interventions to change that behaviour. The more one knows about the determinants of a given behaviour, the more likely it is that one can develop an effective communication or other types of intervention to reinforce or change that behaviour. The purpose of this study was to show the relevance of behavioural theory for developing communications to promote healthy and/or to prevent or alter unhealthy behaviours.

B. Parameters of Credibility for TV Programme

The credibility of message design of mass media in general and for a television programme in specific depends on some factors—like the accuracy of the message, openness and fairness of data planning, procurement and presentation, presentation of unbiased content and observation, the use of content in respect of audience's need and the timeliness of programme. These are the thumb rules to design an edutainment/infotainment programme production, as a health communication programme.

From Table 14.10 to 14.15, the numbers in parentheses denote the actual number of respondents considering a specific variable.

Accurate and Unbiased

Table 14.7: Gender vs. Accurate and Unbiased Information in TV Programme (Overall TV Programme)

S. No.	*Gender*	*Agree*	*Disagree*	*Strongly Agree*	*Total*
1.	Female	(14) 25.53%	(3) 6.38%	(37) 68.09%	54 100.00%
2.	Male	(30) 62.96%	(09) 18.52%	(09) 18.52%	48 100.00%
3.	Total	(44) 43.13 %	(12) 11.78%	(46) 45.09%	102 100.00%

Analysis on Accuracy and Unbiased Vs. *Gender*

To know the media credibility (on general and specific content) of rural audiences here is a comparative analysis of the degree of credibility between overall TV programmes (TV serials, drama, film, sports etc.) *vs.* the programme solely on health and hygiene or on public health has been done. In general, it could be stated that a rural society itself is patriarchal. At the same time, children spent maximum time with their mothers. But the literacy rate has yet not reached that level (Table 14.2) where the content of science communication could be discussed in an open forum.

As a subject health communication is under the school of development communication that is dominated by scientific and experimental based terminological communication. The credibility of the content of such communication could interfere on degree of behavioural changes of an individual and/or community.

Among the regular TV viewers (who watched at least three numbers of TV channels spending total time not less than 30 minutes in a day) said that they are strongly supported that programme contents in TV (means audio and visual elements and presentation/production format) are unbiased and authentic (Table 14.7). But when the same behavioural approach was tasted exclusively on health-related programmes, only 7 per cent of respondents expressed their opinion on the 'strongly agree' parameter.

TV has an enormous power to motivate people and a high degree of credibility of programme content helps to reach a high degree of effective innovation in the communication process. Rural women opted for teleserials, drama, reality shows, films and other entertainment programmes as their primary preference list. It was also noticed that they discussed the storyline or climax of the scene or situation of the protagonist character with their family members, friends or neighbours. Normally, the storyline of teleserials mostly focused on conflict, struggle, politics and some domestic violence of daily life. Here it could be assumed that women have been tried to relate these programme content within their family– life or society. Perhaps a degree of physical and cultural proximity has been noticed by the audience and that helped to believe that 'TV programmes are unbiased and accurate'.

A content analysis is conducted on selected health programmes of four leading Bengali TV channels based on their TRP. When 62 such episodes are analyzed it is revealed that private TV channels had focused their production on 'tips of good-life' for the urban upper or middle-class society. Use of refined oil (16 episodes); effectiveness of Amand Badam and Raisin (08 episodes); use of white curd for skin (12 episodes); awareness, symptoms and prevention of heart attack, diabetes, blood pressure and cancer (17 episodes); going to the gym to retain psychical fitness (07 episodes), compare to diarrhoea (03 episodes); family planning

(01 episodes); DOT Programme (zero episodes); or whooping cough (zero episodes)–were the list of produced programmes. The programmes were sponsored by different groups of corporate and normally they try to focus the urban-based market interest regarding health and hygiene. So, considering the rural audiences perhaps these selected episodes were just interfering agents on their existing belief and behaviour of health communication. Desai A.R. commented that physical and cultural proximity are two significant catalysts in any rural society and these catalysts may create rigidity or semi-rigidity feelings over one content if those (designed message) are not matched with their diversified culture.

Timeliness and Authenticity

Table 14.8: Gender *vs*. Timeliness and Authenticity of TV Programme (Overall TV programme)

S. No.	Gender	Agree	Disagree	Strongly Agree	Total
1.	Female	(03) 4.3%	(0) 0.0%	(51) 95.7%	54 100.0%
2.	Male	(31) 64.8%	(08) 16.7%	(09) 18.5%	48 100.0%
3.	Total	(34) 33.33%	(08) 7.84%	(60) 58.83%	102 100.0%

Observation on Timeliness and Authenticity

Three more parameters are also to be considered to study the level of credibility of health-related TV programmes in the selected Bengali channels (as per research design). These parameters are, (i) Timeliness and Authenticity, (ii) Usefulness, and (iii) Simple language. Selections of parameters were governed by cognitive factors—social judgment and constructivism. Constructivism is a combination of observations that help to define the ability to differentiate the way people make sense of things and to the creation of activity. That means it defines personal construction and person-centred message.

Dalal (2016), opined that "social constructionism makes sense if we consider human beings, not as a conceiver of the social and physical world. One must know before one can see. These approaches hold that there is no truth or objectivity. The reality as we see is a mental and social construction. Our expectation, ideology and past knowledge determine what we see as real". Knowledge cannot be independent of the knower. Luckmann believed that, "social constructionism takes the position that there are no truths or objective realities, all realities are socially constructed.

Audiences cannot directly describe our experiences, as all experiences are shaped by our construction of events" (1966, pp. 6-7). Scientific knowledge (like health communication, environmental communication etc.) deals with these constructed realities—everyday subjective construction on the part of people who are studied and scientific construction on the part of the researcher in collecting, treating and interpreting data as well as in the presentation of findings. Based on these socio-psychological reagents the following tables would help to develop an individual's belief, constructivism and aspects of social justice on the television programme of entertainment section and for health as an exclusive format.

Usefulness

Table 14.9: Overall TV Programme by Gender and Usefulness

S. No.	*Gender*	*Agree*	*Disagree*	*Strongly Agree*	*Total*
1.	Female	(21) 38.3%	(07) 12.8%	(26) 48.9%	54 100.0%
2.	Male	(32) 66.7%	(08) 16.7%	(08) 16.7%	48 100.0%
3.	Total	(53) 52.94%	(15) 14.70%	(34) 32.36%	102 100.0%

Table 14.10: Health Programme Only by Gender and Usefulness

S. No.	*Gender*	*Agree*	*Disagree*	*Strongly Agree*	*Total*
1.	Female	(30) 55.3%	(0) 0%	(07) 12.8%	(17) 31.9%
2.	Male	(36) 75.9%	(08) 16.7%	(02) 3.7%	(02) 3.7%
3.	Total	(66) 64.70%	(08) 7.84%	(09) 8.82%	(19) 18.64%

Simple Language

Table 14.11: Overall TV Programme by Gender and Simple Language

S. No.	*Gender*	*Agree*	*Disagree*	*Strongly Agree*	*Total*
1.	Female	(21) 38.3%	(01) 2.1%	(32) 59.6%	54 100.0%
2.	Male	(32) 66.7%	(04) 9.3%	(12) 24.1%	48 100.0%
3.	Total	(53) 52.00%	(05) 10.20%	(44) 37.80%	102 100.0%

Table 14.12: Health Issue by Gender and Simple Language

S. No.	Gender	Agree	Disagree	Strongly Agree	Total
1.	Female	(36) 66.0%	(0) 0 %	(07) 12.8%	(11) 21.3%
2.	Male	(38) 79.6%	(07) 14.8%	(02) 3.7%	(01) 1.9%
3.	Total	(74) 72.54%	(07) 6.86%	(09) 8.82%	(12) 11.78%

How Credibility Helps an Effective Campaign of Health Communication through Television Programme

About 32.36 per cent audiences of total (48.9% of females as against 16.7% of males) expressed that overall TV programmes are very useful where only 18.64 per cent (31.9% males and 3.7% females), rural Scheduled Caste population had agreed to say TV broadcasting on health – hygiene was extremely useful in their daily life (Table 14.9 & 14.10). Berol's SMCR Model of Communication (1960) as opined by Saud *et al.*, (2014), articulated a model of interpersonal communication in any social system. To explain the process, 'from the encoder to decoder', he talked about four factors—source, message, channel and receiver. The message is comprised of content, element, treatment, structure and code, whereas the other two factors, 'Source and Receiver', have been included knowledge, social system, culture and attitude. In this process, 'Language' is a way of making more easy communication. It also helps to express the culture of a person to another one. Again cultural proximity sometimes interferes with one's attitudinal delicacy. Common language is one of the most important features of a community and the constant use of the same language is the most certain proof of continuity of a community of people. Rural society itself practices a high intensity of social cohesion considering its different traits of culture, like language, dialects, religion, occupation, festival, food habit or dress code. In a holistic process of communication when the sender communicates with another one, the language can help him to express his ideas more accurately.

In this context, the present study also identified that just 11.78 per cent (21.3% and 1.9% of females to males respectively), (Table 14.12) rural Scheduled Caste community of total sample has strongly advocated in favour of the simple language of television broadcasting on a health issue. Designing a message for any development communication, like health communication, has some systematic steps for audience involvement both for message design and decoding the message. It is a part of persuasive communication where the articulation of language aids to design a message that communicates in a straightforward simple approach.

In any rural socio-cultural sphere, women are more interactive with their community, like family members, extension workers or neighbours. A continuous mode of discussion (an intrapersonal and group level), in a multi-cluster level, sometimes facilitates to decode a scientific communication like health communication in any mass media platform. Secondly, the rural society has its indigenous knowledge network system, which disseminates basic information on the health and hygiene of an individual and/ or her family. Perhaps, all these are framed to easy the female audiences (compared to males) to grasp the scientific terminology related to health and hygiene.

7. Conclusion

In concluding this chapter, it is important, to sum up, the salient features and findings of the present study. While describing these features, we feel it necessary to repeat the major findings which might have a bearing, however remote, upon the methodology and substantively of Health Communication programme in TV and Rural Scheduled Caste community. At a broad theoretical level, the present study has demonstrated based on substantive data that the TV has an impact and to a certain extent of acceptance among rural Scheduled Caste community. But at the same time audiences are interested to watch Entertainment-Education, E-E, Model of TV programme for any development communication, like rural communication. Johnson (2001) analyzes the role of television in rural life, and the influence it has had on various social, economic and political processes that have been revolutionizing the landscape of village India in recent years. Speaking truly, rural Scheduled Caste community is ruled by socio-cultural taboos and orthodoxy. TV has enormous power on the dynamics of social changes. Not only its speed, authenticity and straight dealing format of communication but the audio and visual support also create a positive reagent on the presentation of any scientific communication, like health communication.

Data from ethnographic fieldwork in two remote villages in the Burdhman District, West Bengal, are presented in the context of development (extent of use of health communication) and social change. In particular, the research establishes the framework and rationale for an ethnographic approach to the research. It discusses the unique characteristics of television that make it an important agent of cultural change. Furthermore, the research revealed various social processes that include behavioural study, behavioural changes, communication, and role of cognitive theory and the emergence of reasoned action from the cognitive network. Health and well-being is a comprehensive model which includes the whole gamut of psychological conditions which are linked with health as causes and consequences (Dalal and Mishra, 2006).

The focus of this chapter primarily depends on the three areas i.e., health communication; rural communication and rural development. These three notions of communication studies would help for a constructive change on awareness and usefulness of information on health and hygiene among rural people in general and SC community in specific. The television programme (designing – message) should be included—cultural compatibility, community-based dialogue/characterization, medical pluralism in the country (both modern medicine and indigenous system) and also considered the relevance of faith healing in the modern scientific age and resorting equilibrium on social, cultural and bio-cultural healing system. It is said composition of the Entertainment-Education (E-E) strategy helps to contribute to social change through mass media in multiple ways. E-E can influence the audience's awareness, attitude and behaviour towards a socially desirable end. Often E-E programmes spark conversation among audience members about the health awareness programme that are addressed, leading to dialogue, decision and individual or collective actions.

An E-E based Television network broadcasting should be introduced on promoting family planning and malaria prevention and other community diseases. It should be a story-based broadcasting, comprising feature or docu-feature format. Regarding communication strategies, an "action-packed script" be designed that takes viewer's perceptions from the ground level, here the rural Bengal. The plot boasts all the ingredients of irresistible television—tragedy, chaos, laughter, love, deception and forgiveness. Through these viewers could be motivated and after seeing this kind of programme either they could adopt the new thing as well as could start an interaction with extension workers of the stated issues.

Script development method should ensure on current data from research on the thematic issues and writers be guided by a crop of content specialists. Before final production, to maximise impact and increase the appeal of Behaviour Changed Communication be pre-tested, and relevant suggestions from the audience should be incorporated. It will be an E-E programme based on horizontal knowledge sharing from audiences.

Considering the present age of media convergence and the boom of social media, the EE Programme could be translated in into various vernacular languages to ensure a high degree of inclusion of rural audiences. It could be also considered that these programmes be available on a mobile phone.

It's true that at present the amount of corporate sponsorship is too little to produce a series of health awareness campaigns on TV. To overcome the stated situation, we recommended the government interference to produce/broadcast such a programme. The wellness of the citizen makes a better and stable social capital of the 'State'. The government through its active governance could take an intuitive to promote baseline health literacy among the rural Scheduled Caste community. Effective governance has it is a 'winning formula'. It is: [Development + Good Governance System = Low and Stable Diseases Prevalence]. A broad-based conclusion from this discussion that social change is directly linked with the degree of awareness of rural people. These social changes could be done through an integrated network among the organization, expert personnel, research institute, peer group and major stakeholders. This network should be effective both on the structural as well as psychological levels. Another major conclusion from the research argues that the village audience is an active and vibrant participant in the use of media. The challenges are whether the form, content, message design and presentation of these programmes are produced according to their level or not. Our observation reads that the selection and message design of TV programmes of health on and hygiene for the rural Scheduled Caste community are not focusing on the ground level reality.

REFERENCES

Atkin, C.K., and Wallack, L. (1990). *Mass communication and public health: Complexities and conflicts* (Vol. 121). New Delhi: Sage.

Centers for Disease Control and Prevention. (1967). *Records of the Centers for Disease Control and Prevention*. Retrieved 20 July 2020, from https://www.archives.gov/research/guide-fed-records/groups/442.html

Center for Disease Control and Prevention (2018). *Annual Report.* Retrieved 20 July 2020, from https://www.cdc.gov/nchs/data/hus/hus08.pdf

Dalal, A.K., and Misra, G. (2006). "Psychology of health and well-being: Some emerging perspectives." *Psychological Studies. 51*(2-3) 91–104.

Dalal, A.K., (2016). *Cultural psychology of health in India*. New Delhi: Sage Publication.

Jaggarajamma, K., Ramachandran, R., Charles, N., Chandrasekaran, V., Muniyandi, M., and Ganapathy, S. (2008). "Psycho-social dysfunction: Perceived and enacted stigma among tuberculosis patients registered under Revised National Tuberculosis Control Programme." *Indian Journal of Tuberculosis*, *55*(4), 179-187.

Johnson, Krik, (1999). *Television and Social Change in Rural India.* New Delhi: Sage Publications.

Johnson, Krik, (2001). *Media and Social Change: The Moderninzing Influence of Television in Rural India. Media Culture and Society 23*(2), 147-169.

Karnik, K. (2008). "Global sourcing of services: Vision 2020." *Journal of Information Technology Case and Application Research, 10*(4), 1-7.

Luckmann, C. (1996). "Defining experiential education." *Journal of Experiential Education, 19*(1), 6-7.

McQuail, Denis (2005). *Mass Communication Theory*, Fifth Edition. New Delhi: Vistaar Publication.

NACO. (2000). "National Strategic Plan for HIV/AIDS and STI." Retrieved 18 July 2020, from http://naco.gov.in/sites/default/files/Paving%20the%20 Way%20for%20an%20AIDS%2015122017.pdf

Nayak, H.S., and Jhadav, S.N. (1996)."Televiewing behaviour of rural televiewers towards farm programmes." *Maharashtra Journal of Extension Education.* 15: 173-175.

Pallikadavath, S., Sanneh, A., Mcwhirter, J.M., and Stones, R.W. (2005). "Rural women's knowledge of AIDS in the higher prevalence states of India: reproductive health and sociocultural correlates." *Health Promotion International*, *20*(3), 249-259.

Radhakrishnan, T. (1988). Impact of agricultural telecast on farmers. M.Sc. (Agri.) thesis, Tamil Nadu Agricultural University, Coimbatore.

Saud, S., Jufri, A., and Rahman, M.A. (2014). "Learning devices development on descriptive writing for foreign language based on Belro's SMER Communication Model of secondary school student." *Journal of Language Teaching and Research*, *5*(5): 1033.

Sharada, P.V. (1992). *Impact of Television on Political Awareness of Masses*. New Delhi: Gyan Publication.

Subbarayan, G. (1991). "The Television and Social Behaviour", *Communicator*, vol. xxvi, No. 4.

The National Institutes of Health. (1997). The National Institutes of Health (NIH) Consensus Development Program: Interventions To Prevent HIV Risk Behaviours. Retrieved 18 July 2020, from https://consensus.nih.gov/1997/1997preventhivrisk104html.htm

Wallack, L., Grube, J.W., Madden, P.A., & Breed, W. (1990). "Portrayals of alcohol on prime-time television." *Journal of studies on alcohol, 51*(5): 428-437.

WHO. (1948). "Working for health." Retrieved 18 July 2020, from https://www.who.int/about/brochure_en.pdf

WHO (1979). WHO handbook for Reporting Results of Cancer Treatment. Retrieved on 18 July, 2020 from apps.who.int/iris/bitstream/handle/10665/37200/WHO-OFFSET_48.pdf?sequence.

WHO. (2007). "HIV/AIDS Programme: Strengthening health services to fight HIV/AIDS". Retrieved 18 July 2020, from https://www.who.int/hiv/pub/guidelines/HIVstaging150307.pdf?ua=

WHO. (2014). "World Health Statistics." Retrieved 18 July 2020, from https://apps.who.int/iris/bitstream/handle/10665/112738/9789240692671_eng.pdf;jsessionid=2E034409E1F75AC82F58F59BC35FFBDB?sequence=1

Woodruff, K. Alcohol (1996). "Advertising and violence against women: A media advocacy case study." *Health Education Quarterly*, *23*(3):330-345.

15

Social Network Systems, Mental Health and Development

A Study of Medical and Dental Students

N. Sharon Sucharitha Gold

Introduction

It is not an exaggeration to say that technology is ruling the modern world. From office work to household work everything is intertwined with different machinery, appliances and electronic gadgets, and the technical knowledge about operating various machinery and appliances is mandatory. Within this domain of technological achievements, advancements particularly in computer technology have overtaken all other applications of scientific knowledge for almost all practical purposes of life. In one word, today technological paradigm has invaded workplaces, homes and culture as never before. Humans, being social animals have the inherent need to connect and communicate with others having been endowed with biological and cultural systems of communication. And, this natural process of communication has now been mediated by technology so much so that world has become a 'global village' as McLuhan (1994) said breaking down the physical and special boundaries. This has led Information and Communication Technology (ICT) to be at the forefront of these advancements. The ICT includes telecommunications, computers, necessary software and audio-visual systems that are integrated to form unified communications. Further, it has created new social spaces where individuals can interact, exchange ideas, conduct businesses, share information etc., fostered by computer-enabled automated information and technologies that are termed 'cyber space'. It is an online virtual world formed by interconnected technology *viz.*, computer systems and networks. William Gibson (1984) is the person who created the term 'cyberspace' in 1984 in his novel 'Neuromancer'.

The networks which create cyberspace are of different kinds of web spaces that allow a person to create a profile of him or her containing the basic bio-data, profile picture and other information that one wants to share with others. They also provide users facilities to interact with other users of the same space to share information or form relationships. The users can even create a list of other users who they want to be 'friends' with online contact. These friends can 'like' or 'comment' on any photo or video uploaded by the user and the user can perform the same action when the friend upload anything. These sites are termed Social Networking Sites (SNS) as they act as a platform for meeting new people with similar interests as well as being in touch with 'offline' friends or regular friends who reside in distant locations. Social networks are largely connected to people's social characteristics reflecting their professional and personal interests. The most commonly used SNS in India are: Facebook, YouTube, WhatsApp, Facebook Messenger, We Chat, Instagram, etc. (Anonymous n.d).

There has been extensive use of cyberspace and social networking sites daily ever since the emergence of SNS. Networking by individuals provides privacy and independence which is not a problem as long as they are unaffected by the perils of the system such as addiction, psychological problems etc. In some cases, increased communication through the internet has affected psychological well-being in a positive direction (Magsamen-Conrad, K. *et al.*, 2014). The other side of excessive usage of social networking sites and cyberspace has proved to have a detrimental effect on the mental health of today's younger generation (Bashir, H. *et al.*, 2017). In a recent news report, it has been said as,

> "In the almost two decades of the 21st century, technology has irreversibly changed our lives. Ever since smartphones invaded the human civilization, people seem to have become more mechanical and insensitive. They have become bereft of real emotions and have started to reside in a fake world. Consequently, depression amongst students is also at an all-time high." (Priyadarshini, 2018)

Thus, SNS has become a sort of menace affecting mental well-being unintentionally which need to be properly understood. Mental health is often neglected or sidelined, which has to be taken care of, for the total health of an individual is very important. It is defined as "a state of well-being in which every individual realizes his or her own potential, can cope with the normal stresses of life, can work productively and fruitfully and is able to make a contribution to his or her community" (WHO, 2004:13). Mental health disorders are usually not caused by a single factor. Biological, psychological and socio-cultural factors together cause mental illness which occurs in a variety of forms with overlapping symptoms. Some categories of mental health disorders are anxiety disorders, mood disorders, psychotic disorders, personality disorders, impulse control disorders etc. In the various mood disorders, major depressive disorder is the most common type. (Anonymous n.d). Depression is a condition where there are persistent feelings of sadness and hopelessness. The affected individual has a marked lack of interest in the things once enjoyed. There are disturbances in eating and sleep patterns. The overall social functioning of the individual is affected. According to the DSM V, the symptoms must be persistent for more than two weeks to be considered as depression.

Depression is a psychological disorder that can be traced back to the classical era, but then, it was called 'melancholia'. Hippocrates takes the credit for describing 'melancholia' as a disease with particular mental and physical symptoms caused due to excessive amounts of black bile (Akiskal, 2000). Cicero, a prominent Roman statesman and philosopher attributed the causes of melancholy to psychological problems such as rage, fear and grief. During the 18th and 19th centuries, depression came to be understood as a weakness of temperament for which a vast number of treatments including shutting the affected people out, immersion under water, horseback riding, enema and vomiting were recommended. Freud theorized that depression is nothing but loss, either the death or loss of a loved one or the inability to attain the desired goal, thus linking melancholy to mourning (Ehlers *et al.*, 1988). Emil Kraepelin, a German psychiatrist is the one who first used the term 'depression' (Ebert *et al.*, 2010). It is derived from the Latin verb 'deprimere', meaning 'to press down' or 'bring down' in spirit, referring to different types of melancholia as depressive states. Meyer worked on emphasizing the reactions of a person's life influenced by a mixed social and biological framework in causing the melancholic conditions and hence argued that 'depression' is the term to be used.

Is the ITC Boon or Bane?

As mentioned earlier, social networking sites and cyberspace has some relation with human communication and mental health. Is the ITC, then, boon or bane? How far the impact is negative in causing psychological problems such as anxiety, depression, loss of self-worth, decreased self-esteem etc., is again a matter of controversial debate as of today. Some studies point out that there are negative consequences while others say that there are positive outcomes such as increased self-esteem, increased sense of self-worth associated with excessive use of cyberspace and SNS.

The earliest study that Kraut *et al.* (1998) conducted in this regard shows that the excessive use of the internet resulted in decreased communication with family members in the household, a decline in the size of the social circle, increased depression and loneliness. Even though SNS were not yet introduced at the time of this study, an increase in the time spent on the internet showed a decrease in mental health and well-being with a decrease in interpersonal communication. This has trigged several studies. For example, Takahira *et al.*(2008), studied the effect of daily internet usage on 10 to 12-year-old Japanese School children. It has been indicated that the use of the internet tended to increase depression, aggression and preference for internet communication, but did not affect loneliness. The study also examined causal relationships which indicated that children with higher depression, aggression and preference for internet communication tended to use the internet more. Another study by Rosen *et al.* (2013) supports the fact that those who spent more time online showed signs of major clinical depression. This study also brought to light the fact that people with high levels of narcissism and high levels of Facebook activity are associated with higher levels of depression. Siobhan McGrath (2012) in 'The impact of new media technologies on social interaction in the household' has said that integration of media technologies into social settings such as household, is having a major influence on social interaction between individuals in a family.

But other studies have indicated quite opposite trend of the relationship between higher-level engagement with SNS and psychological well-being. According to Pantic *et al.* (2014), there is a significant positive statistical correlation between depressive symptoms and time spent on SNS. At the same time, the study shows that there is no positive correlation between depressive symptoms and time spent watching television. Jelenchick *et al.* (2012) in their study have put forth the opinion that depression caused by SNS may also be related to the age factor. Their study shows that there is no evidence supporting a relationship between SNS use and clinical depression. According to Ali *et al.* (2018), there is no positive correlation between depression and addiction to social media among the female teenagers in Buraidah, Al Qassim, and Saudi Arabia.

There does not appear to have been any major study in India to establish any relationship between the SNS and psychological well-being or mental health though several studies are available on the latter. I think it is high time to consider undertaking such studies in India too and participate in the debate and discussion.

Studies in India: There is a growing concern about excessive or intensive use of social media by students as it is believed that their studies are being adversely affected as indicated in the quote made earlier. There are several studies about internet use in India. To cite some examples, the internet use of college students in Kashmir valley is about 44.5 per cent across all disciplines according to Loan (Loan, 2011). In one study it is reported that 93 per cent of the students' access the internet everyday in 7 cities of India. (https://www.livemint.com/Politics/PSq0aCdEQTkbFa3LwghGSM/93-students-in-India-access-Internet-everyday.html). Among the Bombay university undergraduate students, it is found that 90 per cent of students spend 2 hours a day and 40 per cent use the internet for non-academic purposes (Limaye and Fotwengel, 2015). However, there are no studies to reveal the impact of internet use among college students.

There are few studies on internet use by medical students. For example, in a study of medical students in Meerut UP, it is found 78 per cent of students use the internet while 20 per cent of the time only it is used for medical education. More than 22.8 per cent use the internet for more than three hours a week (Maroof, Khan Amir, Pawan Parashar, and Rahul Bansa, 2012). On the contrary, a study with the sample from Bangalore, Mangalore and Trissur has found that 27 per cent of medical students met the criterion for mild Internet Addiction (IA), 10.4 per cent for moderate IA, and 0.8 per cent for severe addictive use of the internet (Anand *et al.*, 2018).

Though few studies show the prevalence of depression, anxiety and stress among college-going students, the association with SNS are not available. In the Amritsar district of Punjab, the depression rate is high among engineering students (22%) compared to medical students (11%) (Kaur, Deepti, and Lal, 2014). However, in Delhi, the depression in terms of provisional depression and disorder depression is found among the medical students of Maulana Azad Medical College, New Delhi, at 21 per cent and 7.6 per cent (Sidana *et al.*, 2012). Yet another study shows prevalence of depression to an extent of 49.1 per cent among the students of a private medical college in Bareilly, Uttar Pradesh (Singh, Lal, and Shekhar, 2010). In a study of medical students in Bhubaneswar, Odisha, depression is found in 51.3 per cent of the sample (Iqbal, Gupta, and Venkatarao, 2015). But in these, studies there is no indication to what extent internet use has contributed to depression, anxiety and stress.

The use of the internet by the dental undergraduate students in Rajasthan seems to be minimum, not more than 5 per cent (Kumari, Tadakamadla, Tibdewal, Duraiswamy and Kulkarni, 2010), but it has been reported high (88.84%) in another study in North India (Marya, Marya, Dahiya, and Gupta, 2013). Nevertheless, there is no study about the relationship between the internet or social media on the students of medicine or dental sciences.

In the background of the above discussion, the present study has the following objectives.

Objectives

1. To understand the prevalence of depression between the genders among college-going students.
2. To find out the difference of time spent on cyberspace/SNS among the genders.
3. To find out the correlation between time spent on the internet and depression.

Methodology

No hypothesis is proposed in this as it is an explorative study. A short survey has been organized with a psychological tool for the collection of relevant data.

Survey and Sample

The sample consists of 100 students from Rajiv Gandhi Institute of Medical Sciences (RIMS), Kadapa, which is run by the Government of Andhra Pradesh providing in Bachelor of Medicine and Bachelor of Surgery (MBBS) and Bachelor of Dental Surgery (BDS). RIMS is affiliated with Dr. N.T.R. University of Health Sciences, Vijayawada. It is located in Putlampalli village, about 7 kilometres from Kadapa town. The medical college with an intake of 150 students per year came into the function from the year 2006. Government Dental College, RIMS, Kadapa was started in the year 2008-2009 with an intake of 100 students per year. Both the colleges are on the same campus and the sample was collected from both the colleges. The college and hospital were started with the noble cause of fortifying treatment to the rural populations near Kadapa, the district headquarters of the YSR district.

Tool for Data Collection

Beck's Depression Inventory (BDI): Psychiatric rating scales based on symptoms were developed more than 40 years ago where patient's behaviour and feelings were assigned numerical values. Galton has been given credit for the introduction of rating scales, however, prior usage can also be traced (McReynolds, and Ludwig, 1987). The hospital anxiety and depression scale available has been widely investigated and validated but not in much use in the clinical setting as it is more time consuming (Snaith, 2003). There is the 20 item Zung Depression Scale which does not have adequate sensitivity to detect change over time and hence is seldom used (Zung, W.K.W. 1965). The Hamilton Depression Rating Scale is the oldest instrument which is a validated instrument and used widely (Kobak, 2010).

The BDI was first published in 1961, created by Aaron Beck. It is a tool that is high in specificity and sensitivity and is valid and reliable in assessing the severity of depressive symptoms (Beck *et al.*, 1988). BDI was developed in such a way to allow patients to describe their symptoms along with a scale to measure the severity of a particular symptom. It is a 21 item self-report inventory for individuals aged over 13. The items relate to symptoms of depression such as hopelessness, irritability etc. Cognitive disturbances such as feelings of guilt and punishment and physical changes such as a change in appetite, sleep pattern, loss of interest in sex are also included in the inventory. The BDI closely agrees with Hamilton Depression Rating Scale. It is widely used by health practitioners and researchers. Its usefulness had led to its translation into various languages such as Arabic, Chinese, Japanese, Persian, Xhosa as well as multiple European languages. The development of the BDI shifted the psychiatrists' and psychologists' view of depression from a Freudian perspective of hidden inner feelings to one by the person's thoughts and cognitions.

BDI categorizes the scores obtained through the scale into mild, moderate and severe depression. A score of 0-9 indicates minimal depression, 10-18 mild depression, 19-29 moderate depression and 30-63 indicates severe depression.

Findings and Discussion

Socio-demographic characteristics of the sample: As can be noted from Table 15.1, the course or gender-wise the total sample drawn is almost in equal proportion. But, within the course, the male representation of the MBBS is greater than the BDS males and similarly female representation in BDS is greater than the female in MBBS (Table 15.1).

Table 15.1: Characteristics of the sample – Gender by Course

Sl. No.	*Gender*	*MBBS*	*BDS*	*Total*
1.	Male	25	13	38
		65.8%	34.2%	100.0%
		49.0%	26.5%	38.0%
2.	Female	26	36	62
		41.9%	58.1%	100.0%
		51.0%	73.5%	62.0%
3.	Total	51	49	100
		51%	49%	100%

When it comes to community, there is almost equal representation of males and females from BCs but female representation from OCs is high. The representation of males from SC/ST categories is relatively high compared to females (Table 15.2).

Table 15.2: Characteristics of the sample – Gender by Community

S. No.	*Gender*	*OC*	*BC*	*SC/ST*	*Total*
1.	Male	7	19	12	38
		18.4%	50.0%	31.6%	100.0%
		17.1%	48.7%	60.0%	38.0%
2.	Female	34	20	8	62
		54.8%	32.3%	12.9%	100.0%
		82.9%	51.3%	40.0%	62.0%
3.	Total	41	39	20	100
		41.0%	39.0%	20.0%	100.0%

OC = Other Class; BC = Backward Class; SC = Scheduled Castes; ST = Scheduled Tribes.

Depression and its Correlates

Gender: The study makes it clear that there is some form of depression to the extent of 55 per cent in the entire sample, however, the severe form is only one per cent which is negligible. The prevalence of depression is almost equal in both genders, 55 per cent (21out of 38) males and 54 per cent (34 out of 62) among females. Mild depression is higher in females whereas, in males, the incidence of moderate to severe depression is higher. The mild form of depression is more prevalent than the moderate form in both genders. If the total sample is considered 55 per cent is affected by depression either mild or moderate form regardless of gender difference (Table 15.3).

Course: So far as the course is concerned there is not much difference between the students of MBBS or BDS. While 29 MBBS students out of 51 i.e., 56.8 per cent and 26 BDS students out of 49 i.e., 53.06 per cent show depression. However, the prevalence of a moderate form of depression is slightly more in the case of the MBBS students when compared to BDS students, while it is the mild form which is more in the case of BDS students when compared to MBBS students (Table 15.4).

Table 15.3: Prevalence of Depression by Gender

S. No.	*Gender*	*No Depression*	*Depression*				*Total*
			Mild	*Moderate*	*Severe*	*Sub-Total*	
1.	Male	17	9	11	1	21	38
		(44.7%)	23.7%	28.9%	2.6%		100.0%
		(37.8%)	24.3%	64.7%	100.0%		38.0%
2.	Female	28	28	6	0	34	62
		(45.2%)	45.2%	9.7%	0.0%		100.0%
		(62.2%)	75.7%	35.3%	0.0%		62.0%
3.	Total	45	37	17	1	55	100
		45.0%	37.0%	17.0%	1.0%		100.0%
		100.0%	100.0%	100.0%	100.0%		100.0%

Table 15.4: Prevalence of Depression by Course

S. No.	*Course*	*None*	*Depression*				*Total*
			Mild	*Moderate*	*Severe*	*Sub-Total*	
1.	MBBS	22	18	10	1	29	51
		43.1%	35.3%	19.6%	2.0%		100.0%
		48.9%	48.6%	58.8%	100.0%		51.0%
2.	BDS	23	19	7	0	26	49
		46.9%	38.8%	14.3%	0.0%		100.0%
		51.1%	51.4%	41.2%	0.0%		49.0%
3.	Total	45	37	17	1	55	100
		45.0%	37.0%	17.0%	1.0%		100.0%
		100.0%	100.0%	100.0%	100.0%		100.0%

Time spent on cyberspace: From Table 15.5, it is clear that among those who do not show any signs of depression (45 out of 100), those who relatively spend little time i.e., less than one hour, in cyberspace or SNS are more in number (34 out of 45). Among those who show depression i.e., 55 out of 100, a majority (20 out of 55 i.e., 36.4%) spend more than 2 hours a day in cyberspace.

Table 15.5: Depression and time spent on cyberspace/SNS

S. No.	*Time spent on SNS*	*No Depression*	*Depression*				*Total*
			Mild	*Moderate*	*Severe*	*Sub-Total*	
1.	< one hour	34	11	6	0	17	51
		66.7%	21.6%	11.8%	0.0%		100.0%
		75.6%	29.7%	35.3%	0.0%		51.0%
2.	1 – 2 hours	6	16	2	0	18	24
		25.0%	66.7%	8.3%	0.0%		100.0%
		13.3%	43.2%	11.8%	0.0%		24.0%
3.	> 2 hours	5	10	9	1	20	25
		20.0%	40.0%	36.0%	4.0%		100.0%
		11.1%	27.0%	52.9%	100.0%		25.0%
4.	Total	45	37	17	1	55	100
		45.0%	37.0%	17.0%	1.0%		100.0%
		100.0%	100.0%	100.0%	100.0%		100.0%

From this, we can infer that there is an increased depression concerning the time spent in cyberspace.

Table 15.6: Independent T-Test between Depression and the Time Spent on Cyberspace usage

	N	*Mean*	*Std. Deviation*	*Std. Error Mean*	*T*	*P*
Depression	20	17.15	7.199	1.610	2.27	0.01
More than 2 hours spent on cyberspace	18	13.00	3.430	.808	2.04	

As shown in Table 15.6, there is a significant difference between the scores of the means of time spent on cyberspace (M = 17.5, SD = 7.19) and depression (M = 13.0, SD = 3.43). The t value of 2.27 is significant for p of 0.01 level. We can infer that the t-test is significant here, as time spent on cyberspace is increasing, there is an increase in the incidence of depression.

Table 15.7: Correlation between Depression and Time spent on Cyberspace.

		Time spent on cyberspace	*Depression Total*
Cyberspace Usage	Pearson Correlation	1	.347**
	Sig. (2-tailed)		.000
	N	100	99
Depression Total	Pearson Correlation	.347**	1
	Sig. (2-tailed)	.000	
	N	99	99

**. Correlation is significant at the 0.01 level (2-tailed).

Table 15.7 indicates that there is a significant correlation between depression and time spent in cyberspace. The Pearson's correlation coefficient p is 0.347 at the 0.01 level.

The symptoms of depression are found to be more in the OC community than the rest. The lone case of severe depression is shown only in this category.

Table 15.8: Depression and Community

Depression	*Community*			*Total*
	OC	*BC*	*SC/ST*	
Mild	18 (81.8%)	12 (54.5%)	7 (63.6%)	37 (67.3%)
Moderate	3 (13.7%)	10 (45.5%)	4 (36.4%)	17 (30.9%)
Severe	1 (4.5%)	0	0	1 (1.8%)
Total	22 (100.0)	22 (100.0)	11 (100.0)	55 (100.0)

Discussion

Unlike several earlier studies, the study demonstrates that there is not much difference between the genders about the prevalence of depression is concerned. Similarly, the course also is found to be not relevant. However, there is a positive relationship between the time spent on cyberspace usage and depression among the students with symptoms of depression. Few students are spending time more than two hours on cyberspace and social networking sites but they do not have significant levels of depression. Yet some students not using cyberspace and SNS for more than 1 hour, yet present with symptoms of depression. Clinical depression is a complex disease that can occur due to a variety of reasons. The predisposing factors can be genetic, physical health issues, any sudden changes in the normalcy of life etc. In this chapter, only the incidence of depression has been taken into account but not the causative factors. Based on the analysis of the results, instead of concluding that spending more time on the internet or social networking sites is a causative factor for depression, there appears another possible inference, and that is, "Could it be that students who are more depressed prone to spending more time on the internet and SNS?"

Do depressed individuals find comfort in interacting with screen friends instead of real friends or classmates? Why is it that they are comfortable with their virtual friends? Is it a feeling of insecurity to interact with others in person? All these questions are vital, and to find answers we need to undertake both extensive and intensive studies on the impact of cyberspace on human behaviour and personality. However, an attempt has been made here to examine the issues in a wider background in terms of information, psychological and sociological perspectives as regards the relevance of the study regarding the role of computer-mediated communication in the development.

First of all, as several scholars argue, we live in global interconnectivity and the digital world brought about by the third revolution with digital technology. At the local level, as the traditional society is transformed into modern society with industrialization, the latter is in the process of transformation into information society through digitalization. Though it is not necessary that all the social transformations shall be viewed as if following this evolutionary sequential order, one stage after the other, the changes can be perceived more or less in this order. Since the technological changes that accompanied meeting the needs of the society, the technology has also been in turn impacting the social and cultural milieu. Digitalization has added to the existing gaps, anomalies and contradictions which are related to gender, rural and urban contrast, areas of developed and underdeveloped etc. In this background, information technology needs to be located and its roles are to be examined.

In the traditional concept of culture, it is a system or pattern of integrated beliefs and values that constitute the basis on which social relations and behaviour of individuals depend or constructed in a given society with constant interaction with the physical environment, and it is bound concerning the groups and communities. However, culture is changing in response to the forces of inside and outside. This sort of conceptualization of culture has helped understanding the role of culture in the socio-economic development processes, culture resisting the change or culture promoting change. In this conceptualization of culture in the conventional wisdom, technology has been considered to play a significant role, and it has been interpreted as traditional societies getting transformed into modern societies.

But when the boundaries become less rigid, one can find trans-culture, and also as one moves from one to the other, such individuals subscribe to dual or multi-culture. In such a situation one dominates the other including the spheres of development. It is a complex situation to conceptualize development as in one's point of view, what is development may not be viewed as development at all. Further, when non-traditional institutions proliferate with different ways of existence mostly aided by technology, and that situation ushers significant culture change, the culture adapts to new situations where technology dominates. In this context, today we notice the emergence of institutional cultures such as corporate culture, technological culture, media culture, cyberculture, industrial culture, modern culture versus traditional culture. It becomes challenging to conceptualize the role of culture in the development process when a multiplicity of cultures is in circulation and when there exist strong opinions on the changing culture.

In this kind of complex cultural context, the role of technology affecting the social and cultural fabric of a community or society comes under question. It is considered positive as it provides solutions to the persisting problems for progress or development in education, health, economic development etc. However, it is seen negatively also as technology creates problems of adaptation for the individuals and thereby to the society. Technology has further been viewed as neutral, as it depends on how the technology is used and misused. The role or contribution of communication technology is required to be understood in this broad framework.

One significant change noticed in the contemporary world over the years is that not only European societies but others are becoming individualistic, and individualism is becoming a global phenomenon. A study conducted across 78 countries collecting data over 51 years has shown that out of 41 countries, 34 have indicated a substantial rise in individual practices and out of 53 countries 39 have shown a similar rise in individual values. The study reports that changes in socio-economic development mediated the effect of time on individualism, and increased socio-economic development preceded an increase in individualism (Santos, Michael, Varnum, and Grossmann, 2017). Further, other studies reveal the fact that the technology is also being individualized with flexible arrangements of work without creating any unemployment (Castells n.d.). Castells refers to several other studies to say that computer-mediated social networks largely connect people's existing practices and existing networks. Further, he writes that new electronic communities emerge from the old communities without replacing them but the latter may become weak or get expanded. Thus, he writes, "Thus, sociability in Internet is both weak and strong, depending on people and content of the relationship, and it is linked to non-electronic communication at various levels of intensity. In other words, there is no virtual world independent from the physical/social world. There is continuity between family life, work life, face-to-face sociability, and electronic communication, with a pattern of interaction that combines in different forms these various expressions of sociability" (n.d. 7). Others have also made similar observations (DiMaggio *et al.*, 2001). New media practices have brought the rich families into individualization as each member in the family possesses a mobile phone, and even Wi-Fi connected laptop or pad and parents have their own that has moved into the bedroom (Bovill and Livingstone, 2001). It has been noted that the time spent on the internet has reduced the time of children with their parents. McGrath (2012) refers to Wellman *et al.* and quotes "internet use increases, social contact offline decreases and depression and loneliness increase" (2001:429). One can also notice quite contradictory observation, electronic communication increases connectedness and decreases isolation (Hiltz and Turoff, 1978; Carley, 1995).

Thus, if we examine the findings of the study about the time spent on social networks and depression among the MBBS and BDS students of RIMS, Kadapa, in the light of the above discussion, there is not much contradiction. The impact of electronic media oftentimes is positive but at times it is negative. This phenomenon can be explained with philosophical ideas contained in the works of Gilbert Simondon, a French philosopher psychologist. His conceptualization of man as a living being is very different from others. In his theory of individuation, man is the object of the second after the physical order and there is a third order of individuation which is simultaneously internal while at the same exceeding extending and exceeding it; it is psycho-social or trans-individual of the third order of the individuation (Barthélémy, 2015:19). According to him, the living being (man) distinguished from the physical, maintains it's own becoming in terms of individuation. Further, there is a tri-dimension division of living animals – action, perception and emotion – which are interlaced with each other in the constitution of culture. While perception is psychosomatic and closely related to science and technology, the psyche is socially decentered; there is continuity and discontinuity. Humans are bio-psychic "subjects" under the condition of 'trnasindividual' responding to external stimuli and thus individuate themselves. There is internality of the individual in bio-psychic terms and externality with social conditions. Thus, he builds up a bio-psychic-socio model of a living subject with the internal structural organization which is capable of individuating within simultaneously continuing without. While the physical individual (body), the external, is of the past, the internal is of the contemporary endowed with the vitality of individuation. The true interiority is the thinking man separated from the world. He says, "The individual is not a being but an act, and being is an individual as the agent of this act of individuation by which it shows itself and exists. Individuality is an aspect of generation, is explained by the genesis of a being, and consists in the perpetuation of this genesis." (2015:26)

Technology is though part of the culture but not entirely as it is natural for man to make tools for survival, and technical objects take the models of a living being. A technical object that man invents is an individual composed of several inner parts and the object comes into existence through the process of concretization. There is an internal functional relationship of the parts in a centralized and also in a decentralized manner and the object would have an external relationship some other. The object or its parts can lead to the development of some other parts or objects, and thus individuation process continues with continuities and discontinuities.

The conceptualization of an individual from the above discussion enables us to realize that the individuals in their interiority continuously engage in the process of individuation responding to the perceptions with the physical sensations, emotions and acting accordingly. The response of the individual depends on all these internal mechanisms. The virtual world with which the individuals encounter remains in semblance and relation with real world. According to the perception of virtual reality, an individual responds positively and maintains balance with the real social world allowing individuation internally leading to certain actions. Similarly, an individual may fail to maintain the balance of developing negativity internally in response to the perceptions of virtual reality.

Finally, a development that manifests in improved health, increased literacy and education, higher incomes etc., also is based on the ideas of progress and development. A school building or a hospital building though concrete structure, it also contains the idea of education and health which need to be positively perceived. But oftentimes it is found there is no people's participation in these programmes due to not only problems of their functioning but also perception that people have about them. The development messages that the media conveys depends on the perception of the targets and individuation that causes that are interior to individuals and connectivity that brings out in the social world.

Conclusion

The above discussion leads us to conclude that yes, there is a relationship that exists between internet usage/SNS usage and depression. However, many factors may be etiological factors that contribute to the occurrence of depression that have not been studied in this context concerning the present sample. To rule out the other factors which may be causing depression, further in-depth collection of data is required which is a limitation in this study. There is another view that needs to be explored further and that is, could it be that depression is a factor causing students to spend more time on cyberspace and social networking sites? Do they want to escape reality to find comfort in some virtual human connection? In this present technological age, is a real human connection being replaced by virtual relations? If so, then is Cyberspace usage a remedy for depression?

REFERENCES

Akiskal (2000). "Mood disorders: introduction and overview" B.J. Sadock, V.A. Sadock (Eds.), *Comprehensive Textbook of Psychiatry*, Lippincott, Williams & Wilkins, New York (2000), pp. 1284-1298.

Ali, Sarah Harbi, H.A.A. and Rahman, S.R. *et al.* (2018). "Relationship between Use of Social Media and Depression among Female Teenagers in Buraidah, Al Qassim, Saudi Arabia", *J Child Adolesc Behav*. Vol 6(3): 374 DOI: 10.4172/2375-4494.1000374.

Anand, Nitin, Christofer Thomas, Pravin A. Jain, Aneesh Bhat, Chriss Thomas, P.V. Prathyusha, Shalini Aiyappa, Shrinivasa Bhat, Kimberly Young, Anish V. Cherian. (2018). "Internet use behaviors, internet addiction and psychological distress among medical college students: A multi centre study from South India." *Asian Journal of Psychiatry*. V 37: 71-77. DOI: https://doi.org/10.1016/j.ajp.2018.07.020.

Anonymous (n.d). *Online Etymology Dictionary*. Retrieved in June 30, 2008, from Dictionary.com.Anonymous (n.d).

Barthélémy, Jean-Hugues (2015). *Life and Technology: An Inquiry Into and Beyond Simondon*. Translated by Barnaby Norman. Leuphana: University of Lüneburg.

Bashir, Hilal and Bhat, S.A. (2017). "Effects of Social Media on Mental Health: A Review". *The International Journal of Indian Psychology* ISSN 2348-5396 (e) | ISSN: 2349-3429 (p) Volume 4, Issue 3, DIP: 18.01.134/20170403 DOI: 10.25215/0403.134 http://www.ijip.in | April - June, 2017

Beck, Aaron, T. Robert, A. Steer Margery, G. Carbin (1988). *Psychometric properties of the Beck Depression Inventory*: *Clinical Psychology Review,* Volume 8, Issue 1. Pages 77-100 https://doi.org/10.1016/0272-7358(88)90050-5

Bovill, Moria and Sonia M. Livingstone (2001). "Bedroom Culture and the Privatisation of Media Use" [online]. London: LSE Research Online. Retrieved February 27, 2012 (http://eprints.lse.ac.uk/672/1/Chapter8_Children%26ChangingMediaEnvironment.pdf).

Carley, Kathleen M. (1995). Communication Technologies and Their Effect on Cultural Homogeneity, "Consensus, and the Diffusion of New Ideas." *Sociological Perspectives, 38*(4): 547-571.

Castells, M. (n.d.) The Social Implications Of Information & Communication Technologies [from www.chet.org.za/oldsite/castells/socialicts.html – no longer available] https://pdfs.semanticscholar.org/368b/9dd76eed6a85efecc2a902e7f305bba3ea5d.pdf

DiMaggio, Paul., Eszter Hargittai, W. Russell Neuman and John P. Robinson. 2001. "Social Implications of the Internet." *Annual Review of Sociology.* 27:307-336. Retrieved February 27, 2012 (http://www.jstor.org.jproxy.nuim.ie/stable/pdfplus/2678624.pdf?acceptTC=true).

Ebert A. and Karl-Jurgen Bar (2010). "Emil Kraepelin: A pioneer of scientific understanding of psychiatry and psychopharmacology". *Indian Journal of Psychiatry. 52*(2): 191-2. doi:10.4103/0019-5545.64591. PMC 2927892. PMID 20838510.

Ehlers, C.L., Frank, E., and Kuper, D.J., (1988). "Social Zeitgebers and Biological Rhythms: A Unified Approach to Understanding the Etiology of Depression." *Arch Gen Psychiatry. 45*(10):948–952. doi:10.1001/archpsyc.1988.01800340076012

Gibson, William (1984). *Neuromancer*. New York: Ace Books.

Hiltz, S.R. and Turoff, M. (1978). *The Network Nation: Human Commtunication via Computer*. Addison-Wesley, Reading, Mass.

Iqbal, S., Sandhya Gupta, and E. Venkatarao (2015). "Stress, anxiety and depression among medical undergraduate students and their socio-demographic correlates." *J. Med. Res. 141*(3): 354–357. PMCID: PMC4442334. PMID: 25963497.

Jelenhick, L.A., J.C. Eickhoff and M.A. Mereno (2013). " 'Facebook Depression?' Social Networking Site Use and Depression in Older Adolescents." *Journal of Adolescent Health, 52*(2013): 128-130.

Kaur, S., Deepti, S.S. and Lal, M. (2014). "Prevalence and Correlates of Depression among College going students of District Amritsar, India." *International Research Journal of Medical Sciences*. Vol. *2*(11), 5-9.

Kobak, A.K. (2010). Hamilton Depression Rating Scale January https://doi.org/10.1002/ 9780470479216.corpsy0402

Kraut, R. Patterson, M., Lundmark, V., Kiesler, S., Mukhopadhyay, T., & Scherils, W., (1998). "Internet paradox. A social technology that reduces social involvement and psychological well-being?" *Am Psychol.* 1998 Sep.; *53*(9):1017-31.

Kumari, S., Jyothi Tadakamadla, Harish Tibdewal, Prabu Duraiswamy, Suhas Kulkarni (2010). *Internet usage among undergraduate dental students in India.* Rev. odontociênc. (Online) vol.25 no.3 Porto Alegre. http://dx.doi.org/10.1590/S1980-65232010000300008.

Limaye, Rewati and Fotwengel, Gerhard (2015). "Use of Internet Among Undergraduate Students From Mumbai, India." *International Journal of Electronics & Communication Technology*. 6.2:26-28.

Loan, Fayaz Ahmad (2011). "Internet use by the college students across disciplines: A Study." *Annals of Library and Information Studies,* Vol. 58, pp. 118-127.

Magsamen-conrad, Kate, China Billotte-Verhoff and Kathryn Greene (2014). Technology addiction's contribution to mental wellbeing: The positive effect of online social capital. Article in Computers in Human Behavior 40:23–30, November 2014 DOI: 10.1016/j.chb.2014.07.014

Maroof, Khan Amir, Pawan Parashar, and Rahul Bansa (2012). "How are our medical students using the computer and internet? A study from a medical college of north India." *Niger Med J. 53*(2): 89–93. doi: [10.4103/0300-1652.103549]

Marya C.M., Marya K.M., Dahiya V., Juneja V., Gupta P. (2013). "Internet usage among dental students in north India." *J Pak Med Assoc. 63*(5):628-9.

McGrath, S. (2012). "The impact of new media technologies on social interactions within the household." *Electronic Culture and Social Change*. Department of Sociology, National University of Ireland Maynooth.

McLuhan, M. 1994 (first published in 1964). *Understanding Media: The Extensions of Man*. Massachusetts: MIT press.

McReynolds, P. and Klaus Ludwig, (1987). *On the history of rating scales*, Volume 8, Issue 2, pp. 281-283.

Pantic, Igore, Damjanovic, A., Todorovic, J., Topdovic, D., Bojovic-Jovic, D., Ristic, S. and Pantic, S. (2014) *Psychiatr Danub*. 2012 Mar; *24*(1):90-3. Association between online social networking and depression in high school students: behavioural physiology view point.

Priyadarshini, Varsha (2018). "Depression Amongst Students In India – A Silent Killer." edInbox. https://edinbox.com/uncategorized/depression-students-india/ accessed on 15.7.2019.

Rosen, L.D. Walling, K., Carrier, L.M., Cheever, N.A., and Rokkum, J. (2013). "The Media and Technology Usage and Attitudes Scale: An empirical investigation." *Comput Human Behav.*1; *29*(6): 2501-2511.PMCID: PMC4338964 NIHMSID: NIHMS658683 PMID: 25722534

Santos, C.H., Michael E.W. Varnum, and Igor Grossmann (2017). "Global

Increases in Individualism." *Psychological Science,* Vol. *28*(9) 1228-1239 https://doi.org/10.1177/0956797617700622.

Sidana, Surbhi, Jugal Kishore, Vidya Ghosh, Divyansh Gulati, R.C. Jiloha, Tanu Anand (2012). *Australasian Medical Journal.* 5, 5, 247-250.

Singh A., Lal A., and Shekhar (2010). "Prevalence of Depression Among Medical Students of a Private Medical College in India." Online. *J Health Allied Scs. 9*(4):8.

Snaith, Philip R. (2003). The Hospital Anxiety and Depression Scale Health and Quality of Life Outcomes1:29 https://doi.org/10.1186/1477-7525-1-29.

Takahira, Mieko, Ando, R., and Sakamoto, A. (2008). Effects of internet use on depression, loneliness, aggression and preference for internet communication: A panel study with 10-12 year old children in Japan DOI: 1504/IJWBC (2008.019191). *International Journal of Web based communities, 4*(3):302-318.

Wellman, B., Anabel Quan Haase, James Witte and Keith Hampton (2001). "Does the Internet Increase, Decrease, or Supplement Social Capital?" *American Behavioral Scientist. 45*(3):436-455. Retrieved February 29, 2012 (http://abs.sagepub.com.jproxy.nuim.ie/content/45/3/436. full.pdf+html).

WHO (2004). Promoting mental health: concepts, emerging evidence, practice. Summary Report Geneva: World Health Organization.

Zung, W.K.W. (1965). "A Self-Rating Depression Scale." *Arch Gen Psychiatry,12*(1): 63-70. doi:10.1001/archpsyc.1965.01720310065008.

http://www.oxford dictionaries.com/us/definition/Americanenglish/cyberspace

https://files.eric.ed.gov/fulltext/EJ1115126.pdf

https://webopedia.com/TERM/social_networking_)site.html

https://www.encyclopedia.com/science-and-technology/computers-and-electrical engineering

https://www.jagranjosh.com/general-knowledge/top-10-social networking sites-by-number-of -users-1317626809-1

https://www.ncbi.nlm.nih.gov/pme/articles/PMC/4183915

https://www.ncbi.nlm.nih.gov/pubmed/23260846

http://www.oxford dictionaries.com/us/definition/Americanenglish/cyberspace

https://files.eric.ed.gov/fulltext/EJ1115126.pdf

https://webopedia.com/TERM/social_networking_)site.html

https://www.encyclopedia.com/science-and-technology/computers-and-electrical engineering

https://www.jagranjosh.com/general-knowledge/top-10-social networking sites-by-number-of -users-1317626809-1

https://www.ncbi.nlm.nih.gov/pme/articles/PMC/4183915

https://www.ncbi.nlm.nih.gov/pubmed/23260846

https://www.edinbox.com/depression-students-india/

https://www.who.int/features/factfiles/mental_health/en/

SECTION 5
Community Radio

16

Community Radio as a Tool for Gender Sensitization

A Case Study of Gurgaon Ki Awaaz

Sreeju V. Nadh

Community Radio in India

Over the past few decades, community radio has evolved as a lively field of study in developmental communication due to its pliability to be a participatory medium for development. Looked upon as an independent, diverse, and democratic medium, community radio has the potential to play a significant role in the development process. According to the Community Radio Handbook of UNESCO, "Community radio catalyzes the development efforts of rural folk and the underprivileged segments of urban societies, given its exceptional ability to share timely and relevant information on development issues, opportunities, experiences, life skills and public interests" (2001, p. iii). Community radio is considered to be a medium that acts as a catalyst for ensuring the participation of community members in developmental activities, especially of those who are marginalized based on caste, class, and gender.

In India, with the announcement of the new community radio policy in 2006, allowing agricultural universities, educational institutions, and civil society institutions to apply for a community radio broadcasting license under the FM band 88–108 MHz, the community radio is now more than a decade old phenomenon. The count of community radio stations in the country has reached about 251 (2019). (mib.gov.in/broadcasting/list-251-operational-community-radio-stations-India)

Indian society, with its multicultural-patriarchal structure, has a long history of confining women in terms of options and opportunities. Urban or rural, educated or illiterate, women are given secondary status in the society with chances of less or no roles in any decision making, both in the private and the public sphere. Radical feminists insist that women's subordination does not depend on other forms of domination, such as class, but totally on patriarchy, or the domination of women by men which existed in virtually every known society, even those without classes. Women's subordination, as it is deeply embedded in individual psyches and social practices, is more difficult to change than class (Parpart, Connelly, Murrey Li, & MacDonald, 2000).

While there exists a strong constitution in India that offers equal rights and duties for every citizen, the reality is bleak with women not having guaranteed freedom or the prospect of having a voice of their own in crucial matters related to their lives. According to Sara Hlupekile Longwe, women empowerment is enabling women to take an equal place with men, and to participate equally in the development processes, thereby achieving a capacity to have control over the factors of production similar to that of men (as cited in March, Smyt, & Mukhopadhya, 1999).

Through the setting up of community radios, the developmental organizations working at the grassroots level intend to provide a platform for women to voice their concerns and be an integral part of their social change initiatives. Most of the community radio stations operating today in the country proclaim to have a gender-sensitive working environment and programmes that specifically engage women in the development process as well as address their concerns. Community radio is looked upon as a tool for augmenting the women empowerment efforts carried out by development organizations and feminists at the grassroots level. However, women empowerment can mean different things in different contexts.

Andrea Cornwall (2000) also asserts that to deal with women's issues more effectively, we need to take both women's and men's perspectives and identifications into account rather than confining our interaction only with women. She observes that the Gender and Development (GAD) agenda seeks to include gender awareness and participation of women in the development initiatives and to give women a voice and the right to speak out. The participatory development approach emphasizes women's access to development institutions as a step towards engaging primary stakeholders in development projects. But there still exists a lack of gender sensitivity in participatory development. However, both feminist and participatory research methodologies that share several common epistemological and political principles, try to address this gap by ascertaining who participates, how, at what stages, to determine the shape and nature of 'participation' that takes place (Cornwall, 2000). According to Sahay, in short, "empowerment is a process of awareness and capacity building leading to greater participation, to greater decision-making power and control, and to transformative action" (Sahay, 1998, p. 22).

Due to many external factors such as limited time and resource management issues, 'community' is usually considered as a whole and often community-based participatory approaches fail to include women's participation. The internal dynamics such as age, economic differences, caste, religious, ethnic, and especially gender differences are ignored while employing participatory approaches to development. Development was always identified with poverty alleviation, and in the process, only caste and economic differences were central to the approaches. Often the internal issues of the communities, such as power imbalances in gender relations tend to be ignored. Sometimes, the community people neglect gender-sensitive development approaches by characterizing it as against their tradition and cultural values (Gujit & Kaul Shah, 1997). The communities that have deep roots in patriarchy refuse to consider women as equivalent human beings and object to the idea of incorporating them in development activities. The oppression and exclusion of women have turned out to be a very normal practice in the mindset and dispositions of community members, even women also espoused it that way.

The Gender Dimension

The instigation of community radio in India has brought opportunities for women to have a voice in their communities as gender equality has been considered a very significant dimension in community radio initiatives (Pavarala & Malik, 2007). Gender Policy for Community Radio states that:

> "Community radio has an obligation to redress the imbalance; facilitate women's involvement at all levels of decision-making and programming; ensure that women's voices and concerns are part of the daily news agenda; ensure that women are portrayed positively as active members of society; and support women acquire the technical skills and confidence to control their communications. Community radio is part of a progressive social movement, and as such stations should initiate and strengthen ties with progressive women's movements. Stations also have an obligation to implement and enforce an ethical policy that includes respect for women and equality as one of its cornerstones." (AMARC-WIN 2008, p. 2)

The Gender Policy for Community Radio was approved by the World Association of Community Radio Broadcasters (AMARC-WIN 2008) in 2010. The main aim of the gender policy spearheaded by AMARC's Women's International Network (AMARC-WIN), is to increase women's access to Community Radio and to assure the continuous participation, including at the decision-making levels (NWMI, 2016). Community Radio Forum (CRF) of India adopted the Gender Policy for Community Radio of AMARC on March 11, 2011, to provide women with more opportunities to have access to information and to promote their involvement in community radio across the country (Malik & Bandelli, 2012). The gender-equal stratagem of community radio appeared to be arduous for India because of its profound history of patriarchy. But today, with 251 operational community radio across the country, including the most remote and backward areas (One World Foundation, 2016), the capacity of community radio in bringing up change is evident.

The transformation from a male-driven society to a gender-equal society is never easy for India. But initiatives by community radio seems to be effective with noticeable examples. During the initial phase of community radio in India, pioneering organizations such as Voices and Drishti Media extracted the essence of community radio through narrowcasting to circumvent the policy restrictions. They worked with NGOs Myrada in Bangalore and Kutch Mahila Vikas Sangathan (KMVS), a woman collective in Gujarat to train rural community reporters to produce audio programmes. The programmes were played out over loudspeakers in common community meeting points such as near temples and at Panchayat (village level governing bodies) meetings, or within "listener groups" of women working together in self-help groups. In 1999, KMVS started airing a 30-minute programme made by them in the Kutchi language on All India Radio's Bhuj station by purchasing a commercial slot. Deriving the model of KMVS, Chala Ho Gaon Mein, a community radio programme aided by the National Foundation for India and produced by community representatives of the NGO Alternative for India Development (AID) started broadcasting once a week on All India Radio Daltonganj in Palamau district of Jharkhand. In 2001 at Budikote in Kolar district of Karnataka, Namma Dhwani (Our Voice), an audio production center initiated by the media advocacy group Voices, started narrowcasting programmes made rural folk trained in the basics of radio production (Pavarala, Malik, & Cheeli, 2005). Namma Dhwani programmes created awareness among its listeners about health and sanitation, education, savings, food habit, and family system, etc. and enhanced the behaviour, and leadership qualities in women (Yalala, 2015).

The first community-based radio station licensed to an NGO was launched on 15 October 2008, when Sangham Radio, licensed to Deccan Development Society, in Pastapur village, Medak district, Andhra Pradesh state went on the air at 11:00 am. Sangham Radio, which broadcasts on 90.4 MHz, is licensed to the Deccan Development Society (DDS) (an NGO which works with women's groups in approximately 75 villages in Andhra Pradesh). The community radio station managed by "General" Narsamma and Algole Narsamma was established as one of the first community radios in the country and managed by a team of *Dalit* women who have been excluded and rendered voiceless in any other public forum (One World Foundation, 2016).

Though the primary goal of community radio in India in its infancy period was the development of the community as a whole, later, through evident examples (as mentioned before), its potentiality in performing further consequential acts such as women empowerment was unfolded. The effort of community radio in India to bring about change in the lives of women inevitably requires recognition.

Gurgaon Ki Awaaz Samudayik Radio Station

The evolving story of community radio in India is inspiring with expeditions and experiments in the form and content of the programmes produced by the communities. Gender sensitization has become a significant component in the community radio sector over the period. 'Gurgaon ki Awaaz' community radio in Haryana with its inspiring experiments in programmes like 'Chahat Chowk' (a programme focused on encouraging community members, especially men and women between 20 and 40 years to talk about sex and reproduction, and about their feelings and their fears), portrays the potential of community radio in empowering women in India. Gurgaon Ki Awaaz Samudayik Radio Station has been working for the community's betterment since its inception in 2009. With the support of The Restoring Force (NGO), Gurgaon Ki Awaaz addresses the needs of the hundreds of villages, semi-urban clusters, and urban slums that fall within a 10 to 15 kilometers radius around Udyog Vihar in Gurgaon. Under the supervision of the station director Arti Jaiman, the team always looks up to serve the development of the community. Gurgaon Ki Awaaz discerns its community as migrants settled in the locality for various purposes, mainly for occupation in garment factories and construction sites. Even though the migrants who have been settled down in Gurgaon find occupation and settlements, they always lacked a space to express their native culture and find it difficult to merge with local communities. Gurgaon Ki Awaaz stands as a platform for the localites as well as for the culturally marginalized migrants to express and experience their culture and it promotes multi-culturalism and cultural convergence. Gurgaon Ki Awaaz aims to reach people like construction workers, factory labourers, housewives, children, etc. who don't have a medium of their own. Vandana (previous station manager) says that "if a big shot's son falls into a manhole, it becomes news, but the people who work on the construction sites and local areas, even if they die, not even local media bother to consider it as a news and cover it. We are for them."

Over the years, with constant efforts in uplifting the lives of the community members, now Gurgaon Ki Awaaz has achieved a friendly image among the community members. Through implementing a localized, bottom-top approach in every aspect of the working of the community radio station, they have created a space for the community to discuss and debate on various issues ranging from entertainment to development. Gurgaon Ki Awaaz provides people with information regarding every minute aspect of life, such as where are the government educational institutions located and how to reach them, how to fill the application form, career development, health concerns, gender equality, etc.

Gurgaon Ki Awaaz as the Voice of Women

Even though Gurgaon is a city, the community that Gurgaon Ki Awaaz serves is underprivileged of any facilities of city life. According to the reporters of the station, women of the community still face a lot of issues such as secondary status in the society and most of them are restricted to household work. Gurgaon Ki Awaaz as a platform that has been constantly trying to look up at the issues of women who are being marginalized in society is only partially successful in bringing women to the community radio. It has been observed that a lot of barriers are there to be conquered to uplift women's status in society. Vandana (previous station manager) says, "In the initial stages of the radio station, reaching women itself was difficult as they don't have their own mobile phones to call or even visiting the houses also were futile since women were scared that their husbands will figure it out and make issues". The scenario has changed when Gurgaon Ki Awaaz started Community Learning Process (CLP), through which they reached women and conducted cascade workshops. According to the team members, creating a feeling of possession of community radio among the community members was the primary task to make them embrace Gurgaon Ki Awaaz which was achieved through regular workshops, focus group discussions, formal and informal interaction and debates on various topics.

Through systematic propagation with the help of the community women, Gurgaon Ki Awaaz could reach to the women who were restricted to kitchens. Gradually women developed a feeling of reassurance about the community radio and began to get involved. But the greatest challenge of Gurgaon Ki Awaaz is that the community women are migrants, often they return to their hometowns or relocate to different regions. So, even after so much hard work, most of the time the impact of community radio in women's lives remains imperceptive. But an evident impact that the community radio has observed over the period since inception is that the locals and migrants have started accepting the culture of one another and seems to be more tolerant towards the cultural differences.

The community radio station is now entirely run by women, who identifies themselves as a part of the migrant community of Gurgaon. The core team members include teenage girls and women of various age groups. The team ensures the participation of community women in every stage of the programme production starting from the field research where they organize meetings and take opinions. As identified by the community radio station team, the major hurdle of the community women is that they lack awareness and education. So, the major task of the community radio remains information dissemination and awareness creation. To create a lasting impact on the community women, Gurgaon Ki Awaaz seeks life stories of women and broadcast it through the community radio which helps other women to relate to things and understand easier. As women empowerment remains one of the prime motives of the community radio, the team mainly focuses on developing capacity and courage among the community women to talk about their matters varying from health issues, sexual life, family planning, domestic violence, education, and career, etc. Pravin, who is a migrant from Uttar Pradesh says, "the radio has reached every woman of the community and it has given them a confidence and strength at least to speak. I am also the part of the male-dominated society where we don't entertain women's concerns, where we don't listen to their issues. Radio act as a mentor for the women, it encourages women to come forward and speak."

Participation of women in community radio is at varying levels even though the team tries to ensure complete participation. Every programmes are made gender-neutral and matters related to women are often given priority in the content. In the career-related programme Career Express, Gurgaon Ki Awaaz provides women with proper guidance and help them to be financially independent. Vocational training and soft-skill tips are given to women for starting small scale businesses that they can run from their houses themselves. Vandana (previous station manager) says that "if we are talking about candle making business in Career Express, rather than we explain it to the community women, we bring any women from the community who are already engaged in candle making business and make them share their experiences which makes it easier for other women to understand and feel that they can also do it." As per Vandana, the community women feel that for having a voice or power to make any decisions, they should have a job and be financially independent. So, the community radio is helping them with information regarding a wide variety of jobs women can easily do. To enable a habit of critical thinking and to break stereotypical ideas, the reporters often debate with the community members on topics like "Why only men do electronic repairing jobs, why can't women also do it" and so on.

In a society that has conventional cultural and moral values, talking about sexual matters were not a possible thing. The 'n' number of doubts and queries about sexual health was never uttered out anywhere at any point of time by women. A space for conversation did not exist until Gurgaon Ki Awaaz with its well-received programme "Chahat Chowk" on sexual health has changed the situation into a positive one where men and women could openly talk about their body and its needs and necessities, according to Sharmila, who is the host of the programme. Chahat Chowk offered a platform where people get information and can clarify their doubts through a non-judgemental conversation where the anonymity of the caller is guaranteed. The radio station encourages young men and women to participate in programmes where an expert doctor or an Auxiliary Nurse Midwife are available to answer their question regarding sex and reproduction. The initial response from the community members was negative as they couldn't accept the openness in the content. But the programme has completed three seasons successfully with the support of the community members which shows the gradual change in the attitude of the community members as a result of the awareness created.

The team ensures that all the programmes made are gender-neutral. Consciously it has been made a habit to keep women at the forefront of every programme. "It's not only about women since Gurgaon Ki Awaaz is the voice of and for marginalized sections of the society, but all marginalized sections are also accepted and addressed, including transgenders. The team positively talk about gender differences and identities through our radio to create awareness among the community members", says Ujala, the station manager of Gurgaon Ki Awaaz. Sweety who works with the community radio as a reporter says that assurance of anonymity is one reason for the women to embrace radio, unlike any other medium. Herself a migrant woman, she mentions the advantage of being a migrant in Gurgaon is getting to enjoy more freedom than in their native place wherein which they feel more restricted by cultural and moral values.

Gurgaon Ki Awaaz community radio station act as an alternative public sphere where women can sit and talk about anything without fear and restrictions. Financial difficulties restrain the community women from frequently visiting the station and spending quality time there. But it doesn't stop them from gathering to discuss what the community radio has told the other day. Amita's beauty parlour in the town area has turned into a hub for the women listeners to sit and chit chat. The community radio team members also join them often to get feedback or sometimes just to talk.

Vandana says that they feel motivated to work efficiently for the community when they receive positive feedback. Women who were scared to talk before now come forward and volunteer to produce programmes saying that community radio has taught us that women are not any less of men. They started realizing the importance of having a voice of their own. But many women are still struggling in the community. To expand the reach of the radio station, Gurgaon Ki Awaaz conducts outreach programmes. A street play "Dastak" (Knock Down) on domestic violence, sexual harassment, and female foeticide were conducted in nearly 50 schools with the support of Asmita Theatre Group in Delhi. The rigorous hard work of Gurgaon Ki Awaaz is to develop the capacity in women to say 'NO' and make the women decide for themselves. To fight against the power imbalances through raising a voice. Gurgaon Ki Awaaz is looking forward to reaching every community member amidst all the restrictions and limited resources. The Gurgaon Ki Awaaz community radio team believes that transparency in governing and working of the community radio station is the ultimate solution to bring community members closer. The community should feel that they know things and they own it. According to Gurgaon Ki Awaaz, rather than suggesting or imposing solutions upon the community for the problems they face, it was found more effective when they held discussion and debates among themselves and identified solutions in the best possible ways they can. Providing a space for having that discussion is the ultimate essence of community radio.

REFERENCES

AMARC-WIN. (2008). Gender Policy for Community Radio. AMARC-WIN. Retrieved from http://www.amarc.org/documents/Gender_Policy/GP4CR_English.pdf (2 March 2011).

Cornwall, A. (2000). Making a Difference? Gender and Participatory Development. Institute of Development Studies. https://www.participatorymethods.org/sites/participatorymethods.org/files/Dp378.pdf

Gujit, I., and Shah, K.M. (1997). "Waking up to Power, Conflict and Process." In Guijt, I. and Shah, K.M. (*eds.*) *The Myth of the Community.* London: Intermediate Technology Publications, pp. 1-23.

Malik, Kanchan K. and Bandelli, Daniela. (2012); "Community Radio and Gender—Towards an Inclusive Public Sphere" paper presented at the India Media. Symposium: Public Spheres, the Media & Social Change organized by University of Queensland (Australia), Brisbane, between November 21-23, 2012.

March, C., Smyt, I., and Mukhopadhya, M. (1999). *A guide to gender-analysis frameworks.* Oxfam GB. Public Action Publishing.

Network of Women in Media (NWMI), India (2016). Gender Equality on the Radio. Retrieved from Network of Women in Media, India (NWMI): http://www.nwmindia.org/research/gender-equality-on-the-radio.

One World Foundation (ed.) (2016). Community Radio in India: Towards Diversity and Sustainability, Community Radio Compendium, New Delhi: One World Foundation of India on Behalf of the Ministry of Information & Broadcasting, Government of India.

Parpart, J.L., Connelly, P.M., Murrey Li, T., and MacDonald, M. (2000). "Feminism and Development: Theoretical Perspectives." In P. Jane L., P. M. Connelly, & E.V. Barriteau (Eds.), *Theoretical Perspectives on Gender and Development.* Ottawa, Canada: International Development Research Centre.

Pavarala, V., and Malik, K.K. (2007). *Other voices; The struggle for community radio in India.* New Delhi: Sage Publications.

Pavarala, V., Malik, K.K., and Cheeli, J. (2005). Community Media and Women: Forging Subaltern Counterpublics. *Gender Perspectives on the Information Society – South Asia Pre-WSIS Seminar 2005.*

Sahay, S. (1998). *Women Empowerment: Approaches and Strategies.* New Delhi: Discovery Publishing House.

UNESCO (2001). Community Radio Handbook (ed.) Colins Frazer and Sonia Restrepo Estrade. Paris Cedex 15: UNESCO. mib.gov.in/broadcasting/list-251-operational-community-radio-stations-India.

Yalala, Nirmala (2015). The role of community radio in empowering women in India, Media Asia, 42:1-2, 41-46, DOI: 10.1080/01296612.2015.1072335

17

Community Radio and Disaster Management

A Study on Role of Kalanjiam Community Radio Station during Gaja Cyclone

R. Shamala, M.B. Devadas and *N. Sivakami*

Introduction

It has been a regular interval that disasters have been hitting the country. Communication is an integral tool of any disaster management. It is the efficacy of communication that is creating awareness among people and helping in mitigating disasters.

Natural disasters are caused by cyclones and floods have a profound impact upon vulnerable people, affecting their life, infrastructure, assets and environment and livestock. Some of the common hazards experienced in the region include typhoons, floods, drought, forest fires, landslides, earthquakes and tsunamis. We can avoid and reduce losses from disasters through effective communication, by either mitigating the hazards or reducing the vulnerabilities of the people living in hazard-prone areas.

The process of disaster risk reduction involves the identification of hazards/vulnerabilities, analyzing their potential impact, identifying priorities for risk reduction and identification and implementation of solutions. To reduce the risks of disasters everybody needs to be informed well about the situation. This includes government departments, research institutions, NGOs, United Nations agencies, donor agencies, the media, and the private sector. The role of at-risk communities and groups is most important in reducing the risks of disasters. All of the above stakeholders have different perceptions about the nature of risks, priorities for risk reduction and the appropriate solutions.

2. Role of Community Radio at the time of Disaster

Community radio emerged as alternative media to mainstream media. The idea of community radio evolved from a situation where organisations experimenting with the concept of participatory communication for social change across the world, citizen groups, community organisations and media activists have been pushing for an institutional space that can be effectively used for revitalising the civil society. The historical philosophy of community radio is to use this medium as the voice of the voiceless, the mouthpiece of oppressed people (be it on racial, gender, or class grounds) and generally as a tool for development (Pavarala & Malik, 2007).

A disaster is a catastrophic event whose impact is undergone by the affected lot in phases. Media prepares the people with factual information about an approaching hazard and the ways and means to adopt, to mitigate their dire impacts during the preparedness phase (Seydlitz, Williams, Laska, & Triche, 1991).

When it comes to the response and recovery phase, the media provides reports based on the damage assessments, attempts to rescue the affected lot, bridge the needs and the needy and support the distressed to recover from the trauma. Mobility post a disaster is often restricted. In such instances, media serves the surveillance function and drives the people who witnessed the disaster to develop an increased dependency on them for any momentous information (Hirschburg, Dillman, & Ball-Rokeach, 1986). Media is found to serve the manifest functions such as providing informational needs to the distressed due to disasters (Perez-Lugo, 2004).

Another usual and frequently noticed function performed by media during disasters is, providing a platform to reconnect displaced members of a social group due to a disaster (Barton, 1969). Some of the local media like local community radio stations announce messages that are related to the safety of missing individuals post a disaster. At such times, the media tends to back the displaced members of a community by connecting them with the outside world (Perez-Lugo, 2004).

Gaja Cyclone

The cyclone Gaja has set the tone towards the end of the North-East monsoon in India. A low pressure intensified into a cyclone that made its landfall during the early hours on 16 November 2018 had hit six districts in the southern state, Tamil Nadu, namely Nagapattinam, Tiruvarur, Thanjavur, Pudukottai, Dindigul and Ramnad. The wind speeds reached as high as 120 km per hour during its landfall. A major disaster was averted due to the elaborate preparedness measures taken by the government supported by the civil society organizations. Approximately 1,50,000 vulnerable people were evacuated to relief camps along with the coastal areas and fishermen were not allowed to go fishing. Despite elaborate preparedness measures, the wind speed and heavy rains have caused deaths, damages to houses and public infrastructure.

3. Review of Literature

Community radio emerged as an easy alternative to public and commercial radio in the late 1970s. In Western countries community radio fulfils the needs of self-expression for groups who have scanty exposure to the mass media. In developing countries, as a Rockefeller Foundation report asserts, community radio is 'one of the best ways to reach excluded or marginalised communities in targeted, useful ways', and in giving them a 'voice' that *matters most in development communication* (Dagron, 2001). It helps to enhance cultural identity and community pride. The widespread ownership of and familiarity with transistor radios make it potentially a people's medium. All over the Third World radio has a proven track record of being a catalyst for social change (Girard, 1992; Dagron, 2001).

Thus, community radio may be owned and managed by one group or by combined groups. It could also be controlled and run by people such as women, children, farmers, fisherfolk, ethnic groups, or senior citizens. Tabbing points out that a high degree of people's participation, both in management and programme production aspects distinguishes community radio from other media. Also, the principal sources of support for community radio operations are individual community members and local institutions (Pavarala & Malik, 2007).

Community radio is thus characterized by access, public participation in production and decision making, management by listeners, and its operations rely mainly on the community's own resources.

K. Anjaneyulu, the initiator of one of the earliest community radio projects, asserted that "Local radio should identify itself so completely the interests of its local population that the heart of the people beats in every pulse of the programme it broadcasts" (Page and Crawley, 2001, p. 37).

Apart from community-level communication processes, media, in general, can be a strategic resource for assisting crisis management, with radio notable for its flexibility and wide availability (Romo Murphy *et al.*, 2011). Radio science pervades society and has an integral role in disaster management and mitigation that is often taken for granted. Radio is a vital element in monitoring the environment, and in feeding data to prediction models that are a major factor in safety and economic well-being.

The media does have a linkage and a social utility function to perform during disasters (Dominick, 2010; Juric, 2006). Apart from the mere transmission of information, the media attempts to bind and link the members affected due to a disaster by creating strong ties, facilitating dialogue through their content. The media stands as a binding factor of the affected people and build strong communities (Cerulo & Ruane, 1998) by breaking the physical barriers.

Media is even found to be filling the void due to the absence of human beings (Perez-Lugo, 2004). The extended functions of media during a disaster are more. The media does not simply act as mediators instead it functions as an actor during such instances. It stands as a pillar of emotional support to the people disturbed due to a disaster (Graber, 1980) and facilitates social cohesion (Perez-Lugo, 2004). Social cohesion is the readiness of the members of a community to come together to survive and come out of a collective crisis like a disaster.

The common man is found to be highly involved in "volunteerism" during disasters with varying manifestations depending on the disasters right from the dawn of humanity (Simon *et al.*, 2015). The normal citizens become the first responders of disasters. Thanks to the media that binds together audience on a universal scale during such a crisis. The media empowers the common man and plays a key role to showcase their inherent altruistic nature.

The advantage of radio over other mediums is that; they provide immediate and comprehensive reports that are flexible in terms of content, coverage and accessibility (UNESCO Chair on Community Media, 2013, toolkit). Not only that the common man has been found involved in presenting communication during disasters in the community radio for ages (Colie, 1997). An effective disaster communication medium should be such that it withstands the onslaught of disasters and does not collapse (Simon *et al.*, 2015).

Radio is one such effective disaster communication medium and saves the communities from communication blackout.

4. Kalanjiam Community Radio

Kalanjiam Community Radio by DHAN Foundation was established aftermath of the Tsunami devastation, on December 26, 2004. The CRS started narrowcasting for two years before its operation in 2006. The station got its official broadcast license and transmitter on 12th July 2009.

The CRS worked in a big way with the affected people, fishing and farming communities along the coast with a long term development as the main focus. Empowering the community in every aspect in building the life of the community, disaster management was felt like an important area of intervention. Implementation of Information and Communication Technology (ICT) were introduced few of the Village Information Centres connected with the set-up of internet facility in all the villages. As an ICT initiative, the Foundation has launched the Community Radio Station of Kalanjiam Samuga Vanoli (90.8 MHz FM) with a vision of creating a Community Media Centre with a mixed media model, combining radio with video and web-based technologies. In the beginning, United Nations Development Programme provided resources under its Tsunami Recovery Support Programme.(Dhanfoundation.org)

The station started its functioning from August 2006. After two years of successful narrowcasting through loudspeakers tied to poles in five villages in and around Vizhunthamavadi, Kalanjiam began broadcasting through a transmitter in July 2009.

4.1 Purpose

The Kalanjiam Samuga Vanoli has been established

- To use information and communication as a tool for change in the areas of poverty reduction, gender and environment.
- To enable the communities in the disaster-prone coastal areas to get prepared for managing disasters and strengthen their livelihoods to cope up with such disasters through Community Owned Media Centre.
- To build skills of the community to prepare and disseminate audio programmes on the areas concerning their socio-economic and cultural development.
- To aid in the promotion and preservation of local wisdom, traditional knowledge and skills by encouraging communities to prepare programmes in these areas.
- To create a platform for local youths and students to develop their skills in communication.

(Source: DHAN Foundation, Kalanjiam CRS).

4.2 Location

The Station for Kalanjiam Samuga Vanoli (90.8 MHz) has been set-up at Vizhunthamavadi village of Keelaiyur Block in Nagapattinam District, Tamil Nadu. Nagapattinam district is a coastal district of Tamil Nadu; the Keelaiyur block of Nagapattinam is next in the south to the pilgrimage and tourist spot – Velankanni. The block is surrounded by sea in its east. Four hamlets located around Vizhunthamavadi village, *viz*., PR Puram, Kameswaram, Pudupalli and Vettaikaraniruppu, are under coverage.

4.3. Socio-Demographic and Listeners' Profile

The total population of the five villages is 34,328 in 8,462 households; except two villages Puthuppalli and Vettaikaraniruppu. The population is predominately an extremely backward community are mostly agriculture labourers, fishing and migration to foreign countries for work is a common phenomenon in these villages. One in every two household has a family member employed in South East Asian countries.

4.4. Programme Production and Distribution

The station is equipped with the very basic infrastructure needed for producing audio programmes. It has a recording and transmission room both without any soundproofing. A team of trained volunteers from the local community mostly women is involved in programme production. Presently, programmes of local interest are broadcasted from 8 am to 10 am and 2 pm to 4 pm every day, including narrowcasting.

For now, the two hour broadcast by Kalanjiam that begins with a unique signature tune at 8 am every day is a package of valuable local information and community needs that revolve around disaster preparedness, livelihoods, local best practices, women empowerment, health, child education, farming, agriculture, Tamil literature, folk songs, fishing and animal husbandry. The volunteers go to the field, interview people, record events like health awareness meetings and also bring resource persons to the studio and transmit live and recorded programmes. They are planning to increase the transmission period to three hours in near future. The additional one hour will be a phone-in programme.

4.5. Type of Programme by Kalanjiam Community Radio Station

1. Tirukkural
2. Local Information
3. Agriculture
4. Fishing
5. Livelihoods Best Practices
6. Women & SHG
7. Children Educational & Entertainment
8. Traditional Health Practices
9. Local Leadership
10. Awareness on Development Issues
11. Government Programmes
12. Local Culture and Songs

(*Source:* DHAN Foundation, Kalanjiam CRS)

5. Need for the Study

In recent years, CRS has emerged as a powerful and unique medium with community development as its major objective. It is something that actually brings the community together, whereas a lot of the other media today seems to be isolating us from society and even from family members. In spite of its uniqueness, the Community Radio sector is struggling to survive due to some factors like broadcast policy in India, lack of strategy to ensure financial sustainability and of course some undiscovered factors which determine the success of CRS. To boost the success rate of CRS, it becomes essential to discover the factors which persuade the community members to actively participate in it. It is also vital to study the community development function of the medium and the role of NGOs in this communication process.

6. Objectives of the Study

Based on the objectives and conceptual framework of the study, a set of research areas were identified and corresponding research questions were formulated (details in Table 17.1). This was done to evaluate the commonalities emerging from the findings across different objectives and case studies. Interview guides and checklists, as appropriate in particular situations, were used for the purpose.

7. Research Methodology

The research work uses a qualitative methodology for accomplishing the objectives of the study. The approach was to gain insight into community radio in India through the application of multiple methods of inquiry. The case study method was used, involving in-depth and open-ended interviews and focus groups, along with analysis of documents.

Document analysis of official publications, factual records, reports and declarations yielded excerpts, quotations, or entire passages, facilitating a historical study of media development, operations and legislative framework of broadcasting in India. Analysis of documents released by organisations involved in community radio initiatives helped in tracing the ideology behind them and the course of the lobbying efforts for community radio in India. In addition, audio material and websites of organisations were also examined. In-depth interviews with members of lobbying groups, representatives of the various civil society organisations, programme coordinators, content producers and policy planners were conducted to generate productive information consisting of direct quotations from the people about their experiences, opinions, feelings and knowledge about the community radio in India. Focus Group Discussions (FGDs) with listeners within the broadcast/narrowcast area were conducted with the aid of a moderator in the sample villages. These discussions were audio-recorded and transcribed for detailed analysis. The focus groups were conducted in the local language and in comfortable settings where the members would normally gather to hold discussions in their villages.

Table 17.1: Research Themes and Questions

Sl. No.	*Research Area*	*Research Questions*
1.	Pre-disaster alert	Did the Kalanjiam Radio was successful in alerting people about the Gaja cyclone?
2.	During disaster	To analyze the extent of support provided by Kalanjiam during disaster rescue operations.
3.	Post-disaster	To understand the role of Kalanjiam in post-disaster community rebuilding?

Informal visits to the villages as well as discussions at the many seminars and conferences, and consultations we attended over the last five years were some of the ways in which we gained familiarity with those associated with both the advocacy and the grassroots facets of the community radio movement in India.

8. Results of Focus Group Discussions

The outcome of in-depth Focus Group interview with member of Kalanjiam Community Radio Station were recorded. The CRS had a wider role to play in the entire Cyclone period in informing the communities to manage the disaster.

8.1. Pre-Cyclone

Information was given by the Meteorological Department, Nagapattinam to the Community Radio Station 20 days before the cyclone. For extensive awareness, a WhatsApp group was created and regular information was disseminated to the stations through local administration.

Regular updates of the cyclones with estimated date and time and speed of the wind along with rain warning was provided.

In the beginning, people were casual about the cyclone as they felt it was a regular affair. Regular awareness programmes and local administration efforts along with people's participation, people started to take measures to deal with the cyclone.

8.2. Post-Cyclone

Regular programmes only on creating awareness about cyclones were carried out informing them about the severity and measures to be adopted.

A WhatsApp group with 115 members, were provided regular updates and they further passed it to other groups. Along with this Kalanjiam, CRS Facebook and Instagram were used to disseminate information.

Due to the impact of the cyclone, the station was damaged and shutdown and for nearly two months, finding a generator was not easy.

A back-up team had been sent to start the station. At the end of January 2019, the station started its operation with one-hour programmes daily.

8.3. Post-Cyclone

The CRS had started collecting information on the devastation. Although there was not much work done with production. Community radio volunteers assisted in rehabilitation work. After a few days, we started doing video recording of the damage and interview of the people affected by cyclone and started the programme VOICE OF VULNERABLE, communities narrated their experience of the cyclone. Which was later used to fund crowding to help the people affected by the cyclone.

A motivation programme was undertaken. Besides this providing basic amenities such as safe drinking water was the main problem. Due to cyclone effect sweet water had turned into saltwater further situation becomes more worst due to lack of timely rain, well waters also turned into saltwater. After cyclone CRS provide information to collect drinking water information through WhatsApp, Instagram and Facebook pages of Kalanjiam.

It is evident from the focus group discussions that the community members, both male and female, are very enthusiastic and excited about the possibility of working with CRS and engaging themselves.

CRS has become very intimate to the lives of the community members, especially, the potential listeners. A feeling of belongingness could be sensed among them.

The information exchange is quick. This helps the community members, especially during crisis situations. The feedback is also very effective and constructive.

8.4. Weakness

Though the level of participation in programme production is considered good, the stations suffer from programme inconsistency. There is a general discontent with the poor signal which is a consequence of the low power transmitter and mediocre grade of audio pieces of equipment.

Poor internet connectivity is a genuine problem faced by the station. Transportation is also a major problem and due to that, the programmers confine their territory to the adjoining villages.

Lack of long-term commitment and coordinated efforts among the community members and volunteers and even the staff of CRS should be considered seriously.

Implementing organizations should incorporate training of management, financial, technical, equipment maintenance, and journalistic skills into their projects. Most importantly, they should prepare project beneficiaries to face and adapt to change.

8.5. Opportunities

The radio stations can make partnerships with other groups, organizations, schools, government, etc., to have a network to facilitate programming and increased listening. CRS can be paired with other ICTs to have a more effective reach. Convergence with new media and the Internet would definitely enhance the ability of CRS during a crisis situation.

Radio clubs and listener groups could be formed which will help the station to retain its audience and create more potential listeners. Also, these groups can be effectively used during disaster mitigation. Networks of community radio stations can serve as an effective and efficient forum for the exchange of programming, creation of national news, and information programmes.

Professional associations can play a vital role in establishing professional codes of ethics, identifying training needs, and establishing training programmes about disaster warning and mitigation.

9. Findings and Discussion

The CRS was severely damaged by the impact of the cyclone, no one was able to pass messages through the radio at that time as the wires were all destroyed due to the cyclone. The tower which transmitted signals got bent harming its functioning. Even the speaker was unable to reach the studio due to the cyclone.

Most of the trees and electric posts were uprooted by this in Nagapattinam and Karaikal district. For rehabilitating places affected by this disaster groups like CRG, SHG and more participated for the same. Collecting people from places affected by this cyclone and giving them necessary things were the main purpose of these people. Velankani was the only place that was least affected in that locality. Some people helped those who needed help by building camps in schools, also by preparing food for them in Velankani and places which were least affected.

Every incident was recorded earlier by people but they couldn't publish it due to the connectivity problem as most of the major forms of message transmitting sources were out of order. From the mid of November till February the radio stations were not working within this locality, hence the people were dependent on radio for getting information. The radio station got the generator in February so all the news which was recorded during those days reached the audience only in February.

So for the time, as the radio was not functioning, they started transmitting messages through this website called www.milaap.org. Milaap is a fundraising website. The broadcasting was done an hour a day through this website. Every person from that place needed light at that time as it was the major issue that the people of that place were facing. "The Voice of the Vulnerable" was the tag line of the programme that had been organized for the people on those days through the website.

The main aim of this programme "The Voice of the Vulnerable" was to make people aware of what they should do in such situations. For every natural calamity, food and money are the major problems during disasters. Because in places where the money is already a problem, disaster like Gaja would have adversely affected the life of the families living in that locality.

Before the occurrence of this cyclone, the farmers were already facing a lot of problems in every manner. By this, many farmers lost their homes, lost their crops, lost their cattles and every single thing that they had as their own. Restarting cultivation was a difficult task for the farmers as they would have a lot of problems for the rehabilitation of their cultivation.

Disease growth became very common at that moment, as maintaining hygiene was a crucial role to be played by the disaster management authority. Many of the women and children faced issues related to hygiene at that time as their homes were destroyed and public toilets were very few and unmaintained. For them, being homeless made them unable to be unaffected by various diseases. Hence, these disaster management authorities were able to help these people to a level when they would have done more at that time.

Fishermen's problem was the other major issue at that time as many fishermen lost their boats and some of them lost their lives. The government didn't provide enough support that they needed for rehabilitating themselves at that time. Also, the problems faced by fishermen were not completely told by the media hence people of other places were not able to understand what happened to their families who were more affected than the fisherman himself. The families of these fishermen were worst affected due to it as for them, it is about poverty. The families of the fishermen were and are still dependent upon the daily wages of the fishermen for basic requirement such as food. The fishermen weren't able to go fishing for months causing their families to be left, starving and unaddressed. The volunteers engaged in rehabilitating people affected by Gaja Cyclone asked the listeners to send postcards to the people affected by this crisis through their organization.

Most people understand things when it's told in the form of a drama. As the world dramatically portrays everything has a huge role to play in it. That's why people only believe in things when it is told dramatically. Hence, the disaster management authority, what they did was that they started dramatically portraying everything so that the people believe in what they were trying to convey, so that could help them out to an extent at that moment.

10. Recommendations

Community Radio stations can make use of the Internet for networking with other stations and they can become community multimedia centres. Incorporating Internet content in their programmes and providing communities with access and expertise, the community radio stations can be made more effective. As new technologies and combinations of technologies make affordable rural Internet possible, connecting Community Radio stations should be a priority and strength by giving them more frequency coverage area to reach the communities.

REFERENCES

Barton, D.K., and Ward, H.R. (1969). *Handbook of radar measurement.* New York: McGraw-Hill.

Cerulo, K.A., and Ruane, J.M. (1998). "Coming together: new taxonomies for the analysis of social relations". *Sociological Inquiry*, *68*(3), 398-425.

Coile, and Russel, C. (1997). "The role of amateur radio in providing emergency electronic communication for disaster management." *Disaster Prevention and Management: An International Journal*. *6*(3): 176-185.

Dominick, J.R. (2010). *The dynamics of mass communication: Media in the digital age*. New Delhi: Tata McGraw-Hill Education.

Dragon, G.A. (2001). Making Waves: Participatory communication for social change: A report to the Rockefeller foundation. Rockefeller Foundation.

Girard, B. (1992). *A passion for radio: Radio waves and community* (Vol. 178). Montreal, Quebec: Black Rose Books Ltd.

Graber, D.A. (1980). *Crime news and the public*. New York: Praeger.

Hirschburg, P.L., Dillman, D.A., & Ball-Rokeach, S.J. (1986). "Media system dependency theory: Responses to the eruption of Mount St. Helens." In Ball-Rokeach, S., and Cantor, M.G. (eds.) *Media, audience, and social structure*, Newbury Park, California: Sage Publications, pp.117-126.

Juri, P. (2006). Mass media usage during a natural disaster: LSU college students and Hurricane Katrina. Retrieved from: https://digitalcommons.lsu.edu/cgi/

viewcontent.cgi?referer=https://scholar.google.com/&httpsredir=1&article=1939&context=gradschool_theses

Page, D., and Crawley, W. (2001). *Satellites over South Asia: Broadcasting, culture and the public interest*. New Delhi: SAGE Publications.

Pavarala, V., and Malik, K.K. (2007). *Other voices: The struggle for community radio in India*. New Delhi: SAGE Publications.

Perez-Lugo, M. (2004). "Media uses in disaster situations: A new focus on the impact phase." *Sociological Inquiry*, *74*(2):210-225.

Romo-Murphy, E., James, R., and Adams, M. (2011). "Facilitating disaster preparedness through local radio broadcasting". *Disasters*, *35*(4), 801-815.

Seydlitz, R., Williams, S.J., Laska, S., and Triche, E. (1991). "The effects of newspaper reports on the public's response to a natural hazard event." *International Journal of Mass Emergencies and Disasters*, *9*(1): 5-29.

Simon, T., Goldberg, A., and Adini, B. (2015). "Socializing in emergencies—A review of the use of social media in emergency situations". *International Journal of Information Management*, *35*(5): 609-619.

UNESCO Chair on Community Media (2013). *Community Radio Continuous Improvement Toolkit (CRCIT), Version 2.0*, New Delhi: CEMCA (English and Hindi versions), Retrieved from: http://uccommedia. in/wp-content/uploads/2014/08/CR-CIT-Version-2.0.pdf

WEBSITE

www.dhanfoundation.org/kalanjiyamvanoli.com

Retrieved from: https://d1wqtxts1xzle7.cloudfront.net/57335173/Perez_Lugo_2004.pdf?1536579018=&response-contentdisposition=inline%3B+filename%3DMedia_Uses_in_Disaster_Situations_A_New.pdf&Expires=1595832705&Signature=e6GDIL2Q6so9A5yYEVtUCUgvEJKa4zl7c6v7OH-lptr9p26GdRQJP81NxgVcq2WP!9mYymtXa0oqhE1i1qgEfn7fW6TDMRdXG1YI3d2nMXOrDedbNPfZk74MS4Phx2vf7V9KQYLBjhP6ttbIpueY7Hlfdr2rLPvMEvUjCzen11gw~n7U9WRRZ3pBImeTK9cWLFvNe~3yDK5I0YmaGf9UXcYKcVue7hctmD1drUIIAy0k2dgetF6klcjtLm5-Cvfs~Z2LTYlo7XyPZ3LACZyr1vYPre4cPvL0zohIBuA9HoSc1x8MXBaDLZmgHIICkXT4fd~yO-cGlyN8JtXR3l-oZw__&Key-Pair-Id=APKAJLOHF5GGSLRBV4ZA

Hurricane Katrina. Retrieved from: https://digitalcommons.lsu.edu/cgi/viewcontent.cgi?referer=https://scholar.google.com/&httpsredir=1&article=1939&context=gradschool_theses

18

Who is Participating?

An analysis of Communities in Community Radio in India

Taijrani Rampersaud

Introduction

In India, there has always been some interest in media that are beneficial to the voiceless society, however, the policy environment within the country was not fertile until after the Supreme Court verdict in 1995 which declared that the airwaves are public property. This resulted in activists strengthening their call for community media which saw fruition nearly one decade later with the establishment of *Anna Community Radio* in Tamil Nadu — the first (campus) community radio station (CRS), in 2004. Since then, there have been the introduction of more than 200 other stations in India (About 251 by 2019)[1] (see weblink).

Overall, community media were introduced with the idea that they are "produced, controlled and owned by the people" (Pavarala, 2015, p. 14). In so doing, communities utilize alternative media to share their perspectives—their challenges, proposed solutions, as well as their unique cultural practises, all of which are often ignored by the mainstream media. A deeper understanding of *'the people'*, whether classified by geography and/or by interest (Pavarala and Malik, 2007), can prove important in enabling stakeholders involved in advocacy and capacity building activities to better represent these communities, and, ultimately, might prove beneficial towards the growth of the community media sector in India (Bailur, 2012; Browne, 2012; Couldry, 2010).

This chapter attempts to provide a generalized description of the types of communities involved in community radio (CR) in India with a focus on four case studies: *Sangham Radio*[2] in Telangana, *Radio Tilonia*[3] in Rajasthan, *Radio Luit*[4] in Assam, and *Waqt ki Awaaz*[5] in Uttar Pradesh. Through quantitative secondary data, the types of participants were categorized using 'children, LGBTQ[6], men, PWD[7], women, youth, and other.' Through qualitative primary data from the cases and stakeholders' interviews, the types of internal and external participants of these CR stations were further categorized in an attempt to provide a deeper understanding of the participants.

Categorizing and Classifying Members of the 'community'

Based on the information available via the stations' social media platforms and the CR compendiums—'*Community Radio for Good Governance*' (2015) and *'Community Radio in India, Towards Diversity and Sustainability'* (2016), I was able to compile and curate the data for operational stations as of December 2017. Of these, 146 of 193 stations (75.6%) had data regarding their communities, in Figure 18.1 based on my analysis.

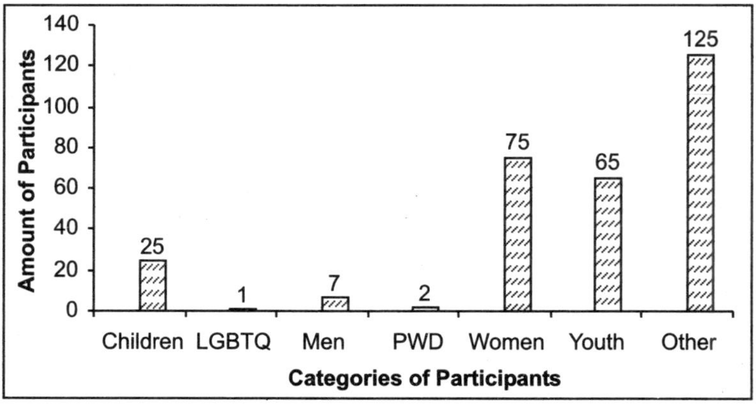

Fig. 18.1: A general categorization of the types of communities in CR in India.

The most popular identified community was 'women' which 75 stations, followed by 'youth' in 65 stations, 'children' in 55 stations, men in 7 stations, PWD in 2 stations, and LGBTQ in 1 station. The 'other' categorization identified by 125 stations was for references made to 'community' or for identified groups which included: apartment and boat dwellers, artists, drivers, ex-child labourers, farmers, fisherfolks, illiterate people, migrants, parents and guardians, scientists, senior citizens, students, trainers, teachers, academicians, tribal groups, unskilled workers, and weavers.

While the secondary data provided some insight, specific information about the internal and external communities were not available. Based on the case study interviews, I was able to classify these communities further, as can be seen in the Figure 18.2.

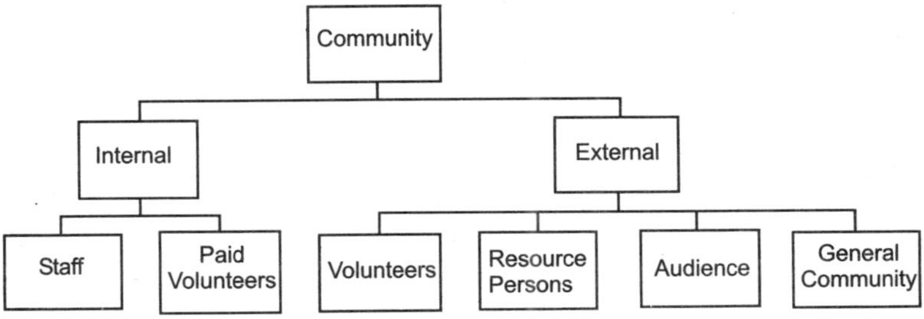

Fig. 18.2: Classification of types of communities in CR in India.

The internal community comprises staff and paid volunteers while the external community comprises volunteers, resource persons, audience, and the general community. *Staff* and *paid volunteers* are paid a salary and stipend, respectively, in order to motivate them to participate directly in the operation of the stations. *Volunteers*, *resource persons* and *audience* (active listeners) have vested interests in the stations' continuity and provide content, information, and feedback to ensure this. The *general community* comprise the population within reach of the station; they are not the 'others' who are not actively involved however are considered as potential participants since at any time they can become direct participants.

Internal Community

The internal community can be further classified into (1) *management personnel* involved with the administration of the station, and (2) *production personnel* involved with the creative aspects involved with programming. In many cases, one individual undertook several tasks in either or both the management and production areas of the stations.

Additionally, I was able to prepare Table 18.1, based on the cases, which depicts the general roles participants undertake within the stations.

The most popular internal community based on gender classification is 'women' followed by 'men'. Of the 47 participants, there were also representatives from the 'PWD' and 'youth' communities. Overall, there were 5 management personnel: 3 paid women, 1 paid man, 1 male volunteer[8]; and, 42 production personnel: 4 paid women, 2 paid men, 21 female volunteers, and 15 male volunteers. *Radio Luit*'s 25 volunteers

Table 18.1: The number of participants performing management and production tasks within the four case studies

Category	*Management*								*Production*								
	Paid				*Voluntary*				*Paid*				*Voluntary*				
	SR	RL	RT	W/A	SR	RL	RT	W/A	SR	RL	RT	W/A	SR	RL	RT	W/A	*Total*
Men		1				1				1		1		15			19
Women	1		1	1					1		1	2	11	10			28
PWD														2			2
Youth												2		19			21

Notes: 1. 'SR' – Sangham Radio; 'RT' – Radio Tilonia; 'RL' - Radio Luit; 'WA' – Waqt ki Awaaz.

2. 'Children' and 'LGBTQ' had not representatives, so they were not represented in the table.

(*radio activists*) are media and communication students of the Guwahati University. *Sangham Radio*'s 11 reporters are employed by DDS; any work done for the CRS is additional to their normal duties.

As can be seen, *Sangham Radio* and *Radio Tilonia* are completely run by women – from the daily management of the station to planning and executing programmes for broadcast. In addition to this, although *Waqt ki Awaaz* has equal numbers of men and women, the station coordinator is a woman. In a traditionally patriarchal society, having women in leadership roles is inspiring; a point supported by Dutta[9] (personal interview, 2018) who highlighted that community media initiatives can eradicate voice poverty[10]—a familiar situation for women, especially those in remote areas.

The fact that there appears to be more women involved, raises the question: *is the internal community truly representative of the wider communities the stations serve?* A question addressed by all four cases is that they agree there is a need for increased representation. As to why this challenge has not been addressed, Aarti Devi from *Radio Tilonia* summed it up best when she stated that the community members need money to survive and cannot volunteer because there is no stable income for volunteers, only for full-time staff (personal interview, March 2018).

When asked if there is any noticeable difference between staff and volunteers, *Radio Luit*'s interviewee[11] said there wasn't, *Radio Tilonia*'s interviewee[12] did not have a response since there weren't any volunteers, and *Waqt ki Awaaz*'s interviewee[13] said there were some differences but did not offer any clarification. *Sangham Radio*'s interviewee[14] alluded to the fact that there is some difference especially with regards to loyalty – the staff of the station are more invested in the station's continuity while the volunteers (staff of DDS) are loyal to that organization first.

Overall, the internal communities within the case studies are reportedly adequate to ensure the stations' continuity. Since funding challenges are preventing this, the CR teams attempt to engage individuals from the external community — explained below.

External Community

All four cases highlighted that their external communities are defined by the reach of the transmitters followed by the interests of the people within these geographically defined areas. Based on the case study interviews, *Radio Luit*'s general community was described as being more than over 5000 individuals, with most of them being part of the campus community, within a 10-12 km radius covered by a 100 watts transmitter; *Sangham Radio* caters to 150 villages within a 35 km radius reach of the 100 watts transmitter; *Radio Tilonia* caters to approximately 60,000 people across 30 villages within a 24 km radius covered by the 50 watts transmitter; and, *Waqt ki Awaaz* has approximately 3,00,000 people from 300 villages within reach of the 100 watts transmitter.

Apart from the geographical reach, the interviewees provided more specific data which I was able to analyse and visually represent in Figure 18.3.

Radio Luit	Sangham Radio	Radio Tilonia	Waqt ki Awaaz
• General categories: men, women, youth, children	• General categories: men, women, youth, children	• General categories: men, women, youth, children, PWD	• General categories: men, women, children, youth, Hijras (LGBTQ)
• Interests: students (university, school), housewives, shopkeepers, Harijans, Dalits, cleaners	• Interests: thematic based groups	• Interests: elderly, tribal communities	• Interests: thematic based groups

Fig. 18.3: Members of the external community with regards to the four case studies.

All four stations produce programmes that cater to 'children', 'men', 'women', and 'youth' communities, while *Radio Tilonia* also focuses on PWD and *Waqt ki Awaaz* focuses on LGBTQ. Apart from these generalized communities, each of the four stations, due to location and demographics of their participants, also cater to various interests expressed by different groups of peoples. With regards to *Radio Luit*, a station established by and housed in an educational institution, this station caters largely to the students of the university as well as nearby schools through educational programming; however, there are also programmes that cater to housewives, shopkeepers, and cleaners as well as religious minorities such as *Harijans/Dalits.*[15] *Radio Tilonia* also has specific programmes for the elderly and tribal communities. *Sangham Radio* and *Waqt ki Awaaz* did not identify specific communities of interest, however, these stations have programmes along with various thematic areas, such as agriculture, culture, and development, since these are important to their communities.

With regards to volunteers, only *Waqt ki Awaaz* highlighted this group. Shukla (personal interview, 2018) stated that they have 303 individuals from the surrounding villages who act as liaisons between the station and the villages. Sometimes, these individuals also act as guides and assist with production tasks; on such occasions, they are paid a stipend for their efforts since the time spent with the CR team is time away from their occupations.

Additionally, each station indicated having resource persons who are consulted depending on the stations' needs. For example, *Radio Sangham* has the policy to broadcast local songs between each programme—all these songs are sung by localities and are not written down anywhere. *Waqt ki Awaaz* highlighted having received multiple pieces of trainings over the years from external resource persons associated with international organizations such as UNESCO and regional organizations such as CEMCA (Commonwealth Educational Media Centre for Asia).

With regards to audience engagement, according to *Radio Luit*, the audience members utilize multiple platforms, including telephone calls, text messages, and social networking, to provide feedback about programmes being aired. Likewise, the audience feedback for *Sangham Radio, Radio Tilonia* and *Waqt ki Awaaz* are similar in nature. *Sangham Radio* highlighted having mixed reactions from their listeners — sometimes they like the content and sometimes they do not, however, they will communicate both to the CRS. *Radio Tilonia* stated that their communities provide feedback through phone calls, during community meetings, by responding to questionnaires, and by participating in focus group discussions. Similarly, *Waqt ki Awaaz* highlighted that their listeners provide constructive criticisms through focus group discussions, telephone calls, and letters.

Overall, all four cases highlighted that feedback is good, however, there is a need for more communities to be represented in the actual station — in decision-making, production and management aspects, and not simply as 'audiences' for programmes.

Conclusion: Participation of Communities

In India, there are many different communities associated with CRS — both internally and externally, some paid, some unpaid. However, the amount of people involved in these processes is considered low by practitioners and are not representative of the wider communities even though there is support from resource persons, volunteers, and active listeners to ensure more inclusive programming.

As Pavarala[16] (personal communication, 2018) highlighted, it is important to get the participation of the marginalized communities into the making of community media, not just the programmes for broadcast. Dutta (personal communication, 2018) adds to this by stating that participation goes beyond content generation; there needs to be involvement of the community at every stage.

However, it is also important to note that there are attempts by the internal communities to ensure greater involvement from the general communities of these stations. Through the radio activists of *Radio Luit*, the reporters of *Sangham Radio*, and the volunteers of *Waqt ki Awaaz,* we can clearly see that there is awareness about the importance of increased engagement of communities. Furthermore, while everyone might not have the time to dedicate to the operation of the station, their voices still have a variety of a to be heard and to influence the processes of social change.

In summary, while there is need for greater representation of the communities to which community radio stations broadcast in India, the challenges associated with funding is a deterrent. To ensure that different communities, whether geographical or communities of interest, are catered to and represented by the stations, there are feedback and consultation sessions where the internal communities can interact with the external communities and ensure they are producing content in keeping with the needs of said communities.

NOTES

1. While the MIB website reflects a total of 251 operational community radio

stations as of May 2019, the secondary data referenced in this paper were gathered and analysed up to December 2017.

2. Established in 2008 by the Deccan Development Society (General Narsamma, *Sangham Radio*, personal interview, April 06, 2018).
3. Established in 2009 by Barefoot College (Aarti Devi, *Radio Tilonia,* personal interview, March 07, 2018).
4. Established in 2011 by Guwahati University (Bhaskar Jyoti Acharjya, *Radio Luit*, personal interview, February 05, 2018).
5. Established in 2013 by Shramik Bharati (Radha Shukla, *Waqt ki Awaaz*, personal interview, March 08, 2018).
6. LGBTQ - Lesbians, Gays, Bi-sexuals, Transgenders, Queers.
7. PWD - Persons with Disabilities.
8. The director of the Institute of Distance and Open Learning who holds the portfolio of 'station director' and is the final signing authority for the station—is not involved in the day-to-day operations of the station (Acharjya, personal interview, 2018).
9. Dr. Ankurran Dutta is an associate professor and the HOD at the Department of Communication and Journalism, Gauhati University, Assam, India. With approximately 13 years of experience in the development communication field, he has been working towards the advancement of community media, especially in the North-East regions of India, in his capacities as an activist and academic. (Dutta, personal interview, 2018.)
10. Voice Poverty addresses the lack of "attention that is being paid to the local production of content" as a result of "the need to listen to the voices of the poor in order to both understand and tackle poverty." (Jo Tacchi, 2008.)
11. Bhaskar Jyoti Acharjya, Programme Executive, *Radio Luit*, personal interview, February 05, 2018.
12. Aarti Devi, Station Co-ordinator, *Radio Tilonia*, personal interview, March 07, 2018.
13. Radha Shukla, Station Co-ordinator, *Waqt ki Awaaz*, personal interview, March 08, 2018.
14. General Narsamma, Station Manager, *Sangham Radio*, personal interview, April 06, 2018.
15. The word 'Harijan' roughly translates to "children of God" a term that was first used by Mohandas Karamchand Gandhi to refer to 'Dalits' in 1933 as he found the term *Dalit*, which translates to "untouchable", to be offensive. Regardless of the preferred term, *Harijan* or *Dalit*, people so-called belong to the lowest group within the Hindu caste system of India. (Ramanathan S., 2017.)
16. Prof. Vinod Pavarala is the chairholder for the UNESCO Chair on Community Media and a professor at the University of Hyderabad. He has been working in the development communication field for over 20 years in the capacities of activist, teacher, and researcher.

REFERENCES

Bailur, S. (2012). "Who is the community in community radio?" *Economic and Political Weekly*, April 28, 2012, *47*(17), pp. 92-99.

Browne, D.R. (2012). "What is 'Community' in Community Radio? A Consideration of the Meaning, Nature and Importance of a Concept." In J. Gordon. (Ed.). (2012). *Community Radio in the Twenty-First Century* (pp. 153-171). Switzerland: Peter Lang.

Community Radio for Good Governance [Compendium]. (2015). New Delhi: One World Foundation.

Community Radio in India, Towards Diversity & Sustainability [Compendium]. (2016). New Delhi: One World Foundation.

Community Radio Stations. (n.d.). Retrieved September 2017, from https://www.mib.gov.in/broadcasting/community-radio-stations-0.

Couldry, N. (2010). "Voice as value." In *Why Voice Matters: Culture and Politics After Neoliberalism* (pp. 1-20); Goldsmiths, University of London, UK: SAGE Publications Ltd.

Pavarala, V. (2015). "Community Radio 'under progress': Resuming a Paused Revolution in South Asia." *Economic and Political Weekly*, Vol. L. No. 51.

Pavarala, V. (2018, July 11). Personal interview.

Pavarala, V. & Malik, K.K. (2007). *Other Voices – The Struggle for Community Radio in India*. New Delhi: Sage Publications.

Ramanathan S. (2017). *Stop calling Dalits 'Harijan': SC calls the term abusive, as we remain ignorant and insensitive.* Retrieved July 2019, from https://www.thenewsminute.com/article/stop-calling-dalits-harijan-sc-calls-term-abusive-we-remain-ignorant-and-insensitive-59315.

Rampersaud, T. (2019). *Community Media Database for South Asia V.01* [Microsoft Access Database]. Unpublished, University of Hyderabad, Telangana, India.

Rampersaud, T. (n.d.). *Community Media Directory*. Retrieved July 2019, from http://cmd.sancomonline.net/.

Tacchi, J.A. (2008). "Voice and Poverty." *Media Development*, 2008/1. mib.gov.in/broadcasting/list-251-operational-community-radio-stations-India.

SECTION 6
Media

19

Media Awareness among the School Going Students

A Study of Math Village in Raipur District of Chhattisgarh

Vinod Pandey and *Satyabrata Das*

Introduction

Media has turned into a basic piece of our everyday life. It has impacted us to such an extent that individuals need newspaper with their morning tea. Media, print or electronic web-based life has developed as the fundamental wellspring of data. Internet-based life is going to be one of the most well known and popular media for correspondence nowadays. Web-based life has brought various individuals from the diverse topographical territory to one stage on which they can share their inclination, thoughts, feelings, data and substantially more. With the progression of science and innovation, the world has approached one another. Today individuals don't need to hang tight for the dispersal procedure yet the condition is with the end goal that each web-based life client has turned into a wellspring of data all alone. The everyday news and perspectives to which the online networking client scores overspread a wide scope of points. These points or subjects are identified with the happenings of our encompassing. Individuals like to show feelings through the rundown of emojis or even remark like manner. Online networking goes about as an umbrella that comprises an assortment of fascinating highlights that have our life exceptionally simpler. Highlights of labelling companions, area sharing, photographs and video transfers, message talking, video calling, looking through companions and so on have made our lives all the more captivating. Culture, Communication and Development are unpredictably related ideas that are exceptionally important with regards to creating nations in the contemporary Global South. While the points of view of improvement has been changing from monetary development to social advancement, human improvement, and maintainable advancement, both correspondence and human sciences have been instrumental in making advancement to the following level. Correspondence rose as an important field with regard to the development of the purported Third World in the post-World War II period with the rise of broad communications, i.e., papers, radio, and TV. Wilbur Schramm, Daniel Lerner and Everett Rogers, among other Western researchers made a start with their models and ways to deal with the investigation of modernization and the job of communication in that procedure, establishing the framework for what came to be known as the 'overwhelming worldview'. The development of sciences has added a lot in creating ideas and research strategies that helped to understanding the connection between language, human communication, culture, broad technologies, and the association of the executives of development and social change.

Mike Moran, Jeff Seaman and Hester Tinti-Kane believed for a long time that the term social media does not have a clear definition. However, when one platform emerged that gave people an opportunity to be content creators, controllers and transparent users, the situation changed to a great extent. Once this content is shared, it become a conversation, because all users who have accounts on social media platforms could interact with all posts (Moran, Seaman and Tinti-Kane, 2011).

The present chapter has explored the media behaviour of school children between the ages of 16 to 19. A few students use Facebook, YouTube, Google, and numerous others that will be talked about in the discoveries of this exploration. The people of this age that will lead our real lives, later on, should be knowledgeable about the option that affect this world and make India a superior nation by making steady progress. Accordingly, we look into what they present to us that may impact them adversely or favourably. This exploration planned a survey for understanding long-range interpersonal communication, and whether it has any impact on their school education. If there is an effect on their academic achievements we shall find out, how it has impacted their education? The advanced web resembles a worldwide town permitting everybody boundless access to anything, whenever and any place. It rises above all physical limits permitting an individual to stand up to an expert level. All the more significantly, the excellence of the web lies in the way that it is intelligent and supports investment just as a feeling of a network when contrasted with some other types of media. The 21st century is a technological world. Wherever you look, you will find everybody is having a device: regardless of whether it's a telephone, tablet or workstation. You can't get away from this innovation since it is integrated with our living in this world. New media has gradually found its way into homerooms and it is reshaping our education and eventually leading to the development of our country. Our development depend on innovations in our educational systems and resultant positive change. Innovation makes our training productive, connect with the world, and allow our education effectively available. There are numerous points of interest relating to new media that have an impact on school children's learning and eventually influence their future.

This world of social media gives scope to everyone to express and share ideas, thoughts and feelings who want to be a part of it. Within the past ten years, social media, such as Twitter, Facebook, Myspace, YouTube, Flicker and, others have grown at a tremendous rate, enlisting an astronomical number of users. Social media have inevitably become an integral part of the contemporary class-room, advertising and public relations industries, political campaigning, and numerous other aspects of our daily existence (Matyszczyk, Chris, 2013).

A study covering 120 school children in the Math town close to Tilda Tehsil of the Raipur region, Chhattisgarh was conducted of which about 100 students responded to the questions asked. The present chapter presents an analysis of data thus collected on the utilization of new media by the students, their knowledge about the new media, and the effect of the new media on their education.

Literature Review

Kaveri Subrahmanyam and Patricia Greenfield write that utilization of web correspondence has both negative and beneficial outcomes due to unsafe manners by which the web could be utilized. They likewise feel that these days schools are attempting their best to control students in the use of advanced media in school premises (Subrahmanyam and Greenfield, 2008). In certain schools, authorities accept that online life positively affects the academic achievements of students. In some schools, informal web access has been prohibited for the fear of students getting into undersirable habits though they know the positive effect of online life on the students' education (Ahn, 2010). Ahn likewise writes youth use YouTube to share their options and stream recordings, use Facebook to display their total personality on the web and develop companions. Ahn says client specialists examining grandeur of the profiles of the web-based life of claim these as a feature of the procedure required for the students to build up their character (Ahn, 2011a). Gwenn Schurgin O'Keeffe and Kathleen Clarke-Pearson accept that there are negative effects brought about by web-based social networking due to incorporation of unseemly behaviour and matters. Students get involved not "understanding on the web security." They additionally state that there is online badgering and cyber-bullying, which will have a bad effect on the youth (O'Keeffe and Clarke-Pearson, 2011). Paul Kirschner and Aryn Karpinski characterize Facebook and other interpersonal communication organizing locales as online catalogues that enable individuals to discover their companions, family and partners finding them on informal community destinations (Kirschner and Karpinsk, 2010). Curtis expresses that youth everywhere throughout the world are beginning to lose enthusiasm for the utilization of Facebook and are utilizing Snapchat, Twitter and Instagram (Curtis, 2013). Victoria Rideout states, the time that the youth spend via web-based networking as 'diversion media'. It is "more than double the normal measure of time went through in school every year." (Rideout, 2012, p. 5) She likewise includes that an American youth spends overall seven and a half hours daily only for having some good times on the media, yet they perform multiple tasks, between all the various media they use. For instance, they can be tuning in to music, sending a tweet and furthermore posting on Facebook. Rideout says, that since online networking is seven days, in contrast to class or having an all day's work, throughout the years the measure of time one could spend over the web "has detonated" (Rideout, 2012, p. 5). Abelardo Pardo accepts that innovation offers a stage for advancement, and enables its clients to express their assessments about how they feel towards the data being distributed. He adds that online life additionally enables students to interact with each other, and with their instructors and network with those that offer their equivalent training. Pardo states that these kinds of connections are "a fundamental piece of how people learn." (Pardo, 2013, p. 45). Kirschner and Karpinski, examine Wim Veen's new term, "Homo Zappiens", which alludes to the students of the new age, and the new ways they learn. This new way is known as "meta-subjective abilities", which means that they learn individually without guidelines, it is called "find based learning." They likewise add that more youth possess distinctive abilities for innovation since their introduction to the world, driving them to perform various tasks. They note that 46 per cent of the youth take the assistance of web for their school assignments (Kirschner and Karpinski, 2010). June Ahn talks about her exploration of a hypothesis called 'Flagging Theory'. This hypothesis alludes to how people in the informal community present themselves, build up their characters and fabricate trust with others. She adds that by having numerous companions on various stages, individuals lose the trust of their companions since they begin including individuals they don't have the foggiest idea to demonstrate to others how well known they are (Ahn, 2011b).

According to O'Keeffe and Clarke-Pearson, these are two or three advantages in the use of the internet as revealed by the American Academy of Pediatrics. One of the most significant advantages of the internet is that it improves comprehension of an indivdual himself by drawing in with others, and getting to be imaginative through blogging. This prompts better results in the individual school work. Another significant advantage is the way the web offers students the chance to improve their learning, since they get the opportunity to impart information to each other and direct gathering activities all the more effectively (O'Keeffe and Clarke-Pearson, 2011).

Victor Lavy and Edith Sand's exploration in a Tel Aviv school to decide the impact of the kind of companions that the students choose via web-based networking media. They isolated the kinds of companions into classes like "Proportional companions" who are companions that share something for all intents and purpose with one another, for example, scholastics and interests. A subsequent gathering was the "non-proportional companions", the individuals who turned down the "kinship offer" of another understudy student. They found that the students with complementary companions in their group had a hugely beneficial outcome on three of their test scores; Hebrew, Math and English. Then again, students that had no normal companions demonstrated that there was a negative impact on a similar three test scores. This reveals that if students are in contact with companions who offer similar interests, objectives and training via web-based networking media, at that point they are bound to help each other in performing admirably in their investigations, because of inspiration and different elements (Lavy and Sand 2012).

Singh, Amiri and Sabbarwal (2017) have shown the relationship between web-based networks and informal communication sharing idea, benefits, bad low marks and so on. The chapter has attempted to compare this study with the findings of other studies.

Chawla, Khan and Pandey (2016) tried to show an association that exists between Higher Education and Social Networking Sites. They examined the use of mining calculations given by NASA instruments such a Like-Analyser, Gephi, Wolfram Alpha and Node XL to survey nearness and investment factor of students and instructions. It has also been found that diagrams are used in the informal organization. It is discovered that interpersonal organization with long-range informal communication on Facebook and advanced education work go parallel. In the midst of customary print media, there used to be a single direction of data scattering which was confined as far as possible to nearness. The procedure of data dissemination with the use of the Internet changed essentially.

Sanzhar Naizabekov concluded that social media causes procrastination as a result of its distracting nature. It would take an individual who uses social media much more time than it would take a focused individual to finish a task. Through procrastination emerges the second negative impact, which is lack of motivation, because using social media with studying develops a negative attitude towards their individual work at school (Naizabekov, 2012).

Purva, Yadav, Abbasi and Toshniwal (2015) have studied online long-range interpersonal communication platforms like Facebook and Twitter for gaining an understanding about correspondence. The users are from different locations spread across the world, and the subject matter includes everything. The Twitter users exchanged information relating to any occasion at any time. The subject matter of these messages could be either short or long, urgent or not urgent, local or non-local, and common or uncommon matters. Devmane and Rana (2015) analysed the online informal communication with regard to the occasions, time spent, reasons for the communication, and participants' demeanour and conduct etc. The data for the study come from more than 700 respondents conducted in a survey of 27 locations in India.

Objective

The present study has focused on the Indian youth: The reason for selecting youth as the target audience is that the direction of a country and culture is decided by the direction taken by youths of that country. This chapter is an attempt to analyse the pattern of social networking usage and to investigate the impact of new media (Social media) on the students and their addiction to it. Further, it is also to find the impact of new media (social networking sites) on the academic performance of the students.

Research Method and Sampling

As in other disciplines, in the field of communication too, a large number of studies conducted by academics are related to the category of basic or pure research and applied research as these are carried out to understand a phenomenon or to gain new insights into it. The phenomenon of social media and its addiction among the young is rich in pure research.

The sample for the study consisted of 100 students (boys and girls) aged 16-19 years. They are from different socio-economic backgrounds. Four intermediate schools near Math and Tilda tehsils of Raipur district were selected for the study. The researchers conducted a survey administering a questionnaire at these four schools: Swami Vivekanand Kanyasala, Gyanjyoti School, Bharat Dewangan Higher Secondary School and Maa Sarada School.

Results and Analysis

Out of a total of 120 students, 100 (60 students were boys and 40 girls) of the 12th standard of four schools responded to the questionnaire. Out of which 85 students had mobile and smartphone to use the internet and 15 students didn't have phones.

The following responses were received:

- Out of the 80 students who were using the mobile and smartphone, girls were 20 per cent and boys were 80 per cent who were using new media technology through internet.
- About 70 per cent of students (56) used new media technology for the education purposes like sharing digital study materials. Teachers also share important news related to academic session, notice and other important information required for students. The rest 30 per cent use the computers at a particular period to get the required information.
- 80 per cent of the students (64) use new media technology like WhatsAap, Facebook, Instagram, YouTube, Google etc., for the purpose of entertainment.
- 30 per cent of the students (24) use this technology for other use than education and entertainment like railway reservation, online bill payment, online movie booking, online money transfer, online merchant, offline merchant through Apps etc.

Conclusion

Only 70 per cent of the students use new media technology for studies. Still 30 per cent is not getting any benefit from the new media platform as they are not having mobile phones. They get the benefit from the internet only during the computer periods in the schools where these facilities are not up to the mark. Abouth 80 per cent use new technology for entertainment purposes and only 30 per cent use it for getting other facilities like bill payments, online money transactions, online and offline merchants through this new technology platform. From the study, it is obvious that the reach and use of new technology are average and it needs to be developed. Media awareness among the students is still required. ICT in Math village and its Tehsil is yet to cover those areas which are lacking its functioning so as to make it more powerful and developed.

REFERENCES

Ahn, J. (2010). The Influence of Social Networking Sites on High School Students' Social and Academic Development. Diss. Faculty of the USC Graduate School University of Southern California. http://digitallibrary.usc.edu/cdm/ref/collection/p15799coll127/id/352705.

Ahn, J. (2011a). "Digital Divides and Social Network Sites: Which Students Participate in Social Media?" *Journal of Educational Computing Research, 45*(2), 147-63. http://dx.doi.org/10.2190/EC.45.2.b.

Ahn, J. (2011b). "The Effect of Social Network Sites on Adolescents' Social and Academic Development: Current Theories and Controversies." *Journal of the American Society for Information Science and Technology, 62*(8), 1435-1445. http://dx.doi.org/10.1002/asi.21540.

Chawla, M., Khan, M.N and Pandey, A. (2016). "A Study of Information Technology Usage Behaviour of University Students", *AIMA Journal of Management & Research, 10*(2/4):1-16.

Curtis, A. (2013). The Brief History of Social Media. Retrieved from: http://www.uncp.edu/home/acurtis/NewMedia/SocialMedia/SocialMediaHistory.html.

Devmane, M. and Rana, R. (2015). "Usability Trends and Access of Online Social Network by Indian Population and its Analysis", paper presented in International Conference on Nascent Technologies in the Engineering Field (ICNTE'15), IEEE, 2015.

Kirschner, P., and Karpinski, Aryn (2010). "Facebook® and Academic Performance." *Computers in Human Behavior, 26*(6), 1237-45. http://dx.doi.org/10.1016/j.chb.2010.03.024

Lavy, V., and Sand, E. (2012). "The Friends Factor: How Students' Social Networks Affect Their Academic Achievement and Well-Being?" *The National Bureau of Economic Research.* Hebrew University, University of Warwick, CEPR, and NBER. DOI:10.3386/w18430Corpus ID: 16534057.

Matyszczyk, Chris. (2013). "Facebook Entry Gets Office Worker Fired." https://www.cnet.com/news/facebook-entry-gets-office-worker-fired/

Moran, M., Seaman, J., and Tinti-Kane, H. (2011). *Teaching, Learning, and Sharing: How Today's Higher Education Faculty Use Social Media,* pp. 1-32. Boston, MA: Pearson Learning Solutions and Babson Survey Research Group.

Naizabekov, S. (2012). "Negative Impact of Social Networking Sites on Academic Performance of Students." Retrieved from https://www.academia.edu/1810511/Negative_impact_of_social_networking_sites_on_academic_performance_of_students.

O'Keeffe, G., and Kathleen, C. (2011). "The Impact of Social Media on Children, Adolescents, and Families." *Pediatrics, 127*(4):799-805. http://dx.doi.org/10.1542/peds.2011-0054.

Pardo, A. (2013). "Social learning graphs: combining social network graphs and analytics to represent learning experiences." *International Journal of Social Media and Interactive Learning Environments, 1*(1):43-58. http://dx.doi.org/10.1504/IJSMILE.2013.051652

Purva, P. Yadav., Abbasi, F. and Toshniwal, D. (2015). "How Has Twitter Changed the Event Discussion Scenario? A Spatio-temporal Diffusion Analysis", in International Congress on Big Data (BigData Congress'15):733-736.

Rideont, V. (2012). Children, Teens, and Entertainment Media: The View from the Classroom. Commonsense. www.commonsense.org/research.

Singh, M.M., Amiri, M. and Sabbarwal, S. (2017). "Social Media Uses: Positive and Negative Effects on the Lifestyle of Indian Youth", *Indian Journal of Social Sciences and Humanities Research*, *5*(3):123-127.

Subrahmanyam, K., and Greenfield, P. (2008). "Online Communication and Adolescent Relationships." *The Future of Children. 18*(1), 119-146. http://dx.doi.org/10.1353/foc.0.0006

20
Role of Social Media in Social Transformation

Pradeep Mallik

Introduction

Social media are challenging several well-established notions of media and look poised to emerge as the predominant media in the very near future, if they are not already that. Like their traditional counterparts, they too are contributing to social transformation. There are some instances of scholars and social workers treating the two terms – 'change' and 'transformation' – as synonyms and using social change and social transformation interchangeably. However, this chapter treats them differently and the difference has been explained. There are several issues concerning social media but this chapter discusses only those concerning their role in and use for bringing about social transformation.

Social media are simultaneously playing multiple roles: the dual role of an agent of change and transformation as well as of an index of free exchange of ideas and information in a society, the tool of social and political mobilization leading to overthrow of dictators and other rulers whom even the powerful militia and military could not ruffle, the platform for carrying out business and tracking one's sales and marketing, the vehicle for political campaigns and governance, and many others.

1. Social Media Explained

Developments in science has given the humankind information and communication technology, which, in turn, is a convergence of microelectronics, computing, telecommunications, broadcasting, and optoelectronics. Social media are essentially Western in origin and refer to an array of internet-based services that people use for online exchanges, create/co-create content and join online communities.

Social media networks are defined as "online tools and utilities that allow communication of information online and *participation and collaboration*" (Newson, *et al.*, 2008: 03) (*accent added by this author*).

Social media are also referred to as Web 2.0 and have in their ambit blogs, wikis, bookmarking, networking sites, status update services, virtual world content and media sharing sites (Dewing, 2012).

There is some overlap in the nature of the individual tools of social media. Weblogs, often shortened as blogs, are hosted on websites like WordPress, Blogspot, Weebly, Tumblr, etc. Wiki is where users create, host and edit content, the most prominent example being Wikipedia. In bookmarking, participants organize and share links to websites. Digg and Reddit are two very popular bookmarking sites. Social networking sites like Facebook and Linkedin let users construct a public profile and also allow the articulation of a list of participants with whom they are connected. Status update services let participants microblog so that they can tell others about their status or an event and follow such posts by fellow users. People use virtual world content to interact with each other individually or as members of groups in a game-like virtual environment. For example, in Second Life participants create an "avatar" of themselves and interact with others through those avatars (OECD, 2007). Last but not the least, media sharing sites like YouTube, Instagram and Pinterest help users to share photographs, audio, video, etc.

The enormity of these tools can be understood by taking the example of the popular site Facebook. It was launched in 2004 for Harvard students to help them network with each other. In 15 years, i.e., by 2019, it has become popular across the globe and has a whopping 2.38 billion active users (www.statista.com, 2019). In other words, if facebookers were to be treated like a nation, then "facebook nation" will be larger than China and the US combined. People of a few European and Asian countries will have to join them to outnumber the "facebookans". Facebook users interact among themselves (Facebook friends) by updating their status, contributing texts and images on each other's walls or pushing direct messages. They can create interest groups, join such group(s) created by others, "like" pages, import and search for contacts, and upload texts, photos and videos.

1.1. Significant Other

There is another significant platform: WhatsApp. Instant messaging platform WhatsApp has been acquired by Facebook. The app had more than half a billion daily active users (DAU) across the globe. As against this, the figure in the second quarter of 2018 was 450 million global DAU. It is extremely popular in India which has logged more than 200 million monthly active users by the turn of 2019. With more than 460 million internet users, India ranked the second largest in the internet market in the world. By 2023, this figure is likely to move past 666 million (www.statista.com, 2019).

The instant messaging platforms are built around the notion of private communication. The ease with which WhatsApp can be installed on most phones, its easy interface, and group features that allow bulk messages to be sent (though the promoters have imposed several restrictions to ensure security and misuse of the application), has made it one of the hottest tools of communication. WhatsApp is being used to disseminate messages, engage with fellow users, be they a college group, a cultural collective, a scientific group or voters. WhatsApp allows people to send text and multimedia messages using mobile data or Wi-Fi networks free of charge, thus avoiding costly SMS messaging. A user does not need to create profiles or add friends, the app links directly to his contact list so that someone can send a message to anyone in his phonebook. In the last couple of elections in India, the volunteers or social media coordinators of the political parties worked with the campaign's main WhatsApp channel to send out image posts and messages in hope that the receivers will forward them to others and create a "human chain" of communication.

1.2. Social Media as Alternative Press

Inventions and innovation have been used to bring about social change for ages. Back in the 15th century, Gutenberg's movable typeface played a significant role in loosening the power of the medieval church over the state and people at large. This, in turn, ushered in Renaissance. Reformation and Scientific Revolution followed.

In keeping with the times, people now use social media for citizen journalism. Citizen journalists use digital media tools to report and upload text and videos on the Internet. Many a time they send their content to media outlets. During Arab Spring, citizens used Facebook, Twitter and YouTube to good effect to mobilize people, plan their activities and publicize them. The mainstream media made use of the content flowing on various platforms during the protests in the Arab world. Popular news and current affairs television channel Al-Jazeera used blogs and tweets to augment its real-time reporting of the uprisings. For example, the TV channel used the citizen's media platform Sharek which filtered the posts by citizen journalists.

Personal blogs have spread across the globe thanks to low and soft barriers. According to Arabic Network for Human Rights Information (Storck, 2011), there were 40,000 active blogs in the Arab region in 2010, showing an increase of 5,000 over 2009. However, the number shot to about 6,00,000 since the 2011 uprisings.

2. Social Transformation

As against social change that is viewed as "gradual or incremental changes over a period of time", social transformation implies a fundamental change in society. "Studies of social transformation include a range of institutional and cultural changes in society throughout history" (Khondker, Habibul and Ulrike, Schuerkens, 2014:1).

Looking at changes in societies, Scott (2011) holds that they could be analysed with respect to time. Schuerkens (2001a, 2001b) points out that not every aspect of a social system transforms simultaneously. In other words, several elements change in the initial phase and then these elements force other elements to change. This cycle continues until a new structural model emerges.

> "The transformation of a system happens at the moment when the system has attained its limits of *diversity* and *integration*. Then, a new principle of integration of a society appears, which, at the same time, represents a transformation of the system and its characteristic structures" (Teune and Mlinar, 1978: 43).

3. Social Media and Social Transformation

Curiously, among the first transformation social media have brought in is the very space they operate in. Gone are the days when mere mortals had to depend on the editors, producers and other storytellers to tell their stories. Communication was mediated in which the gatekeeper had the all-important control of the flow of information and exchange of ideas. Anybody can be a content creator what with technology becoming cheaper and the internet becoming ubiquitous.

The examples and discussions above make it clear that social media tools (i) are online utilities, (ii) are about the flow of information and communication, (iii) involve participation of people and collaboration among them for co-creation of content. These utilities are nothing but websites that not only interact with the users but also allow users to interact among themselves without the interference of the hitherto powerful gatekeepers: the editors of the traditional media houses which owned newspapers or radio and television stations. Like the traditional mass media tools, they too inform, educate, entertain people and work as a platform to bring consumers and manufacturers-service providers on a common platform. Media consumers use social media to gratify their needs just as the consumers used and are still using the traditional media.

Social media have emerged as a great leveller. They are contributing in a big way in blurring the distinction between the two distinct groups of people who were seen as media content producers and media content consumers. The two are rapidly catching up with each other's production and consumption. It would not be an exaggeration to say that the media space is getting rid of hierarchy and getting democratized.

Indeed, the traditional media today are using the content floating on social media to prepare news reports. Newman, *et al.* (2012) also reflect the fact that the Fourth Estate—the organized news media—is using content from social media to enhance its own role in the propagation of news.

4. A Few Case Studies

Looking into a few big movements or initiatives could be a good way to appreciate the role of social media in social transformation. This section deals with some movements that were global in scale and had ripple effects in different regions.

4.1. Case study 1: Ice Bucket Challenge

Around the middle of 2014, several video clips of people pouring a bucketful of ice water over their heads appeared on Facebook. They were part of an initiative by the ALS Association. Two friends, Pete and Pat who were diagnosed with ALS (Amyotrophic Lateral Sclerosis), designed this innovative challenge with the aim to mobilize funds to help their ALS counterparts.

Once thrown the gauntlet at, a person needed to shoot her/himself pouring a bucket of ice-cold water over the head and post the shoot on the web. The person needed to nominate three more people to do the same. If s/he could not do so in 24 hours, the person had to pledge and donate some money for the cause.

Media, celebrities, politicians, entrepreneurs and philanthropists-donors took notice of the campaign as it spread across the globe. The campaign brought attention to ALS (also called Lou Gehrig's disease) and the need to find a cure for it. The initiative also shaped into an example of "slacktivism". To name a few, global tech wizards Bill Gates and Mark Zuckerberg, political leader George Bush, Indian film actors like Mamooty, Akshay Kumar and Sonakshi Sinha took up the challenge.

Using its media intelligence platform, media monitoring major Meltwater found that the ice bucket challenge got 1,70,000 mentions in the news media in the second half of 2014. Slacktivism, too was mentioned 3,000 times along with the challenge. This underlines a "trending association" (Vance, 2016).

Meltwater reported that between July 2013 and June 2014, i.e., in the 12 months before the challenge, ALS Association was referred to 6,819 times in the media, and the news media covered the association 64,056 times. It received a whopping 37,205 references in the second half of 2014. In terms of money, *The New York Times* reported that the ALS received more than $40 million (or approximately Rs 2.8 billion) from 7,00,000 donors within 30 days. In August 2014, ALS Association acknowledged donations touching $100 million (or about Rs. 7 billion).

The Challenge had Clearly made an Impact

In July the same year, ALS Association invested the donations that had poured in Project MinE and got the genomes of thousands of ALS patients sequenced. An ALS gene, identified as NEK1, was discovered. This in turn, led to identifying the causes of the disease. True, similar results could have been obtained without the money raised by the ice bucket challenge, but certainly not so quickly. A spike in media coverage of the beneficiaries ensured that the donations kept pouring in and the donors were assured that their money was reaching the right people.

4.2. Ripple Effect

Ice Bucket Challenge had its ripple effect. Ganeeshan (2016) has compiled it for digital marketing and data science organization Digital Vidya.

4.2.a. My Tree Challenge

Inspired by Ice Bucket Challenge, popular actor Mamooty initiated this challenge in Kerala. The activity involves planting a sapling and challenging others to do so. Mamooty planted the first sapling to start the campaign on 30 August 2014. He challenged film celebrities Shah Rukh Khan, Suriya and a few others to do the same. Mamooty's collaborators had created a Facebook page and it garnered more than 1,60,000 likes.

4.2.b. Rice Bucket Challenge

Rice Bucket Challenge spread to several South Asian countries from India. It involves gifting a bucket full of rice to the poor and the needy. The moving force of the initiative was Manju Kalanidhi who saw the merit in the Ice Bucket Challenge but felt that it led to a waste of precious water. She started a Facebook page on 23 August 2014 in support of the cause and in a day, the page attracted 7000 odd likes. There were more than 11,000 tweets in a month after the hashtag #ricebucketchallenge was created. International publications of repute such as *The Huffington Post* and *Chicago Tribune* covered the initiative.

4.2.c. Rubble Bucket Challenge

Some people in trouble-torn Gaza Strip in West Asia started the "Rubble Bucket Challenge". The small region has witnessed some of the deadliest bombings and firing of missiles by militants in Gaza and Israeli armed forces for decades now. The challenge was designed to turn the focus of the global community to the suffering of the Gaza residents. They chose the novel way of emptying a bucket full of debris on the head!

4.2.d. Love Bucket Challenge

Leading Kerala news daily *Malayala Manorama* started Love Bucket Challenge. It asks people to fill buckets with goodies and present them to those whom they think to deserve those goodies.

4.2.e. Kaapi Challenge

There were some commercial offshoots, too, of the ice bucket initiative. As Chennai city was celebrating its 375th anniversary, India Premier League (cricket) team Chennai Super Kings (CSK) decided on a spin off. The CSK players were asked to copy a *lungi*-clad man making filter coffee. Apparently, some players were hesitant in the beginning, but international cricket players like Brendon McCullum (New Zealand), Dwayne Bravo (West Indies), Ashish Nehra, Mohit Sharma and Mithun Manhas (all India) accepted the challenge. Each of the player's videos received more than 2,00,000 views on YouTube.

4.2.f. Wake Up Bucket Challenge

With several challenges floating on the web, Racold Thermo, a water-heating equipment manufacturer, joined the bandwagon in January 2015 to promote its products. Calling it "Wake Up Bucket Challenge", Racold asked people to pour a bucket of warm water on themselves. The participants were supposed to record the act and send the recording to Racold Thermo. The company pledged to give away a water heater to the underprivileged for every 25 such videos it received. The campaign had more than 500 participants and thereby helped several underprivileged people have a warm bath.

5. Social Media as Agents of Transformation

Social media have definitely emerged as an important tool to bring out a political change and this phenomenon has been accepted the world over. Several studies have proved the strength of social media networking when it comes to bringing about a political change or transformation. A case in point is the political transformation brought about in Egypt in 2011 which was termed as "Revolution 2.0". This revolution last just for eighteen days but it was beyond comprehension that a revolution could be borne out of social media networking in a country like Egypt.

Case Study 2: Egyptian Uprising

It began with an individual and then a whole lot of people joined in not so distant past to throw out a president who ruled with an iron fist. Millions of Egyptians rose against Hosni Mubarak in 2011 and in a span of eighteen days, the president of more than 30 years was gone and driven to cool his heels behind bars. (He walked free after six years in prison.)

The role of social media has been beautifully explained by quite a few authors. Johnny West (2011) is one of them:

> "A young Internet executive called Wael Ghoneim helped organize a call for a demonstration for 25 January in Cairo's

> Tahrir Square through a Facebook page entitled 'We Are All Khaled Said'. Fifty thousand people came, not just the dedicated hard core, but fresh faces, old and young. They came back the next day, and the next and the next, swelling to millions, and the rest is history." (West, 2011: 145)

(Young blogger Khaled Said was accused of posting a video of Egyptian police officers that implicated them in wrong-doings. He was thrashed and killed. Wael Ghoneim was the marketing director of Google's Middle East operations.)

The uprising began on 25 January 2011 with thousands of protesters gathering at Tahrir Square in Cairo. It ended with President Hosni Mubarak stepping down on 11 February 2011. The first massive protest on 25 January was christened the "day of rage" by the protesters. Egypt observes 25 January as National Police Day, to pay tribute to the fallen policemen of the 1952 revolution. However, to the activists, the Egyptian police force stood for "repression by the state, the problem of torture and arbitrary arrest symbolizing the corruption and sense of a loss of dignity that cast a shadow over Egyptian society throughout Mubarak's presidency" (Elizabeth Iksander, 2011:1230).[1] However, it must be mentioned here that though Mubarak stepped down after only 18 days of protests, the movement itself was a result of a long process. People found in the movement a way to give vent to their years of frustration. Political mobilization had become easy, thanks to the liberal use of social media platforms by the protesters.

A few theories of communication explain the use of social media as a vehicle for organizing and mobilizing the masses. Laswell and Granovetter gave their 'functionalist theory of the media' and 'theory of weak ties' years before the social media came into being, yet these theories give one an insight into the reason(s) protesters in Egypt chose social media as their communication platform.

Case Study 3: One Tough Job

Children's Trust is a Boston-based non-profit organization, the mission of which is to prevent child abuse in Massachusetts. It funds and operates a variety of programmes for parents. Mantus (n.d), who worked specifically on the One Tough Job programme which is a parenting education website designed to help parents of children 0-6 years of age, sums up her experience of using various social media platforms, namely Instagram,

Facebook, YouTube, Twitter and Pinterest. Her primary job was to drive users to the Children's Trust website using these social media platforms.

Facebook: Facebook was found to be one of our most successful platforms. The organization added many new followers and used various strategies to up its programme. The platform suited the organization's content well helped it reach the people it wanted to reach out to. However, it was a challenge to actually get users to go to the website. This is something OTJ tackled by posting more content that originated from the trust's website and doing so in a way that did not feel like spamming or gaudy self-promotion.

Instagram: This platform was not found to be the best choice for One Tough Job, just because the organization did not create a lot of visual content that would lend itself well to the platform. It was noticed that the platform would get busier during an event when photos are being taken and posted, but otherwise, Instagram was on the back burner. "The creation and posting of branded images and visual quotes is great, but if our goal is to direct users to our website, Instagram doesn't exactly make that easy", she concluded.

Twitter: Along with Facebook, Twitter was found to be doing well, especially when content revolved around text and links. The parenting community appeared to be active on both, making these platforms perfect for the audience the organization wanted to reach. "There is a conflict when it comes to the nature of Twitter and its user sometimes. Twitter is all about individuals and a sense of spontaneity. Using Twitter as an organization can be difficult at times especially when one needs to balance content between what is scheduled and what is actually spontaneous", Mantus (n.d) concluded.

YouTube: This platform was useful when the popular videos came out. However, it became more of a burden after that. If there was time, the Children's Trust team could explore revamping the YouTube account and putting extra effort into maintaining it. However, the platform was not found to be particularly vital for driving users towards the website or the content the organization wanted parents to be seeing.

Pinterest: According to Mantus (n.d), Pinterest is often an undervalued platform because it is designed less for organizations and more for individuals. Twitter is similar except that Pinterest does not have the same communal feel and offers little in terms of engagement. However, if one can create the right kind of content, Pinterest can be great for spreading a message or a resource.

Case Study 4: #End Violence campaign

UNICEF's #End Violence campaign on social media is one of the most recognizable campaigns against violence against children.

Launched in 2013, the campaign has been commended by celebrities through music videos, reports, and infographics. The hashtag '#End Violence' became so popular that it is also used to tweet on violence against women in many countries. People also use the hashtag for posting their response to violent events like acts of terrorism and mass shooting. The campaign became popular especially in the US and Canada where a majority of #End Violence tweets were posted. However, the hashtag is also used in Asia, and Central and South America.

6. Conclusion

Some lessons could be drawn from the examples and case studies cited above: the Ice Bucket Challenge, the ripple movements, the Egyptian uprising, the One Tough Job campaign and UNICEF's #End Violence campaign.

6.1. Essence of Social Media: At the core of social media is people's participation in the communication process (Mayfield, 2008). Social media users co-create content as the platforms encourage contributions and feedback from the participants. Co-creation of content blurs the line between the media and the audience. The platforms and services are mostly open to voting, posting comments and the sharing of information. While broadcast or one-way communication to the audience dominates traditional media, social media are mostly a two-way conversation and also involved horizontal communication. This leads to the quick formation of communities and effective communication among the members. Social media mostly thrive on their connectedness, cross linkages among sites and people.

Now, a look at the four major case studies described earlier.

As pointed out in Section 4.1 that discussed the ice bucket challenge, in the 12 months before the challenge was initiated (July 2013-June 2014), ALSA was mentioned 6,819 times in the media. The disease itself got 64,056 references. But in 2015, after the ice bucket challenge had more of less lived its life in 2015, ALSA attracted attention 10,358 times. This was up 51.9 per cent from the year before the campaign. Similarly, the disease was mentioned 93,299 times. This was up by 45.6 per cent in the preceding duration.

In the latter half of 2014, ALSA was mentioned 37,205 times. This was more than twice the number of articles it featured in the previous year and the following year combined. Between July 2013 and June 2014, the association featured in 10.65 per cent of write-ups that talked about the disease. In the second half of 2014, however, ALSA featured in 22.42 per cent of the articles mentioning the ice bucket challenge or ALS. This enabled the readers know what the campaign was about and to whom it benefitted. Needless to say, this helped in ensuring donations end up in the right place.

Even today, the brand correlation between ALSA and the disease is "still significantly higher than it was prior to the ice bucket challenge, which continues to help funnel donations to the right recipient" (Vance, 2016).

Social media and the figures cited above underline the importance of mass appeal. The initiative was not aimed at only the people who suffered from ALS or only the moneyed people who could make donations. The appeal of the campaign was broad enough to inspire anyone to join in, have some fun, soak in an important message, donate money to a cause, and inspire others to do the same.

6.2. Takeaways: Some takeaways are (i) social media can be more than handy in attracting people to a cause and making them act for the cause if used in the right way; (ii) ideas travel across geographical and physical boundaries faster with the help of social media; (iii) audio-video content has massive power; (iv) a campaign should be timed well; (v) the cause should be genuine; (vi) the campaign should call for simple actionable steps; (vii) a good mix of fun, social cause and ease of participation helps the cause immensely. Some of these takeaways have similarities with the idea of the use of communication in social marketing and social mobilization (Mallik, 2016).

Thanks to their essence – people's participation – social media blur the line between media producers and media audience. The two-way communication between the producers and the audience, and the horizontal communication among the social media users lead to the quick formation of communities and effective communication among the members. All this means that if the cause is genuine and the campaign is well-timed, people do act for it. Traditional mass media are seen as 'magic multiplier' (Schramm, 1964), but as ideas travel across geographical and physical boundaries faster on social media and also because the social media platforms allow for one-to-one communication in the manner of mass communication, the latter can be used with tremendous effect in social and political mobilization, an essential first a step towards social transformation.

6.3. A caveat: The significant role social media played in Egypt uprising has led to the romanticization of social media.

Someone said. "Democracy is just a tweet away."[2]

Google executive Wael Ghoneim famously said, "If you want to liberate a society, just give them the Internet."[3]

New York Times columnist Nicholas Kristof labelled the "quintessential 21st-century conflict", in which "on one side are government thugs firing bullets...[and] on the other side are young protesters firing 'tweets'."[4]

It was aptly summed up by an anonymous activist: "We use Facebook to schedule the protests, Twitter to coordinate, and YouTube to tell the world."[5]

However, one must guard against glamorizing and exaggerating the importance of social media. It must be recalled that though Mubarak gave up power only after 18 days of the uprising, his fall was in the making: the oppositional movement that forced him to step down was a product of a buildup, a product of years of repression and disenfranchisement of Egyptians that fomented political mobilization.

NOTES

1. Elizabeth Iksander in "Connecting the National and the Virtual: Can Facebook Activism Remain Relevant After Egypt's January 25 Uprising?" *International Journal of Communication,* 5 (2011), 1230, in Storck, 2011.
2. See Storck, Madeline (2011).
3. *Ibid.*
4. *Ibid.*
5. Anonymous Cairo activist, quoted in Nadine Kassem Chebib & Rabia Minatullah Sohail, "The Reasons Social Media Contributed to the 2011 Egyptian Revolution", *International Journal of Business Research and Management, 3* (2011): 139.

REFERENCES

Chebib, N.K., and Sohail, R.M. (2011). "The Reasons Social Media Contributed to the 2011 Egyptian Revolution", *International Journal of Business Research and Management.* 3: 139.

Dewing, Michael (2012). *Social Media: An introduction,* Social Affairs Division, Publication No. 2010-03-E. Ottawa: Library of Parliament.

Ganeshan, Krithika (2016). Case Study on Ripple Effects of Ice Bucket Challenge on Social Media Channels. https://www.digitalvidya.com/blog/case-study-on-ripple-effects-of-ice-bucket-challenge-on-social-media-channels/ (Accessed on May 25, 2019).

Iksander, Elizabeth (2011). "Connecting the National and the Virtual: Can Facebook Activism Remain Relevant After Egypt's January 25 Uprising?" *International Journal of Communication* 5:13-15, as quoted in Madeline Storck, (2011) The Role of Social Media in Political Mobilisation: A Case Study of the January 2011 Egyptian Uprising. MA Dissertation. University of St. Andrews, St. Andrews. Scotland.

Khondker, Habibul and Ulrike, Schuerkens (2014). "Social Transformation, Development and Globalization." Madrid: International Sociological Association. www.sagepub.net/isa/resources/pdf/SocialTransformation.pdf (Accessed on May 25, 2019.)

Mallik, Pradeep (2016). *Communication for Social Marketing: A Study in Literacy*. Shanti: Philadelphia/Rohtak.

Mantus, Maggie (undated). *Social Media for Social Good; Case Study: The Children's Trust*. https://socialmediaforsocialgoodblog.wordpress.com/case-study-the-childrens-trust/ (Accessed on June 1, 2019).

Mayfield, Antony (2008). What is social media? An e-book iCrossing. www. icrossing.com/...pdf.../What%20is%20Social%20Media_iCrossing_ebook. pd (Accessed on June 1, 2019).

Newman, N., Dutton, W., and Blank, G. (2012). "Social Media in the Changing Ecology of News: The Fourth and Fifth Estates in Britain." *International Journal of Internet Science.* 7(1), 6–22.

Newson, A., Houghton, D. and Patten, J. (2008). *Blogging and Other Social Media: Exploiting the Technology and Protecting the Enterprise*. Farnham, Surrey: Gower.

OECD (2007). *Participative web and user-created content: Web 2.0, Wikis and Social Networking,* Paris: Organization for Economic Cooperation and Development.

Schramm, Wilbur (1964). *Mass Media and National Development.* Stanford University Press: Stanford.

Schuerkens, U. (2001a). *Du Togo allemand aux Togo et Ghana indépendants: Changement social sous régimecolonial*. Paris: L'Harmattan in Teune H. and Mlinar Z. (1978) *The Development Logic of Social Systems*. Beverly Hills, CA and London: Sage.

Schuerkens, U. (2001b). "Transformationsprozesse in der Elfenbeinküste und in Ghana: Eine historischvergleichende Analyse des Verhältnisses von Lebensgeschichten und strukturellen Wandlungsprozessen." Münster: Lit. (in Teune H and Mlinar Z (1978) *The Development Logic of Social Systems*. Beverly Hills, CA and London: Sage)

Scott, J. and Carrigton, P.J. (eds.) (2011). *The SAGE Handbook of Social Network Analysis*. London: Sage.

Storck, Madeline (2011). The Role of Social Media in Political Mobilisation: A Case Study of the January 2011 Egyptian Uprising. MA Dissertation. University of St. Andrews, St. Andrews. Scotland.

Teune, H. and Mlinar, Z. (1978). *The Development Logic of Social Systems*. Beverly Hills, CA and London: Sage.

Vance, Johnny (2016). Social Media and PR: Insights from the Ice Bucket Challenge on Creating Lasting Impact. https://www.meltwater.com/blog/social-media-and-pr-insights-from-the-ice-bucket-challenge-on-creating-lasting-impact/ Accessed on May 25, 2019.

West, Johnny (2011). *Karama!* London: Heron Books.

WEBSITES

http://www.iamai.in/media/details/1371

Know Violence in Childhood, http://www.knowviolenceinchildhood.org/blog/social-media-best-practice-a-case-study-of-the-endviolence-campaign/

Number of monthly active Facebook users worldwide as of 1st quarter 2019 (in millions) https://www.statista.com/statistics/264810/number-of-monthly-active-facebook-users-worldwide/ Accessed on June 1, 2019.

Number of daily active WhatsApp Status users from 1st quarter 2017 to 1st quarter 2019 (in millions) https://www.statista.com/statistics/730306/whatsapp-status-dau/ Accessed on June 1, 2019.

21

Role of Social Media in Tribal Development

An Empirical Study of Gujarat Tribes

Shashikant Bhagat

Aim

The chapter aims (a) to describe and analyze the extent to which social media has helped tribal development programmes in the state of Gujarat, especially for education among the Scheduled Tribes and (b) to discuss what extent the media has helped in accelerating the process of development among Scheduled Tribes? For this purpose, Gujarat has been selected as one of the western developed states. Gujarat state is having 8.9 million Scheduled Tribes according to the Census of India, 2011. Most of the tribes live in 14 eastern districts.

Bhil is the second-largest tribe in India. According to the Census 2001, the population of Bhil tribe was 34,41,945 (17,49,813 were males and 16,95,132 females). The Bhil tribal community mainly resides in Rajasthan, western Madhya Pradesh, Gujarat and northern Maharashtra. Some families have migrated to other states like Tripura for jobs in tea gardens. In the Bhil tribe, sub-tribes Bhil-Garasia and Dholi Bhil are included. They are 46 per cent of the total tribal population of the state. The population includes people of sub-tribes like Bhil Garasia and Dholi Bhil. The Bhil tribal community mainly live in Banaskantha, Sabarkantha, Panchmahal, Bharuch, Vadodara, Surat and Dang districts. Bhil tribe is the dominant tribe in Gujarat. In north Gujarat they are close to Rajasthan Bhil and their sub-tribes. In Panchmahal, Vadodara and Bharuch districts Bhil tribe is in close contact with Rathava, Dhanaka, Patelia and Nayaka tribes who live in Gujarat and Madhya Pradesh. In south Gujarat, Bhil tribe is in close contact with other tribes of the area and tribes of Maharashtra too (Chaudhury and Singh, 2006).

They speak in Bhili, which belongs to the Indo-Aryan family of languages. As they do not have script, it is a dialect. Rajasthani, Gujarati,

Marathi, Hindi and other regional languages, depending on the state to which the group belonged have somehow, influence their Bhili-dialect (Divatia 1921, Mansukh 1871). According to census 1981, 4,293.314 persons were using the Bhili language. But all are bilingual and use the regional language. In Gujarat, Bhils also use Vaghari as a spoken language, which is a mix of Mewari and Gujarati. Literacy among the Bhil tribe is not very high, 44.3 per cent were literate by 2001 and they read and write in Gujarati language only. It is believed that deities will protect the crop and cattle. The deity Khetlo or Khetarpal who looks after the farm is worshipped from time to time. The coloured thread, coconut and chicken or he-goat are offered to Khetarpal—the deity of the farm (Lodha, 2008; Mehta, 2006).

Bhil tribal families subscribe a newspaper; listen radio and most of the villages have T.V. Thus, modern means of communication have created a widespread impact on consciousness of Bhil youths. In all tribal districts, there are colleges and some have well known universities. The mobile phone has increased contacts that unites them. It is used for many purposes like information sharing in connection with finding jobs, finding marriage alliance, information about illness, place of treatment, and assembling for some events.

For this purpose, fieldwork was carried out in ecologically three distinct districts of Gujarat, namely, Aravalli (plains), Dahod (semi-hilly), and The Dangs (fully hilly) that are bordering Rajasthan, Madhya Pradesh and Maharashtra state. From each district, two villages were purposively selected one close to the district headquarters and another close to the three states bordering Rajasthan, Madhya Pradesh and Maharashtra respectively. From these six villages, in each village, a sample of 50 adult Scheduled Tribes, above 18 years of age, were interviewed, and that comprises of 258 (84%) males and 48 (16%) females. The interview were carried out with the help of structured interview. A schedule for interview was originally prepared in English for data collection. However, respondents were interviewed in Gujarati.

Table 21.1: Age and gender profile by district and type of village (*In Percentage*)

Gender	District Aravalli			Dahod			The Dang			Total		
	Village nearby Taluka	Village in remote area from Taluka	Average Total	Village nearby Taluka	Village in remote area from Taluka	Average Total	Village nearby Taluka	Village in remote area from Taluka	Average Total	Village nearby Taluka	Village in remote area from Taluka	Average Total
Male	86.0	80.0	83.0	84.0	84.0	84.0	82.0	88.0	85.0	84.0	84.0	84.0
Female	14.0	20.0	17.0	16.0	16.0	16.0	18.0	12.0	15.0	16.0	16.0	16.0
Total (N)	100	100	100	100	100	100	100	100	100	100	100	100

Source: Bhagat (2018), p. 106.

Table 21.1 shows an uneven male and female ratio due to author's limitation of not being able to reach women who were 16 per cent in the sample, and 84 per cent of respondents were male. These Scheduled Tribes had indicated their religion as Hindu religion, except 2 per cent who were converted to non-Hindu religious that included Islam and Christianity. Further analysis shows that not more than 27 per cent of respondents had any level of education. No pattern of age at marriage can be found in the study, though, it seemed the Scheduled Tribes of Gujarat generally marry after 18 years of age though they get engaged at an early age.

Table 21.2: Occupation-wise Distribution of Respondents

(In Percentage)

Family Main Occupation	Aravalli			Dahod			The Dang			Total		
	Village nearby Taluka	Village in remote area from Taluka	Average Total	Village nearby Taluka	Village in remote area from Taluka	Average Total	Village nearby Taluka	Village in remote area from Taluka	Average Total	Village nearby Taluka	Village in remote area from Taluka	Average Total
Farmer	42.0	72.0	57.0	28.0	88.0	58.0	72.0	84.0	78.0	47.3	81.3	64.3
Government Service	18.0	6.0	12.0	12.0	2.0	7.0	6.0	0.0	3.0	12.0	2.7	7.3
Private Job	4.0	6.0	5.0	42.0	0.0	21.0	4.0	6.0	5.0	16.7	4.0	10.3
Labour	36.0	14.0	25.0	6.0	8.0	7.0	14.0	6.0	10.0	18.7	9.3	14.0
Own Business	0.0	2.0	1.0	12.0	2.0	7.0	4.0	4.0	4.0	5.3	2.7	4.0

Source: Bhagat (2018), p. 114.

Table 21.2 shows that almost two-thirds or 64.3 per cent of Scheduled Tribes were farmers, whereas, only 14 per cent were labourers, thereby, indicating that a large number of Scheduled Tribes household were engaged in agriculture or farming.

The economic condition of Scheduled Tribes according to official State of Gujarat records belonged to relatively poor households as Table 21.3 indicates. The term Above Poverty Line (APL) is referred to as all those households who earned enough to have daily meals, whereas, Below Poverty Line (BPL) respondents were categorised as all those who had struggled to have even daily meals from their income and occupation.

The socio-economic profile of the Scheduled Tribes indicated that they were largely Hindu who followed farming as an occupation having a small piece of land and by and large lived Below Poverty Line. Social Media utilization of Scheduled Tribes is presented in the next section.

Table 21.3: Distribution of Respondents according to their Economic Condition

(In Percentage)

Economic Condition	Aravalli		Dahod		The Dang		Total	
	Village nearby Taluka	Village in remote area from Taluka	Village nearby Taluka	Village in remote area from Taluka	Village nearby Taluka	Village in remote area from Taluka	Village nearby Taluka	Village in remote area from Taluka
Above poverty line (APL)	48.0	18.0	58.0	28.0	24.0	18.0	43.3	21.3
Below poverty line (BPL)	52.0	82.0	42.0	72.0	76.0	82.0	56.7	78.7
Total (N)	100	100	100	100	100	100	100	100

Source: Bhagat (2018), p. 119.

Social Media Utilization

Table 21.4: Media access and use by district

(In Percentage)

Media Sources	*Aravalli*			*Dahod*			*The Dangs*			*Total*		
	Village nearby Taluka	*Village in a remote area from Taluka*	*Average Total*	*Village nearby Taluka*	*Village in a remote area from Taluka*	*Average Total*	*Village nearby Taluka*	*Village in a remote area from Taluka*	*Average Total*	*Village nearby Taluka*	*Village in a remote area from Taluka*	*Average Total*
Newspaper/ Magazine/ Journals/ Periodicals	8.0	8.0	8.0	72.0	18.0	45.0	18.0	26.0	22.0	32.7	17.3	25.0
TV	56.0	18.0	37.0	74.0	18.0	46.0	50.0	50.0	50.0	60.0	28.7	44.3
Radio	0.0	2.0	1.0	40.0	0.0	20.0	8.0	10.0	9.0	16.0	4.0	10.0
Computer	4.0	0.0	2.0	44.0	2.0	23.0	0.0	4.0	2.0	16.0	2.0	9.0
Laptop	2.0	0.0	1.0	18.0	0.0	9.0	4.0	4.0	4.0	8.0	1.3	4.7
Telephone	0.0	2.0	1.0	24.0	0.0	12.0	0.0	4.0	2.0	8.0	2.0	5.0
Mobile	60.0	14.0	37.0	74.0	22.0	48.0	32.0	36.0	34.0	55.3	24.0	39.7
Total	50	50	100	50	50	100	50	50	100	150	150	300

Source: Bhagat (2018), p. 134.

Due to the high level of availability of electricity in the villages of the Scheduled Tribes and a tradition of watching a variety of visual performances apart from a low level of literacy, television viewing seemed to have attracted a large number of Scheduled Tribes (Table 21.4). Among all electronic media, Table 21.4 indicates that television viewing was high (44.3%) followed by mobile phone (39.7%). It should be mentioned that both television and mobile phones belonged to oral means of receiving information and entertainment that have attracted the attention of Scheduled Tribes like their neighbour non-Scheduled Tribes.

Table 21.5: Social Media Use

(In Percentage)

Social Media	*Aravalli*			*Dahod*			*The Dangs*			*Total*		
	Village nearby Taluka	*Village in remote area from Taluka*	*Average Total*	*Village nearby Taluka*	*Village in remote area from Taluka*	*Average Total*	*Village nearby Taluka*	*Village in remote area from Taluka*	*Average Total*	*Village nearby Taluka*	*Village in remote area from Taluka*	*Average Total*
Social Media Use												
Yes	10.0	2.0	6.0	68.0	4.0	36.0	4.0	10.0	7.0	27.3	5.3	16.3
No	90.0	98.0	94.0	32.0	96.0	64.0	96.0	90.0	93.0	72.7	94.7	83.7
Total	50	50	100	50	50	100	50	50	100	150	150	300

Table 21.6: Purpose of Social Media Use

(In Percentage)

Education	40.0	0.0	33.3	82.4	100.0	83.3	100.0	100.0	100.0	78.0	83.3	78.7
Entertainment	80.0	0.0	66.7	94.1	50.0	91.7	100.0	100.0	100.0	92.7	66.7	89.4
Competitive exams preparation	40.0	0.0	33.3	82.4	50.0	80.6	100.0	100.0	100.0	78.0	66.7	76.6
News/views/opinion	80.0	100.0	83.3	94.1	100.0	94.4	100.0	100.0	100.0	92.7	100.0	93.6
Knowledge	60.0	0.0	50.0	88.2	100.0	88.9	100.0	66.7	80.0	85.4	66.7	83.0
Social relationship	100.0	100.0	100.0	82.4	100.0	83.3	100.0	100.0	100.0	85.4	100.0	87.2
Job search	40.0	0.0	33.3	79.4	0.0	75.0	100.0	100.0	100.0	75.6	50.0	72.3
Information	80.0	100.0	83.3	85.3	100.0	86.1	100.0	100.0	100.0	85.4	100.0	87.2
Total	5	1	6	34	2	36	2	3	5	41	6	47

Source: Bhagat (2018), p. 141.

Table 21.5 and Table 21.6 indicates a relatively low level of social media use (16.3%) by the Scheduled Tribes. Further analysis of the use of social media indicates a relatively smaller number of respondents for various purposes (Table 21.6). Out of 300 respondents only 47 have indicated a variety of social media use in which highest uses was for "news, views and opinion" (93.6%) followed "entertainment" (89.4%)

and "social interaction, social relationships and sharing of information" at the same level (87.2%).

Concluding Remark

The analysis about social media penetration and use among Scheduled Tribes shows low as compared to their non-Scheduled Tribe neighbours. However, it is predicted a higher level of social media penetration and future utilization. It is because of the inherent technology advantage that allows individual privacy and freedom from literacy barrier.

REFERENCES

Bhagat, Shashikant (2018), *Contribution of Media in Tribal Development: Special Reference to Tribal Area Sub-Plan of Gujarat*, Unpublished.

Chaudhary, S.N and Singh, R.P. (2006). *Tribes of Panchmahal Biosphere and Their Indigenous Knowledge*. Bhopal: Indira Gandhi National Museum.

Divatia, N.B. (1921). *Gujarati Language and Literature*, 2 vols., Bombay, p. 32.

Lodha, M. (2008). *Samachar Jagat mai Abhutpurva Kranti*. New Delhi: Classical Publishing House.

Mansukh, M.K. Sh. (1871). *Shahnamu Gujarati*. Bombay.

Mehta, C.P. (2006). *Development of Indian Tribes*. New Delhi: Discovery Publishing House.

22

Giving Voice, Building Community, and Bringing Change One Story at a Time

Can Social Media Live Up to the Hype?

Devina Sarwatay

Storytelling: Giving Voice, Building Community, and Bringing Change

Stories can help in building awareness, comprehension, recognition and empathy (Singh and Sonnenburg, 2012). Stories can be used to empower, humanise and repair broken dignity (Adichie, 2009). When we say "Storytelling", we mean something more visceral than charts, graphs, and a three-part structure of the main idea (Schwertly, 2014). Inclusive storytelling helps piece together a fragmented narrative of society by including often excluded people/groups and building a community (Fajer, 1991). Inclusive storytelling, i.e., telling as wide a variety of stories as possible, serves at least two functions. It both builds community among members of the storyteller's group and adds missing tiles to the mosaic of history that enrich society's understanding of itself (Delgado, 1989). When members of excluded groups begin to create their own histories, the growth of a greater sense of community within the group often follows. Their stories often reflect circumstances and emotions common to many in the group. Community building through storytelling has been a particularly important aspect of the modern women's movement. Women report finding solidarity and strength through sharing the details of their lives with each other. Storytelling creates a common ground between the storyteller and the listeners, validates the listener's own undiscussed experiences, and provides both incentive and protection for the listener to relate stories of her own (Massaro, 1988). Once experiences are shared, no member of the group needs to feel as though her problems are unique. Delgado

(1989) noted that stories are important because they forge ties and bring about cohesive understanding and shared meaning to the group which makes for a strong union; outsiders can tell their own stories but they are shared as counter-narratives to the ones already existing in the group. In the book, "Narrative across Media: The Languages of Storytelling" edited by Marie-Laure Ryan (2004), the discussion is focused on what does it take in static images to evoke story that extends over time. In the words of Áron Kibédi Varga quoted in Hoogvliet (2010), static images are used to evoke stories. Almost everyone has experienced this form of storytelling, which ranges from the exchange of personal reminiscences to family and cultural histories. These powerful stories, hence, have the potential to bring change as narratives evolve and counter-narratives are either challenged or used to add to, modify or replace existing stories. This is especially true of inclusive storytelling that encourages the representation of voices that are otherwise ignored.

Digital and Social Media

Lister *et al.*, in the second edition of their book *New Media: A Critical Introduction, described*, write "... the term 'new media' actually refers to a wide range of changes in media production, distribution and use. These are changes that are technological, textual, conventional and cultural." (2009, p.13). They added that since the mid-1980s, some of the main terms in discourses about new media are digital, interactive, hypertextual, virtual, networked, and simulated. Boyd and Ellison define Social Network Sites (SNSs) as, "... web-based services that allow individuals to (1) construct a public or semi-public profile within a bounded system, (2) articulate a list of other users with whom they share a connection, and (3) view and traverse their list of connections and those made by others within the system. The nature and nomenclature of these connections may vary from site to site." (2008, p. 211)

In an essay for Social Media + Society, Boyd gave some further insight into social media which has, "... more to do with its cultural positioning than its technological affordances. Rooted in the broader "Web 2.0" landscape, social media helped engineers, entrepreneurs, and everyday people reimagine the role that technology could play in information dissemination, community development, and communication." (20[illegible] p.1) The characteristics of new media augur a democratic and participatory environment, the promise of which raises expectations of a freer flow of ideas and content (Jenkins, 2006). Couldry (2008) brings to focus the role of digital and social media in storytelling and how production, dissemination and reception of stories have changed with the emergence of new media; storytelling has evolved and become an activity of co-creation.

Storytelling on Social Media

Storytelling has always been a social activity where a narrator/characters tell(s) a story with or without different setups, props, etc., to an audience who had very little role to play except being at the receivers'end of the communication exchange. However, with social media, these roles are no longer as easily defined. Interactivity and co-creation are two affordances of social media platforms that allow senders and receivers to exchange positions and blur the clear-cut boundaries of these roles. Storytelling in social media is a continuously ongoing and improvisational process, made up of interlinked content (Singh and Sonnenberg, 2012). In fact, most brands have caught onto the fact that storytelling on social media is an effective way of engaging consumers and marketing to them (Pulizzi, 2012).

Page (2013) identified that social media is a highly effective platform for storytelling given its affordances are well suited to different features like formats e.g., seriality, and narrative styling and its various types. Elaborating on this, Alexander and Levine (2008) characterised stories as open-ended, branching, hyperlinked, cross-media, participatory, exploratory, and unpredictable because of Web 2.0 and its affordances like co-creation, participation, and changes in the directionality of flow and narratives, thus accelerating the process of storytelling. They also address another social media feature that plays a role in storytelling, i.e., micro-content. This micro-content allows many more entries into storytelling and, with interactivity and easy co-creation possible on Web 2.0, a new environment for storytelling on social media is created.

Humans of Bombay on Facebook

Inspired by Humans of New York, Karishma Mehta (2014) started Humans of Bombay in 2014 without any specific training in photography or storytelling. She literally walked on the streets of Mumbai and spoke with strangers urging them to share their stories and requesting a photograph. These are stories of joy and sorrow, success and failure, hope and heartbreak (Singh, 2015; Behal, 2016; Joshi, 2016). Mehta believes everybody has a story and they want to share it; all we have to do is ask them simple questions to pull out their powerful, touching narratives. These narratives have not only moved people to share them further on social media but also driven people to express support verbally and through actions like donating money for causes. Mehta has started several funding campaigns on Facebook to raise money for social causes (Singh, 2015; Behal, 2016).

Joshi (2016) interviewed Mehta to find her childhood was driven by storytelling and her craft secret is bringing out narratives of people who have battled abuse and exclusion and came out of their struggles with a hopeful eye towards the future. The secret which allows her to do that is asking strangers who are willing to talk about what their happiest memory is. Mehta said they are more willing to start conversations with this question and are usually smiling while talking about their happiest memory which makes for a good photograph. Mehta spoke to Behal (2016) and highlighted how her audience participates in her stories by reacting (like, love, etc. on Facebook), commenting and sharing on social media. They also shut people with negative comments down without her having to do anything.

Mehta (2014) writes on the about section on her Humans of Bombay Facebook Page, "Humans of Bombay catalogs the beat of the city, one story at a time." It uses the social media platform of Facebook (among others) to bring us people's stories and has slowly grown to a formidable force that uses storytelling with digital and social media to give voice to people—ordinary and yet extraordinary, included and yet excluded, common and yet uncommon—along with community building and bringing change.

Momspresso on Facebook

Founded in 2010, Momspresso is an online platform by Just4kids Services Pvt. Limited. It has social media presence on Facebook, Instagram, Twitter and YouTube. Marketed as "For the mothers, by the mothers" (Jain, 2018), Momspresso is a content platform that deals with different types of content like blogs, short stories, etc. Based in Gurugram, it is a multilingual platform that has a web and mobile presence. The founders, Vishal Gupta, Prashant Sinha and Asif Mohamed, decided to launch this start-up because they wanted to create a platform that curates content for mothers, and, eventually help mothers contribute content of, for and by them. The founders thought there was potential for a start-up that helped moms by listing essentials like tuitions, activity lessons, etc. (curation of content) and soon they decided to upgrade and engage more with mothers by offering them a platform to share blogs and short stories in several languages (contribution of content).

Jain (2018) further reported that the platform had 7.5 million mother viewers every month with 5,500 mother bloggers and an active video channel with around 500 videos. The founders attributed this high rate of reach and engagement to their platform's affordance of providing active readers and interactions in the mom blogosphere. This success has also led to brand collaborations and digital advertising on their platform. Singh (2018) calls Momspresso a "new resource point for sharing experiences, coping with challenges" for and by mothers especially in this age of nuclear families. The experiential content strikes a chord with many mothers and expecting mothers and has taken off especially after introducing blogs in vernacular languages. Momspresso on Facebook (including other platforms) creates an important avenue for mothers to live and share their experiences and has grown to be a powerful force that combines experiential storytelling with digital and social media to give voice to mothers and build a community of moms who can share their lives, ask and receive advice and build a sisterhood of support.

Method and Findings

This chapter is attempting to unpack Humans of Bombay and Momspresso (both on Facebook), through content analysis of posts in the month of

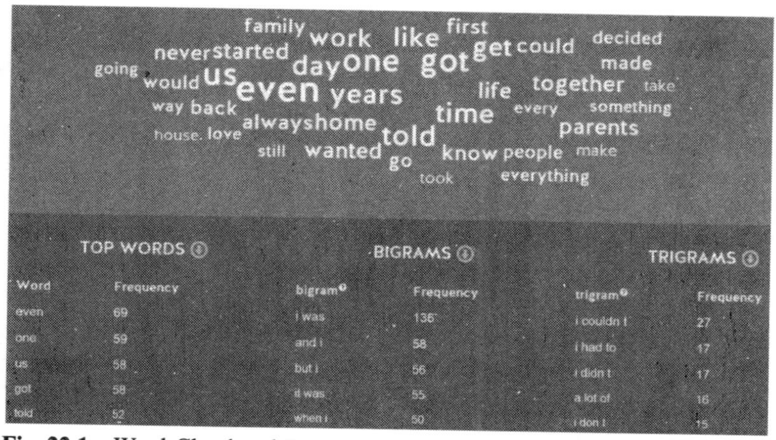

Fig. 22.1: Word Cloud and Top Words, Bigrams and Trigrams of Humans of Bombay on Word Counter by Databasic.

Source: https://databasic.io/en/wordcounter/results/5d51541f5b167809a76223a7

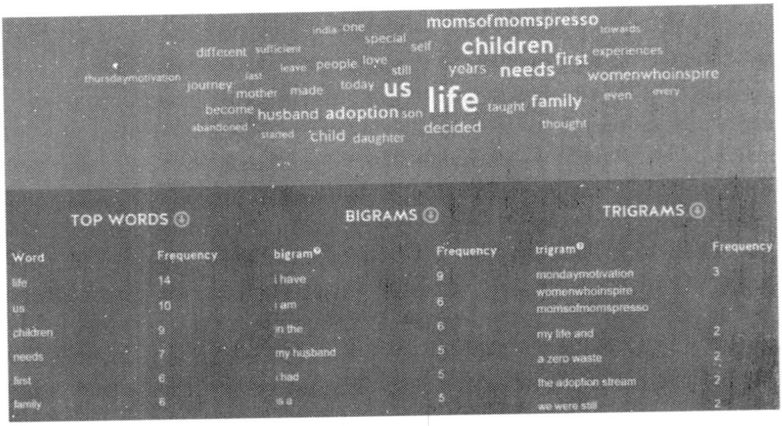

Fig. 22.2: Word Cloud and Top Words, Bigrams and Trigrams of Momspresso on Word Counter by Databasic.

Source: https://databasic.io/en/wordcounter/results/5d53bf2c5b167802703fe243?submit=true

December 2018. Tools available on databasic.io i.e., Word Counter and Same Diff have been used plus, to analyse the two documents together, Overview was used, along with a qualitative reading of selected posts. Word Counter helps identify the most commonly used words in the text and creates a Word Cloud. It also gives the order of the top words, bigrams (two words together) and trigrams (three words together) from the text. Here are the word clouds of both platforms (see Figs. 22.1 & 22.2)

Same Diff is a tool that compares two documents and identifies words that occur solely in one document *vs*. the other and also shows the words which are in both the texts. Here is the result from Humans of Bombay and Momspresso (Fig. 22.3).

They have a cosine similarity (how similar the documents are) score of 0.44, which means that they are more different from each other given that they vary in length, contributions and audiences. Since the two documents were analysed in a limited way by tools from databasic, Overview was used to compare the two together and the following was its word cloud (Fig. 22.4).

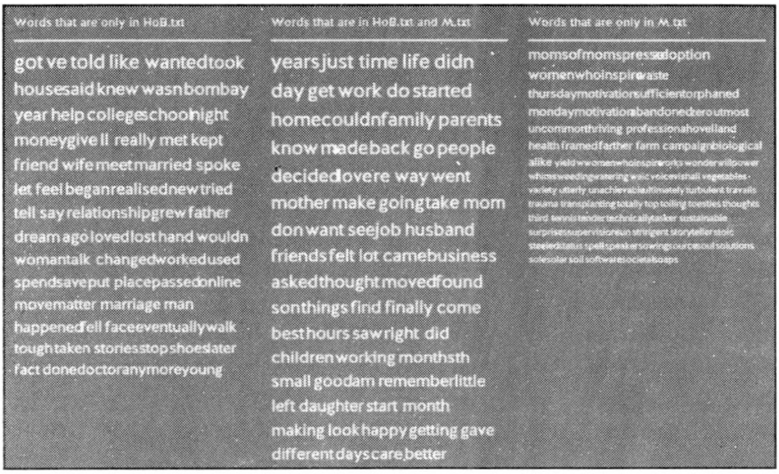

Fig. 22.3: Comparative analysis of words used in Humans of Bombay *vs*. Momspresso AND in both on Same Diff by Databasic.

Source: https://databasic.io/en/samediff/results/5d53ea4f5b167802703fe245?submit=true

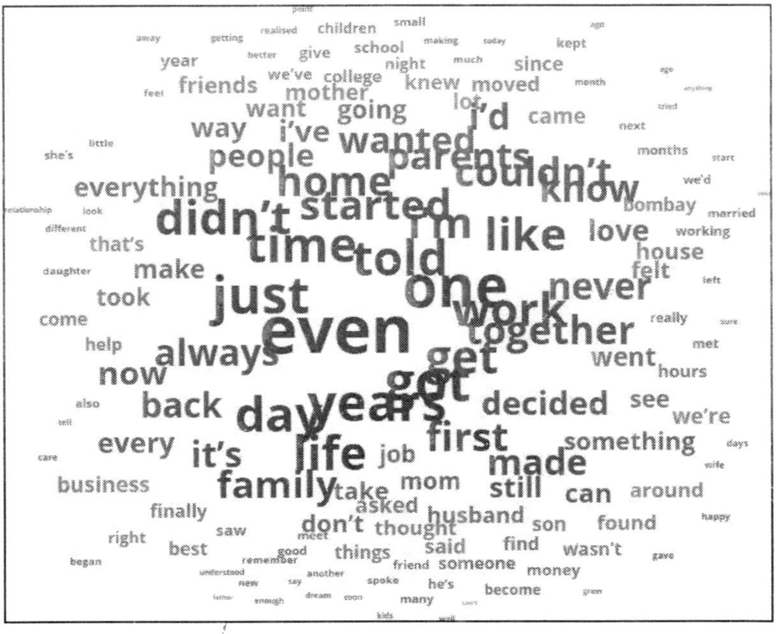

Fig. 22.4: World Cloud of both Humans of Bombay and Momspresso on Overview.

Source: https://www.overviewdocs.com/documentsets/19437/view-33045478407399

On picking out the most used words in Humans of Bombay, Momspresso and both in a CSV, the following graphical representation was found (Fig. 22.5):

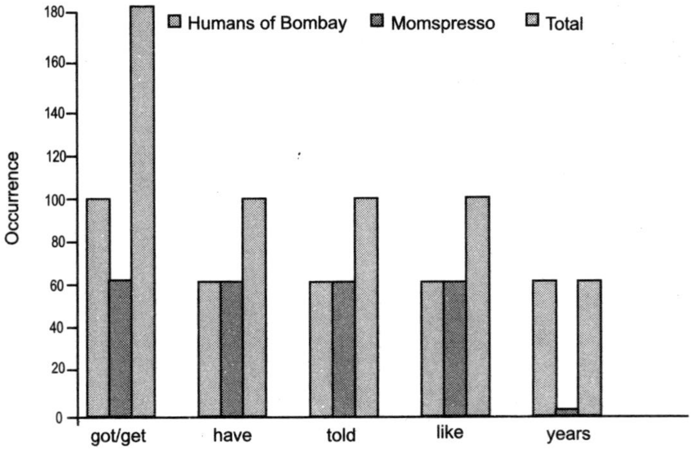

Fig. 22.5: Most used words on Humans of Bombay, Momspresso and Both.

A study of the above figures reveals that on the surface, rather ordinary stories are woven on both Humans of Bombay and Momspresso. While the top words don't divulge, the bigrams and trigrams paint a comparatively clearer picture with people featured talking about their difficulties using words like "I was, I couldn't, I had to, I didn't, we were still, etc." This is no surprise because Humans of Bombay is about inclusive storytelling and showing how different people can be our heroes and sources of inspiration, Momspresso is about creating a space for mothers and allowing them to share experiences and support each other. This is further highlighted when we see results from Same Diff and Overview. There is a closer sphere around words like "years, time, life, told, get/got, etc."

Discussion

Interestingly, when we juxtapose these findings with the social media engagement metrics of the Humans of Bombay and Momspresso Facebook Pages, the following revelations are made. Based on the story most liked/ reacted to, the narrative that pulled people's attention on Humans of Bombay was about a lady who chose to defy all odds and become a doctor despite family opposition. Her inspiration was her grandmother who was a healer herself. Her family opposed her decision because they thought she would never get married if she became a doctor! Nonetheless, she did become a doctor, got married and also set up a free clinic in memory of her grandma. She also happened to deliver the baby of a stranger she met on the train with barely any supplies and realised how grateful she was that some parents don't let their girls settle and helps them pursue their dreams. The findings from the software when collated with this story show that the concepts and themes of "Decided", "Family", "Felt", "Home", "Husband", "Job", "Life", "Married", "Parents", "People", "Time", "Told" "Wanted" and "Work" are related to this narrative.

Fig. 22.6: Stories with the highest social media engagement on the Facebook page of Humans of Bombay.

Similarly, the story most commented on was about the deep bond of friendship and how you keep it safeguarded in your heart, against all odds. The narrative is that of a woman who made a best friend out of someone who was from a very different background than hers. In the face of grave difficulty, they were separated and then, due to the "power" of WhatsApp, were reunited after decades! She equated the deep bond of friendship with cycling because muscle memory never lets you forget how to ride a bike once you've learned. The concepts and themes found here were: "Bombay", "Day", "Decided", "Family", "Felt", "Home", "House", "Husband", "Life", "Married", "Mom", "Mother", "Moved", "Parents", "Time", "Told" and "Wanted".

Finally, one of the most shared stories was that of a train accident survivor whose life completely changed after she lost her right hand. She was studying to become an architect and her dream was heavily compromised after the accident. Incidentally, she braved all odds, received a lot of help and support as well as media attention and had a movie made on her accident and recovery without her knowledge! She narrates how she is now a teacher and does everything any other person does despite many people sharing their reservations about her future. The concepts and themes related were, "Bombay", "College", "Day", "Decided", "Family", "Felt", "Home", "Life", "Mom", "People", "Things", "Told", "Wanted" and "Work".

It is very interesting to find here that the most popular stories are those of women who have fought and won against different difficulties in life. From a feminist perspective, it sure is a clear case of using the tools of storytelling and social media to give voice to a segment that is usually ignored and/or highlighted for very different reasons, especially in mainstream media. When we turn our attention to the posts on Momspresso, the most-liked post was about the story of a mother who quits her job after her son was born and dedicated her life to his upbringing and furthering his career as a tennis player. She learned a lot from this experience and it was a personal choice she made out of her own volition. The experience has also led her to become more disciplined, focussed, independent, confident, and self-assured because it has led her to discover new aspects about herself. These concepts relate to "children", "life", "first", "family", "decided" and "son".

Fig. 22.7: Stories with the highest social media engagement on the Facebook page of Momspresso.

The most commented on and shared posts were respectively about an entrepreneur and environmentalist. The entrepreneur mother is also a special needs mom because one of her children has a rare form of epilepsy and is developmentally delayed. This experience has inspired her to become a motivational writer/speaker because she wants to fight for the social inclusion of special needs children. The environmentalist mother is pegging to become a zero-waste family. She grows her own vegetables, makes her own cleaning material like soaps and detergents, and uses solar energy as well as is working towards a rainwater harvesting system for her home. These concepts relate to "children", "life", "needs", "first", "different", "family" and "self".

Conclusion

Human of Bombay used two powerful tools to become the platform it is today: Storytelling and Social Media. What is unique about this platform is that they give voice to ordinary and yet extraordinary people. The interviewees are using their memories and oral histories to recount their experiences of joy and sorrow, hope and despair and fighting and surviving in life which not only serves the purpose of giving them a voice to share their narratives, but also inspiring readers looking for common and yet uncommon sources of motivation. While their stories are set in the past, their photographs are a window to their present and the hybridity of these narratives of the past with representation of the present brings a temporal juxtaposition that elevates the stories and centres on the inclusion and yet exclusion these people have faced. Additionally, the potential of readers' acceptance by way of reaction, commenting and sharing brings in another temporally hybrid means of giving their voice acceptance in the future. These interviewees that Humans of Bombay has chosen to share stories of on their Facebook Page are rather unique. They fuel and are fuelled by the stories they share and the impact that has on readers. This is, perhaps possible because of the affordances of the art of Storytelling and the new media technology of Social Media. For now, the platform has restricted itself to sharing stories and aiding some support (including funding, in some cases) and only time will tell how far it goes.

In the case of Momspresso, the kind of content that exists on Facebook is limited. Their major use of Facebook is to direct their audiences to their site which hosts several resources among blogs and short stories. They cater to a very specific audience of mothers and enable contributors from among this audience to produce content as well leading to the creation of "prosumers", an affordance of the age of digital and social media and Web 2.0. Their rationale of providing a platform for mothers to share their experiences, anxieties, joys and sorrows is spot on because motherhood is a very personal journey and, given the society we live in, can be quite an alienating experience. At a delicate time like this, an expecting and/or a new mother would definitely look for an avenue that allows questioning, vent, share, and ask without condescension about the new experiences and journey she is undertaking. A common thread of budding writers among mothers was noticed who were well appreciated by their peers without judgment. And, that is how Momspresso empowers mothers; by offering a platform that is no-holds-barred, free-flowing and full of information, emotion, support, and sharing + caring! Clearly, this was created for business interests and the founders are already raking in the money. What remains to be seen is how big this start-up is and will it pop out of the entrepreneurial space and become a full-fledged business.

As far as giving voice, building community and bringing change are concerned; both Humans of Bombay and Momspresso have made a small dent, one story at a time, and included erstwhile excluded population into the mainstream by pitting them as heroes for inspiration or by creating a separate space for them to come together as a support group. Social media is living up to its hype, in whatever limited or small way here by raising money for those in need, in the case of Humans of Bombay or offering a safe space for mothers, in case of Momspresso. However, both are business entities at the end of the day.

REFERENCES

Adichie, C. (2009). *The danger of a single story* [Video]. https://www.ted.com/talks/chimamanda_adichie_the_danger_of_a_single_story: TED.

Alexander, B., and Levine, A. (2008). "Web 2.0 storytelling: Emergence of a new genre." *EDUCAUSE review, 43*(6), 40-56.

Behal, A. (2016). A Humbling Portrayal Of Humanity: Meet The Humans Of Bombay. Retrieved from https://www.forbes.com/sites/abehal/2016/04/15/a-humbling-portrayal-of- humanity-meet-the-humans-of-bombay/#17371a60486a

Boyd, D. (2015). "Social Media: A Phenomenon to be Analyzed." *Social Media + Society, 1*(1), 205630511558014. http://doi.org/10.1177/2056305115580148

Boyd, D., and Ellison, N.B. (2007). "Social Network Sites: Definition, History, and Scholarship." *Journal of Computer-Mediated Communication, 13*(1), 210-230. http://doi.org/10.1111/j.1083-6101.2007.00393.x

Couldry, N. (2008). "Mediatization or mediation? Alternative understandings of the emergent space of digital storytelling." *New Media and Society, 10*(3), 373-391.

Delgado, R. (1989). "Storytelling for oppositionists and others: A plea for narrative." *Michigan Law Review, 87*(8), 2411-2441.

Fajer, M.A. (1991). "Can Two Real Men Eat Quiche Together—Storytelling, Gender-Role Stereotypes, and Legal Protection for Lesbians and Gay Men." *U. Miami L. Rev., 46*, 511.

Hoogvliet, M. (2010). "How to Tell a Fairy Tale With Images: Narrative Theories and French Paintings from the Early Nineteenth Century." *RELIEF-Revue électronique de littérature française, 4*(2), 198-212.

Jain, N. (2018). For the mothers, by the mothers—Momspresso offers content platform; looks at high growth. Retrieved 12 August 2019, from https://yourstory.com/2018/02/mothers-mothers-momspresso-offers-content-platform-looks-high-growth

Jenkins, H. (2006). *Convergence Culture: Where Old and New Media Collide.* New York: New York University Press.

Joshi, P. (2016). Meet Karishma Mehta, the woman behind Humans of Bombay. Retrieved from https://www.hindustantimes.com/art-and-culture/meet-karishma-mehta-the-woman-behind-humans-of-bombay/story-Zwhwt3VJmysEGx62ZsuukJ.html

Lister, M., Dovey, J., Giddings, S., Grant, I., and Kelly, K. (2009). *New Media: A Critical Introduction* (2nd ed.). Routledge.

Massaro, T.M. (1988). "Empathy, legal storytelling, and the rule of law: New words, old wounds." *Mich. L. Rev., 87*, 2099.

Mehta, K. (2014). *Humans of Bombay*. Retrieved from https://www.facebook.com/humansofbombay/

Page, R. (2013). "Seriality and storytelling in social media." *Story Worlds: A Journal of Narrative Studies, 5*, 31-54.

Pulizzi, J. (2012). "The rise of storytelling as the new marketing." *Publishing research quarterly, 28*(2), 116-123.

Ryan, M.L. (Ed.). (2004). *Narrative across media: The languages of storytelling.* U of Nebraska Press.

Schwertly, S. (2014, October 22). The Neuroscience of Storytelling. Retrieved from ETHOS3: https://www.ethos3.com/2014/10/the-neuroscience-of-storytelling/

Singh, G. (2018). Momspresso: A content platform by and for mothers. Retrieved 12 August 2019, from https://www.thehindubusinessline.com/news/mompresso-moms-blog-social-media/article22808951.ece

Singh, S., and Sonnenburg, S. (2012). Brand performances in social media. *Journal of interactive marketing, 26*(4), 189-197.

Singh, T. (2015). Meet the Human Behind "Humans of Bombay", Retrieved from https://www.thebetterindia.com/39315/humans-of-bombay-facebook-karishma-mehta/

23

Hijra Self-Representations on and through Facebook

Negotiating Hijra Identities and Promoting Community Work in Mumbai

Delfi Chinnappan

1. Introduction

This chapter is a maiden exploration of *hijra* community-based organisations and their use of social media for representing *hijra* identity(ies) in contemporary India. *Hijras* are the institutionalised 'third gender' in India. Ina Goel specifies the "*hijra* identity is a unique blend of gendered and sexual identities, underpinned by religion and bound by a tight-knit social structure" (Sapiens website, Goel, 2019). *Hijras* live in residential clusters commonly known as *gharanas*, organised around a social structure and kinship. *Hijra gharanas* are complex apprentice systems of households/residential units that follow a hierarchical structure between *gurus* (teacher/leader) and *chelas* (disciples/learners). The *hijras* are a subset of the broader Indian transgender community, and the general public commonly understands them to be intersex or *napunsak*. *Hijras* are believed to have 'special sanctifying strengths' ordained on them by Hindu deities due to the rigorous formation period undertaken to become a *hijra*. Their connection to the divine confers them a special place in society due to their liminal status—neither male nor female (Nanda, 1990). In recent years, CBOs have emerged from these complex residential and structural units to empower the *hijra* community, promoting welfare, rights, advocacy and equal opportunities for community members.

This study examines three *hijra* CBOs—namely, the Humsafar Trust (HST), Triveni Samaj Vikas Kendra (TSVK) and the Astitva Trust (AT)—located in Mumbai, a city considered the queer[1] capital of India. This chapter primarily explores how the three *hijra* CBOs have used Facebook pages for self-representing *hijra* identities through the presentation of community work to wider Facebook audiences. I examine the *hijra* CBOs and the nature of *hijra* identities in the context of legal recognition and their structural connections to their *gharanas*. Through this examination, I contribute to the domain of how specific groups of sexual minorities, particularly the *hijra* community show resilience in managing underrepresentation and/or (mis)representation and fragmented visibility in digital and public spaces.

2. Background and Research Context

In recent years, India has witnessed historical legislative changes in the understanding of gender and sexual identities. These include the landmark Supreme Court judgement (2014) also known as the National Legal Services Authority (NALSA) that provided legal recognition of the 'third gender' and decriminalisation of homosexuality in 2018. For administrative and official purposes, the NALSA judgement has clustered all the sexual minority groups under the umbrella category of 'third gender'. This judgement specifies that individuals who identify themselves as 'third gender' are now eligible to apply for national identification documents, granting access to basic rights and welfare schemes.

Along with the NALSA judgement, the subsequent introduction of gender-sensitive laws during the last five years in India indicates the changing socio-political climate. This has paved the way for marginalised communities and individuals to identify themselves legally and seek rights to equal educational and employment opportunities. Although *hijras* have now received legal recognition in society, the *hijra gharana* culture that relies on a system of non-biological kinship structure and norms anticipates formal recognition. Thus, the legal changes introduced by the Indian government, together with Facebook's gender categories evolution in 2014, have had a significant impact on the *hijra* community. In 2014, Facebook expanded its gender settings for user profiles by introducing more than 50 options (Bell, 2015).[2] These changes made it possible for users to represent their fluid gender identity on Facebook. The change made by Facebook determines this social media platform as an important site of investigation in the context of the *hijra* community in India.

In early 2017, Vicks India[3], a popular consumer health brand in India, released a video entitled *Generations of Care* as part of its Touch of Care campaign. The video, distributed on television and across various social media platforms using the hashtag #touchofcare, did not advertise any

Vicks product but instead promoted its corporate social responsibility by addressing an important issue in contemporary Indian society. The *Generations of Care* video presents the story of Gauri Sawant, a *hijra* who runs a shelter home in Mumbai for *hijras* who have left their families at a young age to pursue their *hijra* identity. The Vicks motherhood video went viral (Goel, 2018). Having received extensive coverage, both locally and internationally (Sachdev, 2017), it generated global awareness and promoted a discussion of the issues facing the *hijra* community.

Gauri Sawant is a well-known transgender activist based in Mumbai, and Vicks presented her as an inspirational 'trans mommy' in the video. The video narrates Gauri's life, raising an orphaned girl named Gayatri as her own child despite having no legal rights to adopt a child and also facing social stigma. The video demonstrates how 'normal' her motherhood has been. This video positively impacted Indian and international audiences, both online and offline, and contributed to existing debates around the self-representations and gender identity of 'third gendered' individuals on social media platforms. The video was a pioneering initiative for the Indian transgender community. The Vicks advertisement is a seminal case and among very few corporate-made advertisements that, despite being critically reviewed by transgender activists, attracted appreciation for presenting and discussing the social cause and disseminating the novel content to audiences in India and abroad. This mainstream media representation, interwoven with audience responses and the emergence of Gauri Sawant as a *hijra* celebrity, calls for a scholarly investigation about the role social media plays in promoting *hijra* identities in contemporary India. Using the above vignette as central to the study, I build my research and frame the following question to examine *how do hijra CBOs use Facebook to self-represent their identities in contemporary India?* In order to answer this question, I situate the present study at the intersection of a changing socio-political environment and a dynamic digital landscape in India. Using cross-interdisciplinary investigation into contemporary claims of *hijra* identity(ies) on and through Facebook. This study throws light into self-representations of *hijra* identities presented via social media from the *hijra* community perspective; a segment of the sexual minority in India who only intersect with mainstream society on specific occasions.

Contemporary scholars working on issues related to queer communities in India have contributed to the understanding of the uses of digital media as platforms for identity constructions. There are also instances of social media being used as an instrument to raise awareness and galvanise efforts towards seeking social justice via Facebook groups (Dey, 2019). The shifting socio-political climate and dynamic digital landscape in India influences the self-representations made by queer groups. Therefore, this study on *hijra* CBOs and key players in the community operates within the context of these socio-political changes occurring not only within the *hijra gharanas* but also in the broader Indian queer context. To understand the self-representations made by the *hijra* CBOs on social media in contemporary India, it is important to note the advent of technology and social media adoption within the community.

The increased visibility of the *hijra* community is evident even in recent media productions depicting *hijra* community leaders. For instance, a popular tea brand in India named Red Label sponsored project Six Pack Band[4] features six musically talented *hijras* selected through auditions conducted only for *hijras* across the country. Red Label's Six Pack Band provided the *hijra* community with an opportunity to make their presence felt on a larger scale and pursue a potential career in music (Chinnappan, 2019). In addition to the motivations arising from the *hijra* context and emerging media representations, one key catalyst to undertaking this study is a gap in the academic literature concerning digital media and the *hijra* community in existing studies on queer identities in India (see Dasgupta, 2014, 2017; Dey, 2019; Mitra, 2010; Mitra and Gajjala, 2008). By doing so, this chapter contributes to the existing body of knowledge by addressing the gaps in previous queer research in India.

This consideration of transgender issues and concerns in mainstream media has become a potential strategy to secure funding from international agencies to address the plight of the marginalised. For instance, the Vicks advertisement garnered much discussion around various platforms, such as Facebook, YouTube and Twitter. This paved the way for advocacy related to a broad umbrella of rights such as adoption and marriage for the transgender community. Videos and initiatives like Vicks advertisement and the Six Pack music group push the boundaries and definitions of transgender identity(ies) in India. Apart from moving beyond traditional roles, these portrayals also question the traditional occupations historically held by the community. This has also benefited the Indian companies whose sales increased after their unique LGBTQ+ driven advertisements received a widespread response from the general public (Nambiar and Sahani, 2018). The circulation of these multimedia messages has brought these gender-fluid identities closer home. The increasingly visible positive recognition and acceptance in society through these digital platforms has encouraged a process of 'coming out' and accepting *hijra* identities, mediated by digital platforms. These media representations are changing the rhetoric around transgender identities in India and need critical examination.

3. Reviewing Mainstream Media Representations

Hijra portrayals in mainstream media give a narrow perspective of the *hijra* community, and there is a gross underrepresentation of the *hijra* community in mainstream advertisements, films and other content for public consumption. However, there have been efforts to represent these voices and stories in the past few years following the NALSA judgement. Some of earlier portrayals are problematic as they reinforce stereotypes about the community; for example, a stereotype often used in content to sensationalise and caricature *hijras* is that they steal male children. Performances of actors as drag queens and *hijras* in fictional movies are often ridiculed, exaggerated and used for comic relief.[5] Notably, few representatives from the community are available to shed light on the incorrect portrayals of *hijra* lives and identities. For example, Laxmi Narayan Tripathi[6] is the only transgender celebrity regularly seen on national and international news. Other public figures such as Tripathi and Bobby Darling—an Indian actress, who identifies as transgender—fail to represent the community's diversity and cut across occupations and class dimensions. Further, the limited number of transgender voices in the mainstream media, may or may not choose to represent the voices of the community. They are not necessarily bound to advocate issues of sexuality and awareness in the content produced. Hence, a few of these voices perpetuate stigma and stereotypes by participating in the ridicule and comic portrayals. However, there have been some exceptions to the norm. *Tamanna* [Desire] is a film released in 1997, themed around a *hijra* character called Tiku who raises a young orphan. The film sensitively elucidates motherhood themes. Other films, like Mani Ratnam's *Bombay* (1995) and Deepa Mehta's *Water* (2005) feature complex portrayals of *hijras* (Pattnaik, 2009).

The media plays a significant role in forming perceptions of individuals and communities. Due to underrepresentation and misrepresentations of the *hijra* community and related issues, little is known about *hijra* lives other than their engagement in sex work and begging. Their identity portrayals are limited to the 'clap', feminine dressing and their traditional occupations. In the absence of information from diverse perspectives, the community is typified as having these characteristics, and fear of the unknown perpetuates further stigma and misinformation. Documentaries like *Kismet* (2013) and the *Black Sheep* (2017) further demonstrate how mainstream media reinforces myths and represents *hijras* in a negative light.

It is important to explore the idea that being exposed to *hijras*, their life stories and everyday activities via social media, could potentially facilitate greater acceptance. For instance, a study on homosexuality in China presents similar arguments. Wu *et al.* (2018) introduce the concept of 'contact hypothesis' and 'parasocial contact'. The study demonstrated that contact with a marginalised community (such as those with diverse sexual preferences and identities considered in this thesis) is one of the most effective ways to overcome stigma. Social media contributes to generating awareness among people regarding equal rights and opportunities and a greater acceptance of homosexuality because the broader community can experience the lives of a different community through social media.

The accessibility and ease of social media platforms allow marginalised groups to represent themselves and their identities in a manner that is perceived to be safe. There are a few examples of these from India. The Seatbelt Crew project[7], released in June 2014 on YouTube, is an initiative by *hijras* as part of Ogilvy and Mather India and Channel V's ad campaign for road safety. The public service announcement features *hijras* speaking about the importance of seatbelt safety in a funny, quirky and interesting manner that subtly comments on the community's culture and addresses the stereotype of *hijras* badgering travellers on roads for a few Indian rupees. These examples illustrate how a surge in this community's media presence can lead to mainstream acceptance of their issues. This process of inclusion has extended to several netizens who now tweet, share, comment and discuss Indian transgender communities' issues in public and/or digital spaces, as with the *Generations of Care* video and Hijra Project Facebook page.[8] These videos distributed across social media platforms depict the *hijras* in a positive light and attempt to change the status quo. They have created a platform for the general public to engage with the lives and stories of *hijra* community members and discuss the issues concerning them, which paves the way to community acceptance in the Indian context.

Recent socio-political developments and increased social media and public presence have led to a growing sense of acceptance for the community (Chinnappan, 2019; Goel, 2019). Non-governmental organisations (NGOs), along with *hijra* organisations, work to break stereotypes and raise awareness among the general public to increase tolerance of the community and their occupation.[9] Further, writings about the life and culture of the *hijras* by scholars such as Reddy (2010), Nanda (1990), and Khan *et al.* (2009) have added to the depth of knowledge and literature about the uniqueness of the community and their important position in Indian society. The *hijras,* who are the most visible queer community in India, have been a part of Indian culture for centuries, yet they remain underrepresented in the digital discourse (Mitra and Gajjala, 2008). Even though the *hijra* community occupies ritual status, their existence had been considered illegal until the recent NALSA judgement that brought legal recognition.

4. Emerging Debates from Existing Literature

Despite the focus on LGBTQ+ and identity-based representations on digital media in Western research studies, there is a dearth of studies on the role of technologies, digital cultures and social media use among transgender communities in India, particularly among the *hijra* community. The recent studies conducted in this field include Sreyoshi Dey's (2019) focus on numerous Indian LGBTQ+ Facebook groups and Rohit Dasgupta's (2014, 2017) examination of a specific Facebook group, the Pink Kolkata Party, which involves a range of queer identities (mostly gay men) based in Kolkata. To date, the focus has been the aggregates of community identities as inclusive queer identities, which does not represent their internal diversity, although scholars of the diverse queer community in India do acknowledge the diversities of sexual and gender cultures in India. Leading researchers of *hijra* communities, such as Nanda (1990, 1999) and Reddy (2005, 2010), have expressed the need to "increase the visibility of the *hijra* community within disciplinary regimes in India resulting in greater scrutiny of their lives" (Reddy, 2005: 3). The debates in this discussion demonstrates the gap in research on representations of the *hijra* identities by CBOs on social media. This is particularly pertinent due to the recent spurt of *hijra* representation in mainstream media through advertisements (such as the Vicks ad) and initiatives (the Seatbelt Crew and Six Pack Band). In this Chapter, I argue to locate *hijra* communities in the context of changing gender definitions, the existence of queer and trans-social movements and contemporary ideas of sexuality and gender that frame *hijra* identities in India today.

With the recent changes in India's socio-political environment and the subsequent changes in the status of sexual minority groups, there has been greater visibility in the public sphere. This visibility has encouraged the *hijra* communities to represent themselves and present their stories, which go beyond the popular constructions of *hijra*-ness as evidenced by scholars and journalists who have documented the *hijra* community. The narration of *hijra* identities as a collective through their CBOs on wider digital technology-based public platforms sits at the heart of this study. Through an examination of the structure, function and everyday activities of the three CBOs chosen for the study, I seek to understand their narratives of *hijra* self-representations on and through Facebook.

5. Methods

This study is based on three *hijra* CBOs in Mumbai to understand their use of social media platforms for representing *hijra* identities. The study employs qualitative methods to explore and attempt to understand the linkages between social media use and the experiences of individuals involved in negotiating *hijra* identities as presented on Facebook pages. As part of the methodology, this study employs social media ethnography consisting of observations and textual analyses of social media platforms. Additionally, it includes semi-structured interviews with professional members of the CBOs to understand in-depth experiences about the questions outlined and themes identified by a close reading of social media platforms, focusing on Facebook pages that are public-facing and significantly used by the identified CBOs to promote their community work to wider audiences.

5.1. Field-site

From the outset, it is important to stress that I chose to work with CBOs instead of the *hijra gharanas* directly for reasons of accessibility and concerns for personal/individuals' privacy. Mumbai is an ideal site to investigate *hijra* CBOs for many reasons. The city has a large population of *hijras*; the only one with all seven types of *hijra gharanas* (T. Thomas, 2013). Further, the state of Maharashtra houses the largest number of *hijra* CBOs in India (*Humsfar Trust,* 2015). Previous ethnographic studies on *hijra* culture have focused on the Indian cities of Delhi and Banaras (Nanda, 1990), Banaras (Hall, 1995), Hyderabad (Reddy, 2005), Mumbai (Chettiar, 2015) and Delhi (Goel, 2016). Therefore, to build on the existing literature, Mumbai is a relevant site for investigation.

5.2. Selection of CBOs

The sample CBOs were determined based on a pilot investigation into the structure and function of the relevant Facebook pages and were narrowed to Mumbai-based organisations. There were two main criteria for the selection of CBOs for the study: an established area of work and an established social media presence dating from April 2014. For a holistic understanding of both community and individual perspectives of self-representations made on social media, two prominent leaders within the selected CBOs were identified as case studies. Further, considering the role of prominent individual personalities such as activists/celebrities in the *hijra* CBO structure, Gauri Sawant and Laxmi Narayan Tripathi were chosen as case studies based on their association with TSVK and AT, respectively. Based on the selection criteria, the three CBOs chosen were HST, TSVK and AT.

5.3. Social Media Ethnography

In their article 'Social Media Ethnography: The Digital Researcher in a Messy Web', Postill and Pink (2012) describe the approach as:

> [A] plural concept of sociality that allows a focus on the qualities of relatedness in online and offline relationships. This offers a better way of understanding how social media practices are implicated in the constitution of social groups, and the practices in which they engage together (p. 132).

This is an apt method for investigating how the *hijra* community and their practices as a social group are constituted through their social media practices for negotiating their identities. This methodology allowed to explore connections between the subjects' online and offline *hijra* identities. Given the range of possible social media performances, it serves to "make sense of the shifting intensities of the social media landscape as it emerges online, but also interwoven with offline activities" (Postill and Pink, 2012: 132). Additionally, the field of traditional ethnography has changed to incorporate nuances of varied methodologies to include distinct fields of digital ethnography (Pink, 2016), internet ethnography (Hine, 2015), virtual ethnography (Hine, 2000) and digital anthropology or anthropology of communication (Horst & Miller, 2006, 2013). As the subject of the investigation is social media platforms with an added focus on Facebook, social media ethnography allows for fluidity and flexibility in examining these online performances (Postill and Pink, 2012). This study integrates an amalgamation of internet ethnography (Hine, 2015) and principles of on-field traditional ethnographic fieldwork. In her article 'Fieldwork in Social Media: What Would Malinowski Do?' Markham

(2013) urges researchers to adapt their fieldwork based on '21st century networked communication practices and cultural formations' (p. 442). Hence, this study incorporates an eclectic qualitative approach to study a dynamic social media environment, with ethnography at the core of its enquiry process.

5.4. Data Collection

This ethnography involved a close reading and textual analysis of five Facebook pages (three CBO pages and two belonging to *hijra* celebrities within these CBOs) and semi-structured interviews with 30 professional members of the CBOs in Mumbai. The ethnography was undertaken in different stages. The first stage involved the observation and close reading of the Facebook pages operated by the three selected CBOs, and the identification of prominent content patterns across these pages. The content on these pages was studied in-depth and analysed using textual analysis to determine the pattern of activities conducted by the CBOs and the nature of their presence. The themes emerged from the content available to followers or audiences, which is a feature of Facebook pages. In the second stage, semi-structured interviews were conducted with key members of the CBOs to investigate and corroborate the emergent themes. The total duration of the data collection lasted six months involving the initial observation and textual analysis of the pages followed by on-field semi-structured interviews with participants.

5.5. Ethical Considerations

This study took into consideration the ethical issues of using social media data and studying sexually minority groups in India. The ethical considerations for this study comprise two parts. Phase 1 involved the observation and collection of publicly available social media data with a significant focus on five Facebook pages (three CBOs and two celebrities). Phase 2 involved in-depth semi-structured interviews conducted with the professional members of the three CBOs in Mumbai.

5.6. Limitations

Since the study utilised a small sample of *hijra* CBOs and significant stakeholders, the generalisability of the results is limited. However, qualitative studies are designed to capture in-depth experiences, so the emphasis on generalisability is limited. These findings cannot be generalised to *hijra* communities or CBOs in other parts of the country. This is also due to the nature of *hijra* communities, which are unique and context-dependent in the geographically diverse country of India. It is also important to acknowledge the study location and focus—in the metropolitan city of Mumbai, on *hijra* organisations that have an established area of work and social media presence. Such is not the case with other *hijra* CBOs and organisations broadly. CBOs are a nascent concept among *hijra gharanas*; the nature of CBOs studied in this thesis does not represent *hijra* CBOs across India, although potential similarities and differences can be observed and explored in future research.

6. Findings and Discussion

6.1. Creation and Curation of Facebook Pages

The affordances of Facebook are abundant, as evident in transnational literature, particularly among LGBTQ+ communities. The rise of digital media and social networking sites, including Facebook, have created a platform for LGBTQ+ communities to form support groups (Cipolletta *et al.*, 2017) explore identity construction and social justice (Dey, 2019; Lorenzana, 2016), manage their social identities and networks (McConnell, Neray *et al.*, 2018; Y. Taylor *et al.*, 2014) and build relationships that assist with their well-being and mental health (McConnell, Clifford *et al.*, 2017). Creating Facebook pages is a common practice among NGOs for numerous purposes. These include creating a page to help build a brand for an organisation, creating fan pages (Bernal *et al.*, 2016; Mare, 2017), and creating pages to respond to events or issues (Marwick & Ellison, 2012; Matamoros-Fernández, 2017; Schwartz, 2015). Facebook's primary affordances, such as the creation of profiles, friend lists, groups, pages, commenting practices (likes, comment, sharing and reactions) and allowing users to present status updates, are vital channels of public communication that form 'networked publics' (Papacharissi, 2010). Facebook, as a social media platform, expands its social networking options beyond the operation of profiles to also allow users to create a page that contains details of brands, organisations or public figures. These pages allow organisations to promote their work via ordinary text-based posts and rich media content, such as videos, that appear on users' newsfeeds, or to simply use Facebook as a platform to update others on their activities.[10] In the context of this study, the user is the *hijra* community; a collective group that has created Facebook pages under their respective CBO names, based on their culturally specific gender identity and residential segregation. The Facebook pages 'About' sections each provide a short description of the CBO, its foundation date, aims and goals and contact details. This description is indicative of an organisational page, not merely a social or informal one, and provides information to its followers.

Table 23.1: Overview of the CBOs' Facebook pages (updated May 2020)

Name of the CBOs and Establishment Date	*Facebook Page Details*	*Facebook Page Creation Date*	*Likes/Followers*
Humsafar Trust April 1994	@The Humsafar Trust Official	15 August 2009	14,372 likes 18,810 followers
Triveni Samaj Vikas Kendra October 2006	Triveni Samaj Vikas Kendra	23 March 2015	2,729 likes 2,755 followers
Astitva Trust November 2006	Astitva Trust	10 May 2010	869 likes 856 followers

The three organisations were diverse in nature and utilised Facebook pages in varying capacities to present and promote community work to their audience networks.

6.1.1. Humsafar Trust (HST)

HST is located in Santacruz, a suburban area of Mumbai. It is the oldest LGBTQ+ organisation in India and works on a broad spectrum of issues concerning sexual minorities. HST is involved in advocacy, health campaigns, capacity building and research in the field of issues concerning the LGBTQ+ in India (Humsafar Trust, Official Website 2020). HST provides financial and advocacy support to the many *hijra* CBOs under its aegis. Additionally, HST organises training activities and workshops for many *hijra* CBOs in Mumbai.

6.1.2. Triveni Samaj Vikas Kendra (TSVK)

TSVK is a CBO that works with members of the *hijra* community in the surrounding neighbourhood, mentored by the parent organisation Navanirmaan Samaj Vikas Kendra. The main foci of the CBO include a range of activities such as awareness and sensitisation towards HIV/AIDS testing and treatment, counselling services and advice on contraception, lobbying the Maharashtra government for rights and opportunities, and assisting fellow *hijras* to access bank accounts and government-certified identity cards. TSVK also runs a retirement home for elderly *hijras* and caters to the needs of *hijras* who require medical care and assistance. The *hijras* belonging to this household not only work in the CBO, but they are also involved in other traditional *hijras* occupations such as *badhai* functions, begging at traffic signals and on trains, and sex work. Activist and celebrity Gauri Sawant is also actively involved in training and decision-making within TSVK's shelter home for elderly *hijras.*

6.1.3. Astitva Trust (AT)

AT is located in Thane, a central part of Mumbai, and was founded in 2006 by popular *hijra* transgender activist Laxmi Narayan Tripathi. She now runs the trust in collaboration with the members of her *gharana.* It was founded to addressing the stigma and discrimination against the LGBTQ+ community, especially against *hijras,* in Indian society. AT focuses its work on creating awareness about sexual health issues, promoting a safe environment and positive attitudes towards the community, and taking steps towards the integration of the *hijra* community in Indian society. It conducts a host of activities around the health and general well-being of the *hijra* community within the *gharana* premises. The main office is in the Thane-based *gharana* for administrative purposes. Approximately 30 *hijras* work at AT as community welfare developers in conjunction with approximately 1000 *hijras* living in and around Thane.

I designed the following typology classified in Table 23.2 based on similarities in patterns across these Facebook pages. This typology was a systematic way to understand the diversity in the three CBOs' posts and helped to draw out similarities and differences between the pages. The intention was not to compare the CBO pages, but simply depict the diversity of content and presentation of *hijra* identities and community work, as represented on the three CBOs' Facebook pages. During the observation and textual analysis phase of the study, my role as a researcher was limited to being a social media spectator, refraining from participating or engaging in the posts published on these pages in order to maintain an objective stance to analyse data.

Table 23.1 illustrates the emerging position occupied by *hijra* CBOs in promoting their community work on this platform. The affordances of Facebook facilitated the production and sharing of content on the pages. Although the *hijra* CBOs differ in their experience and

Table 23.2: Typology of posts based on the three CBOs' Facebook pages arranged in the order of frequency on the appearance of categories.

No.	*Type/Category*	*Significance*	*Example*
1.	CBO community work in *gharana*	Activities carried out locally or nationally in *gharanas* or other parts of Mumbai Reporting of training, events, seminars, inaugurations	Visit from researchers or neighbouring CBOs Health promotion activities such as camps and counselling/ medical services distribution
2.	Government/ legal/political	Laws, Supreme Court judgement, bills in Parliament, Third gender definitions and categorisations Community activism	Elections Voting Request for toilets for transgender people in public spaces Critics to Transgender Bill Enabling or calling for identification document preparation Transgender ambassadors from the community Commentaries/dialogues/ critique
3.	*Hijra* identity	Promoting cultural significance, community norms, linguistic and gender identity representation, life-cycle rituals	Birthday photos Dance/song/*badhai* perfor-mance Group outings to Mosque/ temple Gifting traditions
4.	Ephemeral events	Announcements, reminders, remembrance, discussion	Job opportunities Annual yearly events, e.g., Annual Day celebrations, Talent shows CBO anniversary and celebrations Topical issues locally; e.g., Rape cases, Caste and Religious Discrimination Motivational posts Significant days: World AIDS Day, Transgender Visibility Day Event notices and call for auditions, e.g., Gulabi Mela casual lunch photos Celebration of Indian festivals
5.	Facebook affordance-based	Capturing events live, capturing and documentation Cross-platform linking Sharing URL's mainstream media links	Speaker sessions Rally/political protests Awareness drive Street theatre acts Post-performance uploads on YouTube Sharing/resharing valuable posts from WHO/UNAIDS (relevant renowned organisations and *hijra* celebrities/activist leaders/ news channels

profile, each has managed to create a network of followers. The typology of posts reveals the range of activities, reflective of the nature of work carried out by the *hijra* CBOs.

The representations of community work as displayed by the CBOs reflect their attempts to increase *hijra* visibility and portray a construction of *hijra* identities to audiences shaped by the legal and social recognition of the *hijra* community. HST took an activist pathway to advocate for equal rights and opportunities, contributing to legal and policy revisions, whereas TSVK focused on disseminating essential information to the community and other audiences. Gauri Sawant's leadership and independent projects provide opportunities for elderly *hijras* and orphaned children to find shelter at homes cared for by the *hijra* community. The reflection of these projects on and through Facebook have generated dialogues for discussion on marriage and adoption rights for the transgender people more broadly in India. AT's page serves as a digital repository, and as a space to participate in discussions, seek information about *hijra* communities and local events, and keep updated about the activities of their leader, Tripathi, who is engaged in multiple awareness and advocacy related activities.

Based on the field observations in Mumbai, a more active and vibrant *gharana* culture was seen at TSVK and AT in the offline settings, which contrasts with their activities on Facebook. These activities highlighted the differences between the three CBOs. Since HST is one of the oldest organisations supporting *hijra gharanas* and CBOs in the city, they had a well-established brand culture communicated through the strategic use of social media. This was dissimilar to TSVK and AT, both small-scale CBOs focused on the *hijra gharana* members. For TSVK and AT, bulk uploads mark the celebration of special occasions, while HST strategically uses social media for promotion and awareness activities. Like other queer CBOs in India, the three Facebook pages are symbolic of the "progressive ideals towards open dialogue and creating queer spaces in the city but at the same time failing to engage, and address issues of diversity among the different class and economic backgrounds that it purports to represent" (Dasgupta, 2014: 276)—particularly for *hijras* and dialogues about the wider *hijra* community.

This chapter mainly argues that community work lies at the centre of *hijra* identities in the post-NALSA phase. The analyses show how *hijra* CBOs use Facebook pages to present a range of community work performed in the *gharana* and CBO premises. The multiple representations of community work by the CBOs and work on information dissemination for and about the community have brought the *hijra* community to the digital forefront. The CBOs have employed innovative strategies and utilised affordances of Facebook pages to represent their personal and collective *hijra* identities, community work and engage in activism to protect the rights of the community members.

6.2. Facebook as a Social Media Platform for Self-Representations

Facebook offers the opportunity for *hijra* CBOs in the Indian context to promote their community work, use the pages along with the existing groups and profiles for various communicative functions. *Hijra* CBOs' representation of their community work on Facebook pages has led to a translation of *hijra* identities, their *gharanas* and CBOs to a broader audience on Facebook. This self-curated representation by the CBO has allowed the *hijra* community to position themselves in contemporary India through their community work. The platform not only promotes their community work, but it also develops a niche for the members by becoming socially distinguished figures; creators and curators of their CBOs' content that includes narratives of the *hijra* community. Hence, Facebook has facilitated *hijras* in digitally mediating their identities, with the benefit of self-representations. Given these complexities around the use and non-use of Facebook pages in the case of the CBOs, it becomes crucial to delve into the context of the *hijra gharanas* that are, in turn, shaping the choices of *hijra* identity self-representations today.

The use of Facebook for self-representations by the *hijra* community is recent, unlike Western counterparts (larger transgender population). The recent surge in usage is closely linked with the growth of media and digital technologies (Dasgupta, 2017) in India, such as the advent of Reliance Jio[11] wi-fi and cheap data plans since 2016. These developments have made it easier for the *hijra* communities living on meagre earnings to afford and utilise the internet for community work and other digital explorations, such as finding friends, reconnecting with family, seeking work and leisure.

These Facebook pages also serve to promote the work of individuals emerging as strong voices and feeding into the collective identity assertions, post-NALSA judgement. The following content originally shared on Sawant's page and reshared on TSVK's page illustrates this point:

> Today, we are five years old as *hijras*, an identity legally recognised in India since 2014. Prior to the judgement, we did not exist for the society; even though we existed in the mythological stories and on the streets in big cities. If using social media today

> is allowing me to express my identity and proclaim the *hijra* community in a progressive manner, I will use the platform to profess it. (Sawant, Facebook post, April 14, 2019)

Representations of *hijra* identities created by the CBOs are informed by the *hijra* culture with specific relation to kinship, religion, class, politics. Apart from these cultural representations, which are popular in nature, the *hijra* communities today wish to be recognised for their professional community work (social work) undertaken for the welfare of their communities. The insights from the study suggest that social media has provided a space for the community to present complexities of their identities, to further contest existing stigma and discrimination. Hence, the self- representations of these diversities in *hijra* identity(ies) have become possible with the dynamic technological affordances.

This mediation supported by digital developments has increased the scope for interacting with a variety of identity self-representations that were otherwise not possible, given the status of the *hijras.* In the absence of real-time interactions with the community (considering the stigma that exists) and religious interaction with audiences, this digital space becomes a medium of interaction. This study shows how self-representations of *hijra* identities were impacted by access to technology issues and restrictions associated with *hijra* social organisation and hierarchy. The traditional organisational structure of the *hijra gharana* was found to control the nature of communication on social media platforms. Hence, the possibilities of identity explorations on these platforms are somewhat limited for ordinary members of the *gharanas* indulging in non-CBO work. Considering these factors that impinge on representations, the narratives of the CBO members helped in understanding what is *shown* to the *hijra* networks (audiences) and what is *withheld.* This study demonstrated more professional community work carried out by the CBOs and their *gharanas* were publicly displayed in comparison to traditional depictions of the *hijra* community in ethnographic texts (largely focusing on health and cultural significance). The study indicates that social media has become an important part of the lives of *hijra gharana* members. These activities displayed on the Facebook pages further reinforce *hijra* culture and community strength as an organisation. The essence of *hijra* identity in contemporary India following the NALSA judgement lies in the presentation of community work to wider audiences, through the medium of Facebook to those that are classified as followers.

7. Conclusion

The NALSA judgement has legitimised the nature of *hijra* CBO work to address rights and advocacy issues for recognition within these marginalised communities. With the introduction of technology and the easy availability of the internet, social media platforms have become available for all. The structurally close-knit and otherwise impenetrable *gharanas* are not immune to these developments, and hence, these social media platforms have made their way into the *gharana* households. This has enabled the CBOs to increase their visibility on social media particularly Facebook, promote CBO work and *gharana* activities, and mobilise support for tolerance towards transgender communities. The active involvement of a CBO in social media activities creates a strong embodiment of the *hijra* identity(ies) on the digital forefront. The *hijra* CBOs have normalised and adapted to using social media to increase CBO reach and visibility for *hijra* identity(ies). The *hijra* CBOs have been able to explore the potential of these digital spaces to connect with the masses about their community work. Hence, Facebook becomes an all-purpose encompassing platform used among the *gharanas* and CBOs.

Acknowledgements

This chapter is produced from my PhD research undertaken and submitted at the Digital Media Research Centre, School of Communication, Queensland University of Technology (QUT), Australia. This work is supported by the QUT Post-Graduate Research Training Scholarship 2017-2020. I am grateful to Prof. N. Sudhakar Rao for his valuable comments that have benefited this chapter immensely.

*All identifying information is anonymised and participant names used in this chapter are pseudonyms.

NOTES

1. The term 'queer' is contentious and could mean different things when used in contexts. In this chapter, I use the term queer to represent a broad range of fluid identities also included in the LGBTQ+ classification. LGBTQ+ is used to refer to people who identify as lesbian, gay, bisexual, trans, queer or alternative diverse gender or sexual identities aside from or in addition to cisgender and heterosexual identities, such as asexual or pansexual.
2. These gender categories were created by Facebook as a means of providing

users with multiple gender options and not restricting users to the binary categories of male and female chosen by default. This strategic move is viewed as a way to let users select the option that best represents their gender identity, thereby allowing each user at least 10 options for identification. Facebook has also made provisions to add more to the list by asking users for comments and suggestions.

3. See https://www.facebook.com/logical.indian/videos/1195943770535340/
4. Y-Films' Red Label project, the Six Pack Band, is India's first transgender band. Popular songs include 'Hum hain happy [We are happy people]' and 'Sab Rab de bande [All people belong to the same God]'. See: https://www.youtube.com/watch?v=msbZUmaUBuI Sab Rab de Bande https://www.youtube.com/watch?v=blvOBnSRfVc Hum hain Happy https://www.youtube.com/watch?v=c3oteSP2OHI Ae Raju
5. Examples of such stereotypical representations in mainstream Bollywood movies like *Page 3* (2005), *Heroine* (2012) and *Traffic Signal* (2007). See http://www.mid-day.com/articles/a-look-at-hindi-films-that-have-explored-the-third-gender-thoroughly.
6. She is the first transgender person to represent the Asia-Pacific region at the United Nations in 2008. Presently she is a transgender activist and runs Astitva, an CBO in Mumbai.
7. See https://www.npr.org/sections/parallels/2014/06/17/323026150/indias-transgender-community-turns-seat-belt-safety-into-video-hit and https://www.youtube.com/watch?v=muCU6_Y_Kyo The Seatbelt Crew Video
8. See https://www.facebook.com/TheHijraProject/
9. For information of *hijra* rallies and protests, see: https://roundtableindia.co.in/index.php?option=com_content&view=article&id=8737:rally-dharna-by-the-hijra-transgender-community-against-the-transgender-persons-protection-of-rights-bill-2016&catid=129:events-and-activism&Itemid=195
10. See https://www.facebook.com/help/282489752085908/?helpref=hc_fnav
11. In 2019, Jio become the largest mobile network in India and the third largest in the world with a total of over 370 million subscribers in India (Jio website, 2020).

REFERENCES

Bell, K. (2015). *Facebook's new gender options let you choose anything you want*. Australia: Mashable.

Bernal, P., I Gascón, J., & Aragón, Ó. (2016). El uso de las brand fan pages de Facebook entre jóvenes y profesionales: Análisis empírico [The use of the brand ran pages of Facebook among young people and professionals: Empirical analysis]. *Enl@ce: Revista de Información, Tecnologíay Conocimiento, 13*(1), 28.

Chettiar, A. (2015). "Problems faced by hijras (male to female transgenders) in Mumbai with reference to their health and harassment by the police." *International Journal of Social Science and Humanity*, *9*(5), 752-759. https://doi.org/10.7763/IJSSH.2015.V5.551

Chinnappan, D. (2019, 7 October). "Digitally mediated hijra identity: The case of the 6 Pack Band." *Critical Asian Studies.* https://criticalasianstudies.org/commentary/2019/10/7/201920-delfi-chinnappan-digitally-mediated-hijra-identity-the-case-of-the-6-pack-band

Cipolletta, S., Votadoro, R., and Faccio, E. (2017). "Online support for transgender people: An analysis of forums and social networks." *Health & Social Care in the Community, 25*(5), 1542-1551. https://doi.org/10.1111/hsc.12448

Dasgupta, R.K. (2014). "Parties, advocacy and activism: Interrogating community and class in digital queer India." In C. Pullen (Ed.), *Queer youth and media cultures*. *London:* Springer (pp. 265-277).

Dasgupta, R.K. (2017). *Digital queer cultures in India: Politics, intimacies and belonging*. London: Taylor & Francis.

Dey, S. (2019). Queering virtual groups: Exploring Facebook groups as a space for identity construction and social justice among the LGBTQ community in India [Doctoral dissertation, Syracuse University]. Surface. https://surface.syr.edu/etd/1088

Goel, I. (2016). "Hijra communities of Delhi." *Sexualities, 19*(5-6), 535-546. https://doi.org/10.1177/1363460715616946

Goel, I. (2018). "What does it mean to be a hijra mother?" *Economic and Political Weekly*, *53*(8). ISSN (online) 2349-8846.

Goel, I. (2019, 26 September). "India's third gender rises again." *Sapiens.* https://www.sapiens.org/body/hijra-india-third-gender/

Hall, K. (1995). Hijra/hijrin: Language and gender identity [Doctoral dissertation, University of California, Berkeley]. eScholarship. http://escholarship.org/uc/item/6m5744jx.

Hine, C. (2015). *Ethnography for the Internet: embedded, embodied and everyday*. London: Bloomsbury.

Hine, C. (2000). *Virtual Ethnography.* London: Sage.

Horst, H., & Miller, D. (2006). *The cell phone: An anthropology of communication*. London: Berg.

Horst, H., & Miller, D. (2013). *Digital Anthropology.* New York: A&C Black.

Humsfar Trust (2015). "Sanchar: Developing a recommended language manual for improved reporting in media on sexual minority issues." http://www.humsafar.org/ResDown/SANCHAAR%20English%20Media%20Reference%20Guide%207th%20April%202015%20with%20Cover.pdf

Humsafar Trust, (2020). Official Website https://humsafar.org/

Khan, S.I., Hussain, M.I., Parveen, S., Bhuiyan, M.I., Gourab, G., Sarker, G.F., Arafat, S.M., & Sikder, J. (2009). "Living on the extreme margin: Social exclusion of the transgender population (hijra) in Bangladesh." *Journal of Health, Population, and Nutrition, 27*(4), 441. https://doi.org/10.3329/jhpn.v27i4.3388

Lorenzana, J. A. (2016). "Mediated recognition: The role of Facebook in identity and social formations of Filipino transnationals in Indian cities." *New Media & Society, 18*(10), 2189-2206. https://doi.org/10.1177/1461444816655613

McConnell, E.A., Clifford, A., Korpak, A.K., Phillips, G., & Birkett, M. (2017). "Identity, victimization, and support: Facebook experiences and mental health among LGBTQ youth." *Computers in Human Behavior, 76*, 237-244. https://doi.org/10.1016/j.chb.2017.07.026

McConnell, E., Néray, B., Hogan, B., Korpak, A., Clifford, A., & Birkett, M. (2018). "'Everybody puts their whole life on Facebook': Identity Management and the online social networks of LGBTQ youth." *International Journal of Environmental Research and Public Health, 15*(6), 1078.

Marwick, A., & Ellison, N.B. (2012). " 'There isn't wifi in heaven!': Negotiating visibility on Facebook memorial pages." *Journal of Broadcasting & Electronic Media, 56*(3), 378-400. https://doi.org/10.1080/08838151.2012.705197

Mare, A. (2017). "Tracing and archiving 'constructed' data on Facebook pages and groups: Reflections on fieldwork among young activists in Zimbabwe and South Africa." *Qualitative Research, 17*(6), 645-663. https://doi.org/10.1177/1468794117720973

Matamoros-Fernández, A. (2017). "Platformed racism: The mediation and circulation of an Australian race-based controversy on Twitter, Facebook and YouTube." *Information, Communication & Society, 20*(6), 930-946. https://doi.org/10.1080/1369118X.2017.1293130

Markham, A. (2013). "Fieldwork in Social Media: What would Malinowski Do?" *Qualitative Communication Research, 2*(4), 434-446. doi:10.1525/qcr.2013.2.4.434

Mitra, R. (2010). "Resisting the spectacle of pride: Queer Indian bloggers as interpretive communities." *Journal of Broadcasting & Electronic Media, 54*(1), 163-178.

Mitra, R., & Gajjala, R. (2008). "Queer blogging in Indian digital diasporas: A dialogic encounter." *Journal of Communication Inquiry, 32*(4), 400-423. https://doi.org/10.1177/0196859908321003

Nanda, S. (1990). *Neither man nor woman: The hijras of India*. Belmont, California: Wadsworth.

Nanda, S. (1999). "The hijras of India." In W. Dynes & S. Donaldson (Eds.), *Asian Homosexuality* (pp. 135-151). Garland.

Nambiar, N., & Sahani, P. (2018). *A manifesto for trans inclusion in Indian workplace*. Mumbai: India Culture Lab.

Papacharissi, Z. (2010). *A networked self: Identity, community, and culture on social network sites*. London: Routledge.

Pattnaik, S. (2009). Outside the frame: The representation of the hijra in Bollywood cinema. Intersections: Gender and Sexuality in Asia and the Pacific, 22. http://intersections.anu.edu.au/issue22/pattnaik.htm

Pink, S. (2016). "Digital ethnography." Innovative methods in media and communication research, December, 26: pp.161-165.

Postill, J., and Pink, S. (2012). "Social Media Ethnography: the Digital Researcher in a Messy Web". *Media International Australia* (145), 123-134.

Reddy, G. (2005). "Geographies of contagion: Hijras, kothis, and the politics of sexual marginality in Hyderabad." *Anthropology & Medicine, 12*(3), 255-270. https://doi.org/10.1080/13648470500291410

Reddy, G. (2010). *With respect to sex: Negotiating hijra identity in South India*. Chicago: University of Chicago Press.

Reliance Jio Website (2020). Official Website https://www.jio.com/welcome

Sachdev, C. (2017, 15 April). 'Mummy' is transgender: A new commercial is the talk of India. KPBS. https://www.kpbs.org/news/2017/apr/15/mummy-is-transgender-a-new-commercial-is-the-talk/

Schwartz, S.A. (2015). "Campaigning and contestation: Comments on politicians' Facebook pages during the 2011 Danish general election campaign." *Social Media + Society, 1*(2). https://doi.org/10.1177/2056305115622480

Taylor, Y., Falconer, E., & Snowdon, R. (2014). "Queer youth, Facebook and faith: Facebook methodologies and online identities." *New Media & Society, 16*(7), 1138-1153. https://doi.org/10.1177/1461444814544000

Thomas, T. (2013). *The clan culture of hijras: An exploration into the gender identity and status of hijras inside and outside gharanas*. Bangalore: Christ University.

Wu, Y., Mou, Y., Wang, Y., & Atkin, D. (2018). "Exploring the de-stigmatizing effect of social media on homosexuality in China: An interpersonal-mediated contact versus parasocial-mediated contact perspective." *Asian Journal of Communication, 28*(1), 20-37. https://doi.org/10.1080/01292986.2017.1324500

24

Sharenting

An Empirical Study on Online Sharing Habits of Indian Parents and its Effects on their Children

Nitesh Tripathi

Introduction

In the age of TMI (Too Much Information) netizens are creating and generating content like memes, blogs, tutorials, do it yourself (DIY) videos. Even Social Media depends more on the users for the creation of content. Whatever they share online is the main fodder that drives these websites and provides the traffic and in turn profits. Now apart from Generation Z, even parents are also equally available and active on the internet. One of the outcomes that have been observed in the past few years is that of Sharenting (sharing+parenting). Parents now shape their children's digital identity long before they open their first email. Parents are supposed to act as gatekeepers of their children's personal information. In the real world, parents are very protective and private about their children but on the digital platform they forget these very rules. Today, many children's social media presence starts with an ultrasound photo/birth announcements and continues till chronicling the first day of school. But this doesn't stop here; parents also post embarrassing behaviour of teens, naked pictures, pictures/videos of tantrums, personal parenting issues, crowdsourcing ideas to address disciplinary issues etc. A 2010 study by the Internet security company, AVG, found that 23 per cent of children had their sonograms posted online before they were even born, and by two years old, 92 per cent had some form of online identity resulting from their parents and family members sharing online. In the United Kingdom, a 2016 study found that the average parent would have posted 1,500 photos on social media by his or her child's fifth birthday close to six pictures a week.

Celebrities like Kim Kardashian and Kylie Jenner have made this trend even more popular. Sometimes, Kim even goes to an extent of enhancing her daughter by slimming the stomach and smoothening the skin. Sharenting is also getting popular as the internet user base in India is already above 500 million (Kantar IMRB ICUBE report). Almost every Indian TV or Film actor is doing this and thus we have star kids who are a celebrity from a very young age (baby Taimur, Abram, Aaradhya etc.). Parents get a lot of gratifications from sharing profit, fame and approval. Even advertisers and social media platforms earn a lot for the "baby pics drive clicks". And thus apart from parent bloggers even some average parents are jumping the bandwagon hoping to make their kids viral or famous.

There have been few examples of kids who got viral in the past such as "Charlie Bit My Finger", "Hey Nora do you pee your pants?", Kid Titus basketball videos, Sammy bottle flipping, Tavaris dancing, "Father telling the daughter that she can't have a boyfriend" etc. International child advocacy organization UNICEF released a report lamenting the dangers of the "bedroom culture" which is leading to reckless sharenting. It can have profound implications on the safety and psychological welfare of the children. Following were the results of the report: One in four children said their parents' sharenting made them feel embarrassed, anxious, worried, or sad. 50 per cent of images shared on paedophile sites are stolen from social media sites. 88 per cent of teens think people are sharing too much online. 14 per cent of American moms maintain their own blogs (of which there are an estimated 3.9 million in North America with the top 10 per cent making six figures in earnings).[1]

Lots of controversies surround Sharenting. Controversial photographer Sally Mann shared stirring and disturbing portraits of her children in 1992. In the book *Battle Hymn of the Tiger Mother*, Amy Chua shared the lives of her children to demonstrate effective parenting techniques. Singer Pink drew the ire of the internet after sharing an image of her 2-year-old son without the diaper. YouTube removed a channel named Toy Freaks, which had more than 8 million subscribers as it featured disturbing content of the father exploiting his daughters' suffering for profits.

In this context, parents must understand that children who grow up with a sense of privacy, coupled with supportive and less controlling parents, fare better in life, create their own sense of both private and public self to thrive as young people and eventually as adults.

Definition: In 2016, the word 'sharenting' was added to the dictionary. Sharenting (or oversharenting) is the overuse of social media by parents to share content based on their children, such as baby pictures or details of their children's activities and is related to the concept of TMI (too much information).

History: As far as the term is concerned, it was coined by *The Wall Street Journal* and they called it "oversharenting", a combination of "over-sharing" and "parenting". It has since been a big topic for discussion throughout the world and was one of Time's Words of the Day in February 2013. As far as Sharenting is concerned, it doesn't have an origin as such but there is a common consensus that since past century, print media in England gave wide coverage about the Queen and her kids. People all over the world have always been keen readers of stories about celebrities and read follow up stories about their personal life. They take a deep interest in what their kids are up to and speculate what they might do in future. As Electronic Media and later New Media came, this trend further increased. Now even celebrities started giving more updates about their children as they got publicity free of cost and also were paid hefty sums from media organizations to post about their personal life and family. With monetizing of parenting for famous parents, parent bloggers entered the field and carried this trend further by giving their personal touch. These bloggers soon turned into celebrities because of their children and began to be called influencers.

Psychological Aspect: Parents who share about their children do so for various reasons, such as—urge/impulse to share their pictures, the greed of earning money, getting approval of others, making their children famous, a matter of pride, showing off or for getting likes. But here, they should draw a line and remember that any action of theirs in present has repercussions in near future. The urge to share and get likes shows attention-seeking behaviour which may turn their sharing habit into an addiction. Parents must understand that some children are extroverts and are fine with sharing but few children are introverts who like to keep things private.

Possible dangers of Sharenting: Sharenting creates a digital footprint of children without their knowledge. The result is that the child grows up to find that most of his/her private life has already been online for years. Funny/awkward childhood pictures can cause embarrassment and cyberbullying from other children in future. Their self-esteem can be affected by negative online reactions as what was cute in childhood may be inappropriate in adulthood. They may have trouble forming their self-identity, separate from the online persona created by their parents. Parents while sharing forget that it's not their information but that of their children. They are directly invading the privacy of their children when they share about them. Also, another concern is that parents share too much and share inappropriate information. Online or Sexual predators may use the information (like location, phone number, favourite ice cream flavour etc.) for child grooming (seducing).

Barclays in its research warns that "Sharenting" may lead to online fraud and identity theft. The bank says parents are compromising their children's future financial security to such an extent that by 2030 it could cost almost £670 million in online fraud. The posts by parents might tamper with the children's reputation. For instance a post on a father's Facebook wall about an argument with them could contribute to their negative online reputation and in turn, may affect their future job prospects. Another impact of Sharenting is that it can turn parenthood into a competition for attention. The case of Mike Martin and his wife who ran a Youtube channel "DaddyOFive" sharenting took extreme form when the couple shared "pranking" videos of their children that bordered on child abuse and thus their Youtube account was suspended in 2017. Also they ended up losing custody of two of their children and were arrested for a brief period.

What can be done?

Police in France and Germany have taken concrete steps to address sharenting concerns by posting Facebook warnings, telling parents of the dangers of sharenting and stressing the importance of protecting children's private lives.[2] Celebrities like Rio Ferdinand (ex-footballer), Robbie Williams (Popstar), Holly Willoughby (presenter) take caution while sharing their children's pictures online by only showing the back of their heads or pixelating their face out. Other celebrities such as Anna Paquin, George Clooney and Rochelle Humes also don't support Sharenting. Ray FitzGerald, a parenting coach asks parents to follow the "three P rules of posting" which are privacy, perception and permission. He asks them to make sure their privacy settings aren't public. Parents should remember that they do not reveal the school address or uniform of children (Use black and white filter instead) and should consider what potential bullies might be able to use as ammunition in near future from a picture. They should be careful not to write about things that would embarrass their children. In fact parents should ask themselves these questions before sharing anything online about their children[3]:

- Why are you sharing it?
- Would you want someone to share it about you?
- Could your child be embarrassed by it, now or in the future?
- Is there anyone in the universe who shouldn't see this about your child, now or at any point in the future?
- Is this something you want to be part of your child's digital footprint?

Objectives

- To assess the pervasiveness of Sharenting in India
- To investigate few cases of Sharenting highlighted in media
- To study Social Media and online sharing habits of Indian parents
- To elicit the opinion of children on various aspects of Sharenting

Research Methodology

The present research is a descriptive one. The Varanasi city Uttar Pradesh was chosen as the study area. Children with different levels of educational qualifications and age group were taken as the sample for the study. The total sample was 83 out of which 69 respondents were found suitable for the study. The age group varied from 11 to 40 years. Survey Method was applied and data was collected by sending Google Forms link of Questionnaire to the respondents via SMS and WhatsApp messaging. Purposive sampling technique was used for data collection. The questionnaire had 22 questions related to attitude and opinion of children on the topic. Later, the data was fed on SPSS and analyzed.

Data Analysis and Interpretation

20.3 per cent of respondents were in the age group of 11-20 years, 69.6 per cent of respondents were in the age group of 21-30 years while only 7 per cent of the respondents were in the age group of 31-40 years. 46.4 per cent of respondents were male and 53.6 per cent were female. 13.0 per cent respondents were School going children, 27.5 per cent were Graduates, 52.2 per cent were Post Graduates and only 7.3 per cent of respondents were doing a PhD. Table from 24.1 to 24.10 provide data on various aspects of Sharenting.

Table 24.1: Showing Parents of Respondents who have Social Media presence

Parents of Respondents having Social Media presence		
	Frequency	*Per cent*
Father	19	27.5
Mother	18	26.1
Both	23	33.3
None	9	13.1
Total	69	100

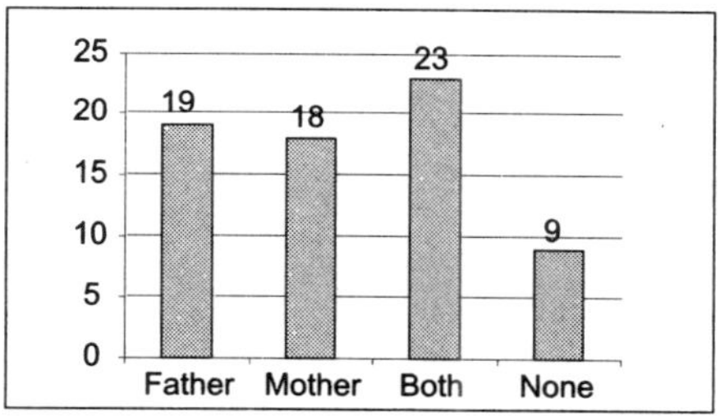

Out of 69 respondents, 27.5 per cent said that only their father while 26.1 per cent said that only their mother was active on Social Media. 33.3 per cent said that both of their parents are on Social Media while 13.1 per cent said that both their parents are not on Social Media.

Table 24.2: Showing Devices Parents possess for personal use

Devices parents possess for personal use		
Device	*Frequency*	*Per cent*
Smartphone	69	100
Tablet	2	2.9
Laptop	8	11.6
Personal Computer	5	7.2

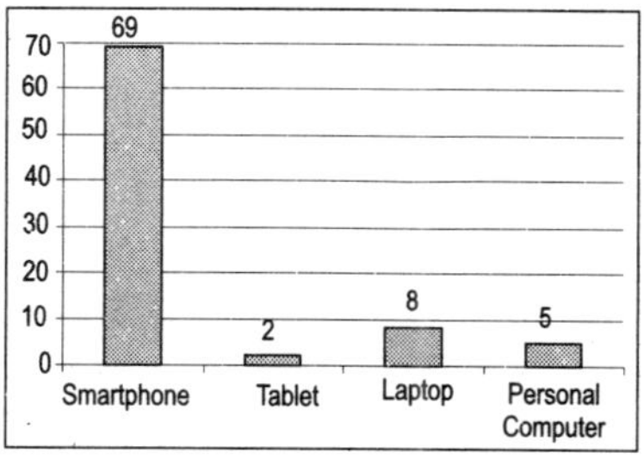

Almost 100 per cent of respondents said that their parents owned Smartphones for personal use; 2.9 per cent of parents owned a tablet; 11.6 per cent owned a Laptop and merely 7.2 per cent owned a Personal Computer.

Table 24.3: Showing Social Media platform that parents use actively

Social Media platform that parents use actively		
Platforms	*Frequency*	*Per cent*
Facebook	50	72.5
WhatsApp	65	94.2
Twitter	4	5.8
Instagram	7	10.1
Tik Tok	0	0
YouTube	1	1.4
Others	1	1.4

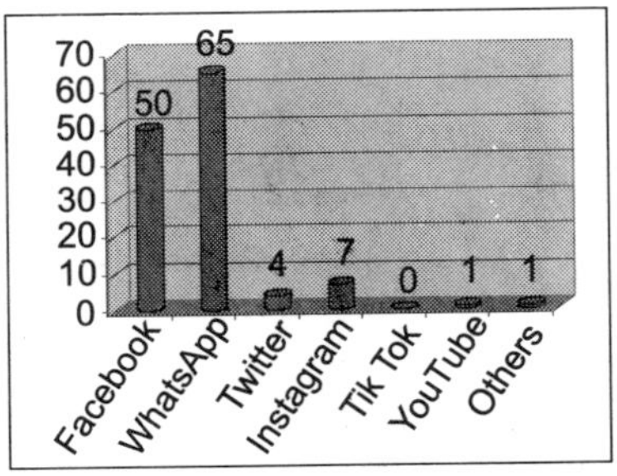

About 73 per cent of respondents said that their parents were using Facebook actively; 94.2 per cent were using WhatsApp and 5.8 per cent were using Twitter. Only 10.1 per cent of parents were active on Instagram; 0 per cent on Tik Tok and 1.4 per cent on YouTube.

Table 24.4: Showing Time that Parents dedicate to Social Media accounts (in hours)

Social Media Usage by Parents		
Duration (in Hours)	*Frequency*	*Per cent*
1 Hour	24	34.8
2 Hour	22	31.9
3 Hour	10	14.5
Above 4 Hour	13	18.8
Total	69	100

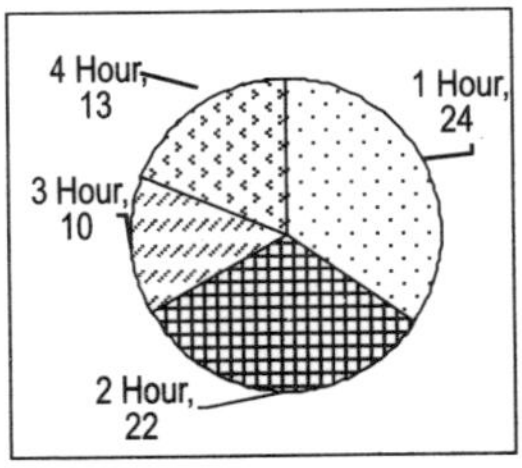

About 35 per cent of the respondents said that their parents were using Social Media for 1 hour or less and 31.9 per cent used it for around 2 hours. 14.5 per cent used Social Media for 3 hours while 18.8 per cent were using Social Media for 4 hours or even more than that.

Table 24.5: Showing Frequency of Parents sharing about their children online

Frequency of Parents Sharing about their children online		
Response	*Frequency*	*Per cent*
Quite Often	5	7.2
Often	2	2.9
Sometimes	27	39.1
Rarely	20	29.0
Never	15	21.8
Total	69	100

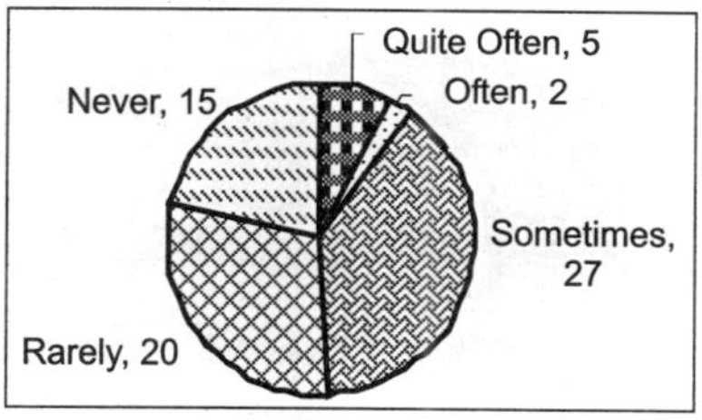

About 7 per cent of parents quite often and 2.9 per cent shared often about their children on Social Media, while 39.1 per cent did it just sometimes. 29.0 per cent rarely shared while 21.9 per cent have never shared about their children on Social Media.

Table 24.6: Showing Pictures/Videos posted by parents that won't be liked by children

Pictures/Videos posted by parents that won't be liked by children		
Options	*Frequency*	*Per cent*
Your Funny pictures/video	29	42.0
Your Awkward pictures/video	35	50.7
Your Personal pictures/video	20	29.0

About 42 per cent of respondents felt that their funny picture/video should not be shared by their parents. 50.7 per cent said the same for awkward pictures/videos and 29 per cent said it for personal video/pictures.

Table 24.7: Showing Pictures of children that parents post online

Pictures of children that parents post online		
Types of Pictures	*Frequency*	*Per cent*
Childhood pictures	17	24.6
Birthday/Happy occasion pictures	33	47.8
Personal Achievement pictures like winning a trophy or topping the class	27	39.1
Holiday/Picnic pictures	25	36.2
Festival pictures	32	46.4
Family gatherings pictures	30	43.5
Intimate/Personal pictures	2	2.9
Casual pictures	12	17.4
Formal pictures	4	5.8

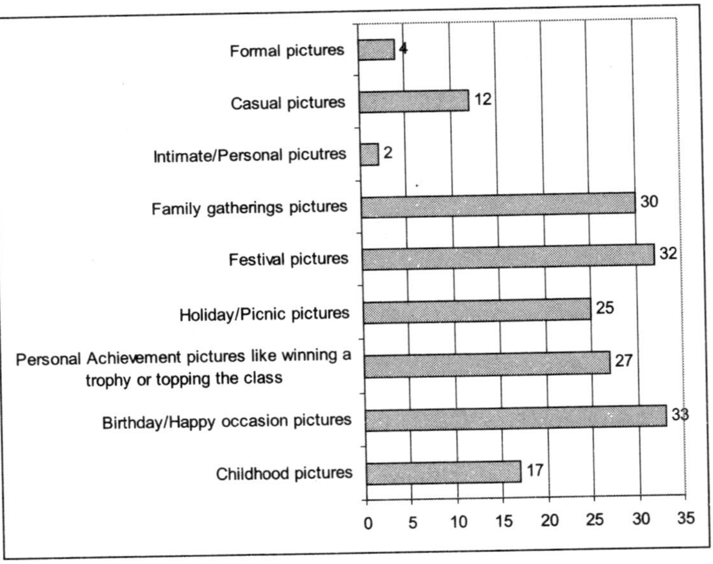

About 25 per cent of respondents said that their parents shared their childhood pictures, 47.8 per cent shared birthday/happy occasion pictures, 39.1 per cent shared personal achievement pictures like winning a trophy or topping the class, 36.2 per cent shared holiday/picnic pictures, 46.4 per cent shared festival pictures, 43.5 per cent shared family gatherings pictures, 2.9 per cent shared intimate/personal pictures and 17.4 per cent shared casual pictures while only 5.8 per cent shared formal pictures of their children.

Table 24.8: Showing Response of Children when their parents post their pictures online

Response of Children when their parents post their pictures online		
Response	*Frequency*	*Per cent*
I'm elated (5)	15	21.7
I'm happy (4)	11	15.9
I'm OK/fine with it (3)	28	40.6
I'm unhappy (2)	8	11.6
I feel terrible/ embarrassed (1)	7	10.2
Total	69	100

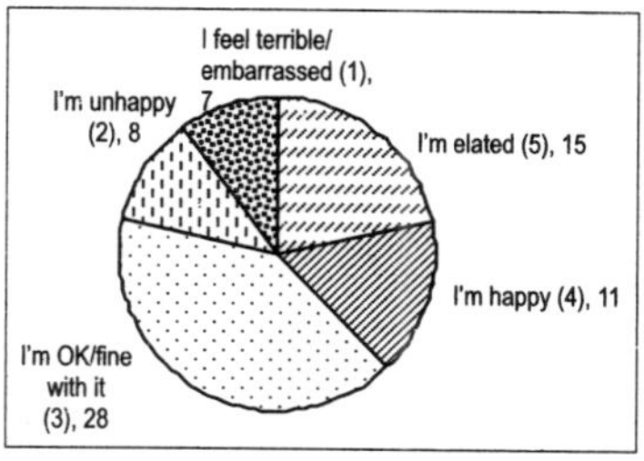

About 22 per cent of respondents feel elated when their parents post about them on Social Media, 15.9 per cent are happy and 40.6 per cent are fine with it. Only 11.6 per cent are unhappy and 10.2 per cent feel embarrassed when their parents post about them on Social Media.

Table 24.9: Showing Response of children on Social Media Platform that their parents should never use

Response of children on Social Media Platform that their parents should never use		
Platform	*Frequency*	*Per cent*
WhatsApp	8	11.6
Facebook	16	23.2
Twitter	15	21.7
Instagram	26	37.7
Tik Tok	45	65.2
Can Use All	4	5.8

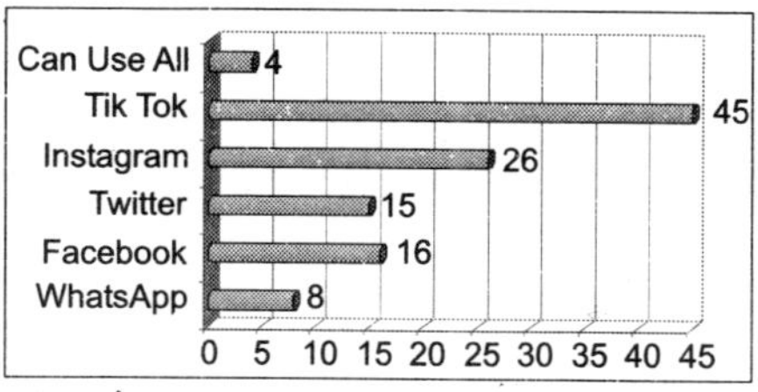

About 12 per cent of respondents feel that their parents should never use WhatsApp, 23.2 per cent feel so about Facebook and 21.7 per cent said the same about Twitter. 37.7 per cent felt their parents should not use Instagram, 65.2 per cent said the same for Tik Tok and only 5.8 per cent feel that they can use all the Social Media platforms.

Table 24.10: Showing Response of children on the aspect of the social media engagements of their parents that they are not comfortable with

Response of children on aspect of the social media engagements of their parents that they are not comfortable with		
Response	*Frequency*	*Per cent*
Lack of technological and social media know-how	35	50.7
Inability to understand what to share and what not to share	20	29.0
Invading your private space	10	14.5
They are keeping a watch on you	13	18.8
Revealing personal information of your life	7	10.1
I am comfortable with their Social Media Use	2	2.9

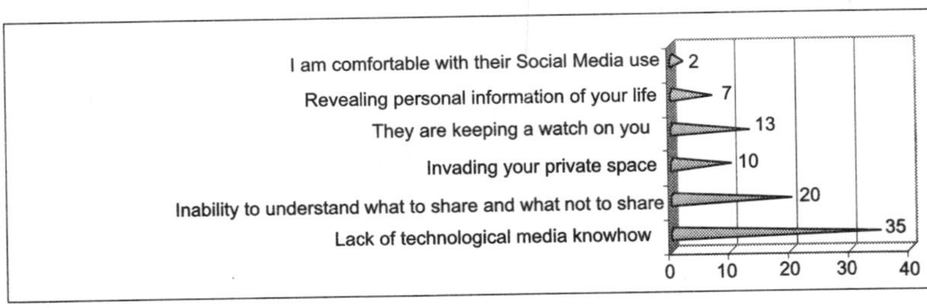

On being asked the aspect of social media engagement of their parents that they are not comfortable with, 50.7 per cent respondents feel that their parents lack technological and social media know-how. About 29 per cent said that their parents cannot understand what to share and what not to share and 10.1 per cent feel that their parents reveal their personal information online. 14.5 per cent feel that their parents invade their privacy on Social Media while 18.8 per cent said that their parents use it to keep a watch on them. Only 2.9 per cent of respondents said that they are comfortable with every aspect of Social Media use by their parents.

Apart from this, few dichotomous questions were included questionnaire to know the opinion of respondents on various asp... of Sharenting. 82.6 per cent of respondents replied that their parents were active on Social Media. On being asked whether their parents take candid pictures of them, 68.1 per cent denied any such action. 78.3 per cent of respondents had added their parents to their Social Media accounts. When asked whether they avoid adding their parents on Social Media accounts, 79.7 per cent said they don't do so. On being asked whether they secretly wished that their parents were less active on Social Media, 82.6 per cent of respondents denied having such thoughts. About 12 per cent of parents always take consent of their children before they post about them on Social Media, 33.3 per cent sometimes take consent while 55.1 per cent never take consent. 11.6 per cent of respondents feel that parents should always take consent before they post their pictures on Social Media. 49.3 per cent feel that it's not needed while 39.1 per cent of respondents feel that sometimes they should take consent before posting online. 5.8 per cent of respondents feel that their parents overshare on Social Media while 33.3 per cent said that their parents did it sometimes. About 61 per cent of respondents said that their parents don't overshare. A descriptive question was asked at the end of the questionnaire on whether there was an incident where parents of respondents posted something embarrassing about them online. Most of the respondents said that there was no such incident. But a few respondents did mention incidents like posting half head photograph, funny childhood photos, father adding his name to his daughter's name, funny haircut picture, a snooping account of children's friends and messaging them.

Discussion and Conclusion

A study was carried out to assess the pervasiveness of Sharenting in India. Most of the respondents were in the age group of 21-30 years. The females and males were equally represented. One of the major findings of the study was that most of the parents are online. From the study, we can conclude that both mother and father, are equally having a Social Media presence. The majority of the parents refrain from taking candid pictures of their children which shows that parents respect the privacy of their children. Most of the children have added their parents to their Social Media accounts which show their acceptance of their online presence. On further enquiry, it was revealed that most of the children add their parents not, because of any pressure and neither they dislike adding their parents in their account barring a few respondents who felt so. On the contrary, the children are very satisfied with the online activities of their parents and seem to have no problem with them being active online. The study reveals that Smartphone is the most popular device among parents personal use including Social Media usage. The most popular Social Media platform among parents is WhatsApp and Facebook. A few of them also have Instagram accounts. Though the time dedicated for Social Media by parents may be debatable still time reported by children was taken into consideration as they are generally aware of their phone usage. Most of the children said that their parents were using Social Media for almost 1 hour and many others said it was around 2 hours. This amount of Screen Time is very much within the internationally accepted Screen Time limit which is 2 hours (although for adults there is no such limit). The Indian parents unlike the Western parents share about their children only sometimes which is good as it shows that they don't believe in showing off. Most of the children said that they would not like their parents posting funny or awkward pictures. Indian parents generally shared pictures/videos of birthdays, happy occasions, personal achievements, festival and family gatherings. Most of the children were somewhat fine with parents sharing their pictures online though a few of them disliked it totally. One of the concerns that the study highlights is that most of the parents don't take consent of their children before they post their pictures online. Meanwhile, even the children felt that sometimes the parents should take their consent if not always. A large number of children also felt that it is not at all needed to take their consent before sharing their pictures online. Most of the children said that their parents should never use Social Media platforms such as Tik Tok, Twitter and Instagram as they are less personal and more public in nature. One of the aspects of Social Media used by their parents that the children are not comfortable with is that their parents are not aware of how Social Media and technology works. There is a possibility that they might become a target of fraud or fakery or might accidentally cause an embarrassment to their children if they share too much. But such scenarios are unlikely to become common as the study revealed that most of the parents don't overshare barring few respondents who felt that sometimes they do so. Overall, the study concludes that a majority of Indian parents don't overshare with except for a few, who sometimes overshare.

The study suggests parents take the consent of their children before posting their pictures online. In case the child is not mature enough to understand the consequences of sharing, they should share pictures/videos in a discreet or curtailed manner so that their children do not become vulnerable to online predators. Parents should check their network of friends and make sure that they are friends with actual friends and not some stranger or a fake account. If they do have some strangers in their account, then they should share it with only selected family members and close friends. They should also ensure that the post does not reveal any personal details of children like home or school address, their likes and preferences etc. Parents should also review their privacy settings on social media accounts and ensure that the pictures that they are sharing are shared only to close friends and relatives.

NOTES

1. See Stadtmiller, M. (2017, December 24).
2. *More Than 80% of Children Have an Online Presence by the Age of Two.* Retrieved from https://futurism.com/more-than-80-of-children-have-an-online-presence-by-the-age-of-two
3. See McCarthy, C. (2017).

REFERENCES

McCarthy, C. (2017). *Sharenting: 5 Questions to Ask Before You Post*. Retrieved from https://www.healthychildren.org/English/family-life/Media/Pages/Sharenting-5-Questions-to-Ask-Before-You-Post.aspx

Stadtmiller, M. (2017). *Kids Don't Have Parents Anymore—They Have 'Sharents'*. Retrieved from https://www.thedailybeast.com/kids-dont-have-parents-anymorethey-have-sharents

25

Phatic Communication on WhatsApp in Indian Family Context

Padma Rani

Bronislaw Malinowski, introduces in his book "Coral Gardens and Their Magic" the term phatic communion, referred to communication for social upkeep. The information communicated has no practical value and is rather mundane. "Phatic communion serves to establish bonds of personal union between people brought together by the mere need of companionship and does not serve any purpose of communicating ideas". (Malinowski, 1935: 151)

Phatic communion has three phatic functions: a social function to establish and maintain social connections; a communicative function to demonstrate that the channel of communication is open and present oneself as a potential communication partner; a validation and recognition function to indicate recognition of one's interlocutor as a potential communicative partner. Philip Riley has added another three functions to the main functions: to provide indexical information for social categorization (to signal social identity); to negotiate the relationship, in particular relative status, roles and affectivity (an indicator of social or affective relationship with the interlocutor); to reinforce social structure (Riley, 2007). Roman Jakobson coined the term "phatic function" which helps understand the social implication in everyday life of a phatic culture. The linguist Jakobson has identified the general functions of language— the metalinguistic (verifying the code), Emotive (expressing the sender's state); Conative (inciting the receiver's response); Phatic (tries to maintain contact with the receiver); Referential (relating to a context); and Poetic (existing as a construct for its own sake). (Jakobson,1960)

The phatic communion by Malinowski and the phatic function by Jakobson, are concepts that together provide a theoretical framework for analysis. The phatic function comprises: (a) social function;

(b) communicative function, (c) validation and recognition function; (d) to provide indexical information for social categorization; (e) to negotiate the relationship, in particular, relative status, roles and affectivity; (f) to reinforce social structure. Conflict-avoidance has been added in relation to social networks helps to keep a balance and harmony, and diminishes the damage caused by conflicts (Jumanto, 2014). By using and stimulating new applications of phatic communication and small-talk, tensions are weakened and the social network in which it is applied could be positively influenced (Senft, 2009).

Web 2.0 led to the development of microblogging culture and social media. The use of mobile devices for social networking sites and chat applications has given impetus to the idea of micro-posts. The origin of tweets, Facebook status updates, likes, comments, Instagram, WhatsApp, and many others is due to the human need for phatic communication. The role of phatic communications is inherent in all human social communication and expect to find it implicated in any online communications system. The functions of phatic communication are: (1) breaking the silence, (2) starting a conversation, (3) making small talk, (4) making gossip, (5) keeping talking, (6) expressing solidarity, (7) creating harmony, (8) creating comfort, (9) expressing empathy, (10) expressing friendship, (11) expressing respect, and (12) expressing politeness.

Online Phatic Posts

Phatic display of a connected presence is expressed through micro-posts, comments, short messages, leet-speak, tweets, status updates, Facebook social add-ons, and embedded applications. All these forms have elements of communicative discourse enabling users to get socially engaged through brief, non-formal messages that have meaning and within their context denote something: interaction, connected presence and fostering and maintaining connections. Human relationships depend more and more on new technologies, such as computers, mobile phones and their social network identities.

In human interaction, it is important to stay in touch and let others know that "I'm here too". To stay in touch and reinforce their relationship participant just write "nonsense", expressing their thoughts freely and make witty comments. For example, Twitter, besides micro-blogging, implies social networking, interacting, text messaging, learning, enabling communication both through the internet and mobile devices. These communications are designed to be instantaneous, spontaneous and connect people globally. These practices have resulted in forming 'phatic media' (Miller, 2008) in which communication without content has taken precedence. For many users, the point of Twitter is the maintenance of connected presence, very similar to saying "what's up?" in an analogue space as you pass someone on the street when you have no intention of finding out what is actually going on. A contemporary digital media scholar, Mizuko Ito, described the appearance of phatic communication processes among Japanese teens in "low-content text message" groups, whose purpose is simply to stay in contact with others. In Japanese culture, the phatic function is called *aizuchi*. The tweets are real-time, continuous, short, two-sided communication where, if one drops out of the communication thread, the dynamics of the aizuchi is lost. Aizuchi's main function is to keep people connected, to be connected they need to have a high degree of alertness.

Some researchers like Licoppe and Smoreda (2005) indicated that non-formal and non-dialogic means of interaction had helped the emergence of small communicative processes and gestures whose purpose at the first glance may appear to lack meaningful information, but in its substance, those gestures and communication expressions foster sociability and maintain social connections. These are communicative processes Malinowski described as phatic communion. Phatic expressions in communication practices are very meaningful because they indicate and imply social recognition, online intimacy, and sociability in online communities. Phatic posts potentially denote a lot more substance and weigh to them than the content itself suggests.

There are numerous possible meanings and interpretations behind the poke and in the context of social networking technologies they can include: (a) showing romantic interest for the other; (b) high visibility, low-pressure way of getting attention; (c) a lightweight interaction.

The phatic process has the function of displaying the other person's online presence, i.e., expressing that one is still "there". This is very indicative to young people (Radovanovic and Regnedda, 2012), who post from the status of their mobile phones updates in the evening after school and look for their peers online. This is the function of online presence— to know that someone is out there. Phatic communication and online connection to the other becomes significant and phatic dialogue enables relationship maintenance as well as the connected presence in social networks. This way the relevance of the phatic function of micro-posts is emerging as a form of online intimacy and social connections in social networks.

WhatsApp

WhatsApp, which has about 1.5 billion monthly active users worldwide, does not really have any major competitor in India. The closest competitor it has in the country is Messenger, another platform owned by Facebook, and Hike, which millions of users check everyday.

WhatsApp is the most popular smartphone application. It was released in 2009 with an active internet connection to use. In 2016 WhatsApp became a free app. As of 5/1/18, we have 450 million daily active users. The number of WhatsApp users in India is 400 million users as of 7/25/19. The number of Indian languages supported by WhatsApp is 19. 90 per cent of smartphones in India having WhatsApp installed on them. There is a significant rise in rural areas as well as users from low-income families. About 65 billion messages are sent through WhatsApp daily. People are chatty on WhatsApp, it gives them an easy way to reach whoever they want, whenever they want. Users spend an average of 195 minutes on WhatsApp weekly.

In WhatsApp, the feature of group chats contributes to its success and changes the way people communicate. The group-based communication paradigm is investigated, particularly focusing on the usage of WhatsApp, communication in group chats, and implications on mobile network traffic. (Seufert Michael *et al.*, 2016)

The reasons for the domestication of WhatsApp are:

1. Users perceive the audiences as Oscillating between "the intimate and the semi-public" (Matassi, M., Boczkowski P., and Eugenia, M., 2019).
2. It is uncontaminated, in the sense they are exposed to content only from direct contacts.
3. Resemblance to offline communication (Chan, 2018).

Oliveria Santos (cited in Matassi, M., Boczkowski P., and Eugenia, M., 2019) uses "kitchen" to describe a WhatsApp group of elderly women. There is continuity in their everyday conversation and socialization. This points to the idea that WhatsApp can be used to explore the interaction between domestication and life stages.

The domestication process and different life stages of users were studied among WhatsApp users in Argentina. The study concluded that in young adults (18-34 years) WhatsApp was a taken for a granted platform where sociability is in groups among friends and always available online mode. Middle adults (35-49 years) used this platform based on their work and care responsibilities. Late adults (60 years and older) used WhatsApp to connect with younger generations in addition to age peers, their availability was less compared to the other age groups. (Matassi, M., Boczkowski P., and Eugenia, M., 2019)

Families with three or more generations either living in the same or different households were studied in Itlay and Argentina. The families in both countries differed in their communication culture but used WhatsApp. WhatsApp is considered to facilitate family interaction across generations. The success of WhatsApp in the family context is first, it reaches the whole family at once; secondly, it promotes "phatic communication" i.e., small messages. The application offers different modalities like text, photo, video, or audio messages depending on the preference and communication skills of the members in the group. The preference for WhatsApp is not only due to its technical properties but also social affordances. They can reach the entire family at the same time using multiple modes. It is used especially for daily phatic communication to help sustain the bonds with family members as their daily schedules may not be compatible with each other. (Taipale and Farinosi, 2018)

The use of a smartphone and WhatsApp among Israeli television viewers of the 2018 World Cup from the quarterfinals onward was studied. The study revealed that most viewers prefer to watch the broadcast of a major soccer game together. The co-viewing is not necessarily done in the physical presence of others. There exists a connection between the viewer's engagement with the game and the enjoyment of watching the broadcast. The use of a smartphone as a second screen, especially WhatsApp mediated the relationship. The co-viewing relationship was mediated with the use of a smartphone, especially WhatsApp. Game-related communication using WhatsApp contributes to a meaningful collaborative viewing experience. WhatsApp influences the degree of engagement with the game and the extent to which it is enjoyed. During the game, if the messages transmitted are related to the game, there is a positive relationship between the levels of enjoyment and the use of WhatsApp. On the other hand, if the messages are not related to the game, there is a negative relationship between the variables. (Weimann-Saks, Ariel, and Elishar-Malka, 2019)

WhatsApp in India: The Study

To understand the use of WhatsApp among family groups in India, five family WhatsApp groups of varying membership were selected for the study. The selection of the group was purposive and convenient. The screenshots of the messages on the group were shared with the researcher. The study was conducted for six months. A manual qualitative content analysis of the messages was done. Five different types of groups were selected. A brief profile of the groups are as follows:

(i) **Group 1**—Family groups which consists of members from three generation, but the second generation were offsprings of the first generation and his grandchildren—25 participants
(ii) **Group 2**—A family group with three generations. The first generation with his/her siblings and spouse, their offsprings with their spouse and grandchildren—35 members
(iii) **Group 3**—Three generations of women belonging to the same joint family—12 members
(iv) **Group 4**—A couple and their adult children and their spouse—5 members
(v) **Group 5**—A couple with their one child—3 members

In all the groups, the day started by members wishing each other "Good Morning". In two groups, the "Good Morning" message is usually accompanied by some motivational quotes. The number of messages in a group per day varied depending on various things. The average number of messages was eight in each group per day. On special occasions like birthday, anniversaries of marriage, work, death and other social occasions and celebration of festivals almost all the members of a group participate. Their participation may be limited to an emoji or a "Pranam" (Indian way of salutation to somebody older in stature) or a "Thank You" message. On special events like children's sports day, annual day and other similar events Photos, Videos and text alone or a combination of all three are shared on the group especially group 1 and 2. As both these groups have grandparents and they are not so technologically savvy like the other members to use social media like Facebook and others. This also helps them to know what their grandchildren are doing. On such occasions, the number of messages would cross double the number of members and the group would be active from early morning into late in the night. Both Group 1 and 2 has members who are based in United States of America currently.

In one of the groups (Group 1), a family member posts her Sunday brunch, which is a special dish. It is customary in that group for other members to react to it with various emoticons. She is a working woman and only finds time on weekends to do something else. Slowly a few more members had also started photos of special dishes cooked by them. In Group 2, one of the members has a transferable job and must shift cities very often. He uses the WhatsApp group to inform his extended family about his transfer, also informs everyone about his new address and new landline number and other things like date of travel, his temporary residence and shifting to his permanent residence. People shifting houses/ or cities inform their new address on the group.

In the same group, one of the members was shifting to a new house in the city by using WhatsApp location he shared with others the location and the route to his new house. In this group, the Display photo of the group is changed based on their birthdays of one of the members of the group. In the case of two people sharing the birthday on the same day, both photos are displayed. Political videos, memes and cartoons were shared on the group during the May 2019 general election. Only the middle generation of the group was involved in discussion and comments on political matters on the group.

In Group 1, a couple was preparing to celebrate their silver wedding anniversary and they announced on the group first and later send invites. This was basically done to keep all the members informed about the dates so that they could plan their travel, leave and other things. Whenever there is a family gathering or some celebration like birthdays of small children or fiftieth-anniversary celebration, the members of the family who are unable to be physically present due to some health issue or other engagement can participate through a WhatsApp video call. Political views are also shared especially during election times. In May 2019, India had a general election; small videos of speeches, memes and funny comments on political leaders and parties. The group members are divided on political opinion and there were occasions when one of the members had to intervene so that the arguments and counter-arguments do not turn into an awkward situation saying no political propaganda on the group.

In Group 3, all the members are mother-in-law, daughters and daughter-in-laws and granddaughters of a joint family which has now split into nuclear families staying in different locations in India and abroad. The group was formed when they met at a family wedding and came up with the idea of having a group for themselves so that they could keep in touch with each other and without sounding trivial in the main family group which has a large number of members from both the sexes. In this group daily there is not much of activity out of the twelve members only three of them are active everyday. The three members generally wish "Good Morning", sometimes it is accompanied by a motivational quote. Occasionally there are small pleasantries exchanged about the weather or health of each other. The group is active on birthdays, anniversaries, special occasions like Dussehra, Teej and other such occasions. They post pictures of how each one is celebrating in terms of dressing for the occasion, food cooked and how they have decorated the house. In case any member has not done it, others ask them to do so. They are two members who are not so active on WhatsApp so whenever they respond or react other members are questioning their well-being and expressing their concern for them. They also share certain jokes, comments or memes which are sexist in nature or are targeted against men in this group. But that happened only twice.

In Group 4, a couple with their two children and a daughter-in-law had formed a small group for themselves. The mother of the group wishes "Good Morning" in the group and informs all of them about birthday, anniversary and other occasions of other members of the extended family. If one of the members is travelling for work, they post about their travel details like when did they leave home, when they are boarding, when they reach their destination, where they are staying? They also share pictures of the places they visit, the food they had for breakfast, dinner. They also share details and pictures of items like clothing, jewellery, and other items if they buy for themselves. They also post pictures of things while they are shopping and seek each other's opinion on what they should buy? Only special pictures are shared on the larger family group but this group as all the members are staying in different cities, keep themselves informed about each other through WhatsApp. Sometimes, they also do a WhatsApp video and seek opinions or advice when they are shopping. The daughter lives in the USA and has gone there only a few years back to do her master's and has started working in the USA. Since she loves Indian food, the mother sometimes posts a recipe for her. She always posts her lunch and dinner. She also shares any new recipe that she has tried.

Group 5 consists of a couple and their daughter who has gone abroad to study. Since she stays in the USA the time difference is almost 12 hours. They have the usual pleasantry of "Good Morning" and "Good Night" in the group. "Good Night" is a common thing in this group, as the daughter has a clear instruction to inform her parents through WhatsApp that she has returned to her accommodation and she is going to sleep through her

"Good Night". As both parents are working, they are not able to have a call with her in their morning and her night so a "Good Night" from her is an assurance that she is back to her home and she is safe. She shares photos of her food, her room, her friends, her labs, and other things with her parents. Sometimes in the evening she has a video call with either of her parents depending on who is free when she is free. She also sends pictures of grocery items and wants her mother to confirm if it is the same ingredient or something else. Like Ladyfinger or *Bhindi* (a Hindi for Ladyfingers) is known as Okra in the USA, similarly many other vegetables like Brinjal is known as Eggplant. Through WhatsApp, she would seek opinion or advice from her mother on what to cook as she has only certain limited ingredients leftover with her. There was a devastating Hurricane in her place and the parents kept in touch with her through WhatsApp. As she did not have electricity, her parents contacted her every two hours through WhatsApp to know her whereabouts and as she was staying alone to also keep her morale high and positive. WhatsApp was used for all sorts of conversation between the mother and daughter and father and daughter from how to cope with loneliness, how to clean a burnt cooking vessel or how to clean a stained bedsheet.

Analysis

Various factors like better educational opportunities, better job opportunities and lack of health facilities have dispersed the families. None of the families studied lived under one roof. At some point in their lives, they lived under the same roof and were part of the same large household. The urge to keep connected with their roots enables them to use WhatsApp. The kinship ties are strong and people want to maintain their family relationship and ties as the extended family has an important role in the Indian scenario particularly during the rites and rituals associated with birth, marriage and death of an individual. The need for maintaining ties with the family is stronger in the older generation in comparison to the younger generation. The younger generation has been brought up as either a single child by their parents or two children and a couple. They have met the larger family only on occasions of a wedding in the family and other similar occasions for a short duration of time. They are connected to their grandparents mainly through the virtual mode of WhatsApp.

In today's scenario, most mobile users from the middle-income families own a smartphone. The cost of mobile and mobile data has reduced substantially over the years. To use WhatsApp, they do not have to spend any additional money to download the app and to form the group. Text or any other feature of WhatsApp can be used from any place at any time of the day. The only thing required is a wi-fi connection and it operates through mobile data also. One of the main reasons for the popularity of WhatsApp is it being inexpensive, simple to use and works on minimal data. A large amount of data is used only while sharing photos and videos.

WhatsApp facilitate family interaction across generations; there is a possibility to reach the whole family via small communication. An emoji or a thumbs up helps the other family members acknowledge their presence. WhatsApp enhances the possibility to reach the whole family via small communication. The option available to utilize text, photos, videos, voice messages helps group members consider others' preferences and communication skills. An attractive tool for the family is the one to one and one to many interactions and provide for intergenerational communication. It helps the older generation to see the engagement and skills of their children and grandchildren. It is also a good leisure time activity for them. The small messages help to sustain the social bonds between family members whose daily agendas and schedules are incompatible. For example, both Group 3 and Group 5 had members who were staying in different time zones. Extended families have harnessed WhatsApp especially for phatic communication dailies such as Good Morning, various emojis, safe journey, happy birthday, congratulations, and many others one-word remarks or reaction. It is evident that WhatsApp fulfils the three functions of Phatic communication listed by Malinowski. WhatsApp helps in establishing and maintaining connections with the larger family group thereby establishing the social function. Through WhatsApp, the channel of communication is open, and all members can participate at their will both in terms of time and in a discussion that they think is relevant.

WhatsApp offers certain features, which makes it compatible with both phatic and familial communication such as enabling to check if the message has been delivered, if the person has read it. In case of any urgency, the individual can be called up and informed through a telephonic conversation. Immediacy in communication is another important feature addressed by WhatsApp. Therefore, even though members are far away from each other physically, they feel they are involved in the group, a sense of community. WhatsApp fulfils the validation and recognition function as the third function of phatic communication.

WhatsApp works dually at one level it acts as an umbilical cord between parents and children, at the second level as a medium it helps to gain a greater degree of independence. WhatsApp can be used to coordinate activities and share information among members who are in the physical proximity of each other or are located far away. WhatsApp family groups offer a dedicated channel to maintain and nurture strong family ties whether near or far. The meaning of sharing photos, video clips and exchanging small text and voice messages is perhaps best captured through the concept of phatic communication. In the case of young children or adults, it helps parents to keep track of their whereabout and activities.

Conclusion

Malinowski outlined the three functions of Phatic communion—a social function, a communicative function, and a validation and recognition function. Phatic communication on WhatsApp is represented by mono-syllabic words or emojis or various forms of salutation and greetings. It was observed that the family WhatsApp group irrespective of the size of the group use phatic communication to keep the conversation going on in the group. The small conversations enable to build and strengthening of ties among the members of the group. Over time the groups can sustain as members keep talking through small conversation and express respect, politeness, and friendship in the group. This helps to build empathy and solidarity within the group.

WhatsApp in the era of smartphones is used by people of all age groups. The inexpensive nature of the app has accelerated the process of communication. WhatsApp also has features that small talk or contacts happen between people who are known to each other. The safety and comfort that no unknown person is there in the group also provides impetus to the older generation and women to use it freely and frequently. As seen in the study groups could be formed for various purposes. There was an all-women group. On the other hand, a group had only three members. The various modes by which messages can be exchanged has also contributed to its adaptability to communication. The study also has pointed out that most messages were small and on occasions, all the group members participated. On normal days in each group, there were only one to three members who were active. They usually post messages such as "Good Morning" but that helps build a connection between the various members of the group.

Further studies can explore to see how WhatsApp is used beyond the family for Phatic communication. The idea of reciprocity can be explored in the messages and other material shared through WhatsApp. In this study, only the content analysis of the messages was done, the family members should also be interviewed after analyzing the message to throw light into various aspects of communication. Further detailed analysis by looking at various themes which emerge in the communication can be analyzed to understand the role of WhatsApp in communication.

REFERENCES

Chan, M. (2018). "Mobile-mediated multimodal communications, relationship quality and subjective well-being: an analysis of smartphone use from a life course perspective." *Computers in Human Behavior*, Volume 87:254-262.

Jakobson, Roman (1960). "Concluding Statement: Linguistics and Poetics". In T. Sebeok (ed.) *Style in Language*, Cambridge: MIT Press.

Jumanto, Jumanto (2014). "Phatic communication: How English native speakers create ties of union," *American Journal of Linguistics, 3*(1): 9-16.

Licoppe, C. and Smoreda, Z. (2005). "Are social networks technologically embedded? How networks are changing today with changes in communication technology", *Social Networks*, *27*(4): 317-335.

Malinowski, B. (1935). *Coral Gardens and their magic*, 2 vols. Allen and Unwin.

Matassi, M., Boczkowski P.J., and Eugenia, M. (2019). "Domesticating WhatsApp: Family, friends, work and study in everyday communication", *New Media and Society*, *21*(2). DOI: 10.1177/1461444819841890.

Miller, Vincent (2008). "New Media, Networking and Phatic culture", *The International Journal of Research into New Media Technologies, 14*(4). https://doi.org/10.1177/1354856508094659.

Radovanovic, D. and Regnedda, M. (2012). Small Talk in the Digital Age: Making sense of Phatic Posts, http://ceur-ws.org/vol-838.

Riley, Philip (2007). *Language, Culture, and Identity: an ethnolinguistic perspective*, London: Continuum, Advances in Sociolinguistics Series.

Senft, Gunter (2009). "Phatic Communion", In G. Senft, Jan-Ola Ostman and J. Verschueren (ed.) *Culture and Language*, Amsterdam: John Benjamins Publishing Company, pp. 226:233.

Seufert, Michael, Hebfeld Tobias, Schwind Anika, Burger Valentin, and Tran-Ga Phuoc (2016). Group-Based communication in WhatsApp, IFIP Networking, ISBN978-3-901882-84-5. https://irp-cdn.multiscreensite.com/d3de1972/files/uploaded/Conference_27_Michael_Seufert.pdf.

Taipale, Sakari and Farinosi, Manuela (2018). The Big meaning of small messages: The use of WhatsApp in Intergenerational family communication, https://doi.org/10.1007/978-3319-92034-4-40.

Weimann-Ska Dana, Ariel Yaron and Elishar-Malka Vered (2019). Second Screen: WhatsApp and watching the world cup; Communication and Sport. DOI:10.1177/2167479518821913.

Index